WEB SITE MEASUREMENT HACKS™

Eric T. Peterson

O'REILLY®

Beijing · Cambridge · Farnham · Köln · Paris · Sebastopol · Taipei · Tokyo

Web Site Measurement Hacks™

by Eric T. Peterson

Copyright © 2005 O'Reilly Media, Inc. All rights reserved.
Printed in the United States of America.

Published by O'Reilly Media, Inc., 1005 Gravenstein Highway North, Sebastopol, CA 95472.

O'Reilly Media, Inc. books may be purchased for educational, business, or sales promotional use. Online editions are also available for most titles (*safari.oreilly.com*). For more information, contact our corporate/institutional sales department: (800) 998-9938 or *corporate@oreilly.com*.

Editors:	Andrew Odewahn	**Production Editor:**	Jamie Peppard
	Mary T. O'Brien	**Cover Designer:**	Ellie Volckhausen
Series Editor:	Rael Dornfest	**Interior Designer:**	David Futato
Executive Editor:	Dale Dougherty		

Printing History:

August 2005:   First Edition.

 This book uses RepKover,™ a durable and flexible lay-flat binding.

ISBN: 0-596-00988-7

[C]

Contents

Foreword

One of the most interesting aspects of web site measurement is that it overlaps with so many areas of a company's business. A company's web presence covers the whole of its interaction with the public. It is marketing and sales and customer relations and press office and recruitment. It has to inform the public, create new customers, and support existing customers.

Web analytics is the study of whether the web site is meeting its diverse goals. Just as important, it is the presentation of the results to the various divisions of the company in a comprehensible format. It is now an industry worth hundreds of millions of dollars annually.

It wasn't always that way. I started writing Analog in 1995 when I was a student at the University of Cambridge Statistical Laboratory. Our department had just set up a web site, and we were keen to know how many people had been visiting it, but we found that none of the existing three programs worked well. So I decided to write my own little program, not guessing how it would take off.

Back then, the terms "web site measurement" and "web analytics" hadn't yet been coined: it was usually called something like "web logfile analysis." And the programs had a different emphasis than today's commercial programs: they focused on more technical statistics, such as which pages had been viewed most often and how many bytes had been transferred, rather than on visitor behavior.

Several things happened to broaden the scope of web measurement. The most obvious is the growth in commercial activity on the Web in the late 1990s. As the Web became a major part of a company's business and a major expenditure, it became necessary to justify that expenditure. This perhaps became even truer during the weaker economy of the last few years, as all expenditure had to be examined, and the Web came to be regarded as a marketing channel like any other.

Another important development was the growth in pay-per-click advertising in the last four or five years. When Overture and Google introduced the ability to place text ads on search engine results pages, it brought web advertising within the reach of many more companies. Compared to traditional banner ads, these new ads were better targeted, and charged only for actual clicks. They were also self-service, which made them cheap to set up and easy to change, and allowed companies to experiment with many different ads. Just as the Web gave everyone the ability to become a publisher, pay-per-click ads gave everyone the ability to become an advertiser.

One technical development also deserves a mention. JavaScript was invented in 1995 as a way to embed small programs within web pages. Its relevance to web measurement is that a piece of JavaScript code can alert a dedicated data-collection server when the page is displayed. This allowed vendors to offer measurement as an outsourced service, instead of as a software purchase. There is an ongoing debate as to whether the JavaScript method or the traditional logfile method is superior—each has advantages and disadvantages, as this book will discuss—but it is certain that JavaScript made web measurement available to many companies with less technical expertise, and to those whose web sites were hosted on third-party web servers.

In this environment, where companies were spending large amounts of money on their web sites and needing to examine the expenditure, web measurement vendors began to focus less on technical statistics, such as browser types and bytes transferred, and more on commercially relevant statistics, such as conversion rate and return on investment. The web measurement field gradually changed emphasis from "server analytics" to "visitor analytics."

In addition, vendors invented new ways to present data to wider audiences. Web statistics are useful to a business only if they can be understood by the people who have the authority to change the web site. If the statistics cannot be understood by people who can act upon them, they are merely an expensive curiosity. It was this that attracted me to making a career, not just a hobby, out of web analytics. I had refused previous job offers, but I joined ClickTracks because they wanted me to develop innovative ways to present the data—ways that were intuitive but still with an underlying mathematical rigor.

In this book, you'll learn techniques to use today's web measurement programs most effectively, written by many if not all of the leading experts in the field. To be successful, every modern business needs to understand the behavior of customers and potential customers on their web site; and if they do, they can see substantial reductions in costs and increases in revenue. It is the aim of the authors to give you new insights into the visitors to your web site: insights that will directly improve your business.

—Dr. Stephen Turner, Cambridge, England

Credits

About the Author

Eric T. Peterson is an author, analyst, and self-described "web measurement geek" from back in the day. Having been introduced to web traffic analysis in the late 1990s as a webmaster and web developer for WebTrends Corporation, Peterson has progressively become more deeply involved in the web measurement space and currently holds the position of senior analyst at JupiterResearch, focusing primarily on web measurement and search technologies. Peterson's first book on the subject, *Web Analytics Demystified* (*www.webanalyticsdemystified.com*), has been extremely well received and served as the basis for a number of measurement-related side projects, including the founding of the world's first web measurement discussion group (*http://www.webanalyticsdemystified.com/discussion_list.asp*).

Contributors

The following people contributed their hacks, inspiration, and writing to this book:

- Akin Arikan (*www.nettracker.com*) is a senior product manager at Sane Solutions responsible for ensuring customer satisfaction and success with the NetTracker line of web traffic analysis solutions. In this role, Akin has worked with many clients over the years on defining and interpreting reports based on their business goals. Akin first stumbled upon the wonderful world of web analytics while working at a leading business intelligence vendor managing enterprise analytic applications.

- Matt Belkin (*www.omniture.com*) has been involved in web measurement and business analysis for over a decade. As a former customer of multiple web analytics solutions, he brings real-world experience and a fresh perspective to the industry. He currently serves as the vice president of best practices at Omniture, where his passion and expertise help customers maximize their success. Prior to Omniture, Matt spent time at Macromedia, Adobe, Yahoo!, and JP Morgan.

- Jason Burby (*www.zaaz.com*) is director of web analytics for ZAAZ, a full-service online agency specializing in web site development, optimization, and business strategy for Fortune 1000 companies such as Microsoft, Converse, Wachovia, and Hallmark. His team works with tool providers, including WebTrends, Omniture, and HBX, to optimize sites using analytics and testing. Burby frequently speaks at premiere industry events and writes a column for ClickZ. He is co-chair of the Web Analytics Association Metrics/KPI Committee.

- Xavier Casanova (*www.fireclick.com*) is Fireclick's co-founder and former chairman, prior to the company being acquired by Digital River in 2004. A recognized expert and innovator in the analytics space, Xavier is a patent holder and pioneered technologies that have advanced the sophistication of analytics, such as real-time path analysis, browser overlay tools, and industry benchmarking. Xavier's client services expertise has also helped highly reputable e-businesses increase revenues through the use of analytics.

- Bryan Eisenberg (*www.futurenowinc.com*) is co-founder of Future Now, Inc., co-founder and chairman of the Web Analytics Association and co-author of *The Marketer's Common Sense Guide to E-Metrics, Persuasive Online Copywriting, and Call to Action*, as well responsible for over 400 ClickZ and GrokDotCom columns on increasing web site conversion rates and measurement. Bryan has been featured in publications such as the *Wall Street Journal, Inc. Magazine*, and *Target Marketing*.

- Chris Grant (*www.enlighten.com*) is a web analytics strategist at Enlighten in Ann Arbor, Michigan and has been involved in web measurement and technology for years.

- Ian Houston (*www.visioactive.com*) is a seasoned Internet consultant with ten years experience in most aspects of developing and supporting large-scale publication web sites. He spent a majority of those years working for Advance Internet as a leader in the tech department: a primary developer of their stats and advertising technologies. Today, he is an independent consultant specializing in web analytic and online advertising systems and practices. When not working, he enjoys exploring and photographing Michigan's many lighthouses with his wife Cindy and their three children, Keira, Liam, and Conlan.

- Brett Hurt (*www.coremetrics.com*) is a founder of Coremetrics and a former online retailer who has been fascinated by online customer behavior since 1998. The Web is the most insightful channel of all—if you know how to collect and analyze the data. At Coremetrics, he is fortunate to work with 350 retail, financial services, and travel clients to better understand customer behavior. Brett sincerely thanks Marianne Llewellyn, Brant Barton, and Matt Lawson for their many "hack" contributions.

- Dylan Lewis (*www.visualsciences.com*) is a consultant for Visual Sciences, LLC, tasked with assisting customers who implement, use, and analyze their data with Visual Site. Dylan is focused on web analytics, organic search engine optimization, pay-per-click advertising, affiliate marketing, Internet advertising, and conversion optimization. Prior to Visual Sciences, Dylan worked at *SmartDraw.com*, developing ways to increase organic search engine listings, and improve Internet marketing efforts.

- Jim MacIntyre (*www.visualsciences.com*) is the CEO of Visual Sciences. Jim started in "site" measurement with the advent of early BBS systems in the 1980s. Jim has been the CTO of five companies, including a multi-billion dollar holding company and the CEO of five companies, including an ISP, a managed services company, and three software companies. Jim is also a partner in a venture capital fund. Jim thanks Aaron Bird and Karen Brothers for helping to produce his hacks.

- John Marshall (*www.clicktracks.com*) was exposed to the web as a direct marketing tool early on at Netscape Corporation. He came to web analytics as a practitioner, running online marketing programs and using tools to measure them. Increasingly frustrated with the cost and complexity of the tools available, John founded ClickTracks Web Analytics in 2001 with a mission to make the process simple, the reports understandable, and the data meaningful.

- Jay McCarthy (*www.websidestory.com*) has spent the greater portion of his life in the pursuit of innovative technology, and refers to himself as "a recovering techie." For the last six years, he has been instrumental in the evolution of on-demand web analytics and is an acknowledged pioneer in the area of online privacy.

- Jim Novo (*www.jimnovo.com*) is a customer analysis consultant with 20 years experience using customer data to increase profits. He was VP of marketing at Home Shopping Network before starting his own consultancy in 1997, with clients such as MBNA Bank, CBS SportsLine, Morrison Homes, Radio Shack, Pfizer, and Tupperware. His book, *Drilling Down: Turning Customer Data into Profits with a Spreadsheet* teaches managers how to increase sales while lowering marketing costs.

- Bob Page (*www.bobpage.net*) was CTO and co-founder of Accrue Software, a pioneer in web analytics. After Accrue, he joined Yahoo!'s Strategic Data Solutions group, building new applications to help make sense of massive amounts of data. In his spare time, he's usually taking a picture of something.

- John Pestana (*www.omniture.com*) is the co-founder and executive vice president of customer success for Omniture and is a Web Analytics Association Advisory Board member (Founding). Pestana is one of the pioneers in online analytics, has consulted on e-business strategy for some of the world's most successful web sites, and has been a key driver in Omniture's success, supporting a marquee list of customers such as eBay, Wal-Mart, AOL, ans Overstock.com.

- Jeff Seacrist (*www.webtrends.com*) is director of product marketing for WebTrends, responsible for product strategy and go-to-market tactics. A noted new product development expert with companies such as 3M and Qwest, Jeff joined WebTrends in 1999 to develop a hosted business, which today is a substantial part of the WebTrends product portfolio. He has spoken at seminars world-wide on the topic of web analytics. Thanks to Barry Parshall and Clay Moore for their assistance.

- Dr. Steven Turner (*www.analog.cx*) is best known as the author of the free weblog file analysis program Analog, which he started writing in 1995 while studying for his PhD in probability at the University of Cambridge, and he is still writing 10 years later. After some years of postdoctoral research at Cambridge, he left in 2001 and became CTO of the new web analytics company ClickTracks. His other claim to fame is that he wrote the very first backgammon page on the Web.

Acknowledgments

This book would not have ever happened if not for the efforts of all of my contributors, colleagues, and friends in the web measurement industry: people like Bryan Eisenberg, Jim Novo, and Jim Sterne, who are always happy to provide guidance; Jim MacIntyre, Jeff Seacrist, Bob Page, and Brett Hurt for technical assistance; and Jason Burby and Dylan Lewis for ongoing support.

My extreme gratitude goes out to each of the vendors who provided screenshots and information for the book, including Jane Palocci at Coremetrics, John Mellor at Omniture, Corey Gault at WebTrends, Brett Crosby at Urchin, Erik Brat at WebSideStory, Jay Rudman at OpinionLab, Roger Benyon and Tom Cherry at Usability Sciences, and, of course, all of my contributors. Thanks is also due to the CEOs and VPs of marketing at many of the vendors, including Jeff Lunsford, Joe Davis, Greg Drew, Jim MacIntyre, Josh James, John Marshall, Jim Rose, and Ram Srinivasan for letting their people take the time to contribute content and ideas.

Tremendous credit goes to Andrew Odewahn, my editor at O'Reilly Media, for being patient and understanding and for his enthusiasm about this work.

Thanks to Tim O'Reilly and Rael Dornfest for taking a chance on a book about web measurement in the first place.

Special thanks to Ross Jenkins, Ian Houston, Terry Lund, and Josh Manion for taking the time to provide *excellent* technical reviews of the book. Trust me, the information quality of this entire book is better for the time these four gentlemen spent.

Thanks to JupiterResearch and David Schatsky for being open to the idea of my writing a book about web measurement.

Both Dr. Stephen Turner and Ian Houston have my eternal gratitude for taking the time to write the "build your own" hacks, which turned out to be more work than any of us imagined, but have provided, in my opinion, a handful of the most valuable hacks in this book. Thanks to Dr. Turner, the original "web site measurement hacker," for providing the foreword to this book.

Thanks to Amity, my best friend and most ardent supporter, for helping me create an environment where writing was possible and encouraging me whenever I became lazy or uninspired.

Finally, thanks to Chloe Michelle Peterson, who from age 18 months to 22 months was so sweet and understanding that "daddy had to write."

Preface

When the Internet was first born, most of us were so delighted with the ability to share information across great distances with relative ease that we gave little thought to critical analysis of how that information was being consumed. With the advent of the modern browser giving way to not just information but *nice-looking* information, our delight only magnified. Like children in a sandbox, we built sites, added images and content, and told everyone who would listen, "Hey, you! Come to my web site. My web site is great!"

At some point, somebody asked if anyone was coming. Nobody knew the answer.

The tools had not been developed, nor the practices established, to understand how people were interacting with these rapidly emerging web sites. The direct mailing crowd had cut their teeth on square inch analysis and DMA zones, and the television and radio folks had their Nielsen and Soundscan data. Physical stores had Underhill, his planograms, and spying college students. Even telesales operations had a notion of how well received their outgoing message was, based on the number of hang-ups they were getting.

Web site operators had nothing more than the occasional *webmaster@* email saying someone liked the site and was it OK to copy their code.

Enter web site measurement.

In 1993 at Honolulu Community College, an enterprising young man (Kevin "Kev" Hughes, for the record) wrote and announced getsites 1.4, a simple web server log analyzer (Figure P-1).

All of the sudden, anyone with a reasonable knowledge of C and their local filesystem could finally see what pages people were looking at. It was basic at best, but it opened the floodgates for what is predicted to become a billion dollar industry by 2009.

Announcing getsites 1.4, a Web log analyzer

kevinh@pulua.hcc.hawaii.edu (Kevin 'Kev' Hughes)

- **Mail folder:** WWW Talk Oct 93-present
- **Next message:** Denys Duchier: "HTML+, tables, math, lists"
- **Previous message:** Tim Berners-Lee: "URN: criticism, point and protocol."

```
Date: Wed, 3 Nov 93 10:25:54 HST
From: kevinh@pulua.hcc.hawaii.edu (Kevin 'Kev' Hughes)
Message-id: <9311032025.AA10184@pulua.hcc.Hawaii.Edu>
To: www-announce@nxoc01.cern.ch, www-talk@nxoc01.cern.ch
Subject: Announcing getsites 1.4, a Web log analyzer


        *getsites* is a small C program that will produce detailed, concise,
weekly, or daily reports from your Web server. Here's the details:

        * Works with CERN, NCSA, Plexus, and gn log files.
        * All reports are in the same consistent format.
        * All reports include server name and type, GMT and local date,
          total requests last 7 days, unique hosts last 7 days,
          total unique hosts, number of HTML and non-HTML requests,
          and total number of requests.
        * Detailed report includes IP addresses and host name,
          number of host requests, and last access date.
        * Weekly and daily reports are in vertical bar-chart format,
          with number of requests for each week or day.
        * You can choose to ignore numerical addresses beginning with
          a certain string.
        * getsites can take standard input, so you can pipe stuff to it.
        * getsites can use a previous full getsites report to lookup
          addresses both ways (this really speeds things up).
```

Figure P-1. Announcement of getsites 1.4

In 2005, web measurement applications are as important to the Internet business framework as web servers and commerce engines. Few serious businesses spend money online without having a tool in place to measure the effect of that expenditure, providing data for critical analysis of the question "Was that money well spent?" Today, companies like WebTrends, Omniture, and Visual Sciences routinely close deals worth hundreds of thousands of dollars—all so companies can understand who is coming to their sites, where they're coming from, and what they're viewing in an effort to understand "why."

It is those questions we hope to answer in *Web Site Measurement Hacks*.

Why Web Site Measurement Hacks?

The term *hacking* has a bad reputation in the press. The press uses it to refer to those who break into systems or wreaks havoc with computers as their weapon. Among people who write code, though, the term *hack* refers to a "quick-and-dirty" solution to a problem, or a clever way to get something done. And the term *hacker* is taken very much as a compliment, referring to someone as being *creative*, having the technical chops to get things done. The Hacks series is an attempt to reclaim the word, document the good ways people are hacking, and pass the hacker ethic of creative participation on to the uninitiated. Seeing how others approach systems and problems is often the quickest way to learn about a new technology.

There are plenty of sources for purely technical information about web data—how to parse logfiles, optimize server performance, and write cool JavaScript. Unfortunately, it is usually the "why," not the "how," that leaves businesses hanging. Web data collection is a simple practice, as is parsing the data into relatively meaningful buckets. The hard part is the analysis—figuring out what data is important and what it means relative to the business problem at hand. Web site measurement is something software can do, enabled by a variety of data collection algorithms and parsing strategies. Web analytics is something that requires people—bright people willing to roll up their sleeves, hunker down, and answer the hard questions.

The hacks in this book are designed to help you know what to do to gain insight into how people use your web site—bits and bytes of information that will help you better explore, understand, and unearth information about how people interact with their sites. Sure, there are scripts and technical tricks, but the essence of hacking in this context is analysis. This compendium of interesting ideas, built upon a foundation of relevant and important information about how the Web is measured, is designed to turn you into a sophisticated web data analyst (or at least push you in the right direction).

The result is 100 hacks, over half of which have been written by some of the best and brightest minds in web measurement today, all of which will hopefully push the limits of your understanding of web measurement, give you ideas about how better to answer the intangible "why," and, most of all, encourage you to "hack" into your web measurement data.

How This Book Is Organized

You can read this book from cover to cover if you like, but each hack stands on its own, so feel free to browse and jump to the different sections that interest you most. If there's a prerequisite you need to know about, a cross-reference will guide you to the right hack.

As you can imagine, there is more involved in web measurement and analysis than we could possibly cover in 100 hacks. Each of the four dominant business models (retail, advertising, support, and lead generation) has enough subtly and complexity in how it should be measured to merit a book of its own. Still, the goal in *Web Site Measurement Hacks* is to get your gears turning and mind humming thinking about the most common problems companies encounter, regardless of business model. To this end, the book is broken into seven chapters:

Chapter 1, *Web Measurement Basics*
> In Chapter 1, we'll tackle the most important aspects of web measurement, especially if you're new to the subject, including the languages used and technologies deployed, then take a look at the vendor selection process.

Chapter 2, *Implementation and Setup*
> This chapter is a walk through the litany of things you need to be thinking about when you're implementing a measurement application for your site. We cover the differences between common data sources, integration of commerce and custom data, privacy policies, and the impact that robots and spiders can have on your analysis.

Chapter 3, *Online Marketing Measurement*
> The number one thing that companies do with web measurement applications is collect data that will help them justify their marketing investment. Whether you buy banner ads, send email, bid on search keywords or advertising for your site in the offline world, this collection of hacks will get you focused like a laser beam.

Chapter 4, *Measuring Web Site Usability*
> More than anything, site owners want to believe their creations are easy to use and easy to understand. Unfortunately, this is rarely the case. Fortunately, web measurement tools provide a plethora of data about usability, allowing site owners to iteratively improve the overall visitor experience (hopefully for the better).

Chapter 5, *Technographics and "Demographics"*
> It wouldn't be an O'Reilly book without some geeky stuff about the ugly underbelly of the Internet, would it? Chapter 5 explores how web measurement applications can be leveraged to improve your site's design and your internal testing and refinement strategies.

Chapter 6, *Web Measurement and the Online Retail Model*
> Given the fact that there are four equally valuable business models online, how do we justify devoting an entire chapter to online retail? Simple, online retailers spend a great deal of money on web measurement, more than the other three business models combined by some estimates. This chapter deals with a dozen or so of the most common measurement needs for online retailers, including shopping carts, checkout processes, and the lifetime value of a customer.

Chapter 7, *Reporting Strategies and Key Performance Indicators*
> Many vendors would have you believe that the interface they provide into the data is the only thing you'll need to be successful. They're wrong. Extensive interviews and experience tell us that most companies are successful with web measurement data when it's presented in a format they're comfortable with. In this chapter, we present key performance indicators and discuss how they can be used to improve the likelihood of adoption and action for web data.

About the Use of Screenshots and Vendor Information in This Book

By some estimates, there are well over 100 vendors providing web measurement tools plus nearly as many free solutions—far too many to adequately treat in a single book. The author and editor of this book have worked diligently to be as fair as possible in our coverage of the vendor landscape and have made every effort to distribute the inclusion of screenshots and examples as equitably as possible.

That said, nobody is perfect, and you cannot please all of the people all of the time.

Inevitably, some vendors' work will be represented more frequently throughout this book. Specifically, at the time this book was being written, the author had demonstration access to applications provided by Omniture, WebSideStory, and Visual Sciences. Because of this, these vendors may appear more frequently throughout the book than, say, Urchin, Click-Tracks, or Sane Solutions. Neither slight nor preference was intended. I can assure you, it was only laziness on the part of the author that prevented each and every vendor from being represented with the exact same number of screenshots, contributed hacks, and mentions throughout the book.

Conventions Used in This Book

The following is a list of the typographical conventions used in this book:

Italics
> Indicates URLs, filenames, filename extensions, and directory/folder names. For example, a path in the filesystem appears as */Developer/Applications*.

`Constant width`
> Used to show code examples, the contents of files, console output, as well as the names of modules, variables, commands, and other code excerpts.

`Constant width bold`
> Used to highlight portions of code, typically new additions to old code.

Constant width italic

> Used in code examples and tables to show sample text to be replaced with your own values.

Color

> The second color is used to indicate a cross-reference within the text.

You should pay special attention to notes set apart from the text with the following icons:

> This is a tip, suggestion, or general note. It contains useful supplementary information about the topic at hand.

> This is a warning or note of caution, often indicating that your money or your privacy might be at risk.

The thermometer icons, found next to each hack, indicate the relative complexity of the hack:

 beginner   moderate   expert

Using Code Examples

This book is here to help you get your job done. In general, you may use the code in this book in your programs and documentation. You do not need to contact us for permission unless you're reproducing a significant portion of the code. For example, writing a program that uses several chunks of code from this book does not require permission. Selling or distributing a CD-ROM of examples from O'Reilly books *does* require permission. Answering a question by citing this book and quoting example code does not require permission. Incorporating a significant amount of example code from this book into your product's documentation *does* require permission.

We appreciate, but do not require, attribution. An attribution includes the title, author, publisher, and ISBN. For example: "*Web Site Measurement Hacks* by Eric T. Peterson. Copyright 2005 O'Reilly Media, Inc., 0-596-00988-7."

If you feel your use of code examples falls outside fair use or the permission given above, feel free to contact us at *permissions@oreilly.com*.

How to Contact Us

We have tested and verified the information in this book to the best of our ability, but you may find that features have changed (or even that we have made mistakes!). As a reader of this book, you can help us to improve future editions by sending us your feedback. Please let us know about any errors, inaccuracies, bugs, misleading or confusing statements, and typos that you find anywhere in this book.

Please also let us know what we can do to make this book more useful to you. We take your comments seriously and will try to incorporate reasonable suggestions into future editions. You can write to us at:

> O'Reilly Media, Inc.
> 1005 Gravenstein Hwy N.
> Sebastopol, CA 95472
> (800) 998-9938 (in the U.S. or Canada)
> (707) 829-0515 (international/local)
> (707) 829-0104 (fax)

To ask technical questions or to comment on the book, send email to:

> *bookquestions@oreilly.com*

The web site for *Web Site Measurement Hacks* lists examples, errata, and plans for future editions. You can find this page at:

> *http://www.oreilly.com/catalog/webmeasurehks*

For more information about this book and others, see the O'Reilly web site:

> *http://www.oreilly.com*

Safari Enabled

When you see a Safari® Enabled icon on the cover of your favorite technology book, that means the book is available online through the O'Reilly Network Safari Bookshelf.

Safari offers a solution that's better than e-books. It's a virtual library that lets you easily search thousands of top tech books, cut and paste code samples, download chapters, and find quick answers when you need the most accurate, current information. Try it for free at *http://safari.oreilly.com*.

Got a Hack?

To explore Hacks books online or to contribute a hack for future titles, visit:

> *http://hacks.oreilly.com*

Web Measurement Basics
Hacks 1–13

Many people consider the "basics" of web measurement anything but. Loaded with confusing and ambiguous terminology, dependent on any number of potentially fallacious assumptions, and often considered the domain of data-loving geeks, no wonder business people have historically eschewed web data analysis for softer and fuzzier endeavors like paid usability studies and online surveys.

But no longer!

Web measurement applications and the vendors that provide them have made great strides in the last few years, making their applications easier to understand and easier to use. The major players are starting to agree on a common vocabulary and working through some of the historical problems with data collection. More and more business people have responded, taking interest in web measurement and actually assigning resources to analyze the resulting data.

Funny how a major economic downturn and the enforcement of fiscal responsibility will motivate people to make decisions based on available data, not just their gut instinct.

Why Measure Your Site?

Most companies measure their web activity because they have an interest in knowing how well their marketing and advertising budget is being spent. Consider the plight of the average vice president of Internet marketing for a company of any appreciable size. He is likely responsible for the web site, email messaging, banner advertising, paid keyword marketing, organic search, internal search, content, and the online extension of the brand. Given this list and the associated costs of developing and maintaining each piece of marketing collateral, how could he possibly hope to make good decisions without data?

Whether you're in charge of site design and development, usability, marketing, customer communication, customer support, lead generation, online sales, brand messaging, product marketing—trust me, this list goes on and on—you need web measurement data to help inform your job.

Think about it. Do you want your airline pilot flying based on available atmospheric and flight pattern data or gut feel? Do you want your doctor to recommend a treatment after just glancing at you or would you like her to run a few tests? Do you want your automobile mechanic to recommend service for your car after just giving it a listen?

Our entire world is run using data collected from the environment around us. Why would you think your web site is any different?

A Brief History of Web Site Measurement

The practical history of web site measurement goes something like this:

> In the beginning there was WebTrends and WebTrends was good. Eventually WebTrends became less good and the market rapidly expanded to well over 50 vendors (which is probably about 45 more than the world really needs).

A touch glib, perhaps, but that's really it. WebTrends Corporation of Portland, Oregon struck on the classic "right place, right time" mix and became an overnight success. At one point claiming over 55,000 customers worldwide, WebTrends had a very successful initial public offering but eventually succumbed to their own successes, failing to respond quickly enough to changes in the market. Fortunately, WebTrends has since recovered and is widely considered to be a market leader.

Because web measurement is such a good idea, eventually every Tom, Dick, and Harry started getting into the scene, and applications started popping up like mushrooms in an Oregon winter. Conservative estimates currently peg the number of vendors at well over 100 worldwide. Names like "ClickTracks," "Clicklab," "Clickstream," and "Clickcadence" abound. Analysts are currently predicting a contraction of the web measurement market around the largest and most successful vendors—companies like WebTrends, Omniture, WebSideStory, Coremetrics, Sane Solutions, and a handful of others.

For a visual history of the marketplace, visit *www.webanalyticsdemystified.com/history.asp*, where the author maintains a PDF outlining the emergence of vendors and application functionality.

What Web Measurement Is Not

Web site measurement is a lot of valuable things, many of which you'll read about in this book, but it is none of the following:

- Usability testing
- Performance monitoring
- A replacement for smart, careful marketing
- A proxy for intelligent, informed people
- A silver bullet

The first two items—usability testing and performance monitoring—are closely related fields that can contribute data to and benefit from web measurement, but they are not web measurement. The third and fourth items—careful marketing and intelligent people—are not web measurement; they are the beneficiaries of web measurement data and applications. When you use the hacks in this book, you can do smarter and more careful marketing. The hacks will ideally be run by intelligent, informed data analysts, and these analysts will be smarter and better informed for having read this book. Silver bullets exist only in the movies.

Why Not "Web Analytics?"

The term *web analytics*, though commonly used, is slightly less accurate than the term *web measurement*. Here's the distinction:

Web measurement
> The act of gathering data and parsing it into a useful and human-readable form (e.g., reports)

Web analytics
> The act of interpreting measurement reports so that organizations can take some action.

About the "Build Your Own" Hacks

Interspersed throughout this book you will find "Build Your Own Web Measurement Application" hacks. These hacks will show you how to write a simple program to collect web measurement data and analyze it, adding functionality with each subsequent hack based on the chapter's theme. We included these hacks not because there is any pressing need for another measurement solution—although we do believe this to be the only open source web measurement application that uses JavaScript page tags—but because we believe the exercise to be instructional. Reading these hacks will help you better understand the more packaged (and pretty) applications.

Because of the recent explosion of the use of RSS to syndicate content and publish weblogs, we've also added two hacks showing you how to build your own RSS tracking application. The analyzer, based on a very simple JavaScript page tag, is written in Perl and is based loosely on the "Build Your

Own Web Measurement Application" hacks, essentially demonstrating how to take a good idea and extend it. Because there are no known client-side applications for measuring activity for RSS feeds, our hope is that if you're into that kind of thing, these hacks will be of interest to you.

Requirements

The minimum requirements you should have, or be willing to learn, before attempting to build you own web measurement or RSS tracking application with our guidance are as follows:

- Reasonably strong understanding of the Perl programming language, although we'll make an effort to describe what's going on in plain text, too.
- Reasonably strong knowledge of how your filesystem works so that you're able to correctly set file permissions.
- Access to a Web server, and the ability to modify its configuration.
- Basic knowledge of P3P, including knowing how to change document headers to return a compact P3P policy.
- Patience and a desire to learn how web measurement applications all work at their core!

All of the files and code necessary to run the application described through-out the book are available at *http://www.webanalyticsdemystified.com/byo* and are freely available as open source code.

HACK #1   Talk the Talk

Learning how to talk the web measurement talk is the first step in really taking advantage of the data, especially if your hope is to someday become a professional "web data analyst."

In web measurement, terminology is tremendously important. Because so few people have experience measuring activity on the Internet, it is impor-tant to explain the most important terms and how they're used. If you're technically inclined, this hack is designed to help you understand how the bits and bytes are translated into information about human activities. If you're more marketing oriented, this hack will help you understand where the information comes from.

Figure 1-1 illustrates the relationship between the basic terms. As you can see, as the volume of available data decreases, the value of that information increases. At the bottom of the pyramid and in greatest volume, we have "hits," and at the top, we have "unique visitors," the holy grail of "things that can be measured."

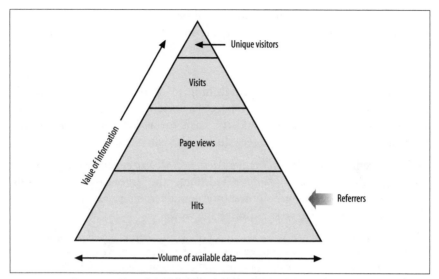

Figure 1-1. The pyramid model of web measurement data

Even if you already "talk the talk," recognize that many of these terms are loosely defined, and the strict definitions that follow serve as the foundation for the rest of this book.

Hits

The term *hit* is perhaps the most overused and misunderstood word in the entire web measurement vocabulary. People talk about "site hits," "page hits," and "hits from search engines" *ad nauseum*. The best definition of a hit is provided by WebTrends:

> (A hit is) an action on a web site such as when a user views a page or downloads a file.

When you read the definition of a page view, you'll be struck by the similarity of the two definitions, but consider the words "or downloads a file." Files, in this context, include executable files; PDFs; sound files; JPEG, PNG, and GIF images; etc. The problem is that the "page" that appears in your web browser is technically the aggregate of potentially hundreds of "hits"—every image and page element is counted as a hit.

So if every time a page loads any number of hits is recorded, but a different number of hits depending on the number of images used to render the page, how can one reasonably expect to use hits in a business context?

You can't. Don't try.

The best you can do with a "hit" is to recognize that it's simply one of those words that people misuse and move on. Use words like "page views" and "referrals from search engines," and you'll be talking the talk. In web measurement, "hits" is an anachronism; the term's time has come and gone.

Page Views

The page view is the fundamental unit in web measurement, ideally recorded when a person sees a web page. Page views are the measurement of a visitor's interest in your site and the basis for a visitor's *clickstream*, the sequential list of pages a visitor sees during his visit.

In their recent document *Interactive Audience Measurement and Advertising Campaign Reporting and Audit Guidelines*, the Interactive Advertising Bureau (IAB), a governing body for Internet advertising measurement standards, had the following to say about page views:

> Page [views] are defined as measurement of responses from a web server to a page request from the user browser, which is filtered to remove robotic activity and error codes prior to reporting, and is recorded at a point as close as possible to opportunity to see the page by the user.

For the sake of this book, the definition of page view is:

> A page view is counted with the successful loading of any document containing content that was requested by a web site visitor, regardless of the mechanism of delivery or the number and frequency with which said content is requested.

While there are a number of problems associated with how page views are defined and used in the web measurement market, it's tremendously important to understand the general concept. Page views, in practical usage, provide an easy way to convey the popularity of a page or section of your site. While not as people-centric as visits and unique visitors, *page view* is a term you'll use frequently when talking the talk.

Visits

A visit, also referred to as a session or user session, is generally defined by the collection of pages viewed when someone browses a web site (the "clickstream"). It is defined by the IAB (in particularly droll language) as:

> One or more text and/or graphics downloads from a site qualifying as at least one page [view], without 30 consecutive minutes of inactivity, which can be reasonably attributed to a single browser for a single session.

While this concept is not particularly complex, ambiguity arises when you consider how people browse web sites. Consider two examples:

- Tammie enters a URL into her browser and methodically clicks links, completing her given task in a reasonable amount of time and then moving onto the next site, hopefully satisfied.

- Tom enters a URL into his browser and drifts around, randomly clicking links, taking breaks of varying duration to drink coffee, make lunch, chat on the phone, and coming and going willy-nilly for hours on end.

Both are reasonable and common strategies for using the Internet. Unfortunately, while it is easy to know when Tammie's visit ends—when she has completed her specific task—the same determination is difficult to make for Tom. Because it is nearly impossible to determine the intent of a web visitor, certain assumptions are required. A fundamental assumption is that *any visitor* who fails to click for more than 30 minutes has mentally "moved on," and her visit should be considered ended.

Why 30 minutes, you ask? An excellent question! Unfortunately, one without an answer; suffice to say, 30 minutes for visit expiration is a widely used standard, something worth remembering when you want to talk the talk.

The most useful definition of a visit is as follows:

> A *visit* is counted when a unique visitor creates activity on a web site, measured using sequential page views (clickstream), regardless of the duration of this activity as long as the period of inactivity between page views does not extend beyond 30 minutes.

You'll see that there is no upper limit on the length of a visit—one visitor can click around for as long as he pleases, as long as he clicks a measured link at least once every 29 minutes and 59 seconds. Visitors can visit a site multiple times a day; the ratio of visits to visitors is a great key performance indicator [Hack #94]. Visits are tied to referring sources like paid and natural search terms [Hacks #42 and #43] and banner ad campaigns [Hack #40]. Visits bridge the gap to truly meaningful information about real people.

Unique Visitors

In the field of web site measurement, people are called "unique visitors." Unique visitors are the top of the pyramid model of web measurement data (Figure 1-1) and exist in three forms—totally anonymous, mostly anonymous, and known [Hack #5]. The important things to remember about unique visitors are that they are human beings, not nonhuman user agents [Hack #23].

In terms of a strict definition of *unique visitor*, the IAB has this to say:

> Unique [visitors] represent the number of actual individual people, within a designated reporting timeframe, with activity consisting of one or more visits to a site or the delivery of pushed content....Each individual is counted only once in the unique [visitor] measures for the reporting period.

Again, while using the least engaging language possible, the IAB has captured the essence of the unique visitor. Especially important is the concept of timeframe and the relationship between unique visitors and visits. I think the best definition of a unique visitor is as follows:

> A unique visitor is counted when a human being uses a web browser to visit a web site, regardless of the number of pages visited or the duration of the visit. A visitor can be unique for different periods of time, and the individuality of a visitor is preferably defined by a truly unique user identifier shared between browsers. A unique visitor for any arbitrary timeframe should be counted one time and one time only on her first visit between the start and end dates.

As long as you remember that unique visitors are people just like you and me, you'll be fine. If you remember that the uniqueness of visitors is associated with a specific timeframe—the day, the week, the month, or the football season—you're golden.

Referrers

Anything online that drives visitors to your web site is said to "refer" traffic to you, hence the term *referrer*. Referrers are generic web sites, search engines, banner ads, weblogs, email, and affiliates: basically online sources that inspire unique visitors to visit your web site and generate page views. All that is required of a referrer is that it can be identified based on information contained in the HTTP request. The following logfile shows some examples referrers:

```
216.219.177.29 -- [15/May/2000:23:03:36 -0800] "GET /index.htm HTTP/1.0" 200
956 " http://www.webanalyticsdemystified.com" "Mozilla/2.0 (compatible;
MSIE4.0; SK; Windows 98)"
212.219.31.219 -- [15/May/2000:23:03:42 -0900] "GET /mail/email_marketing.
htm HTTP/1.0" 200 956 "http://www.altavista.digital.com/cgi-bin/query-bin/
query?pg=aq&text=yes&d0=1%2fnov%2f99&q=email+marketing %2a&stq=30" "Mozilla/
4.05 [en] (Win 95; I)"
121.12.31.45 -- [15/May/2000:23:03:56 -0300] "GET /index.htm HTTP/1.0" 200
956 "http://www.oreilly.com/lists/links.php?link_list_id=134" "Mozilla/4.0
(compatible; MSIE4.01; Windows 98)"
```

The example shows that:

- One visit started when a unique visitor came from *http://www. webanalyticsdemystified.com* at 23:03:36 requesting the file *index.htm*.
- A second visit started when a unique visitor came from an AltaVista search for "email marketing" at 23:03:42 requesting */mail/email_marketing.htm*.
- A third visit started when a unique visitor came from a link list at the O'Reilly web site (*http://www.oreilly.com/list/links.php?link_list_id=134*) at 23:03:56 requesting the file *index.htm*.

The best working definition of a referrer is as follows:

A referrer to any web site should be an undifferentiated and complete uniform resource locator (URL) describing the exact page on the web site that contained the link to the web site. Failing a complete URL, a referrer should describe the source of traffic in as much detail as possible.

The second half of this definition was added in recognition that email is a very important component of Internet marketing efforts, but many email applications don't provide referring URLs. When analyzing a referring URL, you should examine the entire URL—the *http://www.oreilly.com/books/ hacks/websitemeaurementhacks.html* plus any information contained in the query string (the stuff after the *?* in a dynamic URL)—so you can reconstruct the exact and entire page that contained the original link. If you cannot, hopefully you're able to embed information into the requesting URL that describes the medium and message that contained the referring link.

As you can see in Figure 1-2, while this visitor was referred to the *Web Analytics Demystified* web site from an email, we can determine that he came from the December 2004 campaign (`campaign=Dec2004`), he clicked on a "buy now" message (`message=buy_now`), the creative was an image (`creative=image`), and the link identifier was 54412 (`id=54412`). Any good web measurement application [Hack #3] will be able to leverage this information, usually using campaign and email tracking functionality [Hack #41].

Figure 1-2. Referring URL

Tying It All Together

At the end of the day, each term is part of the framework for web site measurement. Make sure you really understand the subtleties associated with each one; using "visits" when you mean "unique visitors" can have a profound effect on someone else's understanding. When you really get this—when you talk the talk, as it were—you're going to be saying things like:

- "We're looking more closely at a dramatic increase in the average number of page views to our corporate policies over the last week."

- "The ratio of visits to unique visitors from our biggest online partners has dropped off significantly, so we've contacted them to see if they've somehow modified the message on their end."

- "We're generating 20 times the page views per visit from our most recent campaign. Since our average advertising CPM is over $30, this is pretty significant from a revenue standpoint."

- "Hits? I'm sorry, we don't use that term around here unless we're talking about baseball."

You get the idea. Talk the talk, and everything else falls into place.

#2   Best Practices for Web Measurement

To truly be successful with your online business, you need to treat web measurement as a business practice and be willing to invest time, effort, and money as necessary.

Web measurement is not a silver bullet; in fact, outside the realm of law enforcement and werewolf hunting, there are no silver bullets. In order to be successful with your web measurement program, you have to treat it like any other business process through such things as customer relationship management (CRM), sales force automation (SFA), and enterprise resource planning (ERP). There needs to be an abbreviation for web measurement—for example, "WMO" for "web measurement and optimization," which captures the fact that you measure for improvement's sake, or "SMI" for "site metrics integration," which expresses the need to integrate your metrics with other site operation strategies. Perhaps that's all that stands in the way of web measurement becoming widely used inside organizations: an appropriate abbreviation.

The following best practices, if rigorously followed, will help you identify changes you can make that will dramatically improve your site.

Identify Your Objectives Before You Begin

A common mistake that many companies make is to rush out to purchase software or services before they develop sound reasons for doing so, a mistake not exclusive to web measurement. While occasionally these companies are able to back into the rationale for the purchase, a better approach is to actually sit down with those in charge and explore what you hope to gain by an investment in web measurement in advance. This is usually the best place to begin implementing a web measurement strategy: clearly identifying your site's business objectives [Hack #38]. Some examples of clear reasons for investment include:

- "We're a retailer and our margins are very low. We want to increase the number and value of online purchases while making sure that our marketing dollars are not wasted."

- "Our customer support costs are very high. We want to optimize our support site so that more customers are likely to find answers to basic questions, decreasing the number of phone calls we get."

- "We have an online banking application that customers have complained about. We want to identify and fix any usability issues so more people will use this application."

- "We're a new company trying to enter a very competitive market. We need to know how best to communicate our value proposition and differentiate ourselves from bigger competitors."

When you're clear about your overall goals, it becomes much easier to explain your needs to vendors [Hack #3], make implementation decisions (Chapter 2), develop a reporting strategy for your KPIs [Hack #91], and explain to your senior executives exactly what you're trying to do.

Make Sure You Have Executive Buy-In

Web measurement works only if you're able to make changes to your web site. Occasionally you're going to realize that you need to make changes to your entire online strategy—something that is easier to do if you have executive buy-in. If you're the owner of your site, great, give yourself permission. However, if you're like most of us and you report to somebody who reports to somebody who reports to somebody, you may want to prepare yourself for an uphill battle at times. One of the best ways to avoid these internal squabbles—fights that often result in no action at all—is to ensure that management understands not only what is required but also what can be gained.

To get management involved, consider having them read the following hacks in addition to Chapter 7:

- Best Practices for Web Measurement [Hack #2]
- Understand Marketing Terminology [Hack #37]
- Define Conversion Events [Hack #39]
- Identify Your Business Objectives [Hack #38]

Build the Right Team

One of the most important things to take away from this book is that regardless of how good the application, there is no substitute for smart people. Companies traditionally over-invest in software and under-invest in expertise to translate insight into action; web measurement is no exception. Research suggests that you're far more likely to make good decisions based on web data if you have at least one dedicated person [Hack #4] maintaining the application and analyzing the data. The ideal situation is two people—one focused on the implementation and vendor relationship, the other charged with making sense of the data and ensuring that the rest of the organization "gets it"—both of whom report to a relatively senior person.

Regardless of how many people you can assign to web measurement projects, understand that zero dedicated resources will return zero valuable insights. That said, if you're willing and able to assign resources, the continuous improvement process will help you translate effort into action.

Measure and Improve: The Continuous Improvement Process

Once you've identified your objectives, received executive buy-in, and built the right team, the real work can begin. The most reliable way to integrate web measurement into your overall business is via the continuous improvement process. Figure 1-3 illustrates an ongoing cycle of "measure, report, analyze, optimize" that takes advantage of your data collection and reporting applications; your smart people; and your desire to improve your site, customer experience, and (hopefully) top and bottom lines.

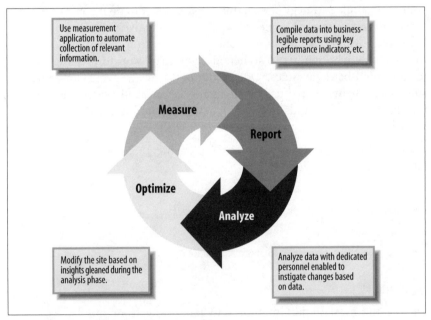

Figure 1-3. The continuous improvement process

This framework is deceptively simple. The majority of companies have a tendency still to use web measurement as an *ad hoc* process: to identify a problem through some other channel (email, phone calls, or the CEO's brother) and then look for an explanation in the metrics. This reactive use is appropriate in some situations, but should never be your only interaction with the data. The most successful companies have adopted the continuous improvement process, a proactive approach to identifying problems *before* the phone rings.

At the end of the day, following each of these best practices will help you align your organization around data, a surprisingly difficult goal. Jim Novo, measurement guru and former vice president of programming and marketing at the Home Shopping Network, has commented on many occasions that the companies who really get web measurement are companies that already "get" the use of customer data to make business decisions. Direct marketers, automobile manufacturers, book publishers, and their ilk are accustomed to mining data so they can make informed decisions. Other types of organizations are more likely to shoot from the hip and make gut-level decisions. According to Novo, the former already get it, and if you're in this group you'll most likely embrace the ideas in this book. If you're in the latter group, well, keep reading.

HACK #3 Select the Right Vendor

One of the most important decisions you will make in web measurement is which vendor you're going to work with, keeping in mind that some are better than others but there is no one "best" vendor for every company's needs.

The web measurement arena is littered with software and service vendors, some good and some bad, yet all eager to take your money. The vendor selection process is often the most painful step in setting up a web measurement program. Understanding the major differences between types of vendors and seeing a brief synopsis of the top vendors in the market can make this process a little less painful.

Vendors can be categorized along two major axes: delivery type and the data collection mechanism. The delivery type characterizes how you use the vendor's services, and falls into two broad categories: *software*, which you install on your own servers, and *hosted services*, which are maintained by the vendor. The data collection mechanism describes how the vendor collects data, such as web server logfiles [Hack #22] or client-side JavaScript page tags [Hack #28]. Since a handful of vendors are now supporting both data collection mechanisms, and since often delivery type defines which data model you'll use, we'll focus on delivery type.

Software

The software model for web measurement applications is essentially the "original" model—one very well understood and widely deployed. Companies generally choose software because they seek flexibility from the application and prefer to own the process from beginning to end. Software may be more expensive in terms of up-front fees and first-year investment, but cost savings are usually appreciated in the second and subsequent years when maintenance fees are 17–22 percent of first-year costs (this will make sense when you read about hosted service model pricing). If you go the software route, you need to be ready to support the application internally, maintaining the software when necessary as well as the hardware it runs on. Software typically uses web server logfiles (Figure 1-4) as a data source.

```
fcrawler.looksmart.com - - [26/Apr/2000:00:00:12 -0400] "GET /contacts.html HTTP/1.0" 200 4595 "-" "FAST-webCrawler/2.1
123.123.123.123 - - [26/Apr/2000:00:23:48 -0400] "GET /images/sponsors.gif HTTP/1.0" 200 6248 "http://www.webanalyticsd
fcrawler.looksmart.com - - [26/Apr/2000:00:17:19 -0400] "GET /news/news.html HTTP/1.0" 200 16716 "-" "FAST-webCrawler/2
123.123.123.123 - - [26/Apr/2000:00:23:47 -0400] "GET /book_home/ HTTP/1.0" 200 8130 "http://search.netscape.com/Comput
123.123.123.123 - - [26/Apr/2000:00:23:48 -0400] "GET /images/author_image.gif HTTP/1.0" 200 4005 "http://www.webanalyt
ppp931.on.bellglobal.com - - [26/Apr/2000:00:16:12 -0400] "GET /download/windows/wad_book.zip HTTP/1.0" 200 1540096 "ht
123.123.123.123 - - [26/Apr/2000:00:23:50 -0400] "GET /images/book_cover.gif HTTP/1.0" 200 1031 "http://www.webanalytic
123.123.123.123 - - [26/Apr/2000:00:23:51 -0400] "GET /images/book.jpg HTTP/1.0" 200 4282 "http://www.webanalyticsdemys
123.123.123.123 - - [26/Apr/2000:00:23:51 -0400] "GET /cgi-bin/perl.cgi HTTP/1.0" 200 36 "http://www.webanalyticsdemyst
```

Figure 1-4. A web server logfile

Hosted Services

The hosted service model—often referred to as the *outsourced* or *application service provider* (ASP) model—takes advantage of the fact that some companies prefer not to run and maintain software internally. In the hosted service model, in-house IT groups are usually involved only during the original implementation and deployment phase, allowing business and marketing resources to tweak reports and data collection mechanisms on an ongoing basis. While first-year costs for hosted services are often much lower than software, the hosted service model is built on a "pay as you go" plan, much like your cell phone. Since you're paying for the page views your visitors generate on a "cost per million page views," you will continue to pay a similar or increasing monthly cost year over year. Hosted services, while not exclusively so, traditionally use a client-side JavaScript page tag as a data source.

Popular Vendors Providing Software and Services

Table 1-1 summarizes the data source and delivery types for a handful of well-known web measurement vendors.

Table 1-1. Popular web measurement vendors

	Delivery type		Data source used	
Vendor	Software	Hosted service	Logfiles	Page tags
ClickTracks	X	X	X	X
WebTrends	X	X	X	X
WebSideStory		X		X
Omniture		X		X

Table 1-1. Popular web measurement vendors (continued)

Vendor	Delivery type		Data source used	
	Software	Hosted service	Logfiles	Page tags
Coremetrics		X		X
Urchin	X	X	X	X
Sane Solutions	X		X	X
Visual Sciences	X	X	X	X
Fireclick		X		X
IBM SurfAid	X		X	X

As you can see, a number of vendors support multiple data collection mechanisms and delivery strategies, and four—ClickTracks, Urchin, Visual Sciences, and WebTrends—support all available options. Here are a few other things you should know about each of these vendors to help you in the selection process.

ClickTracks

ClickTracks are known for popularizing the browser overlay [Hack #62] model for data viewing, letting you view your site and pay-per-click campaign traffic mapped directly on top of your web pages. One of the least expensive web measurement tools, starting at $495.00 for a single-user software license, ClickTracks is a great entry-level product.

WebTrends

WebTrends is a long-standing vendor in the market and offers both hosted and software solutions. With the release of WebTrends 7, the company and products have become more competitive, offering pricing based on page view volume to the enterprise, professional, and small business markets. (The Small Business edition starts at $495.00 for software and $35.00 per month for a hosted service.)

WebSideStory

One of the original hosted service providers, WebSideStory was the first company to allow customers to populate and automate web measurement data directly into Microsoft Excel. WebSideStory recently acquired a hosted search and content management system vendor, allowing them to provide more services to smaller businesses.

Omniture

Known for their visually appealing SiteCatalyst interface, Omniture has built a healthy business around measuring some of the Internet's largest properties. It is appropriate for nearly any online business.

Coremetrics

Coremetrics has made a name servicing online retail, financial services, and travel sites. Built on top of a flexible data warehouse, Coremetrics is able to build complex visitor profiles and has experience integrating outside data [Hack #32] from companies like BizRate, Commission Junction, and Foresee Results.

Urchin

Urchin is another long-time measurement application vendor, which many companies get directly from their hosting provider. Having recently released significant enhancements, including the ability to get Urchin as a hosted service, Urchin provides good value relative to price.

Sane Solutions

Sane's NetTracker application is one of the most widely used web measurement tools. This is a nominally sophisticated analysis application and an industry -eading extract, transform, and load (ETL) tool for converting data collected from the web site into a format useful for business intelligence (BI) tools like Cognos, Business Objects, and MicroStrategy.

Visual Sciences

Visual Sciences, a relative newcomer to the measurement market, is less of a web measurement application and more of a data analysis engine. Capable of analyzing many types of data, the company's Visual Workstation application is among the industry's most powerful and flexible tools.

Fireclick

Fireclick is a hosted service provider that was among the first to offer additional value-added tools, like the ability to benchmark your site against your competitors [Hack #93], a browser overlay for retailers [Hack #62], and direct-to-Excel reporting [Hack #91]. Fireclick is appropriate for cost-conscious online retailers.

IBM SurfAid

IBM SurfAid made an early name by being able to integrate data from a variety of web-related sources, including complex product sale databases. SurfAid is perhaps most appropriate for companies who would normally turn to IBM, Oracle, or Microsoft for business solutions (given that Microsoft and Oracle do not sell web measurement solutions).

Tying It All Together

If you've never looked at web measurement software before, you may want to ask around and see if anyone else you work with is familiar with these types of applications. Because the differences between vendor offerings are sometimes slight and often just a matter of preference, having someone with relevant experience work with you to vet vendors can be very helpful (kind of like taking your dad to buy your first car!). One resource I strongly recommend is the Web Measurement and Analysis Forum at Yahoo! Groups (*http://groups.yahoo.com/group/webanalytics/*). I founded the group in 2004, and as of this book's printing, the membership includes nearly 1,000 members, all happy to provide opinions and assistance.

When looking at different software options, be sure to take a close look at what you'll be getting. Ask for a few demonstrations, and consider downloading and trying copies yourself if possible. (ClickTracks, WebTrends, Urchin, and Sane Solutions all offer downloadable trial versions.) If you're leaning toward a hosted solution, consider asking the vendor to conduct a limited pilot so you can see how *your data* will look in their application.

Whatever you do, don't just jump right in with the first vendor you contact (or who contacts you). Again, like your first car, your first web measurement application is one you'll long remember, for better or for worse.

HACK #4   Staff for Web Measurement Success

Selecting the right vendor is only half the battle in successfully building a web measurement program for your company. You should also be thinking about dedicating resources to manage, maintain, and evangelize the data throughout your company.

Many companies make the mistake of simply selecting an application and assuming that all of their problems are solved. The notion of the "silver bullet" software or service is surely attractive, but unfortunately, no such bullet exists. Companies who assume that a technical or marketing resource will be able to spend a little time each week poking around in the measurement application when they have spare cycles nearly always fail to take full advantage of their investment in analytics. In other words, the old adage that "you get what you pay for" holds true in staffing, as it does in vendor selection.

Staff for Measurement Success

Some companies will inevitably not be able to afford to hire a dedicated staffer to manage their measurement program, especially those companies who are spending less than $25,000 on the entire application and implementation. In these cases, it is recommended that companies at least dedicate one-half of a single person's time to managing the measurement program. Empower a motivated employee to make sure the implementation is good and that people at least understand that the information is available.

Most companies need to dedicate at least one full-time resource to their web measurement efforts. One person who has enough technical skills to manage and tweak the application's implementation but enough business savvy to translate the data into something that the entire organization can use [Hack #91]. Larger organizations should plan to hire more than one resource, especially if the initial investment in a measurement package is particularly large or if a significant number of people in the company will likely use the data on a regular basis. The logic is that no one person can support an army—you need to distribute the responsibility and allow a team of data analysts to support the company.

Skills for a Web Data Analyst

Because very few people have degrees in "web data analysis," it is likely that you'll need to hire someone with relevant skills and adapt them organically into the role of a web data analyst. Some of the characteristics of great data analysts include:

Technical background
> The best web data analysts will not be afraid to roll up their sleeves and write some code when necessary. Web measurement is a nascent enough field and there are enough web measurement hacks to fill a book. You'll need to hire someone who has at least HTML and JavaScript experience so that he'll be able to collect the data the company needs without always having to ask your vendor for support.

Business acumen
> The best web data analysts have a strong interest in the business being successful and understand business and marketing concepts. You don't need to have an MBA to understand concepts like visitor acquisition costs, margins, and return on investment, but you do need to have enough interest and experience to differentiate a good business decision from a bad one.

Strong presentation skills
> Much of what a web data analyst does is help people understand the data and its potential impact on the overall business. If the analyst is afraid to present to groups or is otherwise mousey, more often than not she won't be effective. Having an ineffective web data analyst is like not having anyone in the position. The ability to work with multidisciplinary teams and build consensus is also critical.

The "best" web data analysts are people who are able to successfully bridge the gap between business interests and technical resource allocation—essentially, getting marketing and IT to talk to each other in meaningful and productive ways. When your web data analysts are doing their jobs, they should be getting *everyone* excited about the data and its potential impact on your online business.

Finding a Web Data Analyst

Unfortunately, it's not that easy in this day and age to just hang a "Help Wanted: Web Data Analyst" sign in the front window and wait for the resumes to start pouring in. As mentioned previously, nobody is currently producing college graduates with bachelor's degrees in web analytics—at least nobody known to this author. Without a deep pool of talent, at least in 2005, the need for qualified data analysts far exceeds their availability.

So what can you do?

Well, rather than go back to not staffing for measurement success, you can increase your chances of attracting available talent by doing a few simple things.

Put the word out that you're looking for some serious talent. It's unlikely that the usual path of throwing a listing on Monster.com is going to get the response you're looking for. Likely, you'll get resumes, but experience tells us that most of the candidates will be underqualified and probably didn't even read the posting closely. Consider the following nontraditional avenues for hunting down web data analysts:

- Let your vendor know you're looking for help and ask them to keep their ears to the ground for you. Make sure they know you're not trying to steal their people, but you're serious about getting help.

- Write to the Web Analytics Association (*www.webanalyticsassociation.org*) and see if anyone in their membership is currently looking for a job.

- Join the Web Analytics Forum (*www.webanalyticsdemystified.com/ discussion_list.asp*), a collective of over a thousand web measurement professionals, some of whom may be interested in coming to work for you.

Be prepared to hire someone senior enough to be truly effective. A common mistake that companies make when trying to hire web data analysts is looking for inexpensive, junior people who don't have enough business experience to really succeed on the job. Look for senior-enough people and be prepared to pay them salary commensurate with their experience, increasing the chances that the "right" person will be interested in your position. Most talented web data analysts are making around $100,000 plus other incentives, depending on where they're located geographically.

Provide additional financial incentive based on successful attainment of goals. If one of the key drivers behind investing in web measurement is increasing your conversion rate or average order value, give serious consideration to offering your web data analyst a cash bonus if he helps you reach goals for improvement.

For example, if by increasing your site-wide order conversion rate by 10 percent, your business will bring in an additional million dollars a quarter, it seems logical that you'd work diligently to try things that will make that goal become reality. While your web data analysts will surely work diligently towards that goal, if you agree to pay them a $10,000 bonus if they drive the business to meet that goal, you're still left with $990,000 per quarter in additional revenue, and you'll see your web data analysts work harder than you thought possible.

Fight the temptation to say "I should not have to pay someone a bonus if she's simply doing her job!" If you don't, your competitors will, and the talented data analysts will be working for them (and against you).

In summary, no web measurement application is good enough to work without someone or a group of people supporting it. Companies don't buy sales force automation or customer relationship management tools without dedicating resources (usually administrators) to their care and feeding; why would you think you could avoid staffing around your investment in web site measurement?

HACK #5 Get to Know Your Visitors

Knowing that you have three totally different kinds of unique visitors coming to your web site can save you time, money, and headaches.

Visitors are the fundamental currency in web measurement—the top of the pyramid, as shown in Figure 1-5. The idea of the "known visitor" is important to web measurement because, given the right message, any good salesperson can sell; the sales process breaks down when forced to sell to anonymous groups. Think about the difference between a really good car salesperson and a car commercial on TV—the commercial may sway you one way or the other, but it's the salesperson speaking to you directly who will seal the deal. Because of the universal desire to "know" the visitor, it's important to understand the three major visitor categories: totally anonymous, mostly anonymous, and known (Figure 1-5).

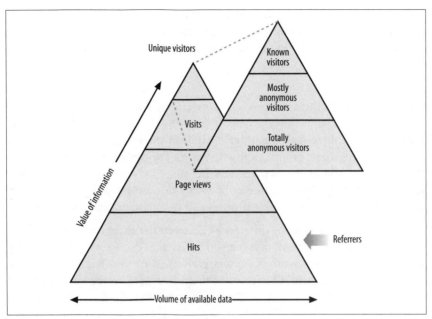

Figure 1-5. The three types of unique visitors

Totally Anonymous Visitors

Some of the visitors who come to your web site will be truly and potentially forever anonymous; there's very little you can truly know about them except where they came from (their referring URLs) and which pages they view during their visits. This small but persistent group may be as many as 15% of Internet users who disable all cookies, surf through proxies that hide their IP addresses, or otherwise work to obfuscate their identities. While there are alternatives to using cookies [Hack #17] to determine the relative uniqueness of a visitor, anyone with motivation, desire, and a basic understanding of how Internet browsers work can prevent you from knowing much about him at all. The fact that this group exists is reason enough to exclusively use first-party cookies in your analysis [Hack #16].

Mostly Anonymous Visitors

The bulk of people who visit your site are *mostly anonymous*: people who don't go out of their way to hide from you but also don't offer up any truly useful personal information. Most of your Internet audience will accept cookies [Hack #15], allowing you to determine whether they have been to your site previously, how they originally found you, whether they are customers or not, and how you can segment them into meaningful categories [Hack #48].

Still, unless you provide a reasonable trade for their personal information (or require it, as is becoming increasingly popular), visitors are unlikely to divulge enough to allow you to feel like you truly "know" them.

Known Visitors

Known visitors are those folks who, for whatever reason, have provided you personally identifiable information (PII) [Hack #26] and allowed you to set some kind of unique user identifier (UUID) in their browsers. Typically the smallest of the three groups, known visitors are tremendously valuable to site operators and Internet marketers because, by virtue of allowing their identification to be known, their online activities can be tied to offline information, including demographic profiles and purchase or support histories.

One way to think about the differences between the three types of visitors is this: truly anonymous visitors force you to say that "some people visited my web site." Mostly anonymous visitors allow you to say that "some people visited my web site, and 30 percent of them had been to the site within the previous week." Known visitors allow you to say that "Bob, Ted, Alice, and Mary visited my web site; Alice looked at a product that she ultimately purchased in my store; and Mary later called to complain about a problem, which was handled by our support group."

HACK #6   Understand Common Data Sources

Before you get started analyzing, determine where the data will be coming from.

In the early days of web site measurement, there was only a single source of data, web server logfiles [Hack #22]. Generated automatically by web servers like Apache and Microsoft Internet Information Server, these flat text files were simply a report of which IP addresses were requesting which objects. At one point, a smart and enterprising soul realized that these files could be parsed and that the results could tell you roughly what people were doing on your web site. Some say, "In the beginning there were logfiles and they were good...." Unfortunately, web server logfiles weren't good enough.

Problems with Web Server Logfiles

People began to see problems creeping into their log-based analysis—missing information and requests that could in no way be coming from a human being—and gradually programmers realized that something better would be needed. Problems arose from the emergence of forward caching devices, the addition of page caching in the browsers, and the explosion of nonhuman user agents attempting to catalog the rapidly expanding Internet. As more and more people came online, the caching devices were needed to improve the overall browsing experience, and while they helped the average surfer connecting with a 28k modem, they dramatically impacted the accuracy of log-parsing applications.

Enter the Packet Sniffers

Packet sniffing, also referred to as the network data collection model [Hack #8], basically puts a listening device on a major node in the web delivery architecture, as shown in Figure 1-6. The listening device would then passively log requests for resources, essentially sitting in front of your web server farm. While sniffing provided some advantages—centralized data collection, more details about failed or cancelled requests, and improved accuracy in server overload conditions—few applications ever supported the model and it never really took off.

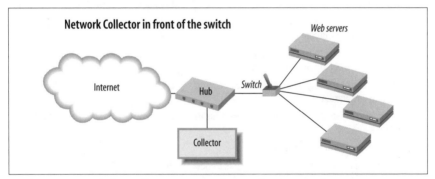

Figure 1-6. Network data collectors in an archetypical web server farm

JavaScript Page Tags Are Born

About the same time the packet sniffers were starting to struggle, a handful of companies realized that by embedding a small JavaScript file into web pages, you could collect a great deal of useful information about the page being viewed and the visitor doing the viewing. The JavaScript would then dynamically generate an image request to an external server, appending all the collected information into the query string, and the client-side page tag was born [Hack #28].

Once initial security and privacy concerns were worked out, JavaScript page tags quickly took off. Companies eagerly bought into the use of tags to render traffic data in real time, and others were delighted by the relative simplicity of the hosted application model.

Eventually, though, companies began to discover the limits in their utility as well. A major limitation of page tags is that if they're not on a page, no data is collected for that page, making deployment mistakes quite costly from a data collection perspective. Also, some companies balk at the seemingly ever-expanding size of the tags, occasionally exceeding 20 KB!

Evaluating Data Sources

Given that each data source has its benefits and limitations, you might be asking yourself "How should I decide which source is best for my business?" For the most part, there are a handful of needs and limitations. In general, a "yes" answer to any of the criteria presented in Table 1-2 will yield a "best" data source to use.

Table 1-2. Criteria to help you determine which data source to use

Need or limitation	Logfile	Packet sniffer	Page tag
Need to access to historical data, generated prior to application implementation	BEST	NO	NO
Do not have the ability to modify each page on the web site, such as by adding a JavaScript page tag	BEST	OK	NO
Concerned about accuracy being affected by caching devices and software agents	OK	OK	BEST
Have no desire to maintain additional hardware inside the network	OK	NO	BEST
Need access to information in real time	OK	OK	BEST
Need information about which software agents (robots and spiders) are indexing the site	BEST	BEST	NO
Concerned about measurement in server overload conditions	OK	BEST	NO
Concerned about ownership of information	BEST	BEST	NO[a]
Need to be able to process and track a variety of different types of data (commerce servers, content servers, proxy servers, and media servers) or determine successful delivery of downloadable files (PDF, EXE, DOC, XLS, etc.)	BEST	OK	NO
Concerned about implementation times and ease of implementation	BEST	OK	NO
Need ability to log data directly to a database	BEST	OK	NO
Concerned about high up-front costs	OK	OK	BEST

[a] While most hosted application vendors will insist that you "own" the data, this is nearly never true since the data physically resides in a different location. Exceptions to this are applications like Visual Sciences and WebTrends SmartSource, which allow page tags to be run from your own infrastructure (and thus the data is wholly owned by you).

While there are no absolutes, it is important decide which source you prefer to use before you start contacting software or service providers. Also, there are often differences in pricing models associated with each data source, with page tags most commonly associated with hosted applications, which are typically paid for on an ongoing basis, and web server logfiles and packet sniffers with software-based solutions, which are typically paid for up front at the beginning of the relationship.

Further complicating your decision making process is the recent emergence of vendors offering hybrid solutions—usually combining page tags and logfiles to create a more holistic view of your data. Vendors like Visual Sciences, Urchin, and Sane Solutions are now offering the ability to blend data sources in new and interesting ways. While hybrid vendors may not be the best solution for you, if you have experience with both logs and page tags and are looking for an alternative, these vendors are worth a look.

HACK #7 Understand Visitor Intent

Despite the great body of knowledge that web measurement applications help you collect and organize, the intent of visitors when they come to your web site is nearly always part of the "great unknown" online. By recognizing this, you can often improve your overall understanding of the metrics, improving their value and use.

If you ask any online retailer why people come to their web sites, they usually answer, "Well, to buy things of course!" While it sounds like a great answer, it is usually not true; if it were, retailers' buyer conversion rates would be much higher than the three percent widely reported. Most people who visit online retail sites are simply browsing or doing research and have no intention of making an online purchase. The problem is that order and buyer conversion rates [Hack #39] are built from the assumption that every visitor is a potential purchaser, a fallacious assumption if there ever was one.

If retailers could build calculations based not on the entire audience, but only on the people who actually intended to purchase, conversion rates would likely shoot through the roof. By eliminating the tire kickers from the equation, business owners could focus on resolving problems experienced by visitors who actually had potential, not just promise.

So if you could figure out the visitor's intent, your measurement problems would be solved.

Indeed.

Easier said than done, but there are two general strategies for determining visitor intent: explicitly and implicitly.

Determining Intent Explicitly

Determining intent explicitly is actually pretty easy if you think about it—
you ask. Simply pop up a window when visitors arrive at your site and ask
them in as polite a way possible "Why are you here today?" Present them
with a reasonable list of options (for example, "To make a purchase," "To
research your products and services," and "To get customer support") and
pass their response to your measurement application.

The best strategy for passing the response to your measurement application
is to create visitor segments [Hack #48] from different "intent groups" based on
their answers. Ideally, your measurement application will be sophisticated
enough to then let you calculate differential conversion rates and generate
value metrics for members of the intent group.

For extra credit, when you can tell a visitor is leaving the site, pop up
another window and ask her how you did in satisfying her stated intentions.
A simple "Do you consider your visit to our site to be successful or unsuccessful?" will usually do, and is quick enough to not seriously impede the
visitor as she's moving on. Knowing when the visitor is actually leaving your
site is difficult to do unless you're keeping track of all the links that leave
your site or using an external technology like Usability Sciences WebIQ
(Figure 1-7). Do your best.

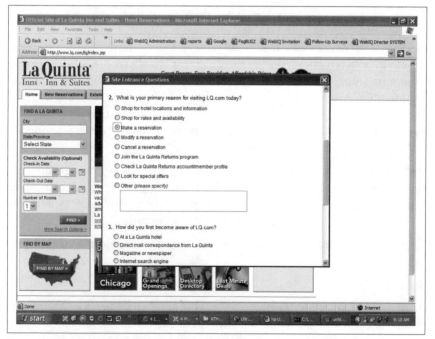

Figure 1-7. Explicitly asking about visitor intent

Determining Intent Implicitly

Determining intent implicitly is the reason visitor segmentation was originally generated; *visitor segmentation* is the ability to make assumptions about visitors based on their clickstream, and then grouping them into segments for further analysis. To extend segmentation to create intent groups, all you need to do is think carefully about the events or actions that visitors are likely to make based on their intent.

Using the retail examples provided above, it is fairly safe to assume that any visitor who clicks on a "checkout" button intends to make a purchase, any visitor who *does not* click on a "checkout" button was merely browsing, and anyone who clicks into your customer support pages is looking for customer support.

These are very simple examples, and most sites aren't that simple. Still, if you start small and then carefully examine the segments you're creating, looking back into the group's general clickstream behavior, it is likely you'll be able to evolve the segment over time to be a more accurate predictor of intent.

Once You've Determined Intent, Then What?

Once you've figured out what visitors actually came to your site to do, you can start building better metrics and key performance indicators [Hack #94]. Many of the KPIs presented in Chapter 7 of this book are dramatically improved by focusing them based on visitor intent.

- *Conversion rates* are improved by looking only at visitors who were likely to convert.

- *Average order values* and *revenue per visitor* are improved by looking only at potential customers.

- *Average page views per visit* is improved by looking at visitors who were actually trying to learn something about your offerings.

- *Time spent on the site* is improved by looking at visitors who were actually researching your products or looking for customer support content.

Since tracking intent is moderately dependent on your application's ability to segment visitors, it is likely worth a call to your vendor to explain what you're trying to do.

HACK #8 Know When to Use Packet Sniffing

Network data collectors, or "packet sniffers," create an alternative data source that has a handful of benefits, provided that you maintain their upkeep.

Users respond not only to a site's *content*, but also to its *delivery*, which include factors such as speed, quality, and reliability. Together, content and delivery influence what users choose to view, how long they view it, how they navigate through the site, and ultimately whether they will return. All the compelling content in the world won't save a web site that can't deliver it well.

Many options exist to get information about what content was served. But to get the delivery information, in order to get a complete picture of user behavior, you can turn to collecting data at the network level. This is commonly referred to as network collection (or using a sniffer, but Sniffer® is a registered trademark of Network General Corporation to describe its line of protocol analyzers, so we won't use that term here).

The Ugly, Ugly Details

Because of the design of the network layers in a computer system, the low-level details about the network packets are unavailable to the web server—this is a good thing, as it allows the web server to concentrate on serving web content. However, by the time the server sees the transaction, much of the underlying performance data is lost, or has been modified into something less useful.

For instance, a web server can log when it sent some content, but cannot know if the client actually got it, or if the client didn't get it, how much it got before the client stopped the transaction. Using collection methods such as page tagging, you can capture more granular information about page deliveries, but cannot determine why a transaction was slow or failed. In general, application-level loggers (web logs, page tagging, server plug-ins, etc.) cannot report:

- Client-initiated disconnects (for example, users hitting the stop button in mid-download)
- Network problems: server retransmissions due to overloaded networks
- Busy signals: requests ignored by the server due to overload
- The time the server took to respond to each request

A network collector (usually just software running on off-the-shelf hardware) is a specialized packet grabber that "knows" all about web traffic. It passively watches the traffic flow across the network and keeps a record—similar to a web server log line—of what it sees. Because a network collector lives on the network, however, it can see and report what application-level loggers cannot.

Imagine an observer on a freeway overpass. If the observer is fast enough, it can count all the cars that go by. If it's really fast, it can log information like the car's color, make, model, or number of people in each car. All this can happen without disrupting traffic flow (Figure 1-8).

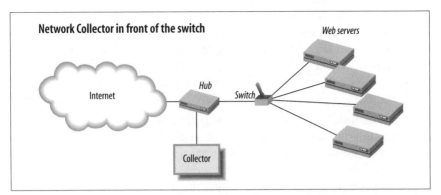

Figure 1-8. Typical placement of a network data collector on a hub in front of your web architecture

From this viewpoint, a network collector can view traffic for all web servers on a particular network. One network collector can gather statistics for many web servers simultaneously, reducing the cost of manually administering logfiles on each web server.

This wealth of information becomes a great foundation on which to analyze a web site. The combination of content and delivery makes for powerful analysis. For example, what happens to the average number of pages a web surfer sees at a site when the server's response time goes from under two seconds to over 10 seconds? Which content is most abandoned during download? What is the relationship between users' connection speeds and page views? Is there a particular CGI program that should be tuned because it's taking too long to run?

How to Use a Network Collector in a Switched Environment

A network collector relies on having a machine watch the network traffic between browsers and the web server, so it must be on the network path between the two. In a shared media environment (such as a hub), the sniffer collects all the information because every port on the hub sees traffic to and from every other port on the hub.

In the more common switched environment, each port on the switch transmits only traffic that is supposed to be for the machine (the web server) plugged into that port. Putting a network collector on a switch port means that it sees only traffic for itself, and not for the web servers. This isn't very useful!

There are several approaches you can take to allow network collectors to work in a switched environment. Each has its advantages and disadvantages.

Get in front of the switch

In this scenario, the network collector lives "upstream" from the switch, where it can see all traffic flowing into the switch. This allows the collector to see traffic between the Internet and all the web servers (Figure 1-8). However, it does not see traffic between two web servers, since that happens through the switch. In practice, this isn't a problem.

The big hurdle with this approach is that there is usually a high-speed point-to-point link between the router and the switch. In order for a machine to act as a network collector, it would have to tap in to the stream. Tapping into a half-duplex stream (such as a normal 100 Mbps Ethernet link) would work by connecting the router, switch, and collector to a hub where they can exchange data. This means the collector will have to process a huge amount of traffic, looking for just the web traffic, so the processor speed of the machine would have to be sized accordingly.

In very high-speed environments, the link between the router and switch could be a full-duplex link, where the link speed is effectively doubled (so traffic may be flowing between the switch and the router at 200 Mbps). Monitoring this traffic isn't possible without specialized hardware and software.

Configure a monitoring port

Most switches can be configured to send traffic from/to specific machines to another port. This "monitoring port" contains duplicates of the traffic, and the collector runs as if it's plugged into a hub (Figure 1-9).

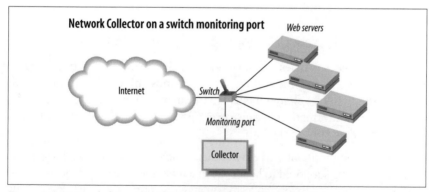

Figure 1-9. Network data collector sitting on a monitoring port

The downside to this approach is that traffic within the switch is increased. Let's look at an example 12-port switch. Ten of the ports are running web servers. The ports are capable of 100 Mbps, but only about 40 Mbps sustained are flowing per port. Thus, the switch is passing 400 Mbps through it, which could easily be within the maximum limit of the internal backplane on the switch. If we then configured one port to be a monitoring port, all the traffic would need to be duplicated to that port. However, now the switch would be trying to put 400 Mbps onto the 100 Mbps monitoring port, which is beyond the capacity of the port.

Put the data collector on the web server itself

If the collector can be isolated to a piece of software, and run on the web server, it can collect network-level statistics. However, this can add an additional load to the web server.

Put a hub between the switch and the web server

This is almost the opposite of getting in front of the switch. Here the collector lives behind the switch. Rather than plugging the web server directly into the switch, plug the web server into a hub, and plug the hub into the switch port (Figure 1-10). Now you can plug the network collector into the hub. Downsides to this approach: you're adding a hub per switch port, and the collector can only see one web server.

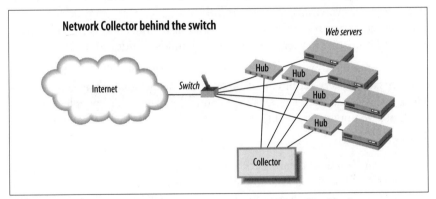

Figure 1-10. Network data collector attached to hubs in front of each web server

Using a Network Collector with Encrypted (SSL) Traffic

Generally, you'd put an SSL frontend device before the web servers. That offloads the web servers from having to manage the encrypted packets. It also allows you to put a network collector behind the SSL box and in front of the web servers, where the traffic is unencrypted.

If there is no good place to monitor all incoming and outgoing traffic due to network layout, a network collector won't work, and you'll forfeit delivery information. In these cases, consider using a network collector for some part of your traffic—say, a particular set of machines—in order to "spot check" some of your delivery data that's not available though other collection mechanisms.

—Bob Page and Eric T. Peterson

Write a Useful Web Measurement Request for Proposal (RFP)

Business people love to create complex RFPs when they're making a purchase decision. Here's why this is a bad idea and what to do about it.

Requests for proposal (RFPs) are a very popular and inefficient way to select a web measurement vendor. Yes, *inefficient*. While you may think that creating a list of your requirements and then asking vendors how well their software satisfies this list would be a great way to get started, it's not. Here's why.

First, I have never in my life come across a company that could assemble a list of requirements in an efficient manner. Usually some poor soul is forced to walk around asking people what their needs are, trying to keep track of whether the same needs have already been mentioned, and compiling a ridiculous list that then needs to be refined.

Second, nobody ever seems to come up with a practical list. RFPs usually read like "we need everything that is currently available, everything on every vendor's development roadmap, and a handful of features not likely to be available until humanity masters cold fusion and builds a bridge to the moon."

Third, no matter how impractical the list, every vendor you send it to will be able to satisfy every requirement better and cheaper than their competition. How is this possible? It's not, but do you really expect sales people to tell the truth in a document where if they do, they will most likely be disqualified?

I didn't think so.

So what can you do if creating RPFs is a complete waste of time, energy, and resources and you'll still end up with the same answer you'd likely get if you just read any good analyst report? One thing you can do is write a better RFP! Here are four simple things you can do to write a better request for proposal, if you really feel you must.

Focus on Your Current Needs

A common mistake companies make when writing RFPs is trying to figure out what their needs will be well into the future and adding those requirements to their list. While it's a good idea to think about the near-term future, it's a much better strategy to focus on the problems that you can solve immediately (or nearly so). While this sounds counterintuitive, experience tells us that most companies that purchase technology to support future measurement needs often pay for functionality they never use. If you focus on the technology you're confident you'll use in the next 12 months, you'll get more short-term wins that will leave everyone feeling better about your decision.

Ask Only Well-Qualified People for Input

Another common mistake is to ask every web stakeholder for input about what the measurement application should do. This opens you up to gathering input from well-meaning folks who have no idea what they're talking about, people who often outrank you. While politics rules in the workplace, a better strategy is to ask only people who you *know* are familiar with web measurement and explain to everyone else that the domain experts have the situation under control.

Send Your RFP to as Few Vendors as Possible

Given that every vendor you send the RFP to will be able to satisfy your requirements better and less expensively than their competitors, do yourself a favor and do your homework ahead of time so you can limit the number of RFP responses you need to review. If you can rely on the advice of analysts, your web measurement specialists or your industry peers who use different applications to limit the vendor recipient list to two or three, you'll save yourself a ton of time. Consider that you're very likely to have to sit through presentations, review pricing proposals, and perhaps run proofs of concept with vendors providing strong responses, and you can start to see how much time this can take if you're considering 6 to 10 vendors.

Remember, Less Is More

When you're being smart about your RFP, you'll already have a pretty good idea of which vendors you like before you begin writing. If you're able to write a request for proposal that focuses on the particular strengths of your favored vendors, you increase your chances of eliminating companies you don't like, even if you're forced to send the document to a set number of vendors. You'll save time reviewing the responses (which you should always do, even if you have a pretty good idea that you'll ultimately reject the proposal, because you never know what you might discover) and waste less vendor time while they're filling in responses.

If you write a better RFP, you'll still end up with a great piece of software, purchased via a process no more biased than a more lengthy process—one that draws on the right resources in your organization and that saves you time.

 HACK #10 Find a Free or Cheap Web Measurement Solution

Free or inexpensive packaged solutions are a great place to get your feet wet with web site measurement.

It's easy to get the impression that web measurement is a costly and time consuming endeavor, one requiring deep pockets and significant expertise.

While time and effort are absolutely required to truly understand your web site visitors, there are also many inexpensive and even free software is available to support your efforts. In fact, the very first web measurement applications, Webstats and Analog, are freely available and nominally supported by the open source movement to this day.

An important consideration regarding free and inexpensive measurement solutions is the old adage *you get what you pay for*. While this does not mean that low-cost solutions are necessarily bad, it's more a reflection that open source and entry-level web measurement solutions are often less well maintained, documented, or supported than their business-class counterparts (at least at the time of this writing). If you go this route, you need to simply be aware of this and be prepared to have to look a little harder or wait a little longer for help when problems arise (and trust me, they always arise!).

Free Web Measurement Solutions

The following table lists several free measurement solutions, where to get them, which data sources they use, how the applications are delivered, and what makes them worth mentioning in this hack (Table 1-3).

Table 1-3. Freely available web measurement solutions

Name and URL	Data source(s) used Delivery type platforms	What's good or cool about this solution
Analog *http://www.analog.cx*	Web server logfile Software Win/Unix/Mac	Analog is highly scalable, ultra-fast, easily configured to report in over 30 languages, and it works on *any* operating system. Analog is purportedly the most popular measurement application in the world.
AWStats *http://awstats.sourceforge.net*	Web server logfiles, FTP logs, mail logs Software Win/Unix/Mac	An open source Perl-based measurement tool, AWStats is a very flexible tool for technically minded folks.
WWWStat *http://ftp.ics.uci.edu/pub/ websoft/wwwstat/*	Web server logfiles Software Unix-based systems	Relatively simple and easily modified Perl-based logfile parser for Unix systems and common logfile (CLF) format web servers.
Webstats *http://www.columbia.edu/httpd/ webstats/*	Web server logfiles Software Unix (Solaris)	Very simple Perl-based logfile parser. Easy to install, easy to run.

Table 1-3. Freely available web measurement solutions (continued)

Name and URL	Data source(s) used Delivery type platforms	What's good or cool about this solution
Log Parser 2.0 *http://www.microsoft.com/ technet/scriptcenter/tools/ logparser/default.mspx*	Web server logfiles Software Windows	Microsoft tool that allows SQL-like queries against Microsoft Internet Information Server (IIS) logfiles.
FunnelWeb *http://www.funnelwebcentral.com*	Web server logfiles Software Win/Unix/Mac	Surprisingly well-supported by moderately active bulletin boards maintained by a regular software company (Quest Software).

Keep in mind that there are likely many more free applications, including hundreds (if not thousands) of page counters. The programs listed above are those that have a solid reputation and have been around for years. Some, like Microsoft's Log Parser, are even documented in great books like *Microsoft Log Parser Toolkit* (O'Reilly).

For the most part, to take advantage of these free applications, you need a good working knowledge of software installations, some Perl in many cases, and lots and lots of patience. Some of the applications, such as AWStats and Analog, are supported by the open source community and incredibly nice people like Dr. Stephen Turner (author of Analog and contributor in this book). Also, if you're really interested in saving some money, don't forget to read the "Build Your Own Web Measurement Application" hacks throughout this book!

Inexpensive Web Measurement Solutions

The next step up from free software is inexpensive software. By *inexpensive*, I mean under $1,000 for either the software license or *two years* of hosted costs. For example, if a hosted application is $500 per year, it would be on this list because it costs only $1,000 over two years. We use two years because that is the average amount of time companies use most web measurement applications before upgrading or switching vendors.

While $1,000 may seem like a lot for you, many of the applications listed in Table 1-4 are significantly less expensive, and I've tried to include the lowest available pricing I could find (but please remember those prices are subject to change).

Find a Free or Cheap Web Measurement Solution

Table 1-4. *Inexpensive web measurement solutions*

Name, URL, and lowest available price	Data source(s) used Delivery type Platforms	What's good or cool about this solution
Web-Stat http://www.web-stat.com $5/month	JavaScript page tags Hosted application	Perhaps the world's least-expensive tag-based solution; provides simple conversion and ROI tracking for under $10 per month.
ClickTracks http://www.clicktracks.com	Web server logfiles, JavaScript page tags Software, hosted application Windows	One of the most usable, visually engaging measurement applications available; very appropriate for those new to site measurement.
VisitorVille http://www.visitorville.com $4.95/month	Web server logfiles, JavaScript page tags Software Windows	The Sims meets web site measurement; hilarious, if a touch impractical for serious measurement; allows real-time chat with visitors.
WebSTAT Premium http://www.webstat.com $9.95/month	JavaScript page tags Hosted application	Basic tag-based measurement application, a step up visually from Web-Stat; able to publish reports in Excel and Adobe PDF formats.
HitBox Professional http://www.hitboxprofessional. com $26.67/month	JavaScript page tags Hosted application	The original inexpensive web measurement application; feature rich and supported by a well known application vendor (WebSideStory).
OneStat http://www.onestat.com $10.82/month	JavaScript page tags Hosted application	Purportedly used by 50,000 subscribers in 100 companies; a feature-rich alternative to HitBox Professional for Europe and Asia.
Deep Log Analyzer http://www.deep-software.com $149.95	Web server logfiles Software Windows	Very inexpensive software-based logfile parser; provides additional functionality via downloadable reports (Professional version only).
IndexTools http://www.indextools.com $19.95/month	JavaScript page tags Hosted application	Tag-based solution highly focused on pay-per-click campaign efforts; has add-on functionality to generate complex keyword ROI metrics and a nifty browser overlay (E-Business Edition only).

Table 1-4. Inexpensive web measurement solutions (continued)

Name, URL, and lowest available price	Data source(s) used Delivery type Platforms	What's good or cool about this solution
Clicklab *http://www.clicklab.com* $50/month	JavaScript page tags Hosted application	Relatively simple application; the only measurement application I know of that focuses on identifying click fraud.
WebTrends 7 Small Business Edition *http://www.webtrends.com* $495 or $35/month	Web server logfiles, JavaScript page tags Software, hosted application Windows (software)	Very flexible, very powerful application for the money; provided by a market-leading application vendor (WebTrends).
NetTracker Professional *http://www.nettracker.com* $695	Web server logfiles Software Win/Unix/Mac	Flexible solution for a variety of platforms; one of a small number of applications that provide visitor segmentation for under $1,000.
Urchin 5 *http://www.urchin.com* $895	Web server logfiles Software Win/Unix/Mac	Very fast, slick-looking interface capable of reporting in multiple languages; improves accuracy of web server logfiles using first-party cookie augmentation.

The advantage of paying even a small amount is that you establish some type of relationship with the software provider—one that you can leverage if you need minor support. Some of the programs listed in Table 1-4, including WebTrends, Urchin, NetTracker Professional, ClickTracks, and HitBox Professional, are sold by very reputable companies that also sell business- and enterprise-class applications; these companies have an added advantage of a larger, measurement-focused organization supporting their inexpensive products and are worth a closer look.

I'm not advocating free and inexpensive solutions if you're absolutely committed to web measurement being a critical aspect of your online business; there is a pretty strong correlation between the amount companies spend and the attention they pay to software applications. Still, if you're just getting your feet wet and want to test the waters, any of the applications listed in this hack are worth a look.

Use Analog to Process Logfiles

HACK #11

Analog is purportedly the most popular web server logfile analyzer in the world. If you're just getting your feet wet in web measurement, you might want to give it a quick try.

Analog, written by Dr. Stephen Turner (one of the original web measurement hackers), is an easy-to-install and highly flexible web server log analyze—one that hundreds of thousands of people have likely tried at one time or another just to get a taste of web measurement. Since it's completely free, you might want to take the time to download and install the application and generate a few reports just for fun.

Analog: Where to Get It!

Analog is made freely available by Dr. Turner at *www.analog.cx*. At the time this book was written, versions of the application were available for Windows; Macintosh OS 8, OS 9, and OS X; dozens of flavors of Unix, including BSD, Linux, HP-UX, and Solaris; and a motley collection of non-Unix platforms like BeOS, Novell Netware, and OpenVMS. You can also download the source code to compile on any known platform, if it suits your fancy.

Visit *http://www.analog.cx/download.html* and select the version of Analog that works best for you.

How to Install Analog

Once you've downloaded the application, on most platforms all you need to do is extract it using whichever application you normally use to extract archives. The archive will uninstall into an install directory, usually *analog [version]*, where *[version]* is the version of Analog you've downloaded. For example, if you downloaded Analog Version 6.0, you're going to end up with a directory called *analog 6.0*.

To test your installation, simply navigate to the directory created and run Analog in the normal way for your operating system. For example, on Linux, you would just type `./analog`, and on Windows, you would click on the executable *analog.exe*. In Windows, a DOS window will open and close, but a report file called *Report.html* should be created in the *analog* directory—one that when opened will present you with a sample report. If something went wrong, look for the *errors.txt* file, open that, and look for an explanation of what went wrong.

Telling Analog Where Your Logfiles Are

Analog doesn't have a Windows-style user interface. Instead, you configure it by putting commands in the configuration file *analog.cfg*. The first thing you need to tell it is where your web server logfiles can be found. The command for selecting a logfile is

```
LOGFILE logfilename
```

You can have several LOGFILE commands, and you can also include wild-cards in the logfile name. For example, on Windows, you might use the command:

```
LOGFILE C:\WINDOWS\system32\Logfiles\W3SVC1\*.log
```

Creating Basic Reports in Analog

Once you've told the application where to look for your logfiles, all that's left is to generate basic reports based on those logs. The most basic command to get Analog to create a report is simply to click on *analog.exe* or run it from the command line. Still, Analog is very powerful, and you may choose to modify the reports to suit your specific needs in hundreds of different ways. Here are a handful of commands you can place in the *analog.cfg* to modify your reports:

OUTFILE {*filename*}
> You can use the OUTFILE command to change the name of the report generated from *Report.html* to anything you like.

HOSTNAME *and* HOSTURL
> You can use the HOSTNAME and HOSTURL commands to change the name and URL at the top of the reports you generate. Use the following format:
>
> ```
> HOSTNAME "Web Analytics Demystified"
> HOSTURL http://www.webanalyticsdemystified.com/
> ```

LANGUAGE {*language*}
> You can change the language in which the report is written to any of over 30 languages. For example:
>
> ```
> LANGUAGE UKRAINIAN
> ```

For a more complete list of basic commands that can be issued to Analog, visit *http://www.analog.cx/docs/basiccmd.html*.

Running the Hack

Once you've successfully downloaded and installed Analog, simply execute it on the command line. On a Windows system, for example, simply type analog.exe on the command line. The program will read the configuration file and place its output in a file called *Report.html* (or the file specified in the OUTFILE setting in *analog.cfg*). You can then open this report in a web browser to see the results. Figure 1-11 shows a typical example.

Hourly Summary

(**Go To**: Top | General Summary | Daily Report | Daily Summary | Hourly Summary | Search Word Report | Browser Summary
File Type Report | Internal Search Query Report | Request Report)

This report lists the total activity for each hour of the day, summed over all the days in the report.

Each unit (■) represents 100 requests for pages or part thereof.

hour	reqs	pages	
0	15105	2155	
1	12807	1972	
2	12097	1920	
3	12611	2932	
4	12383	2184	
5	12448	1540	
6	12072	1686	
7	13256	1799	
8	16725	2300	
9	19731	2765	
10	20365	3166	
11	19534	2923	
12	17757	2913	
13	20557	3135	
14	25140	3896	

Figure 1-11. Hourly summary report from Analog

Consider combining Analog with Report Magic (*www.reportmagic.org*) to improve the visual appeal of the reports (Figure 1-12).

Analog is a simple but powerful web measurement application—one that will perhaps satisfy your entry-level needs if you're just getting into web data analysis.

—Dr. Stephen Turner and Eric T. Peterson

HACK #12 Build Your Own Web Measurement Application: An Overview and Data Collection

If you've got passable Perl skills and the desire to control your own destiny, you can use our code and build a simple page-tag analyzer.

The first hack in our "Build Your Own Web Measurement Application" series describes how the data will be collected. We'll be using a JavaScript page tag [Hack #28] and, to the best of our knowledge, ours is the only freely available tag-based reporting application available today.

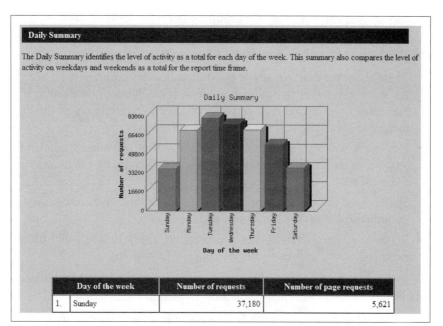

Figure 1-12. Analog reports modified using Report Magic

Collecting the Data

There are two components in our data collection strategy. The first is a piece of JavaScript code that must be inserted into every page on your web site. When the visitor's web browser renders the page, the script is executed, causing a request for an image to be made to the web server. For now, the image URL contains basic information about the page and the referrer, although we shall see how to augment it in [Hack #90].

The second component is a program that runs on the server. It writes the page and referrer information into a web server logfile, and then returns the image the browser is waiting for, which is an invisible one-pixel transparent image.

The logfile we build will look something like this:

```
1104772080 192.168.17.32 /index.html?from=google http://www.google.com/
search?q=widgets 192.168.17.32.85261104772101338
1104772091 192.168.17.32 /products.html http://www.example.com/index.
html?from=google 192.168.17.32.85261104772101338
```

The first field on each line is the time of the request in *Unix time* (seconds since 1/1/1970). The second field is the client's IP address, which the server knows. The third is the URL of the page; the fourth is the URL of the referring page (the page linked to this one); and the fifth is the visitor's cookie (in this case, generated by Apache's mod_usertrack module).

It might occur to you that all this information is already present in the web server's own logfile. Why do we want to produce a second logfile to duplicate the data? In fact, there are several advantages to this approach.

- The web server that is running the data collection program need not be the same web server that is hosting the web site. Sometimes the web site may already be hosted on a server from which you can't access the logfiles, or the web site may span more than one server.

- Our logfile will record only some of the data. That will make it quicker to analyze. In particular, we ignore hits [Hack #1], which may be important for technical analysis, but are not useful for analyzing visitor behavior.

- Spiders and robots do not execute JavaScript, so we automatically exclude them from the logfile [Hack #23].

- When the page is rendered a second time, the JavaScript will be re-executed, so we automatically bust the cache [Hack #24].

We shall see in [Hack #90] that our approach makes it easy to add additional data fields that are not normally recorded in the web server logfile.

The disadvantages of this approach are similar to those observed with other client-side page tags. For example, it can be more difficult to set up, it won't measure visitors who have disabled JavaScript, and you can't go back and analyze historical data. But we believe the benefits associated with accuracy and the ability to gather customized data outweigh the problems for many people.

The JavaScript part of the code is very simple:

```
<script>
document.write('<img src="http://www.yourserver.com/cgi-bin/readtag.
pl?url='+escape(document.location)+'&amp;ref='+escape(document.referrer)+'">');
</script>
```

This script has to be inserted at the top of the <BODY> element of every page you want tracked, and the *www.yourserver.com* reference needs to be changed to the real location of this script on your servers. Some web servers are set up to insert a template at the top of every page, in which case you can do this once and it will appear on all of your pages. But usually you will have to edit each page.

When the browser renders the page, it will execute the script and insert into the page an HTML image tag like this one.

```
<img src="http://www.yourserver.com/cgi-bin/readtag.pl?url=http%3A//
www.example.com/index.html%3Ffrom%3Dgoogle&ref=http%3A//www.google.com/
search%3Fq%3Dwidgets">
```

This is just the URL of the current page and the referring page, slightly encoded to avoid ampersands and equals signs looking as if they belonged to the image URL.

When the browser requests that image from the server, the server will record the current page and the referrer in our web server logfile and send a one-pixel transparent GIF back to the browser.

Returning the Image and Logging the Page View

The image tag calls a script called *readtag.pl* that is listening for requests. To deploy *readtag.pl*, you should adjust your web server configuration as follows:

- The server must execute programs in the */cgi-bin/* directory.
- The server must be able to write to the logfile chosen below.
- You should plan to cookie your visitors [Hack #15]. The program will work without this, but the visitor tracking will be less accurate. If you are using Apache, the mod_usertrack module will produce cookies.
- You should set up a P3P policy on the server using compact policy headers [Hack #27]. This is essential if the program is running on a different server from the web site; otherwise, Internet Explorer will reject the cookies. The minimum CP headers you'll need to set to make this code function properly are:

```
P3P: policyref="http://www.yourserver.com/w3c/p3p.xml",
    CP="COR NID NOI OUR COM NAV STA"
```

- If you are using Apache, you should use the mod_perl module. This will reduce the load on the server by starting Perl only once, instead of every time this program is run.

If you have any questions about these requirements, we recommend you consult with your web system administrator and explain what you're trying to accomplish. Making changes to your Apache configuration is not without risk and should be attempted only by an experienced professional.

The Code

All of the following code should be saved in a file called *readtag.pl* into your web server's */cgi-bin* directory. The #!perl line may need to be adjusted to point to the location of Perl on your machine—for example #!/usr/bin/perl.

```
# Remember to change the next line to your Perl location
#!perl -w
use strict;
# Declare the location of the logfile. The CGI program needs to be given
permission to write to this file.
my $logfile = '/var/log/apache/page.log';
# The name of the cookie you are using. 'Apache' is the default for mod_
usertrack cookies.
my $cookie_name = 'Apache';
# We shall use the standard CGI module. This does all the work of extracting
the parameters from the query string and decoding them.
use CGI;
```

```perl
my $cgi = new CGI;
my $url = $cgi->param('url');   # Get the url= and ref= parameters
my $ref = $cgi->param('ref');
# Strip the server name off the front of the URL (we don't want to repeat it
on every line of the file).
$url =~ s!^https?://[^/]+!!;
# As long as we've got a non-empty URL and a (possibly empty) referrer,
write a line in the logfile.
if ($url && defined($ref)) {
# Look up the current time, the client name, and the cookie.
  my $time = time();
  my $client = $cgi->remote_host();
  my $cookie_val = $cookie_name ? $cgi->cookie($cookie_name) : "";
  if (!defined($cookie_val)) { $cookie_val = ""; }
# We need to open the logfile.
# We also need to lock it, to make sure that we're not writing two requests
at the same time.
# If we can't open it or can't lock it, write a diagnostic message to
STDERR, which is the server's error log.
  use Fcntl qw/:flock/;   # Import the definition of LOCK_EX
  unless (open (LF, ">>", "$logfile") && flock(LF, LOCK_EX)) {
    my $lt = localtime;
    my $progname = $0 || 'readtag.pl';
    print STDERR "[$lt] $progname: Can't open logfile\n";
  }
# Everything worked, so jump to the end of the logfile (this is necessary in
case something was written between the time we opened it and the time we
locked it), and write the line.
  else {
    seek(LF, 0, 2);
    print LF "$time\t$client\t$url\t$ref\t$cookie_val\n";
    close LF;
  }
}
# Finally, send a one-by-one pixel transparent GIF image back to the browser
(the long list of numbers just happens to be that GIF, byte by byte).
print "Content-Type: image/gif\n\n";
print 'GIF89a';
print v1.0.1.0.145.0.0.0.0.0.255.255.255.255.255.255.0.0.0.33.249.4.1.0.0.2.
0.44.0.0.0.0.1.0.1.0.0.2.2.84.1.0.59;
```

That's it!

Running the Code

Provided you've copied the code correctly, and set permissions and P3P policy correctly on your web server, all you need to do is add the following code near the top of the <BODY> element of each of your web pages:

```html
<script>
document.write('<img src="http://www.yourserver.com/cgi-bin/readtag.
pl?url='+escape(document.location)+'&amp;ref='+escape(document.referrer)+'">');
</script>
```

That's it. The scripts handle everything else. As soon as you turn them on and traffic starts flowing on your site, the scripts start to generate a logfile similar to the following:

```
1106000655    204.210.27.229    /discussion_list.asp    http://www.
webanalyticsdemystified.com/free_kpi_worksheet.asp    204.210.27.229.
319011106000542572
1106000657    204.210.27.229    /    http://www.webanalyticsdemystified.com/
discussion_list.asp    204.210.27.229.319011106000542572
1106001299    207.111.202.223    /            207.111.202.223.319061106001281430
1106001303    207.111.202.223    /free_preview.asp    http://www.
webanalyticsdemystified.com/    207.111.202.223.319061106001281430
```

You'll learn more about how to add variables to the script and how to generate reports based on the script in subsequent hacks.

—Dr. Stephen Turner and Eric T. Peterson

HACK #13 Build Your Own RSS Tracking Application: An Overview and Data Collection

Content syndication via RSS and XML and blogging are extremely hot topics, but there are few tools available to track people reading and interacting with your content and articles. With a little bit of Perl knowledge, you can use our "build your own" hack to write a bare-bones RSS traffic analyzer.

If you're willing to roll up your sleeves a bit and dig into some Perl, you can significantly enhance your ability to track syndicated content compared to the little you're likely able to learn using only web measurement tools [Hack #47]. Using the following scripts to track your own RSS feeds and posts will tell you:

- What articles and posts people read
- Who refers people to your work
- Where readers click out to from your posts (which links are clicked)

For syndicated content, this is pretty much it: the information you need to determine the reach and response to your blogging activities. While it depends on a little bit more code—and it won't work on every blogging platform or every RSS reader because there is really no better source for this data—the results are very satisfying.

The Data Collection Code

The code for this hack is relatively simple and broken into four parts:

- The code that goes into each RSS feed or article you want to track
- The code that the RSS feed will call (*track_rss.js*)

- The code that will process the resulting request, generated by the first two blocks of code (*write_rss_tag.cgi*) and generate a log of your RSS activity (*rss.log*)

This code functions in nearly the same way as a client-side page tag [Hack #28] by leveraging a "round trip" call to an external JavaScript file.

Tracking code to be placed into the feed or article you want to track. In order to enable measurement, you need to add the following code to each post you want tracked.

```
<DIV ID="NAME OF ARTICLE">
<!-- YOUR ARTICLE OR CONTENT WOULD GO HERE -->
</DIV>
<SCRIPT LANGUAGE="JAVASCRIPT">n="NAME OF ARTICLE";</SCRIPT>
<SCRIPT LANGUAGE="JavaScript" SRC="http://www.yourserverlocation.com/scripts
/track_rss.js"></script>
```

Remember to change the NAME OF ARTICLE to the actual name of the article as you'd like tracked and the location of the http://www.yourserverlocation.com/scripts/track_rss.js file to the actual location where that file is kept:

> The NAME OF ARTICLE must be identical in the DIV and Java-Script definition for this code to work.

For example, if you had written a weblog post about how great Firefox is, the whole code might look like this:

```
<DIV ID="Firefox is so super cool!">
I love Firefox, it is so cool. <a href=mailto:me@mysite.com>Mail me</A> if
you love Firefox as much as I do.
</DIV>
<SCRIPT LANGUAGE="JAVASCRIPT">n="Firefox is so super cool!";</SCRIPT>
<SCRIPT LANGUAGE="JavaScript" SRC="http://www.yourserverlocation.com/
scripts/track_rss.js"></script>
```

Be sure to include the SCRIPT portion of the code after the text of the article since the JavaScript for tracking clicks depends on being run after the page has loaded. Assuming you've done everything correctly, once you deploy the article or feed via XML, you'll end up with the JavaScript code embedded in the appropriate XML container.

> Unfortunately, this code will not work in all weblog publishing applications, since not all of them allow JavaScript to be embedded.

Tracking code to be referenced externally (the track_rss.js file). The following code is the *trackrss.js file* referred to in the JavaScript you're placing in the article proper. This code is referenced externally to minimize the amount of code that needs to be placed in the article itself. You need to save the file in a publicly available directory on your web site (for example, */scripts/*).

```
// Declare and call the tracking image passing name, location, referrer and
// random number in the query
i=new Image();
i.src="http://www.yourserverlocation.com/cgi-bin/write_rss_tag.
cgi?n="+escape(n)
+"&t=v&u="+escape(document.location)+"&r="+escape(document.referrer)+'&rn='
+eval(RSSRandomNum());

// Get the article container by id and the links within and iterate through
them
var articlecontainer = document.getElementById(n);
var articlelinks = articlecontainer.getElementsByTagName('a');
for(i=0;(link=articlelinks[i]); i++) {
  // Build the new function to add
  var addfunc = "RSSClickTrack('" + escape(link.href) + "','" + escape(n) +
"');";
  // Test if the link already has an onclick event defined
  if (link.onclick) {
    // Get the existing onclick function
    var previousstart = link.onclick.toString().indexOf('{')+1;
    var previousend = link.onclick.toString().lastIndexOf('}');
    var previousfunc = link.onclick.toString().substring(previousstart,
previousend);
    // Test if exisitng onclick already has the RSSClickTrack  call
    if (previousfunc.indexOf('RSSClickTrack')<0) {
      // define and write the new onclick wih both the existing and the new
      var newfunc = addfunc + previousfunc;
      link.onclick= new Function(newfunc);
    }
  } else {
    // No esisitng onclick, create it with the new
    link.onclick= new Function(addfunc);
  }
}

function RSSClickTrack(link,name){
  // declare and call the click tracking image passing link, name, location
and
  //random number in the query location is passed as the referrer to the
click
  c=new Image();
  c.src="http://www.yourserverlocation.com/cgi-bin/write_rss_tag.
cgi?n="+name
+"&t=c&u="+link+"&r="+escape(document.location)+'&rn='+eval(RSSRandomNum());
}
```

```
function RSSRandomNum( ) {
  //get a random number to break caching
  rnum = Math.random( ) * 1000000;
  rnum = Math.round(rnum);
  return rnum;
}
```

 Use this code at your own risk! Because content syndication is still an emerging field, it is difficult to know how all RSS readers and applications will deal with JavaScript.

For this code to function properly, you need to change the location http://www.*yourserverlocation*.com/cgi-bin/write_rss_tag.cgi to the location of the *write_rss_tag.cgi* file (see below). It is worth noting that the variable t is set differently, depending on whether the article is viewed (t=v) or a link is clicked (t=c).

Code to parse the JavaScript into an RSS logfile (write_rss_tag.cgi). The following code is very similar to the "page tag" generated in the "Build Your Own Web Measurement Application" hacks [Hack #12]. It is written to accept input from the JavaScript tag above. You need to save this code on your web server in a location where it can be executed by an external script (for example, your */cgi-bin/* directory). The #!perl line may need to be adjusted to point to the location of Perl on your machine—for example, #!/usr/bin/perl.

```
# The #!perl may need to be adjusted to point to the location of perl
# on your machine, for example #!/usr/bin/perl
#!perl -w
use strict;

# Declare the location of the logfile. The CGI program needs to be given
# permission to write to this file. Exactly how to do that is
# system-dependent.
my $logfile = '/var/log/apache/rss.log';

# The name of the cookie, if any.
# 'Apache' is the default for mod_usertrack cookies.
my $cookie_name = 'Apache';

# We shall use the standard CGI module. This does all the work of extracting
# the parameters from the query string and unescaping them.
use CGI;
my $cgi = new CGI;
my $name = $cgi->param('n'); # Get the RSS STORY NAME
my $type = $cgi->param('t'); # Get Event TYPE
my $param_url = $cgi->param('u');  # Get the u= url that is quantified of
the event
my $env_url = $cgi->referer(); # Get the referrer from environment for
noscript/image calls for url
```

```perl
my $ref = $cgi->param('r'); # Get the r= Referrer to the event (will only be
captured for javascript executed tracking calls))

# Use the referrer from the image call for the url of the page with the tag
# if it exists and the incoming value for the param_url does not exist.
# if neither exist set the value to UNKNOWN. The use of UNKNOWN is to cover
# requests from RSS Readers that don't execute javascript and/or don't send
# a referrer to an image request.
my $url = "UNKNOWN"; # declare url with default value
$url = $env_url if ($env_url); # use referrer to the image request if it
exists
$url = $param_url if ($param_url); # use param_url for url if exists

# Referrer is not always specified for brevity in image tracking calls. If
it is not
# defined define a blank one.
$ref = "" unless (defined($ref));

# As long as we've got a non-empty NAME and a non-empty TYPE
# write a line in the logfile.
if ($name && $type) {

  # Look up the current time, the client name and the cookie. The
  # cookie may not be present for requests from some RSS readers or it
  # might not be set prior to some events.
  my $time = time();
  my $client = $cgi->remote_host();
  my $cookie_val = $cookie_name ? $cgi->cookie($cookie_name) : "";
  if (!defined($cookie_val)) { $cookie_val = ""; }

  # build the log line
  my $logout = "$type\t$time\t$client\t$name\t$url\t$ref\t$cookie_val";

  # We need to open the logfile. We also need to lock it, to make sure that
  # we're not writing two requests at the same time. If we can't open it or
  # can't lock it, write a diagnostic message to STDERR, which is the
  # server's error log.
  use Fcntl qw/:flock/;  # Import the definition of LOCK_EX
  unless (open (LF, ">>", "$logfile") && flock(LF, LOCK_EX)) {
    my $lt = localtime;
    my $progname = $0 || 'readrsstag.pl';
    print STDERR "[$lt] $progname: Can't open logfile\n";
  }

  # Everything worked, so jump to the end of the logfile (this is necessary
  # in case something was written between the time we opened it and the time
  # we locked it), and write the line.
  else {
    seek(LF, 0, 2);
    print LF "$logout\n";
    close LF;
  }
}
```

```
# Finally, send a 1x1 pixel transparent gif back to the browser.
# (The long list of numbers just happens to be that gif, byte by byte).
print "Content-Type: image/gif\n\n";
print 'GIF89a';
print v1.0.1.0.145.0.0.0.0.0.255.255.255.255.255.255.0.0.0.33.249.4.1.0.0.2.
0.44.0.0.0.0.1.0.1.0.0.2.2.84.1.0.59;
```

Running the Code

Assuming that you've copied the code correctly and set the appropriate permissions for *write_rss_tag.cgi* on your web server, you should be all set. Again, the most important things to double check are that:

- The ID in the <DIV> tag in your post matches the value of n exactly.

- The reference http://www.*yourserverlocation*.com/scripts/track_rss.js in the JavaScript has been changed to the location of the file on your server (likely in your */scripts/* directory).

- The http://www.*yourserverlocation*.com/cgi-bin/write_rss_tag.cgi reference in the *track_rss.js* file has been changed to the location of the file on your server (likely in your */cgi-bin/* directory).

Also, because some applications for deploying content via RSS (most notably, the blogging tools) will insert HTML tags automatically (usually the </BR> tag), you should double check that the JavaScript renders correctly when the post is viewed.

The Results

Once you've successfully deployed the data collection code, you'll generate a logfile similar to the one in Figure 1-13.

```
v    1109272096    64.248.172.99    Scoble, who I normally enjoy reading, says something typical of RSS evangelists http:
v    1109272193    66.92.1.40       Scoble, who I normally enjoy reading, says something typical of RSS evangelists http:
c    1109272260    66.92.1.40       Scoble, who I normally enjoy reading, says something typical of RSS evangelists mailt
v    1109272801    64.81.52.179     Scoble, who I normally enjoy reading, says something typical of RSS evangelists http:
v    1109272866    66.159.231.6     Scoble, who I normally enjoy reading, says something typical of RSS evangelists http:
v    1109273523    172.164.94.16    Scoble, who I normally enjoy reading, says something typical of RSS evangelists http:
v    1109273708    172.164.94.16    Bringing RSS to the masses, part II    http://weblogs.jupiterresearch.com/analysts/p
v    1109273708    172.164.94.16    Danny Sullivan on simplifying RSS subscription http://weblogs.jupiterresearch.com/ar
v    1109273872    129.10.157.60    Scoble, who I normally enjoy reading, says something typical of RSS evangelists http:
v    1109273894    129.10.157.60    Scoble, who I normally enjoy reading, says something typical of RSS evangelists http:
v    1109273908    66.184.181.186   Scoble, who I normally enjoy reading, says something typical of RSS evangelists http:
v    1109273956    205.201.15.142   Scoble, who I normally enjoy reading, says something typical of RSS evangelists http:
v    1109274471    171.159.64.10    Scoble, who I normally enjoy reading, says something typical of RSS evangelists http:
v    1109275048    69.92.229.44     Scoble, who I normally enjoy reading, says something typical of RSS evangelists http:
```

Figure 1-13. Sample RSS log generated by the write_rss_tag.cgi script

All that's left is to parse this log and generate reports [Hack #36]. We'll do this using a series of Perl objects, a strategy similar to the "build your own" hacks in this book, and one that allows greater flexibility if you want to modify this code for your own purposes.

—*Ian Houston and Eric T. Peterson*

## CHAPTER TWO

Implementation and Setup
Hacks 14–36

A significant amount of investment on both your and your vendor's part will go into implementation and setup. Why? Because if you screw up your implementation, the chances that you'll do or learn anything meaningful from your analytics application decrease significantly.

The largest numbers of hacks presented in this book are implementation and setup hacks, because this is where the greatest opportunity really is. The more attention you pay, the more useful data you collect, the better the "hack" in your implementation, and the better your overall experience with web measurement will be.

Once You've Selected a Vendor

This is when the really hard work begins. Crazy, huh? You thought sitting through all those demonstrations and negotiating contacts was the hard part. Unfortunately, for the most part, the process you've been through will seem like a piece of cake compared to implementation and training. And, more unfortunately, implementation will seem like a piece of cake compared to getting people to actually use and respond to the reports.

But don't despair!

The hacks in this chapter are written to help you do a great job with your implementation process. My recommendation is not to just read the hacks that seem relevant to you, but rather to read them all. You'll never know where that fantastic piece of trivia will show up, the one piece of information you need to better explain to your vendor what you're trying to do. Remember, knowing is half the battle. Use that knowledge to your advantage.

Relax, and Don't Forget to Breathe

Just in case your implementation is not going as planned, don't panic. Keep in mind that despite years of investment in web measurement and analysis this is still pretty complicated stuff, and you'll inevitably make mistakes. If you find yourself becoming frustrated with the setup or implementation process, here are a few useful questions you should ask yourself before coming unglued:

Whose fault is it really?
> Many companies assume that problems with their implementations are the sole responsibility of the vendor. Practically speaking, though, there is usually ownership on both sides. When you're clear about what is yours and what is theirs, a productive conversation about how to resolve the problem can usually occur.

Was there a realistic timeline and were realistic expectations originally established?
> Ask yourself whether you perhaps bit off more than you (or anyone) could reasonably chew. Keep in mind that the sales person's only job was to say "Yes, we can do that" and "Yes, that sounds realistic." While certainly your vendor should be working with you to establish realistic goals, sometimes a reset is necessary (and yes, this can be painful to message to internal stakeholders, but it's better to bite the bullet than try to dodge it).

If you're still not satisfied, or at least pacified, after answering these questions, my best advice is to call someone else at your vendor's organization and ask for "other help." There is no shame in asking for help, and if you don't ask, opting instead to muddle through with the help you have (or lack thereof), then the only person you have to blame is yourself.

HACK #14   Optimize the Implementation Process
Implementation is over half the battle in web measurement, so you want to make sure you do it right.

Once you've selected a vendor [Hack #3], the next step is to get the application up and running and begin collecting data. Regardless of whether you've gone the software or hosted service route, or whether you're using JavaScript page tags or web server logfiles as a data source, taking time to optimize the implementation process can prevent real headaches later on.

Know What to Collect in Advance

Given the complexity of data collection afforded by top measurement applications, knowing what you want to collect before you start is critical. Especially when working with a hosted service provider [Hack #3] or using page tags [Hack #28], having clear expectations about which data will be collected [Hack #19] can save you time and prevent having to explain why you can't generate critical reports. It's also worthwhile at this point to compare the list of data you'll collect to your original request for proposal (RFP) [Hack #9] to double-check that you're getting what you need. If you don't spend the time getting this right, you'll regret it later.

Work Closely with Your Vendor

Unless you're working with the most bare-bones of applications [Hack #10] or building software yourself [Hack #12], I *strongly* recommend that you plan on spending some time with implementation support staff from your vendor of choice, especially early on. While you may have a clear vision of how you want your data collected and reports generated, many vendors do a poor job documenting their products, making it difficult to rely on the do-it-yourself attitude that so many technologists have.

Most vendors provide at least nominal implementation support for free; if you're spending more than $50,000 on software or data collection, you should seriously consider purchasing (or better, negotiating at no additional cost) at least one full day of implementation support (reported vendor pricing* is listed in Table 2-1).

Table 2-1. Implementation and professional service fees for top vendors

Vendor	Provide account support for every customer?	Professional service fees (per day)
ClickTracks	No	$1,200/day
WebTrends	No[a]	$2,250/day
WebSideStory	Yes	$2,500/day
Omniture	Yes	$1,000/day
Coremetrics	Yes	$1,500/day
Urchin	No	$1,200/day
Sane Solutions	Yes	$2,500/day
Visual Sciences[b]	Yes	$1,600/day
Fireclick	Yes	$1,500/day
IBM SurfAid	Yes	$2,000/day

[a] WebTrends provides dedicated account support to their largest customers.

[b] Visual Sciences was not covered in Terry Lund's Buyer's Guide; this information was independently gathered.

---

* As reported by Terry Lund in MarketingSherpa's *Buyer's Guide to Web Analytics* (*http://sherpastore. com/store/page.cfm/2146*)

As a general rule and based on my experience both as an analyst and a director of professional services, I recommend one day of implementation support for every $50,000 spent, given that an average *initial* implementation takes anywhere between a few hours and a few days. Depending on which data source you choose, you'll face either a nominally complex software implementation or an occasionally arduous page tag deployment, either of which will be made easier with vendor support. If you don't use all of your time during the initial setup, you'll be happy you have that time throughout the course of the relationship.

Once the data collection process is in place, the next step it to start generating reports.

Get the Five Most Important Reports Right Away

Ideally, you already have an idea of what I mean when I say "the five most important reports." These are the reports that either the senior-most decision maker will want to see or the reports that will help quantify a problem that you already know exists and would desperately like to correct. You want to get these reports as quickly as possible once you're up and running. Obviously, if you have to ask someone for a large sum of money, it's prudent to demonstrate as quickly as possible that the money was well spent. Producing the "five most important reports" in short order will help you do that, provided the reports are meaningful and you're prepared to explain them.

Why five reports? Because it's two less than seven and three more than two, of course! Seriously, depending on your company's particular focus, some of the following might be likely candidates for the "most important reports" list:

- Campaign response and conversion
- Most popular pages and content groups
- Product browse-to-buy ratios
- Top referring sites
- Key page "stickiness"
- Checkout process (conversion and sales)
- Top keywords and phrases
- Top internal searches
- Top affiliates by visits and conversion
- Visitor geographies

Also, if your particular measurement application has a browser overlay [Hack #62], you should plan on showing that to management, encouraging its use by providing basic training.

Get Training, but Have the Right Expectations

Once the system is collecting data and generating reports, you should arrange to provide application training to the appropriate people. While companies often try and gather together all possible people who may ever, in their lifetime, have any reason to use the measurement application and subject them to training, often this is a huge mistake. Instead, a more effective strategy to promote adoption of tools like these inside organizations is to create a group of "power users" and have them stimulate interest. Despite the fact that web measurement tools are a must-have for companies hoping to succeed on the Internet, these tools are widely believed to be for the technically inclined (a polite way to say "data analysis geeks"), so you'll need to allow people to self-select into this group, at least in the beginning.

Ideally, you'll be able to provide training to a group of three to five power users, again by working with your application vendor to ensure that you're sharing the right information. These power users can then start to generate and distribute the right reports [Hack #91] and help other folks in the organization understand what the data is saying. Even when everyone is trained and getting reports, you still want to be sure you have a backup plan, just in case training alone is insufficient to get the results you require from your measurement application.

Know Who to Call

There is no "911" call you can make when you have a web measurement problem. Because there will be problems, make sure that when you're done with your implementation, you have a few phone numbers on hand to call if you need help. Many vendors, particularly the hosted service providers who depend on your annual renewal, have started providing dedicated account management teams to their mid-tier and high-end customers (Table 2-1). This team is your first line of support when you need help.

If you're lucky enough to be provided dedicated account management, take advantage of it! Develop a relationship with your account manager, ensuring that he knows enough about your business strategy and web site to provide relevant answers to your questions. The best vendors provide these folks at reasonable customer-to-agent ratios (about 20:1 is pretty good) so that any one agent is not too overloaded to assist you. Ideally, these people aren't sales people, so you know when they call that they may actually have important information for you. Conversely, if your account manager never calls or calls only to sell you something, or when you email or call him you don't hear back for days, ask for "other help" and let his manager know you need better support. Being proactive in this regard pays off every time, because you're letting your vendor know that you're serious about web measurement and they need to treat you as such.

Assuming you're able to follow the advice I provide in this hack relatively closely, you should be well on your way to web measurement success. Congratulations! You're now better off than an estimated 70 percent of the companies trying to do business on the Internet.

HACK #15 Improve Data Accuracy with Cookies

Cookies are a fundamental component in any web measurement solution and they come in several flavors. Because of the explosion in use of anti-spyware applications, you need to understand how cookies are commonly used and make an active decision about how they'll be used on your site.

In theory, one of the simplest ways to improve the accuracy of your analytics data is to use cookies as a data tracking mechanism. A cookie is a piece of information that is stored by your web browser and comes in two minor variations: session cookies and persistent cookies. Session cookies last only as long as the visitor is on your site and are deleted after the user closes her web browser or after some period of inactivity (typically 30 minutes [Hack #1]). Persistent cookies last beyond a single visit and have an expiration date some time in the future. Session and persistent cookies use identical technology but differ in how they're treated by security and privacy applications like the Platform for Privacy Preferences (P3P) [Hack #26].

Session Cookies for Short-Term Accuracy

Session cookies are typically set by web server applications and allow your analytics solution to group interactions with your web server at the visit level. With logfile-based solutions, you should enable your web server to set session cookies and configure your analytics solution to track these session cookies in your logs. Tag-based solutions [Hack #3] will typically set their own session cookies, so you should get this functionality for free. Once session cookie tracking is enabled, you can start to analyze a number of useful visit level statistics, including total visits, pages per session, entry pages, exit pages, and clickstream data.

Persistent Cookies for Long-Term Measurement

Persistent cookies allow your analytics solution to track visitor behavior across multiple visits, which is absolutely critical in web site measurement. This is useful when you are trying to understand customer retention information, such as repeat visit and purchase activity, or understand the frequency of visit and lifetime value [Hack #84] of your visitors and customers. Persistent cookies come in two flavors: first party and third party, depending on how they're set.

First-party cookies. Cookies set by the business from their own web servers and domains are called *first-party cookies*. For example, if eBay is setting their own tracking cookies from the *ebay.com* domain, these cookies are said to be set by the "first party." While not exclusively so, the use of first-party cookies is most common in software-based web measurement solutions that rely on web server logfiles for data.

Third-party cookies. Any cookie set from a domain other than that of the accessed web site are *third-party cookies*. For example, if Disney were using a WebSideStory tracking domain, *ehg-disney.hitbox.com* on their *www.disney.com* web site, the WebSideStory cookie is a third-party cookie. More and more, the hosted application providers are moving to provide a first-party cookie option to their customers, a reflection of accuracy issues associated with third-party cookies.

When a first-party cookie is a third-party cookie. The determination about whether a cookie is first or third party is made by comparing the domain for the web page being served to the cookie domain. Some large organizations have several "brand" web sites that need to be measured as if they were a single site, so sometimes the lines between first-party and third-party cookies become blurred. Consider the following scenarios:

- If Microsoft sent data to and got a cookie from SageMetrics *sageanalyst.net* domain from *www.microsoft.com*, this cookie is definitely a third-party cookie. *Microsoft.com* domain visitors are making third-party requests to *SageMetrics.net* domain, from which a third-party cookie is set. This practice is somewhat deceptive, because the customer did not explicitly ask to send data to SageMetrics.

- If Microsoft sent data to and got a cookie from SageMetrics by modifying DNS and creating a *sageanalyst.microsoft.com* domain, when the data is sent from *www.microsoft.com*, this cookie is said to be a first-party cookie set from *microsoft.com* domain. Microsoft owns and controls the domain and contracts management of the subdomain to SageMetrics as its vendor.

- If Microsoft sent data to and got a cookie from SageMetrics by modifying DNS and creating a *sageanalyst.microsoft.com* domain, when the data is sent from *www.msn.com* to *sageanalyst.microsoft.com*, this cookie is said to be a third-party cookie. The cookie is sent to the *microsoft.com* domain from the *msn.com* servers (different servers in a different domain.)

The third example is usually limited to very large organizations with multiple web sites trying to gather data across multiple domains.

Improve Accuracy with Persistent Cookies

While there are alternatives to cookies [Hack #17], they remain the most popular strategy for determining the uniqueness and visitation history in web site measurement. Unfortunately, because of the proliferation of anti-spyware applications, many designed to remove or disallow third-party cookies, as well as legislation around the world designed to limit the use of "information gathering applications" (which a cookie arguably is, depending on your perspective), the use of cookies is increasingly at risk. Data recently published by JupiterResearch indicates that third-party cookies may be inaccurate as much as 28 percent of the time, and that all cookies might fail as much as 15 percent of the time.

If you are using cookies to track your online visitors—and it is very likely you are—the following recommendations will help improve accuracy.

Use true first-party cookies whenever possible. Because anti-spyware applications are much less likely to block or delete tracking cookies from non-tracking domains, whenever possible, set cookies from your own servers. The logic here is that visitors and anti-spyware applications are less likely to delete your cookies than those of a third party they don't know (or one that is known to be a tracking domain). Most log-based tracking solutions offer some type of web server add-on that will handle this for you, as will any tag-based solution that runs in your data center (as opposed to an external location).

Use DNS to make it look like you're using first-party cookies. One trick that a number of vendors use is mapping a first-party tracking domain to an externally located IP address to give the appearance of a first-party cookie, when in fact the data is flowing to a third party. A simple change in the DNS servers, stating that requests for *tracking.yourdomain.com* should be sent along to your external tracking servers and telling those servers what to do with this traffic when it arrives, is all that is required.

Make sure your privacy and P3P policies accurately reflect what you're doing. People block cookies because they're concerned about their privacy and security online, period. The best way to mitigate this problem and help your visitors understand why you're using cookies is to tell them via your privacy policy [Hack #26] and P3P compact policy [Hack #27]. If you're clear with your visitors, hopefully they will trust you and allow cookies to be set from your site.

The most important thing you need to know about cookies is to not take them for granted. Data suggests that the number of Internet users who are deleting and disallowing cookies is still increasing and that as many as 15 percent of your web visitors are blocking *all* cookies as a rule. By working closely with your measurement vendor to implement the "right" data collection strategy, you will increase data accuracy and the overall quality of your web data.

—Xavier Casanova and Eric T. Peterson

Know When to Use First-Party Cookies

As consumers become more sensitive to potential invasions of their privacy, many are moving to limit your access to information about them via the use of cookies. Here's how to know when to use first-party cookies and what effect their use will have on your analysis.

There are two kinds of persistent cookies used in web measurement: first and third party [Hack #15]. The answer to the question "When should I use a first-party cookie?" is basically "Whenever possible." In this era of increasing awareness about security and privacy, it is preferable to use first-party cookies over third-party cookies, period. It seems like rarely a week passes when we're not hearing about some other privacy intrusion or black hat hack; you and I may know that these intrusions rarely have anything to do with cookies, but the majority of Internet users have no clue.

Given the popularity of anti-spyware applications and the simplicity with which third-party cookies can now be removed or blocked, it is no wonder that research is beginning to show that cross-visit accuracy for these types of cookies is slipping as low as 70 percent. Sure, 70 percent is a lot, but wouldn't you prefer 100 percent accuracy from your web measurement solution?

Cookies are becoming increasingly easy to control, thanks to functionality built into the most popular browsers. Firefox has very simple tools for controlling what cookies are set, from where, and by whom (Figure 2-1) and Microsoft has provided strong controls for cookies via their implementation of the Platform for Privacy Preferences (P3P) [Hack #27]. As more and more Internet users learn about these kinds of tools, can the end of third-party cookies be far behind?

The Advantage of First-Party Cookies

First-party cookies have many advantages. They are not subject to tightening default security settings in many of today's web browsers. They are also not likely to be deleted by anti-spyware and anti-adware programs, which go through your browser's cookies to delete any they deem to be spyware. Consequently, the accuracy of your web measurement data will be much higher if your analytics solution uses first-party cookies to track the majority of your web site activity.

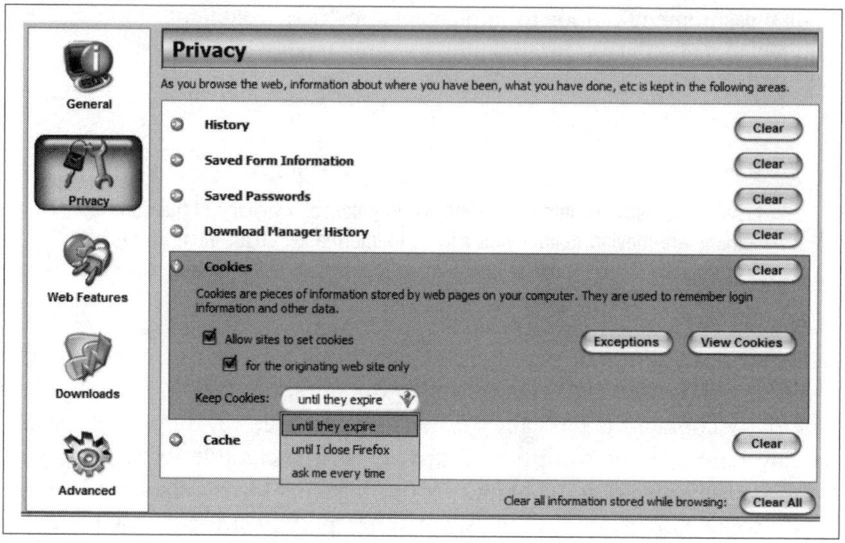

Figure 2-1. Changing cookies in Firefox

Third-Party Cookies Have Their Place

While most measurement vendors support both first- and third-party cookies, it is important to note that third-party cookies do have their place. If you are interested in tracking your users as they navigate across multiple sites, it will be necessary to use third-party cookies.

For example, suppose you manage two sister sites, *www.lawnchairs.com* and *www.lawnfurniture.com*, and you wish to track your users as they navigate across the two sites. Without third-party cookies, if a user clicks on a link from *www.lawnchairs.com* that takes them to *www.lawnfurniture.com*, your web measurement solution would track this as two separate visits.

For sites in this situation, the best compromise is to find a web measurement vendor that uses first-party cookies for internal site activity and uses third-party cookies only to track users as they move from one site to the other. This way, you can use third-party cookies to follow users across your sites, but still retain the accuracy advantages of first-party cookies for all other activity.

How Can I Tell If I'm Using a First- or Third-Party Cookie?

There are a handful of things you can do to determine whether your organization is using third-party cookies. Perhaps the easiest is to grab a copy of Bugnosis for Internet Explorer from *www.bugnosis.org*. Bugnosis is a great little plug-in for IE that will warn you when you're loading a web page that has any potential privacy violations embedded in it (Figure 2-2).

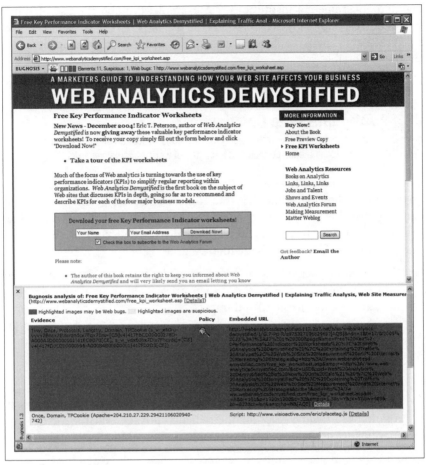

Figure 2-2. Bugnosis report

If you have an aversion to using Internet Explorer (as so many of us do) you can also do a simple search of your page's source code (View → Page Source) for the following strings that identify the most common third-party cookies:

- .hitbox.com
- .webtrendslive.com
- .2o7.net (the second character is a lowercase letter "O")
- .sageanalyst.net
- .wtlive.com
- .coremetrics.com

You'll need to consult the overall privacy policies of your organization before deciding which type of cookie is ultimately best for you. Many financial and governmental institutions, for example, prohibit the use of third-party cookies, and many even prohibit the use of persistent first-party cookies. While third-party cookies have their place, it is best to avoid their use whenever possible.

—Xavier Casanova and Eric T. Peterson

HACK #17 Alternatives to Cookies

While cookies are the most widely used means to identify unique visitors, they are by no means perfect, and a handful of worthy alternatives exist.

Cookies, when properly used, provide a great service to web measurement applications, allowing unique visitors to be tracked from visit to visit and enabling valuable measurements like frequency of visit and lifetime value. Sadly, web site analysts must sometimes do without cookies. There are many reasons for that, such as the following:

- Some visitors actively and consciously disable cookies in their web browsers due to concerns about their privacy. They are essentially opting out of being measured and tracked.

- Some visitors may allow regular cookies set by your web site but disallow tracking cookies set simultaneously by third-party web sites.

- Some visitors may browse your web site from handheld devices that are not always capable of keeping cookies.

- Some web sites make a conscious decision not to cookie their visitors as a symbol of their respect for their clients' privacy. Most typically, this may be the case with web sites of banks and other financial services.

Even if your web site attempts to set cookies, there will be a portion of your visitors for whom cookies are unavailable. Web server logfile-based site measurement tools typically uncover that 15 percent of visits to a web site do not carry a cookie. This hack will show you some alternatives.

Reasonable (If Not Great) Alternatives to Cookies

The more sophisticated the web site measurement application, generally the more alternatives to cookies it will offer. Some vendors allow their customers to choose alternatives to cookies to enable the determination of a unique visitor and visit (sometimes referred to as "sessionization").

The following are less accurate but still often useful strategies for determining the uniqueness of a visitor.

Using the IP address. One piece of information that is always available is the IP address of the computer from which the web site received the page request. In the absence of cookies, the most basic web site measurement tools assume that all page requests that were received from the same IP address within a given period of time were issued by the same visitor. This is an assumption with a high degree of error. Sometimes multiple visitors will share the same IP address—for example when two visitors behind a corporate firewall or proxy server browse your web site simultaneously. At other times, a single visitor will show up in your web site traffic records with differing IP addresses for each page request. This occurs, for example, with visitors using services like America Online—each page request may reach your web site from a different proxy server in AOL's pool of servers.

Using IP address and user agent strings. More sophisticated web site measurement tools will not rely on the IP address alone, but at least combine the IP address with another piece of information that is also always available for each page request, the so-called "user agent" string. The user agent is a piece of text that identifies both the computer operating system and the web browser version from which a page request was issued. For example:

```
Mozilla/4.0+(compatible;+MSIE+6.0;+Windows+NT+5.1;+.NET+CLR+1.1.4322)
```

Two visitors sharing the same IP address while browsing your web site are unlikely to be using the exact same operating system and browser versions, unless they're in a corporate environment, in which case the likelihood improves. On the average, traffic counts are typically 10 percent more accurate when the measurement tool uses the user agent string along with the IP address versus using the IP address alone.

Using the authenticated username (when available). Measurement tools can also use authenticated usernames to identify unique visitors. If your web site requires visitors to log in with a username and password, you can usually pass the username to your web measurement application. Your measurement software can then use the authenticated username to identify all requests that originated together from a visit. In the ideal case, this is the most accurate method for identifying unique visitors. Alas, the ideal case is rare due to the following two reasons:

- Even if you have a registration web site, there are often public portions of your site that don't require authentication. Any page requests viewed before a visitor logs in will not record the username. Therefore, a measurement tool relying on usernames alone may not be able to make a connection between the portions of the visit before authentication and those after authentication and may mistakenly count two visits where there was only a single visit.

- Even if you have a registration web site, the authenticated username is not always recorded in your web site traffic data. For the username to be recorded automatically, the authentication process needs to use the obscure and unattractive HTTP authentication method. If, however, you use an online form for the visitor to input his username and password, the username will not be recorded as an authenticated username.

In the latter case, you could tag the visitor with his username, but we recommend that you never pass unencrypted personal information via HTTP for security and privacy reasons. Alternatively, you may choose to set a session cookie with the user's name, assuming you have session cookies available.

Using a session identifier (when available). Application platforms like Microsoft's Active Server Pages or Macromedia's Cold Fusion often allow an application-based session ID, one that can easily be passed along using either a session cookie or by appending each page's URL with a session ID. By combining such a session identifier with the authenticated username, measurement tools are able to achieve a high level of accuracy without the need for a permanent browser cookie.

Alternatives to Cookies for Identifying Repeat Visitors

Among these alternatives to cookies, an authenticated username is the only method suitable for identifying repeat visitors to your web site, and is even more accurate than using cookies because:

- When using cookies, multiple users may be recorded as a single repeat visitor. For example, users sharing a home computer or using a kiosk computer appear the same unless they explicitly log in and reset the cookie.
- The same person may mistakenly be counted as multiple unique visitors in your measurements if she is connecting to your site on multiple computers, each with its own unique cookie.
- Cookies have an expiration date that may cause them to expire, or the user may simply delete them at will. In both cases, the connection to previous visits by the same person is lost.

Consequently, for the most accurate web site analysis, try to make intelligent use of authenticated usernames if you have a registration web site. In fact, you may want to use a combination of authenticated usernames and persistent cookies to further improve your chances of making an accurate measurement.

Tying It All Together

Here are three recommendations to consider if you absolutely cannot use cookies to track visitors to your web site:

- Make sure you understand *exactly* why you won't be able to use cookies. Keep in mind that there are good reasons to avoid cookies, but they are few and far between. Double-check that someone in your organization is not simply making an irrational decision.

- Work backward through the list of alternatives above, starting with session identifiers plus authenticated usernames. You want to use the most accurate strategy possible, given that none of these methods are perfect.

- Make sure you consult with your web measurement vendor. Vendors often have additional insight into your specific problem (the reason you cannot use cookies in the first place); leverage that insight. Never do alone what you can get others to do for you—it worked for Tom Sawyer and it will work for you!

Remember, a big part of your success using web measurement tools is tied to understanding how visitors interact with your site over time. By doing everything possible to determine the uniqueness and return visit status of your online visitors, you increase your chances for success.

—*Akin Arikan and Eric T. Peterson*

HACK
#18 Use Macromedia Flash Local Shared Objects Instead of Cookies

Leverage the ubiquity of Macromedia's Flash and Local Shared Objects instead of cookies.

Recent data presented by JupiterResearch suggests that the availability of cookies for use in measurement applications is at greater risk than many previously believed. One response to the "decline of cookies" is to look for other systems for tracking new and returning visitors. This hack describes a workaround based on Macromedia Flash's Local Shared Object. According to the fine folks at Macromedia:

> Shared Objects are used to store data on the client machine in much the same way that data is stored in a cookie created through a web browser. The data can only be read by movies originating from the same domain that created the Shared Object. This is the only way Macromedia Flash Player can write data to a user's machine. Shared Objects can not remember a user's e-mail address or other personal information unless they willingly provide such information.

The important pieces of this definition are "much in the same way that data is stored in a cookie," "can only be read by movies originating from the same domain that created the Shared Object," and "Shared Objects can not remember a user's e-mail address or other personal information unless they willingly provide such information." Put another way, Local Shared Objects are a perfect replacement for cookies because they're just as secure and just as harmless.

The JavaScript Code

The following script tests for when the Flash movie should be embedded in the page and provides a function for setting the secondary cookie. There are three main configuration parameters:

- myUIDCookie is the name of the unique ID cookie employed on your site. The default for Apache's mod_usertrack module is "Apache."

- myUIDFlashCookie is the name you wish to be used for the secondary cookie created by this system.

- myTrackingURL is the URL on your tracking server where the set and recover events are to be recorded.

Additionally, you will need to specify the location of Flash in the object and embed tags written into the page by the script. Be sure to change the URL in both locations.

```
// A simple system for testing the ability to recover
// from deleted user cookie using Flash's local
// shared objects.

// Configure Cookies to use. The first is the normal
// user cookie name employed on the site. The second
// is an additional cookie to be used for identification
// of cookie removal and cross deletion tracking.

var myUIDCookie = "Apache";
var myUIDFlashCookie = "FlashID";

// Configure a trackable image request that can be
// used to count the resets. The URL must end with
// a ? or an & as the flash will be appending a few
// name value pairs.
// Modify the URL with the tracking server
var myTrackingURL = escape('http://www.yoursite.com/some/tracking/call?');

// Test if the Cookie set by the flash movie exists and
// if it doesn't embed it while passing it TrackingURL and
// the value of the myUIDCookie cookie.

var Cookies = document.cookie;
if (Cookies.indexOf(myUIDCookie + "=") != -1) {
  // myUIDCookie does exist - system requires it even if it is a new one
  var CookieStart = Cookies.indexOf(myUIDCookie + "=") + myUIDCookie.length + 1;
  var CookieEnd = Cookies.indexOf(";", CookieStart);
  if (CookieEnd == -1) CookieEnd = Cookies.length;
  var myUIDCookieValue = Cookies.substring(CookieStart, CookieEnd);

  //write value of user id cookie
  document.write('<p><font color="red">Your Unique ID Cookie is '
    + myUIDCookieValue + '</font></p>');
```

```
if (Cookies.indexOf(myUIDFlashCookie + "=") == -1) {
  // myUIDFlashCookie doesn't exist embed the flash
  document.write('<object classid="clsid:d27cdb6e-ae6d-11cf-96b8-
    444553540000" codebase="http://fpdownload.macromedia.com/pub/
    shockwave/cabs/flash/swflash.cab#version=6,0,0,0" width="1"
    height="1" id="flashtrack" align="middle">');
  document.write('<param name="allowScriptAccess" value="sameDomain" />');
  document.write('<param name="movie" value="/scripts/flashtrack
    flashtrack.
swf?UIDCookieValue='+myUIDCookieValue+'&TrackingURL='+myTrackingURL+'" />');
  document.write('<param name="loop" value="false" />');
  document.write('<param name="menu" value="false" />');
  document.write('<param name="quality" value="best" />');
  document.write('<param name="scale" value="noscale" />');
  document.write('<param name="wmode" value="transparent" />');
  document.write('<param name="bgcolor" value="#ffffff" />');
  document.write('<embed src="/scripts/flashtrack/flashtrack.
swf?UIDCookieValue='+myUIDCookieValue+'&TrackingURL='+myTrackingURL+'"
  loop="false" menu="false" quality="best" scale="noscale" wmode=
  "transparent" bgcolor="#ffffff" width="1" height="1" name="flashtrack"
align="middle" allowScriptAccess="sameDomain" type=
  "application/x-shockwave-flash" pluginspage="http://www.macromedia.com/
  go/getflashplayer" />');
  document.write('</object>');
} else {
  // Code may be placed here to do something with the value of
  // the flash set cookie when it already exists.

  //write value of the Flash Cookie
  var FCookieStart = Cookies.indexOf(myUIDFlashCookie + "=") +
myUIDFlashCookie.length + 1;
  var FCookieEnd = Cookies.indexOf(";", FCookieStart);
  if (FCookieEnd == -1) FCookieEnd = Cookies.length;
  var myUIDFCookieValue = Cookies.substring(FCookieStart, FCookieEnd);
  document.write('<p><font color="blue">Your Flash UID Cookie was already
    set to ' + myUIDFCookieValue + '<br>so the flash was not loaded
    and no tracking call made.</font></p>');
}
}

// A special function is called by the flash to set
// the cookie that returns the user id stored
function setFlashCookie(value) {
  var expiration = new Date();
  expiration.setTime(expiration.getTime() + (365*86400000));
  document.cookie =  myUIDFlashCookie + "=" + value + "; expires=" +
    expiration.toGMTString() + ";path=/;";

  //write value of cookie being set
  document.write('<p><font color="blue">Your Flash track UID Cookie has been
set to ' + value + '</font></p>');
}
```

Remember, for this code to function properly, you need to change both references to /scripts/flashtrack/flashtrack.swf to the actual location of the *flashtrack.swf* file presented in the next section. You must also modify the reference to *http://www.yoursite.com/some/tracking/call?* to a URL on your tracking server where the set and recover events are to be recorded.

The Flash ActionScript Code

The next step is to create a Flash movie (*.swf*) to store and read from the local object. First, create a blank Flash document and set the stage size to one by one pixel. Create a movie file called *flashtrack.swf* that contains nothing more than a single blank key frame and the following ActionScript:

```
stop( );

// create the local Shared Object to store the uid
myLocalSO = sharedobject.getLocal("flashtrack" );

// initialize the time variables that will be used
myDate = new Date( );
myTime = myDate.getTime( );

// test that the required TrackingURL UIDCookieValue parameters were passed
//      and aren't null
if ((UIDCookieValue != null) && (FlashCookieName != null) &&
    (TrackingURL != null)) {
        // test if the local shared object exists and create the appended
        // tracking url with a name value at the end to illustrate it is being
        // recovered.
        if (myLocalSO.data.uid != null) {
            myTrackingURL =
unescape(TrackingURL)+"&uidvalue="+UIDCookieValue+"&flashvalue=
    "+myLocalSO.data.uid+"&origination="+myLocalSO.data.origination+"&action=
    recover";
        }
        // else set local shared object data if it didn't exist and then the
        // appended tracking url with a name value at the end to illustrate
        // it is being set for the first time.
        else {
            myLocalSO.data.uid = UIDCookieValue;
            myLocalSO.data.origination = myTime;
            myTrackingURL =
unescape(TrackingURL)+"&uidvalue="+UIDCookieValue+"&flashvalue=
    "+myLocalSO.data.uid+"&origination="+myLocalSO.data.origination+"&action=set";
        }
        // define and call the special javascript function that sets the cookie
        myCookieURL = "javascript:setFlashCookie('"+myLocalSO.data.uid+"')";
        getURL(myCookieURL);
        // use loadMovie to call the tracking url from the server to log the event
        loadMovie(myTrackingURL,_root);
}
```

Running the Hack

Assuming you've set everything up properly, your should see results that look like the following:

```
Your Unique ID Cookie is 204.210.27.229.6793111293290684
Your Flash track UID Cookie has been set to 204.210.27.229.29421110768119167
it was originally stored on Wed, 16 Mar 2005 15:14:56 UTC
```

If the two cookie values are the same, it means you currently have the same UID cookie used when the Flash Local Shared Object was stored. Clear your cookies and hard reload the page to see how they will differ.

You can see an example of this script in action by visiting *www.visioactive.com/ scripts/flashtrack/*

A Note About Whether This Is a Good Idea

While we have clearly shown that using Flash's Local Shared Objects is possible as a replacement for cookies, what we have not demonstrated is whether this strategy is actually a good idea. Because concerns among Internet users regarding security and privacy of data persist and may in fact be getting worse rather than better, there is a substantial debate over whether using Flash as a replacement for cookies does more harm than good.

One side argues that any available technology can and should be used to improve the quality of information available to marketers and technologists, working under the assumption that you cannot improve on what you do not truly know. The other side argues that nobody has the right to spy on an anonymous web visitor's activities, and that the contents of this hack do nothing more than enable spying.

While you're free to judge and decide for yourself, consider this: if Flash begins to be used widely for this purpose and the privacy advocates complain loudly enough, Macromedia might be forced to remove the functionality from their application, returning everyone to square one.

You have the information you need. Make your own decision, but choose wisely.

—*Ian Houston and Eric T. Peterson*

HACK

#19 Fine-Tune Your Data Collection

One of the most important steps during implementation is fine-tuning your data collection to suit your specific needs.

One of the things that web measurement in no way lacks is available data— there are hundreds of primary reports that can be generated and thousands of secondary reports available when you begin to drill down and cross-tab within the data. While some paint the plethora of data as "good news," the converse is often true: there is definitely such a thing as "too much information" in web measurement.

This is one reason key performance indicators [Hack #94] are such a valuable management tool: they help simplify data presentation and dissemination. After you have carefully considered your data needs before you set everything up [Hack #14], the next step is to fine-tune the data you collect so that you can make effective use of the KPI framework.

From a technical standpoint, the decisions you make about data collection are driven by your choice between using web server logfiles and JavaScript page tags. The sections below describe some techniques for eliminating some of the clutter in your data for each technique.

Web Server Logfiles

One of the first steps in reducing clutter is to log only data that you might like to eventually analyze. In the web measurement world, a web server logfile [Hack #22] refers to a combination of as many as four individual files: error logs, access logs, referrer logs, and agent logs. Fortunately, the combined and extended log formats used by Apache, Internet Information Server, and other popular web servers remove the need to process four separate files by combining useful elements into a single entry in the access log (often called the NCSA Extended or "combined" log format).

The combined logfile looks something like this (from *http://httpd.apache.org/ docs/logs.html#combined*):

```
127.0.0.1 - frank [10/Oct/2000:13:55:36 -0700] "GET /apache_pb.gif HTTP/1.0" 200
2326 "http://www.example.com/start.html" "Mozilla/4.08 [en] (Win98; I ;Nav)"
```

An excellent overview of log formats is available in *HTTP: The Definitive Guide* (O'Reilly).

The combined logfile provides a record of every request for every resource made to the web server. You're technically not required to record every hit [Hack #1] in the logfile. In fact, many people choose to exclude image requests from logging to cut down on the sheer volume of requests logged. In Apache, a change to mod_log_config will allow you to exclude image (GIF, PNG, or JPG) requests from your logfile:

```
SetEnvIf Request_URI "(\.gif|\.png|\.jpg)$" image
CustomLog logs/images.log common env=image
CustomLog logs/access.log common env=!image
```

The described functionality also requires mod_setenvif, which may need to be installed by your system administrator.

Making this change to mod_log_config, and restarting Apache will exclude requests for images from your primary access log and instead write them to a separate file (*images.log*), which can periodically be erased to save space.

Keep in mind that making this change will cause your image requests to be logged in a separate file, resulting in extra work if for some reason you need that information at a later date. Make this change cautiously and consciously.

JavaScript Page Tags

Deciding which data to keep and which to ignore when you're using a JavaScript page tag is trickier than simply tweaking your web server configuration files. Most often, you'll need to consult with your vendor since they're usually the ones dealing with data collection and storage. You may be thinking to yourself, "Now, why would I want to go messing with my page tags?" There is a good reason to consider tag modification.

Because JavaScript page tags [Hack #28] *always* come with some performance overhead, if you can identify which data you're pretty sure you won't need, you can ask your vendor to build a smaller file that excludes unnecessary code. Smaller files equal faster downloads for the users of your site. Until every customer is on high-speed broadband, smaller code is better code. Period.

While the majority of tag vendors have optimized the bulk of their code to live in the browser's cache, this code still needs to be loaded on the first visit or any time a visitor clears his cache. Put another way, most vendors have employed a "round-trip" strategy that places a small JavaScript file in your pages that sets some variables and then calls a larger script. The script that is called is placed into your pages on the "return trip" and is also usually stored in the visitor's browser cache. This allows easier maintenance on the bulk of the JavaScript and a faster load on subsequent page views. Still, that first page view, when your visitor is required to download the external file, can sometimes be a doozy!

Every little bit of code reduction improves the initial performance of a page tag, something important to accuracy of measurement and, in some instances, the perception of page load time into the visitor's browser. In the same way, you should always strive to present visitors with the most optimized page possible. Any code used on your site should also be optimized.

Here are some categories you should consider eliminating:

Technographic data

The code that gathers data like monitor color depth, JavaScript status, and Java status is suspect because technographic data is rarely valuable [Hack #74]. Unless you have a really good reason to track details like monitor color depth, you should consider having this code stripped out.

Data about plug-ins

Unless you're deploying some kind of specific program to collect data about plug-ins [Hack #73], you should consider having this code removed.

File downloads

If you're absolutely sure you don't have any downloadable files on your site—no PDFs or EXEs or DOC/XLS/PPT files that anyone would be requesting from your site—this code is often suitable for removal. If in doubt, keep this code in place for 90 days to be *absolutely sure* you don't have downloadable files. Once you're sure that no such files exist, consider removing this code.

Commerce data

If you know you're not doing any online commerce and you're not going to be either leveraging commerce variables in some other fashion or assigning a dollar value to a nonrevenue event [Hack #39], removing code for collecting commerce data can often reduce files sizes significantly.

Again, you want to be careful to *never* change your JavaScript page tag without your vendor's help (bad things will almost assuredly happen). Still, every few bytes you can save in your page tag are bytes you can use elsewhere to delight your visitors!

Why Not Just Collect Everything?

Given all you've read so far, you may perhaps be tempted to hedge your bets and just collect everything. This is not a bad idea in theory, but reality dictates that there is a cost associated with data collection—one you should be conscious of to prevent surprises down the road. Depending on your data collection and storage strategy, you need to consider reprocessing time for data and storage and collection costs.

It takes time to reprocess data. Given the volumes of data you can collect from web server logs, page tags, commerce applications, CRM databases, and the like, surely you can appreciate the problem associated with "Can I get a summary of the last two years' data?" By taking the time to streamline data collection, you will save yourself time if you need to look back and generate historical reports.

There are costs associated with collection and storage. While disk I/O and storage gets less expensive every year, it's unlikely that it will ever be free, regardless of whether you house the data internally or keep it with a hosted provider. In fact, many hosted analytics vendors put a limit on the amount of time they keep your data (or at least keep it in a readily accessible format). From a financial perspective, ongoing data storage is a clear case of "more is more."

Finally, always remember, when in doubt, ask your vendor. They will undoubtedly have an opinion on what you should collect and how long that information should be kept. Don't necessarily take their word as gospel, but don't discount their opinions without consideration.

HACK #20 Define Useful Page Names and Content Groups

Make sure that everyone in your organization can decipher your page and content group names.

One aspect of implementations that is often overlooked is the importance of establishing meaningful page names and content groupings. Fight the temptation to take shortcuts during implementation, and instead strive to define useful and human-readable names for your web pages. For example, rather than allowing the overworked implementation team to create incomprehensible page names like pv_133221, invest the few extra seconds it takes to make a more meaningful name like Product View: Product ID 133221. Translating developer-speak into human-readable names dramatically increases the likelihood that non-techies will be able to make use of the information.

Good Names, Bad Names, I Know You've Had Your Share

If you're using a web measurement solution based on a JavaScript page tag [Hack #28], make sure you actually set a page name programmatically instead of using the document <TITLE> or script name (for example, *index.asp*) and always make sure you follow any directions your vendor provides regarding the script, such as converting spaces and removing illegal characters. If your data source is a web server logfile, you start at a disadvantage; generating useful page names usually requires some type of translation table [Hack #22]. Some examples of good and bad page names include:

index.html
> BAD. This default filename provides little or no insight into what content is presented to the visitor. Even when this page is reported in context of the document location (*/products/productA/details/index.html*), it is only nominally better.

index.asp?skuid=45552cb122

BAD. This default filename, again, even in context, because of its dependence on the information contained in the query string (skuid=45552cb122), is perhaps the worst possible page name. Without some kind of translation, the reader will have no idea what the visitor saw when this page was requested.

Shoes Home Page | Shoe Company.com | The Online Leader in Shoes and Socks

BETTER. This page name, likely pulled directly from the document's HTML <TITLE> tag, at least lets the reader know that they're looking at the "Shoe Home Page." The problem with the name is the extraneous information (| Shoe Company.com | The Online Leader in Shoes and Socks), which provides no additional value to the reader and will likely be repeated throughout a page report.

Nike Air Jordan product view (SKU 45552cb122)

BEST. This page name tells you everything you need to know: what type of page it was (a product view), which product was seen (Nike Air Jordans), and even the specific SKU for the product (45552cb122). It's human readable, insightful, and brief.

Content groups are virtual containers for your web pages that are similar to your directory structure or the folders on your computer. Content groups can also be tricky. Sometimes it's actually a good idea to leverage your document path (the */products/shoes/mens/running* in *http://www.shoes.com/products/shoes/ mens/running/index.html*), especially when your web developers have been moderately thoughtful in how they've organized pages. Problems arise, however, when sites are generated dynamically or built from content management systems. In these instances, translation is necessary to make content groupings useful to nontechnical users. Treat content groups the same way you treat page names whenever possible, defining human-readable, insightful, and brief names for each content group.

Rules for Naming Pages and Content Groups

Here are a handful of page naming guidelines to help you create more meaningful page names:

Use human-readable names.

Your page and content group names shouldn't require any special knowledge of your web site's underlying technology.

Be consistent in your naming.

Try not to vary your page naming conventions, including use of whitespace and case, from page to page. This is most often a problem on dynamically generated sites where different templates are used.

Be brief, but not too brief.

Try to use relatively short page names to increase the chance that the full name will appear in the reporting interface, but remember that the page name needs to be descriptive enough to identify one page in a hundred (or a thousand, or ten thousand).

Greater granularity often answers deeper questions.

Especially in content grouping, if you have to choose between "flat" and "deep," go deep. Since many web measurement applications provide page view, visit, and visitor metrics for individual content groups, take advantage of this whenever possible and increase your chances of answering the "How many visitors saw these pages?" question.

Once you've selected the names, don't change them.

Changing page names makes it difficult to trend traffic to pages over time. Some vendors allow you to edit the names of things via the reporting interface, but this often creates problems down the road.

When in doubt, remember that simplicity rules the day. You may also want to read *Information Architecture and the World Wide Web* (O'Reilly) for more information about naming pages and content groups and how, in general, to think about the relationship between information and site visitation.

HACK #21 Understand Where Data Gets Lost

In web measurement, there are a number of ways that data can be lost. By understanding these sources of loss, you can work to minimize their likelihood.

Losing valuable data can taint your web measurement efforts. The more data that is lost, the more inaccurate the web measurement information you produce will be. Data loss generally occurs as a result of one of the following scenarios:

Measurements are not taken.

The web data that you collect begins with the measurements that you take to record the activity on your site. If a measurement is not taken, usually you have lost that data forever. For this reason, it is important that you carefully plan your measurement strategy in advance.

A vendor loses your data (and won't recover it).

Many companies rely on third-party vendors to collect data for them. Because of the volume of this data and the pressure to reduce costs and stay competitive, vendors often extract parts of your originally collected data for their databases and throw away the rest. In still other cases, vendors mix your data with the data of other customers, making the future extraction of your data time-consuming and expensive.

Your data is incorrectly indexed, misplaced, or destroyed.

Whether your data is collected in your facilities or at the facilities of a vendor, it must be reliably indexed and stored. While you may have a reliable contact with your web measurement vendor, at the end of the day, it is *always* your responsibility to ensure that your data is reliably protected.

Data loss also depends on the data collection method that you use. Each data collection method used in the field of web measurement is associated with specific potential causes of data loss.

Data Collection Issues Common to Page Tags

Client-side ("page tagging") data collection [Hack #6] methods have become a common way of acquiring web measurement data. The following points describe some of the additional ways data can be lost when a client-side data collection method is used.

A page tag did not get placed in the page. The most difficult aspect of this threat is that if a page is not tagged due to some mistake, there is no indication that data is lost. If you rely completely on a page tagging–based method for collecting data throughout your site, then you must build and maintain a process for ensuring that a page tag gets placed in every page before that page goes live.

The page tag doesn't work as intended. Page tags are generally implemented using JavaScript. Over time, there is a danger that the JavaScript in the page tag will no longer function as originally intended as modifications are made throughout the site. In addition, many types of errors may be made in JavaScript that cause a page tag to not collect data, such as forgetting to correctly close a statement in the JavaScript code. For this reason, each page that is page tagged must be tested to make sure that the page tag functions correctly.

Page tagging is your only data collection method. When page tagging is the only data collection method, pages are tagged to the exclusion of all other types of content accessible through HTTP on the Internet, and you are measuring only pages being loaded by web browsers. If there are other types of measurement that are important to your company (such as media downloads, server error responses, software downloads, or image impressions), then you should consider a log-based data collection method to collect those measurements.

The visitor's browser has JavaScript turned off. Because page tags rely heavily on JavaScript and the document object model [Hack #30], if a web visitor has

JavaScript disabled, data collection is often minimized or disabled as well. Most tag-based solutions support a <NOSCRIPT> tag as a fallback to ensure minimal data collection. Fortunately, browsing the Internet with JavaScript disabled is a painful process, and so few people actually do it.

The request was blocked by security software. An increasing number of software products that block such third-party requests are being used with Internet browsers. Popular HTML email clients already allow the blocking of third-party and other requests when the page is loaded by the email client's browser software. To decrease the number of times that page tag requests are blocked by such software, have your page tags make their requests to your own domain on a first-party basis instead of to third-party domains [Hack #16].

The information is never received by the data collector. Data is often lost when a page tag is implemented correctly but the HTTP request is never received or recorded. This problem may be caused by a number of factors, one of which may be the DNS "black holing" of certain data collection service provider domains. In other cases, network or network equipment may fail and cause this result. To avoid this problem, use first-party tracking services and regularly verify the capacity of their network infrastructure.

Data Collection Issues Common to Web Server Logfiles

Log-based data collection [Hack #6] methods are the mainstay of web measurement data collection on the Internet. Web and application servers by default collect data about all of the HTTP requests made to them. The following points describe some of these ways in which data can be lost when log-based data collection is used.

The browser serves the request from the local cache. Most web browsers cache web page HTML and the embedded objects called by that HTML. If the page HTML is cached by a browser, then no request is made to the server to record the page request. This can occur on page reloads and on back button or forward button actions. This kind of problem can be overcome by some additional work on your part [Hack #24].

The content is served from a content distribution network (CDN). Data may be also be lost when a request made by a browser is served from the cache of a content distribution network (CDN), such as those provided by Akamai, Speedera, or AT&T. Since it's served from an external server, no request will be made to the original web server, and no request will be logged.

This type of data loss may be prevented by inserting cache control headers into your HTML pages or setting the cache control headers on your web servers as noted above. As an alternative, a site operator may also set the CDN configuration for its site to forbid the CDN to cache HTML pages but allow it to cache images and other content. If you use a CDN, consult your provider directly about concerns related to web data measurement.

Knowing All This, What Should You Do?

At the end of the day, knowing where the data can be lost is the first step in ensuring that it isn't. Specifically, make sure you have answers to the following questions before signing any contract:

- How will your data be collected? Will you use page tags, logfiles, or a combination of the two? Knowing how the data will be collected will let you better understand where the data could be lost.

- Who will take day-to-day responsibility for data storage? If you're outsourcing, this is likely the vendor, but you want to make sure they're not outsourcing that responsibility to yet another party, thus increasing your risk. If you're planning to maintain the data in-house, who will be doing that? Make sure you know which group or person in your company will be on the hook if problems occur.

- How the data is being stored and maintained? Regardless of where the data is stored, ask about the hardware your data will be stored on and the backup/rotation plan. If your data is "unrecoverable" in case of a catastrophe, you want to know that, allowing proper expectations to be set. Ask the seemingly stupid question, "What if a bomb goes off?" and see if the answer makes you comfortable enough.

- What kind of cookies are used to collect the data? Cookies, while tremendously important to web measurement, are not without risks. You should always be using first-party cookies [Hack #16] to increase your chances of collecting the data in the first place.

- Who is responsible for placing page tags on your pages? Since the most common problem with tag-based data collection is simply "the tag was broken," make sure you know who is on the hook if (some would say "when") this happens. Understand your strategy for deploying and testing page tags, looking for weak spots like, "Well, we'll probably just have whoever is available place the code."

- Does your organization use a content delivery network? If you're using a log-based solution, make sure you know if the data is likely to make it back to you or if you need to be thinking about busting the cache to increase accuracy [Hack #24].

Finally, ask yourself these questions and review these issues with your web measurement provider *before* signing any contact to make sure you know how they deal with data collection and what guarantees you have that the problems described herein won't occur.

—Jim MacIntyre and Eric T. Peterson

HACK #22 Deconstruct Web Server Logfiles

The history of web site measurement is, for the most part, the history of web server logfiles. Understanding the data logfiles provide and their limitations will help you better plan for their use.

Web measurement got its start over 10 years ago with simple log analysis tools. These early tools did little more than scan the logfiles produced by web servers to count hits and visits, report on server errors and page load times, and process other data pertinent to early site administrators.

Anatomy of a Web Server Logfile

Generally speaking, each entry in the logfile will contain the IP address of the requesting client, the requested URL, the number of bytes transferred to the client, the date/time of the request, the URL from the which the request was made (also called the referring URL [Hack #1]), and much more. The log will not only contain each explicitly requested page (commonly a file with an extension of HTM, HTML, ASP, or JSP), but also each image (e.g., GIF and JPG), JavaScript file (JS), and other objects needed to complete the loading of the page. Not surprisingly, logfiles can get excessively large [Hack #19].

Using the following sample line from the author's web server logfile, let's step through the fields captured in the combined log format (see below for more formats).

```
216.219.177.29 - elvis [15/May/2000:23:03:36 -0800] "GET /index.htm HTTP/1.
0" 200 956 "http://www.webanalyticsdemystified.com/index.asp" "Mozilla/2.0
(compatible; MSIE4.0; SK; Windows 98)"
```

Each element tells us something about the visitor or application making the request.

Remote host (remotehost)
> The 216.219.177.29 entry in the logfile tells us the remote hostname or IP address for the requestor. Sometimes the entry is resolved to a domain name (e.g., *webtrends.com*), depending on how your web servers are set up.

Authentication server (RFC931)
> The second element of the logfiles is called RFC931, or the authentication server. This poorly understood and little-used element provides us some

insight into the extremely technical history of web server logfiles. For more information, see the FAQs.org document on RFC931 (*www.faqs.org/rfcs/ rfc931.html*).

Authenticated username (auth-username)

If the visitor has been required to log into your site, as is extremely common on intranets and some extranets [Hack #33], this entry will contain the username portion of their login (elvis, in this example). When this entry is available, a variety of additional tracking options are available to you, including individual identification of activities on the site.

Date and time (timestamp)

The date and time the request was made as recorded by your web server ([15/May/2000:23:03:36 -0800], in this example). The -0800 is the offset from Greenwich Mean Time (GMT).

Requested information (request-line)

Arguably the most important component in the log entry, the "request" is the name and location of the actual object being requested by the visitor to your web site, including the method and HTTP protocol of the request. In this example, the visitor is asking for the web site's home page (*index.html*):

```
GET /index.htm HTTP/1.0
```

You can ignore the GET and HTTP/1.0 information and instead focus on the /index.htm component—that's what your log analyzer will do.

HTTP status (response-code)

The numeric HTTP status code returned with the document, letting the requestor know whether the document is available or if some error has been generated. A better overview of status codes is available in [Hack #34] or online at *www.w3.org/Protocols/HTTP/HTRESP.html*.

Content length returned (response-size)

The length in bytes of the content that was returned to the requestor—a data point that becomes especially interesting if your visitors are complaining about your web pages (the download is not complete, causing rendering issues in the visitor's browser) or if one of your business goals is to have visitors download a document (PDF, EXE, etc.). In the latter case, content length can be mined against the known file sizes, looking for incomplete downloads (where the number of bytes delivered is different than the known file size).

Referring URL (referrer)

The referring URL is the exact URL that contained the link to the requested document (http://www.webanalyticsdemystified.com/index.asp, in this example). Arguably the second most important element in a web server logfile, the referrer is present *only* when a link has physically been clicked (and not always even in that case due to a number of technologies that for whatever reason remove the referrer from the HTTP request). The referring URL is usually available only in combined or extended log formats (see below).

User Agent (user-agent)
  The user agent is the description of the application making the request (e. g., the web browser, robot, or spider, Mozilla/2.0 (compatible; MSIE4.0; SK; Windows 98), in this example). User agents can help you understand your visitor's distribution of browser usage [Hack #71], but recent proliferation of user agent strings has made deeper analysis nearly impossible.

For more information on the details of web server logfiles, see the W3C document on logging control (*www.w3.org/Daemon/User/Config/Logging.html*) or Chapter 21 of *HTTP: The Definitive Guide* (O'Reilly).

Requests from clients are interspersed throughout the logfile in the order they are received. The job of the logfile analysis tool is to parse up this large file to stitch together the individual visits from their respective clients. This can be a difficult problem if the only means of identifying the client is the IP address, as IP addresses are apt to change for a given client (especially when the IP address is dynamically assigned by a corporate DHCP server or commercial ISP service, such as AOL [Hack #78]).

Fortunately, vastly superior visitor tracking methods are available to site designers, including session parameters [Hack #17] and cookies [Hack #15]. Use of a session parameter or cookie to identify visitors will dramatically improve the accuracy of your analysis results.

Types of Web Server Logfiles

Logfiles also come in a variety of formats and types (Table 2-2). While industry standards exist for web servers, there are many other types of servers that can use other logging formats. Streaming media servers are one example of this, dedicated to serving media-only files and using a unique, often proprietary logging format that often requires a special processing engine to prepare for analysis.

Table 2-2. The most widely used web server logfile formats

Format	Description
Common Log Format (CLF), also referred to as the NCSA Common format	The most widely used logfile format. Originally defined by the NCSA, it is now available in a variety of server applications, including Apache and Microsoft's Internet Information Server. More information can be found at *www.w3.org/Daemon/User/Config/Logging.html#common-logfile-format.*

Table 2-2. The most widely used web server logfile formats (continued)

Format	Description
Combined Log Format	An extension of the Common Log Format that includes the referring URL and User Agent fields. More information is available at *httpd.apache.org/docs/logs.html#combined.*
W3C Extended Logfile Format	A customizable log format based on the Common Log Format that allows you to collect only the information you need for your analysis. More information is available at *www.w3.org/TR/WD-logfile.html.*
IIS Logfile Format	A fixed format used in Microsoft's Internet Information Server based on the Common Log Format but that allows collection of additional information, including elapsed time and number of bytes sent (different than bytes received in the CLF). More information is available at *msdn.microsoft.com/library/defaultasp?url=/library/en-us/iissdk/iis/iis_log_file_formats.asp.*

The (Occasional) Need for Translation

Content management servers, commerce servers, portal servers, and other "dynamic" application servers also produce special logfiles. In these instances the files themselves are usually easily parsed by a logfile analysis tool, but the resulting reports may contain unintelligible code values in place of the actual page names, document names, product names, or other elements.

To solve this problem, some analysis tools provide "look up" capabilities into the underlying database used by the application server to translate the code values into names or titles that are commonly understood. Figure 2-3 illustrates the SKUs before translation.

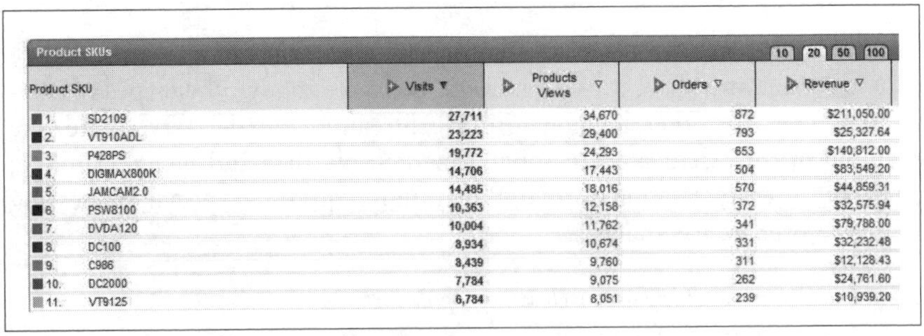
Product SKUs

Product SKU		Visits	Products Views	Orders	Revenue
1.	SD2109	27,711	34,670	872	$211,050.00
2.	VT910ADL	23,223	29,400	793	$25,327.64
3.	P428PS	19,772	24,293	653	$140,812.00
4.	DIGIMAX800K	14,706	17,443	504	$83,549.20
5.	JAMCAM2.0	14,485	18,016	570	$44,859.31
6.	PSW8100	10,363	12,158	372	$32,575.94
7.	DVDA120	10,004	11,762	341	$79,788.00
8.	DC100	8,934	10,674	331	$32,232.48
9.	C986	8,439	9,760	311	$12,128.43
10.	DC2000	7,784	9,075	262	$24,761.60
11.	VT9125	6,784	8,051	239	$10,939.20

Figure 2-3. Untranslated product SKUs

Figure 2-4 illustrates the SKUs after translation.

If you are using an application server, such as BEA WebLogic, BroadVision, or Microsoft SharePoint, and client-side data tagging is not a viable data collection technique, make sure your web analysis tool can perform the required database lookups for your reports to be usable.

Products						
▤ Product Drilldown		▷ Visits ▼	▷ Products Views ▽	▷ Revenue ▽		▷ Orders ▽
▦1.	▽ Electronics	199,904	239,772	$939,342.10	99.98%	6,963
	▷ Imaging	51,515	61,690	$223,178.03	23.75%	1,870
	▽ DVD Players	50,101	60,789	$384,344.11	40.91%	1,660
	▽ Brand Name DVD Players	38,608	47,403	$296,774.10	31.59%	1,241
	▽ DVD Changers	38,034	46,768	$293,898.93	31.26%	1,223
	▷ Toshiba SD2109 DVD Player	27,711	34,870	$211,050.00	22.46%	872
	▷ Panasonic DVDA120 DVD Player	10,004	11,762	$79,788.00	8.49%	341

Figure 2-4. Translated product SKUs

When all is said and done, web server logfiles remain among the most popular and widely deployed web measurement data sources and will likely continue to be popular for years to come. While there has been a noticeable
trend in the last three years towards the use of client-side page tags [Hack #28],
many businesses now realize that the decision is not necessarily black and
white, and that both sources of data have their intrinsic value.

—Jeff Seacrist and Eric T. Peterson

Exclude Robots and Spiders from Your Analysis
#23

One of the major complaints about web server logfiles is that they are often
littered with activity from nonhuman user agents ("robots" and "spiders").
While they are not necessarily bad, you need to exclude robots and spiders
from your "human" analysis or risk getting dramatically skewed results.

Robots and spiders (also known as "crawlers" or "agents") are computer
programs that scour the Web to collect information or take measurements.
There are thousands of robots and spiders in use on the Web at any time,
and their numbers increase every day. Common examples include:

- Search engine robots that crawl over the pages in sites on the Web and
  feed the information they collect to the indexes of search engines like
  Google, Yahoo!, or industry-specific engines that search for information
  such as airfares, flight schedules, or product prices.

- Competitive intelligence robots that spider a site to collect competitive
  analysis data. For instance, your competitor may construct robots to
  regularly gather information from your online product catalog to understand how they should price, or to make product and price comparisons in their marketing.

- Account aggregator robots that regularly collect data from online
  accounts (usually with the permission of the account owner) and feed
  that data to web-based "account consolidators." Users of such account
  management sites benefit from having current information from their
  financial accounts, loyal program memberships (for hotel points or frequent flyer miles), or other accounts on a single site. Examples include
  Everbank, Yodelee, MilePro, and MaxMiles.

- Performance measurement robots that make requests of web sites to simply determine how long it will take a page on the Internet to load. Companies like Keynote and Gomez operate such robots for their clients to take measurements of their clients' site(s) or the sites of their clients' competitors. Your IT department or your IT vendors may use similar agents for system testing—i.e., to test that your site is up and running as intended.

While great benefits are conferred when robots and spiders visit your web site, the fundamental question will always remain: are you able to *distinguish* requests to your site from humans from those generated by nonhuman robots and spiders?

Strategies for Limiting the Impact of Robots and Spiders

The established practice in web analytics with regard to such robots is to exclude them from your analysis and reporting. The Interactive Advertising Bureau (IAB) has published the *Interactive Audience Measurement and Advertising Campaign Reporting and Audit Guidelines*, which include minimum requirements for excluding robots and spiders based on "specific identification of nonhuman suspected activity" (known robots and spiders) and "pattern analysis." For more information on the IAB and its requirements, please visit *http://www.iab.net/standards/measurement.asp*.

To exclude robots from your analysis and reporting, provide lists of known robots to your web analytics software and configure it to filter their activity out of your web analytics data before you produce your metrics and reports. It is recommended that your robot lists are based both on IP addresses and user agents, because different user agents may use the same IP address and many robots may display the same user agent name.

Identify known robots and spiders. Start with a list of known robots and spiders; such a list is likely available from your web analytics vendor. The IAB, in conjunction with ABC Interactive (ABCi), maintains a list of robots and spiders that is available to IAB members free of charge. Next, supplement the list of known robots and spiders with the names of specific user agents that have been identified by your company, such as testing agents used for site monitoring by you or your vendors. The following is a list of just a few robots that have probably visited your site:

- 4anything.com LinkChecker v2.0
- Alligator 1.31 (*www.nearsoftware.com*)
- Express WebPictures (*www.express-soft.com*)

- DaviesBot/1.7 (*www.wholeweb.net*)
- GomezAgent
- Inktomi Search
- InternetLinkAgent/3.1
- MediaCrawler-1.0 (Experimental)
- Mozilla/2.0 compatible; Check&Get 1.1x (Windows 98)

For more information on the IAB/ABCi list, see *http://www.iab.net/standards/spiders.asp*.

Be on the lookout for new robots and spiders. As a next step, establish a regular process and procedure for detecting robots that may be new to the Internet or specific to your site. When you find a new robot, add it to your robots lists and have its activity filtered from your web analytics data. Save all of your old robot lists and the time range over which they were used: You'll need to maintain versions so you can reproduce the numbers in your old reports if you ever need to.

Regularly review your web server's access logs, starting with requests for the file *robots.txt*, which indicates to a robot which content on your web site should be indexed. Requests for this file almost always come from a spider or robot. Don't forget to record the user agents and IP numbers from these requests and add them to your robot lists so they are filtered from your web data.

Your web measurement application should also allow you to search your web data for patterns that are common to robots. Such patterns include:

- Visitors to your site that have very high numbers of page views in single sessions
- Visitors to your site that have many very rapid page views or very low page view duration times
- Visitors that return to your site at exact or seemingly routine times (e.g., every day at midnight)

You should perform this type of pattern analysis at least once per quarter.

Build and deploy a robots.txt file. The *robots.txt* file, which is placed within the root directory of the web site, tells spiders which files they may download and index. Most search engines will honor the *robots.txt* file, but there is no specific requirement that they do. The format of the *robots.txt* file contains two primary elements:

- User-agent line
- One or more Disallow lines

The User-agent line is used to specify particular robots to be targeted with the use of the *robots.txt* file. A wildcard may be used to indicate all robots, as illustrated with the following syntax:

```
User-agent: *
```

The Disallow lines are used to specify particular files and/or directories that the identified user agents are not allowed to download. The format for such exclusion statements are as follows:

```
Disallow: /homepage.asp
```

This example instructs specified user agents not to spider the */homepage.asp* file.

To allow specified user agents to spider the entire web site, use the following:

```
Disallow:
```

To prevent specified user agents from spidering any file within the web site, the Disallow statement would be formed as follows:

```
Disallow: /
```

The most common format for the *robots.txt* file is as follows:

```
User-agent: *
Disallow: /
```

Modifications may be required if your site *does* desire search engines to index only parts of your web site or if other system visitors such as account aggregators need to access particular files/pages served from the web server. If this is the case, you should construct your *robots.txt* file to disallow only those parts of your site that you do not want indexed. The following is an example from a site:

```
# robots.txt for http://www.site.com
User-agent:*
Disallow:/feedback
Disallow:/images
Disallow:/cgi-bin
Disallow:/system
Disallow:/inetart
Disallow:/maps
```

You can view any web site's *robots.txt* file, if it has one, by requesting *http://www.domain.com/robots.txt*, the standard naming convention for this file. (Replace the *domain* variable with the name of the site you want to check.)

Remember That Some Spiders Are Good!

What if you are interested in analyzing robot and spider activity rather than filtering it out? For instance, you may want to track visits from Google's robot, Googlebot. Many web measurement application vendors offer solutions that can collect robot activity data from your web measurement data, providing the ability to analyze robot traffic for various purposes such as optimizing your pages for search engine indexing. The specifics of this procedure will vary based on your particular application, but most mature products allow you to analyze robots separately from human traffic, essentially doing the opposite of what is suggested above in this hack. It is important to know that a solely client-side data collection model (page tags) may not be able to collect all robot/spider traffic information, because some robot/spider agents do not execute JavaScript and generally do not accept cookies.

—Jim MacIntyre and Eric T. Peterson

HACK
#24

Bust the Cache for Accuracy

Measurement solutions based on web server logfiles suffer from a variety of factors that decrease their accuracy. Caching devices are the primary culprits but, in some cases, the cache can be beaten and accuracy improved.

Web server logfiles suffer from a handful of accuracy issues, perhaps the most significant arising from caching devices on the Internet. A *caching device* is any piece of hardware or software designed to store temporary copies of a file, most often to improve delivery performance. There are two types of caching devices that create problems for web server logfiles: client-side caches and server-side caches.

Client-side caches are deployed locally in corporate network operation centers and at Internet Service Providers to improve performance. The most extreme example of a client-side cache is the browser cache, software built into your Internet browser that is designed to save local copies of files. Server-side caches are often placed in front of your own web servers to reduce load. (See *Web Caching* [O'Reilly] for a complete treatise on the subject, or, if you prefer going online, Wikipedia has an excellent entry on the subject at *http://en.wikipedia.org/wiki/Web_cache*.)

The essentials of caching are as follows: because the document is served from a cache, the request never actually makes it into the web server log. Depending on how many of your pages are cached, the result can be a dramatic undercounting of page views, which then cascades into a number or related problems (gaps in path analysis, misleading calculation of key ratios, etc.). So what's a web measurement guru to do?

One thing you can consider is *busting the cache*: adding code to your pages that forces caching devices to request the page from your web servers so you're able to see the request.

Bust the Cache Using Document Headers

Through relatively simple modification of your document headers and the use of META tags, you can request that the document not be cached. Use the HTTP cache-control and pragma directives (HTTP 1.1 and HTTP 1.0, respectively) as follows, remembering to change the expires content from CURRENT DATE AND TIME to the real date and time the page is generated. The complete description of how these headers work can be found at *http://www.w3.org/Protocols/rfc2616/ rfc2616-sec14.html#sec14.9* (HTTP 1.1) and *http://www.w3.org/Protocols/ rfc2616/rfc2616-sec14.html#sec14.32* (HTTP 1.0). To bust the cache, place the following tags in your document's header section:

```
<HEAD>
<TITLE>Your document's title</TITLE>
<META HTTP-EQUIV="cache-control" CONTENT="no-cache">
<META HTTP-EQUIV="pragma" CONTENT="no-cache">
<META HTTP-EQUIV="expires" content="CURRENT DATE AND TIME">
</HEAD>
```

You may also want to hedge your bets, writing each directive directly to the document header—something easily done if you're using a dynamic page generation platform like ASP, PHP, or JSP.

If you're using PHP, simply add the following at the top of each page:

```
<?php header("Expires: 0"); header("Last-Modified: " . gmdate("D, d M Y H:i:
s") . " GMT"); header("cache-control: no-cache"); header("pragma: no-
cache");?>
```

In Microsoft's Active Server Pages (ASP), add the following:

```
<%
Response.Buffer = false
Response.Expires = 1
Response.ExpiresAbsolute = Now( ) - 2
Response.AddHeader "pragma","no-cache"
Response.AddHeader "cache-control","no-cache"
Response.CacheControl = "no-cache"
%>
```

Finally, in Java Server Pages (JSP), use something like this:

```
<%
response.setHeader("pragma","no-cache");
response.setHeader("cache-control","no-cache");
response.setDateHeader("expires", 0);
%>
```

The best recommendation would be to save your header control code as a small file called *cache-control.inc* and include that as a server-side include at the top of every page.

Using both the document header and META tag strategy described above allows you to hedge your bets. Since some caching devices and browser types may ignore one or the other directives, doubling up increases your chances of seeing the request.

 Busting the cache may affect your visitors' experience, especially if they would otherwise be taking advantage of a client-side cache and are physically far away from your web servers.

How Cache Busting Affects the Visitor Experience

One of the great deliberations for web data analysts relying on web server logfiles is the choice between improved visitor performance and improved data accuracy. Unfortunately, it's a pretty binary issue: you're either for performance or accuracy. While the most widely used argument is that doing anything that compromises the user experience should be avoided, the counterargument is that unless you have an accurate picture of what visitors are doing, you cannot hope to improve usability.

You can mitigate some of the problems associated with cache busting by delivering other documents as quickly and efficiently as possible. Here are some suggestions for how to do this to improve performance.

"Unbusting" the Cache for Images and Scripts

Because your primary concern is the measurement of page views and not the successful delivery of images and other document objects, one strategy for optimizing page delivery is "unbusting" the cache for non-content objects. There are three moderately simple things you can do to make this happen.

Deploy an "images never expire" policy. The idea behind "images never expire" is that, for the most part, once images, multimedia files, and PDF documents are created, they rarely change. You can use Apache's <FILESMATCH> directive in mod_headers to set the expiration date for images well out into the future:[*]

```
# Works with HTTP/1.1 only
<FilesMatch "\.(gif|jpe?g|png|pdf|wav|rm)$">
  Header set Cache-Control \
      "max-age=315360000"
</FilesMatch>

# Works with both HTTP/1.0 and HTTP/1.1
```

---

[*] Thanks to Michael J. Radwin for this code, presented at the O'Reilly Open Source Convention on July 28, 2004. Slides are available at *http://public.yahoo.com/~radwin/talks/http-caching.htm*.

```
<FilesMatch "\.(gif|jpe?g|png|pdf|wav|rm)$">
  Header set Expires \
      "Mon, 28 Jul 2014 23:30:00 GMT"
</FilesMatch>
```

Make sure that the regular expression list (gif|jpe?g|png|pdf|wav|rm) contains the file extensions of images and multimedia files contained on your servers, each separated by a pipe character (|). (The max-age=315360000 is 10 years measured in seconds, just in case you were wondering.)

> If you employ the "images never expire" policy, web designers will be forced to rename image, PDF, and multimedia files if they make changes to the files—something many consider a pain.

Now your visitors will be required to download the images on your site only once, very handy for those images that are used frequently throughout the site (navigation elements, logos, bullets and buttons, etc.).

Use caching defaults for occasionally changing content. While your images and PDFs are unlikely to change, the same cannot be said for CSS and JavaScript files. While you may be tempted to add the *css* and *js* file extensions to the <FILESMATCH> directive, fight the urge. While uninteresting from a measurement standpoint, these files are often necessary for rendering your pages. Practically speaking, these files *do* change, and forcing your web developers to rename their code every time they make even a minor update will incur their ire—perhaps even their direct and immediate wrath.

Consider a content distribution network (CDN) for images and code. One alternative solution to the "images never expire" policy you may want to consider if you have some money to spend is a content distribution network (CDN). The idea behind a CDN is that the closer you can get a large object to users, the faster they'll get those files. A CDN acts as a proxy server for the static content you're unconcerned about measuring, but it often provides the ability to manually control their expiration dates, simplifying the refresh process.

While the details of content distribution networks are outside of the scope of this book, I would refer you to two vendors well known for their CDN platforms: Akamai (*www.akamai.com*) and Speedera (*www.speedera.com*). A more complete list of caching device and network vendors can be found at *http://www.caching.com/vendors/index.htm*.

The Obvious Alternative to Cache Busting

Something to consider if this hack was a bit overwhelming is the fact that the JavaScript page tag data source [Hack #6] completely sidesteps the issue of caching. Page tags are cleverly designed to report back, regardless of where the document they're contained in was delivered from, nullifying the caching effect. Moreover, page tags even beat the browser cache, again because they appear to be a completely new request every time the code is executed (based on random number generating functions and other cache-beating technology baked into the tags). Perhaps best of all, often any externally housed code required for page tags [Hack #28] can be thrown on a content distribution network to reduce latency associated with that file, again improving performance for your visitors.

HACK #25 Use Query Strings Effectively

The query string (the stuff after the "?" in a URL) is a powerful tool for web measurement and data collection.

Because of the stateless nature of HTTP, many sites use query strings in their URLs to pass information from page to page or request to request. The query string is a specific portion of a URI that begins after the URI stem and a question mark (?), as shown in the following example:

```
http://www.mysite.com/page.htm?name=value
```

Where www.mysite.com is your server DNS or (s-dns) name, page.htm is your URI stem and name=value is your query string. The query string in this example contains one query string, which is composed of a parameter, variable, or name=value pair.

Within the structure of a query string, there may be multiple pairs, each consisting of a variable, followed by an equal sign (=) and then the data or value associated with each variable name. If there are multiple query string variables in your query string, they will be separated by an ampersand (&). Simply put, the query string is a sequence of name=value pairs separated by ampersands (&) as in:

```
?page=product%20view%20page%2Fprodid123&campaign=123
```

Query strings can be used to carry almost any type of data back to your web servers for a very wide range of purposes. Any query string parameters added to the URL typed into the address bar of the web browser will likely be captured and logged along with the rest of the URL by a responding web server. Finally, certain "unsafe" characters (generally, non-alphabetic or non-numeric characters) in the value of a query string must be encoded to ensure that the data will be correctly interpreted across all platforms. For example, the "space" character must be encoded as its hexadecimal equivalent (%20) or as a + sign.

Some Common Uses for the Query String in Web Measurement

The query string may be used for a wide variety of web measurement purposes, and the figures in this section provide just of few common examples.

Properly identifying dynamically generated pages. In some dynamic web sites one or more name=value pairs in the query string of a URL may be important to determining the actual page requested by a visitor. For instance, many URLs for dynamic pages (those generated by a script on the server, rather than a static file) are structured like those below:

```
http://www.mysite.com/pageserved.asp?PAGENAME=HOME
http://www.mysite.com/pageserved.asp?PAGENAME=NEXTPAGE
```

This structure often results from the use of personalization or dynamic content management systems, in which the actual content served in a page is determined on the fly by the URI, the cookie, related data, and application logic. In the previous example, PAGENAME indicates what page will be served to the requester of this URI.

Many web measurement systems can be configured to use the query names to define unique pages. This is important because most measurement systems would otherwise interpret all requests for *pageserved.asp* as the *same page*, despite the fact that the page serves different content (identified by the PAGENAME attribute in the query string).

Identifying marketing campaign response. Site developers and applications often add many query string variables into a site's URLs that both identify the actual page to be served and provide additional information about which marketing campaign [Hack #37] caused a visitor to see and then select the particular URL. An example of this would be:

```
http://www.myserver.com/pageserved.asp?PAGENAME=HOME&CAMPAIGN=10001
```

Collecting HTML form data for analysis. You'll often be interested in analyzing information that visitors enter into forms on your site. Typically, this information is passed to the web server within a POST type request, signified as follows:

```
<form method="POST" action="formthankyou.asp">
```

Modifying the method from a POST request to a GET request results in the form values entered being displayed as query string name=value pairs within the web browser address bar on the resulting *formthankyou.asp* page (Figure 2-5)

The result of modifying the form action value from a POST request to a GET may not be desirable given the fact that the entered values are displayed

---

Figure 2-5. Sample query string

within the address bar as illustrated in Figure 2-5. Using JavaScript within the form page, a POST method can be used, while still allowing you to collect the provided information as a part of a query string, by appending the posted form values as query string parameters to the action value as illustrated in Figure 2-6.

Form Entry Page	Form Process Page (Visitor does not see)	Form Thank You Page
Visitor completed form and submits	Page processes POST data and redirects visitor to Thank You page	Form Submission Confirmation

Figure 2-6. Using POST data with a query strings

The following JavaScript code modifies the POST action value:

```
<form method="POST" action="formprocesspage.asp" onSubmit="AppendFormValues
    ();">
<script language="JavaScript">
var formvalues="";
function AppendFormValues()
{
for (i=0; i<document.forms[0].length; i++) {
    var item = document.forms[0].elements[i];
    if (item.type!="hidden" && item.type!="submit" && item.name!="undefined"){
    var formitem = item.name;
    var formvalue = item.value;
    formvalues += formitem + "=" + formvalue + "&";
    }
}
document.forms[0].action = document.forms[0].action + "?" + formvalues;
}
</script>
```

The example shown in Figure 2-6 results in three requests to the web server: *formentrypage.asp*, *formprocess.asp*, and *formthankyou.asp*. Inserting the JavaScript example in the *formentrypage.asp* file will modify the form action value to contain query string name=value pairs corresponding to the `formfield=enteredvalue` submitted by the visitor. In the example, the request for *formprocess.asp* will be appended with a query string containing the `formfield=enteredvalue` pairs, but they will not be presented to the visitor within the web browser address bar. The request will be made to the web server for *formprocess.asp* as follows:

```
http://www.mysite.com/formprocess.
asp?firstname=Joe&lastname=Smith&state=VA&zip=20148
```

Putting the Query String to Work

To take advantage of the three most common examples described above, the critical step is knowing how your particular measurement application allows you to access information contained in the query string. Unfortunately, not all applications make it easy; it is very common for page tag-based applications to require you to transcribe information out of the query string and into custom variables [Hack #31] before that data can be passed to the data collection device. The following code, written using VBScript and JavaScript, demonstrates the most common strategy for this type of translation:

```
rev="<%= request.querystring("dollar_value") %>";  <!-- Change 0.00 to the
actual value of the transaction -->
document.write('<img src="/cgi-bin/readtag.pl?url='+escape(document.
location)+'&amp;ref='+escape(document.referrer)+'&amp;rev='+rev+'">');
```

The `request.querystring("dollar_value")` in the code demonstrates an easy solution to get the document's query string values inserted one by one into the necessary JavaScript code.

Logfile analyzers and hybrid solutions usually make this process easier, providing you some type of interface into the different name/value pairs found in the logfile and allowing you to generate reports based on that data (Figure 2-7).

In this case, you would simply identify a particular "name" in the name/value pair and tell your log analyzer how to deal with that information. This is the essence of tracking URLs [Hack #43], which are so critical to most marketing measurement and analysis.

If your web pages are dynamically generated, a common practice for nearly all retail web sites, you need to ensure that relevant information contained in your URLs is translated and made available for analysis. Because there is so much variation in the measurement marketplace in how query strings are made available for analysis, we strongly recommend you contact your vendor for specifics.

—Jim MacIntyre and Eric T. Peterson

Figure 2-7. "Search terms with Revenue" report, based on query-string parameters

Web Measurement and Visitor Privacy

The relationship between web measurement and visitor privacy is complex due to the extensive use of cookies, making it essential that you both understand the issues and establish a robust privacy policy that describes your use of cookies for measurement.

Web site measurement and online marketing offer the allure of infinite measurement possibilities. Because of this, digital marketers sometimes rush to collect and use all the visitor information they can without considering the privacy implications. It is easy to forget that visitors to your web site have the same need to feel safe and secure as they would if they were visiting your real-world office or store. If you are to be successful in convincing visitors to do business with you, you will need to gain their trust. Privacy and security therefore are not about compliance or nice-to-haves, but essential trust-building activities that will help you gain and retain visitors or customers.

It's Not About the Technology, It's About the Practices

As with most technology, web measurement technology may be used in good and reputable ways, or in ways that will cause harm to unsuspecting individuals. Whether it's a video camera or a browser cookie, it's not the technology that is the problem, but the way in which it may be used or misused that presents the real danger. Unfortunately, early debate and legislative work in the area of digital privacy spent much time focused on technology such as cookies and failed to address the real issues surrounding how this technology is used.

In May 2000, the FTC published a report to the U.S. Congress: "Privacy Online: Fair Information Practices in the Electronic Marketplace" (*http://www.ftc.gov/ reports/privacy2000/privacy2000.pdf*). Although controversial, this paper gave the online community a useful framework and an important set of guidelines. Privacy professionals today use this framework as a way to discuss the major online privacy issues: notice, choice, access, and security.

Notice. The idea that sites should have a privacy policy comes from the idea that users deserve to understand what sort of information you are collecting from them and how you are using it. Although most sites agree with this, there's still much debate about when and how notice should be given. Of course, most web sites would like to simply create a privacy policy and link it to their home page. However, some privacy advocates would argue that when you are collecting personal information or sensitive personal information you should provide greater notice with special messages in places where information is collected. Of course, in the case of web site measurement, this would be problematic because information is collected at potentially every interaction with the web site.

Choice. Users should have a choice about what information is collected about them. There are two types of choice you hear about: opt-in and opt-out. Opt-in refers to the users' choice to actively provide information to the site when consent is explicit or it is obvious that the information will be collected through a web form. Opt-out refers to the users' ability to decide that they do not want any more data collected about them by the web site. This typically refers to data that is collected by sites where it is not necessarily obvious that it is happening. This is extremely important for web data collection when implicit consent is necessary. Implicit consent refers to the users' knowledge of a site's practices through the notice provided in the privacy policy.

Access. This is perhaps one of the most controversial areas of privacy practice today. The reason has less to do with the concept than the practicality of providing complete access. This concept says that users should be able to gain access to all the data collected about them. While this may be practical for simple things like contact details, it is much less practical for things like web data when massive amounts of behavioral data may be collected for an individual. For this reason, most sites today do not provide full access to an individual user's web data, but will often provide access to the less data-intensive personal information the site has collected.

Security. It is clear that privacy and security are joined at the hip, for you cannot have privacy without proper security of the information collected. We've all seen stories in the news about massive breaches of security when credit card numbers and other personal information were compromised at a site. This certainly speaks to the trust that you wish to gain from your visitors. If you collect personal information yet leave yourself vulnerable to attack by hackers who will use this information in unscrupulous ways, then you will most certainly lose those customers who have entrusted you in the past.

How to Assemble a Good Privacy Policy

The key to putting together a good privacy policy is knowledge and communication: knowing what you're collecting and what you're going to do with that information, and then clearly conveying your intentions (Figure 2-8).

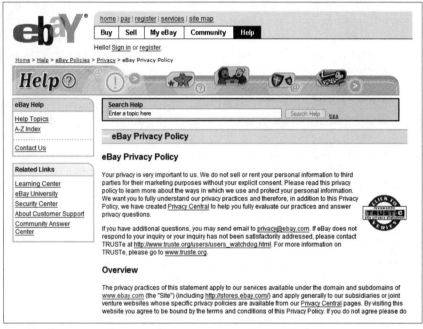

Figure 2-8. Privacy policy at eBay.com

Know where you're collecting personably identifiable information. Personally identifiable information (PII) is data that can be used to identify or contact a person, including name, address, telephone number, and email address. PII also includes any other data, such as, but not limited to, anonymous identifiers, demographics [Hack #77], and behavioral data when such data is linked to PII and identifies a person to the party holding such data.

Explain clearly and truthfully what you're going to do with the data. Even if you aren't collecting personal information, you should disclose all of your data collection practices. It is a good idea to disclose the use of technologies like cookies [Hack #15] or web beacons [Hack #29]. When you are collecting personal information, you should tell users exactly what information it is that you will collect, how it will be used, and with whom you will share it. If you outsource your web measurement to a service provider, you should disclose that you do so.

Consider third-party privacy certification. Although the United States has two industry-specific privacy laws governing the financial and health care industries, a general omnibus law has not yet been adopted. Therefore, privacy practices are largely self-regulated. Depending on your audience, you may want to certify your privacy practices through TRUSTe or BBBOnline. These organizations help you assess your privacy policies and provide an extra level of assurance to your visitors. Any sites that collect personal information or who are in the financial or healthcare industries should seriously consider these seal programs.

Beware of the spookiness factor. Many privacy-related problems occur when something happens that a user does not expect. If information is used in a way that differs from the expectations of your users and they realize it, you have a certain spookiness factor that may make users uncomfortable or doubt your intentions. For instance, if you told your users that you would collect personal information for billing purposes, but then they started receiving large amounts of email from you, they might then become disillusioned.

P3P Technology

In 1997, the World Wide Web Consortium (W3C) started work on a technology that could be used to describe the privacy practices of a site in an automated way. This technology could then be used by browsers to give users more control over their personal information. The Platform for Personal Preferences (P3P) [Hack #27] gives users of browser technology a way to assess your site's privacy policies and make decisions about how to react to them through browser controls. Today, Microsoft Internet Explorer uses P3P technology to decide how to treat cookies issued by sites (Figure 2-9). So if your site sets cookies with personal information in them, the user can set preferences to reject those cookies on the basis of the privacy preference, and not simply because the site may use cookies or not use them.

For More Information

Table 2-3 contains a list of sites providing more information about web privacy, privacy policies, and legislation that may affect your site's ability to collect and use personally identifiable information.

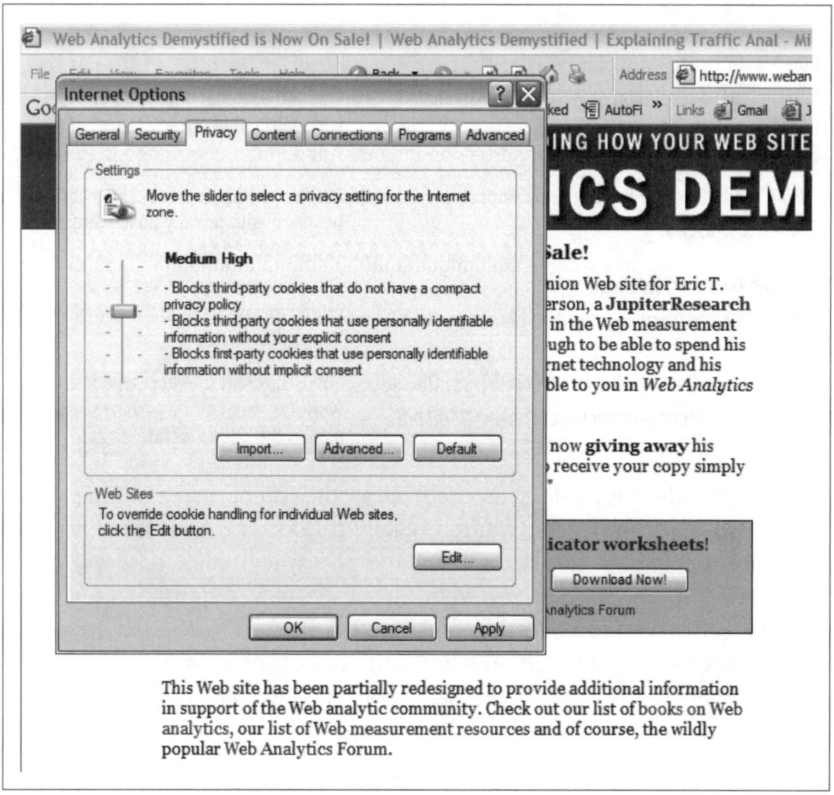

Figure 2-9. P3P in Microsoft Internet Explorer 6.0

Table 2-3. Privacy resources on the Internet

Site and URL	About the resource
Network Advertising Initiative (NAI) *www.networkadvertising.org*	The NAI is an industry group that works to build consensus on privacy-related issues, build best practices, and educate industry and lawmakers.
Search Engine Marketing Professional Organization (SEMPO) *www.sempo.org*	This industry trade group is concerned with search-engine marketing issues.
Internet Advertising Bureau (IAB) *www.iab.net*	The IAB sets standards for online advertising and web analytics.
TRUSTe *www.truste.com*	TRUSTe is the most thorough third-party privacy certification organization.
BBBOnline *www.bbbonline.com*	Part of the long standing Better Business Bureau. BBBOnline is a third-party certification entity.

Table 2-3. Privacy resources on the Internet (continued)

Site and URL	About the resource
International Association of Privacy Professionals (IAPP) *www.privacyassociation.org*	This professional organization deals with worldwide privacy issues of all types.
W3C P3P Platform for Privacy Preferences *www.w3.org/P3P/*	P3P technology is a robust way to describe your privacy policy through automated means.
NAI Web Beacon Guidelines *www.networkadvertising.org/Web_Beacons_11-1-04.pdf*	This document describes the best practices surrounding the use of web beacon technology.
Federal Trade Commission Report on Privacy Online *www.ftc.gov/reports/privacy2000/privacy2000.pdf*	The FTC report that acts as a frame-work for much of the privacy discussion in the online world.

At the end of the day, as long as you're clear and intentional about how you collect and use visitor data, you're unlikely to have any problems, legal or otherwise. Remember to place a link to your privacy policy on every page, highlighting it on those pages where it's especially important (any page through which you're collecting personal or financial information). Also, don't forget to use your web measurement application from time to time to see how many visitors are reading your policy; a big spike in readership can indicate a looming problem.

—Jay McCarthy and Eric T. Peterson

Establish a P3P Privacy Policy

#27   The convergence of privacy concerns and widespread use of cookies necessitates a published commitment to privacy on your part. The Platform for Privacy Preferences provides an easy way to let your visitors know what data you're collecting and how you plan on using it.

According to the World Wide Web Consortium, the Platform for Privacy Preferences (P3P) initiative provides "a simple, automated way for users to gain more control over the use of personal information on web sites they visit." By allowing site operators to answer a standardized set of questions covering their site's privacy policy [Hack #26], P3P provides a mechanism for reporting your site's commitment to privacy so it can be compared to the visitor's expectations. By simplifying the interface to the browser's privacy controls via a set of predefined settings (ranging from "low" to "high" with "accept all cookies" and "block all cookies" options), P3P is helping consumers make better decisions about first- and third-party cookie acceptance.

Sounds Great, How Do I Set One Up?

Once you decide you want to set up a P3P policy—and if you haven't already done this, you need to immediately—the rest is relatively easy and can be done in six steps.

Step one: Create a written privacy policy. Before you can codify anything, you have to have a privacy policy [Hack #26]. Make sure you've carefully outlined what data you're collecting, where you're collecting it, what you do with that information, who has access to the data, and how long you plan on keeping it around. You want your privacy policy to cover every aspect of data collection and sharing, not just regarding your web measurement program.

Step two: Determine which policies apply to which pages. You'll most likely need different privacy policies for different pages and different visitor activities. You may want to establish a different policy for visitors who browse the site that explicitly states that you're using cookies to track visitor activity, and a more detailed policy for pages from which you're collecting personal information.

Step three: Select a P3P policy generator. Policy generators are applications that will assist you in converting the information you've assembled in steps one and two into a machine-readable policy. The generator is going to be interested in who you are and how you can be contacted, the location of your written policy on your web site, assurances that your commitment to privacy is as you say it is, and information about the data elements you're collecting, including your web measurement.

While a more complete list of policy generators is available at *p3ptoolbox.org*, the following are generators recommended by the W3C:

IBM P3P Policy Generator
http://www.alphaworks.ibm.com/tech/p3peditor

PrivacyBot.com
http://www.privacybot.com/

IAjapan's Privacy Policy Wizard (also available in Japanese)
http://fs.pics.enc.or.jp/p3pwiz/p3p_en.html

P3PEdit
http://policyeditor.com/

Customer Paradigm's P3P Privacy Policy Creation
http://www.customerparadigm.com/p3p-privacy-policy3.htm

Step four: Enter the information. Once you've selected a policy generator, simply follow the steps sequentially to generate your policy. Make sure you use any error-checking facilities the generator has to ensure accuracy and, if you've determined that you need more than one policy, save each as sequential filenames (e.g., *policy1.xml*, *policy2.xml*, *policy3.xml*, etc.).

Step five: Create a policy reference file. The generator should allow you to generate a policy reference file (called *p3p.xml*) that describes how each individual policy is applied to documents and directories on your web server. The following is an example policy reference file taken from the W3C's document on creating P3P policies and the basis for this hack:

```
<META xmlns="http://www.w3.org/2001/09/P3Pv1">
    <POLICY-REFERENCES>
        <POLICY-REF about="/P3P/Policy3.xml">
            <INCLUDE>/cgi-bin/</INCLUDE>
            <INCLUDE>/servlet/</INCLUDE>
            <EXCLUDE>/servlet/unknown</EXCLUDE>
        </POLICY-REF>
        <POLICY-REF about="/P3P/Policy2.xml">
            <INCLUDE>/catalog/</INCLUDE>
        </POLICY-REF>
        <POLICY-REF about="/P3P/Policy1.xml">
            <INCLUDE>/*</INCLUDE>
            <EXCLUDE>/servlet/unknown</EXCLUDE>
        </POLICY-REF>
    </POLICY-REFERENCES>
</META>
```

This file and the associated policies should then be uploaded to a directory called */wc3* off of your web server's root directory. You should also, at this point, set up your web server to return a compact policy (CP) with each document's headers. A complete treatment of the fields used in the CP is available at *http://www.microsoft.com/presspass/press/2001/mar01/PrivacyToolsIEfs.asp*, but the header modification will look something like this (taken from *http://www.w3.org/TR/p3pdeployment#Using_HTTP_Headers* at the World Wide Web Consortium's description of P3P):

```
HTTP/1.1 200 OK
P3P: policyref="http://www.yoursite.com/w3c/p3p.xml",
    CP="NON DSP COR CURa ADMa DEVa CUSa TAIa OUR SAMa IND"
Content-Type: text/html
Content-Length: 8104
Server: CC-Galaxy/1.3.18
```

The emphasized code shows how the compact policy is rendered to the browser so determination about third-party cookies can be made as the page is loaded and rendered.

Step six: Validate your policy. To validate your policy, you can either see the list of policy validators at *p3ptoolbox.org* or use the W3C's validator at *http://www.w3.org/P3P/validator.html*. You are able to enter any URL from your web site into the URI box to make sure a policy has been properly set for that page (Figure 2-10).

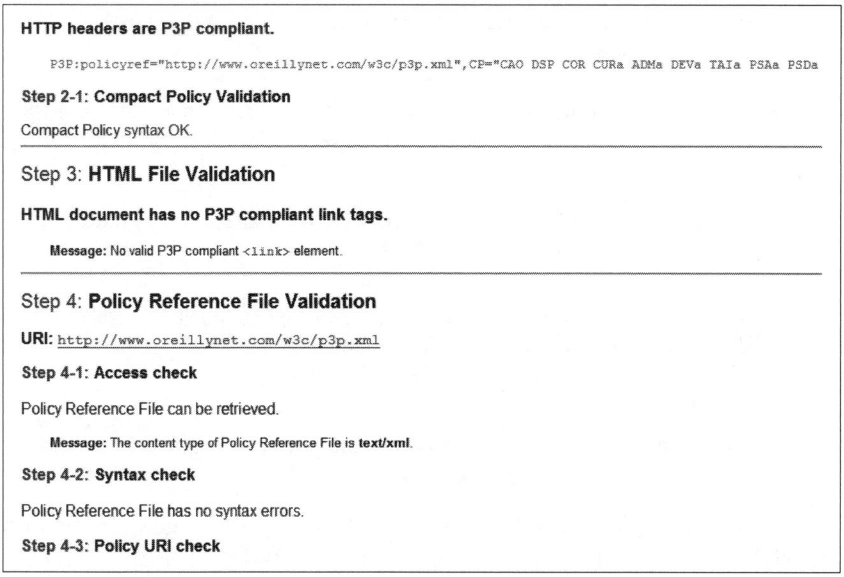

HTTP headers are P3P compliant.

P3P:policyref="http://www.oreillynet.com/w3c/p3p.xml",CP="CAO DSP COR CURa ADMa DEVa TAIa PSAa PSDa

Step 2-1: Compact Policy Validation

Compact Policy syntax OK.

Step 3: **HTML File Validation**

HTML document has no P3P compliant link tags.

> **Message:** No valid P3P compliant <link> element.

Step 4: **Policy Reference File Validation**

URI: http://www.oreillynet.com/w3c/p3p.xml

Step 4-1: Access check

Policy Reference File can be retrieved.

> **Message:** The content type of Policy Reference File is **text/xml**.

Step 4-2: Syntax check

Policy Reference File has no syntax errors.

Step 4-3: Policy URI check

Figure 2-10. Policy validation

It is worth noting that if you're an Internet Explorer user, you can view any web site's privacy policy via the View → Privacy Policy report in the menu bar.

Wait, How Do I Deliver the Compact Policy?

The compact policy tokens must be sent as a part of a P3P HTTP header sent by the web server within the HTTP response for the object attempting to set a cookie in a third-party context. The following steps describe possible implementation for Microsoft IIS and Apache web servers.

For Microsoft Internet Information Server:

1. Open the Internet Services Manager (Microsoft Management Console).

2. Expand the Default Web Site or a specific web site under Internet Information Services.

3. Right-click on the web site, page, or object (image, JavaScript file, etc.) of which you wish to add the P3P HTTP header in the pop-up menu and select Properties.

4. Select the HTTP Headers dialog tab.

5. Click the Add Custom HTTP Header button.

6. In the "custom header" field, enter P3P.

7. In the "custom header value" field, enter your compact policy exactly as follows:

```
policyref="http://www.mysite.com/w3c/policy1.xml", CP=" NOI DSP COR PSA PSAa
OUR IND COM NAV STA"
```

Apache Web Server. A compact policy HTTP header response can be added by including the following line in the appropriate configuration file (*httpd. conf* or *.htaccess*):

```
Header append P3P "policyref=\"\http://www.mysite.com/w3c/policy1.xml\"\,
CP= "NOI DSP COR PSA PSAa OUR IND COM NAV STA"
```

> Apache's mod_headers module needs to be included to push headers to the browser. Make sure that you're using mod_headers if you notice that the CP headers are not pushed.

For a little more information on implementation, you might take a look at *http://www.w3.org/TR/p3pdeployment*.

If you wish to implement a P3P policy on a per-HTML page basis (within the HTML code itself), Table 2-4 illustrates examples of such document headers in various languages.

Table 2-4. How to set P3P compact policies on a variety of application delivery platforms

Language	Code
HTML	`<META http-equiv="P3P" content="policyref='http://www.mysite.com/w3c/policy1.xml', CP='NOI DSP COR PSA PSAa OUR IND COM NAV STA'">`
PHP	`Header("P3P: policyref='http://www.mysite.com/w3c/policy1.xml', CP='NOI DSP COR PSA PSAa OUR IND COM NAV STA'")`
ASP	`Response.AddHeader "P3P","policyref='http://www.mysite.com/w3c/policy1.xml'","CP='NOI DSP COR PSA PSAa OUR IND COM NAV STA'"`
JSP	`Response.setHeader("P3P","http://www.mysite.com/w3c/policy1.xml","CP='NOI DSP COR PSA PSAa OUR IND COM NAV STA'")`

Obviously, the last few code examples cover the setting of P3P HTTP headers for the document as a whole. Since most page-tag–based data collection solutions rely on the request-response headers of an embedded object such as an image or JavaScript file, the server-side P3P HTTP header response mechanism described above is the method to use.

Consequences of Omitting a Privacy Policy

Despite the fact that five of the six steps described above are pretty trivial (writing your privacy policy in the first place can take time, but you really need to do it anyway), you may decide to blow this off. I mean, what's the worst that could happen?

The "red eye". The red eye is a small icon that appears in the lower-right corner of your P3P-compliant browser that lets you know that the site you're visiting is in some way violating your privacy expectations (Figure 2-11). Obviously, if you don't have a policy, you'll be serving many red eyes; they're served with greater or lesser frequency, depending on the type of information you're trying to collect and your use of cookies.

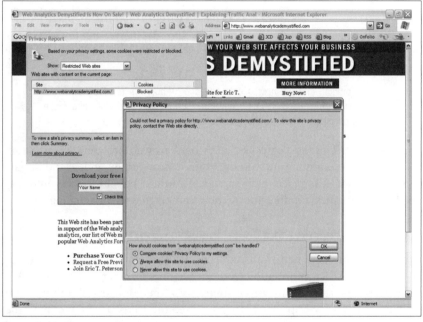

Figure 2-11. Privacy violation warning

Visitors will wonder why you don't care about their privacy. More and more people have become attuned to P3P, thanks to the relatively easy Internet Explorer implementation (if not explained well from a consumer-benefit standpoint), and have become used to watching for the red eye and complaining when they see it. Because these policies are so easy to set up, there really is no excuse for not doing so. Trying to hide from your use of first- and third-party cookies for web measurement is a lousy idea—one that will eventually return to haunt you.

Eventually, the press will wonder why you don't care. As demonstrated in an August 2000 debacle over the lack of adequate customer notice, the media does actually care when companies aren't very careful about how they collect information.* Depending on how big you are and how closely people are watching you, failing to establish a P3P policy that describes your use and collection of web measurement and personal identification could create a PR nightmare that you really don't want.

For more information on creating a P3P policy, see either the W3C's P3P 1.0 Specification (*http://www.w3.org/TR/P3P/*) or description of how to make your site P3P-compliant (*http://www.w3.org/P3P/details.html*), or Microsoft's take on P3P as it relates to Internet Explorer (*http://www.microsoft.com/presspass/press/2001/mar01/PrivacyToolsIEfs.asp*). You may also want to pick up Lorrie Cranor's *Web Privacy and P3P* (O'Reilly).

—*Eric T. Peterson with Aaron Bird, Stephen Turner,*
Jim MacIntyre, and Jay McCarthy

HACK #28 Deconstruct JavaScript Page Tags

Page tagging and the hosted data collection model are relatively new, but becoming more popular. Learn how JavaScript page tags work and make better decisions about deploying them on your site.

JavaScript is a scripting language that is used in web browsers to enable an HTML page to communicate with the visitor's browser. By understanding JavaScript and how it interacts with variables, you can pass in friendly information like page names, product information, campaign data, or anything else.

How Do Web Measurement Tools Use JavaScript?

Not all web measurement tools collect data the same way, but many use JavaScript to collect information from the visitor's browser and act as an API to the web server that displays the content. All the popular web browsers on the market use JavaScript, so it is a good medium to use to interact with the browser application and any server-side technology you may have deployed (Active Server Pages, Cold Fusion, etc.).

Since JavaScript resides in the HTML page, it can access variables populated by the application server and the document object. If you are looking at a web page URL, it normally does not contain all the information you would like to collect. For example, only JavaScript can collect the browser resolution of a visitor to your web site.

---

* See the Wired article "Lack of Notice Snags E-Service," by Chris Oakes, August 2, 2000 at *http://www.wired.com/news/business/0,1367,37949,00.htm*l.

How a JavaScript Page Tag Works

The basic JavaScript page tag functions in what is loosely referred to as a "round trip"—the embedded code is delivered with the web page, but it programmatically builds another script request that is sent back to the original server (hence the round trip) to get additional code necessary for the tag to function. In most instances, this is a four-step process.

Step one: JavaScript in web pages is executed. JavaScript and variables embedded into the application templates (HTML pages) are executed while the web page loads into the visitor's browser, depending on where the tag is located in the file (Figure 2-12). Most vendors recommend putting your tags at or near the top of the page to ensure data collection even in very large HTML pages (knowing that sometimes visitors click "stop" or back up, resulting in an incomplete page load).

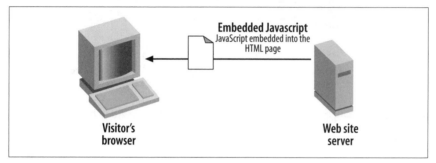

Figure 2-12. Embedded JavaScript page tag

Step two: JavaScript source file is requested and returned to the browser. Java-Script source file referenced within the embedded JavaScript is requested from the original web server (or the browser's cache, or an external content distribution network, Figure 2-13). This code usually provides the bulk of the functionality found in a page tag.

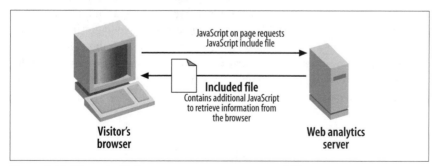

Figure 2-13. The embedded JavaScript requests an external file

Step three: The page tag collects data and reports back. The JavaScript builds an invisible image to send the web analytics collection server. This image request has a long query string, appended to the URL, containing the information gathered out of the visitor's browser about her visit.

Step four: A cookie and P3P privacy policy are returned. In the final step, a cookie is written to the visitor's browser to store a unique identifier and any other necessary information, and the invisible image is returned (Figure 2-14). Also, most measurement applications will send a P3P privacy policy [Hack #26] back to the visitor's browser along with the cookie to prevent cookie dropping [Hack #17].

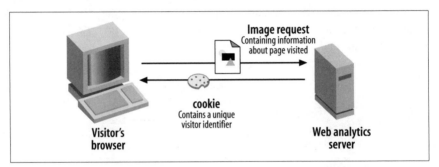

Figure 2-14. A blank image and a P3P privacy compact are returned to the visitor's browser

Deconstructing an Archetypical JavaScript Page Tag

Let's take a detailed look at the JavaScript page tag used in Omniture's SiteCatalyst product. Normally, there is a company copyright at the top of the code.

```
<!-- SiteCatalyst code version: G.7. Copyright 1997-2004 Omniture, Inc. More
info available at http://www.omniture.com --><script language="JavaScript">
```

Next, there is a section of variables that you can customize to collect data about the displayed page. For example, if the web application server displays a product page, it would populate information about the product being displayed into the variables. If the page is on a travel web site, it would pass in information about the hotel or trip someone is viewing. The variable acts as a bridge between the application server and the web analytics application. IDs, instead of friendly names, are frequently passed back and forth, but either will work.

Since JavaScript can happen anywhere on the page, there are times that you will not see the code completely laid out together. For example, some variables may sit at the top of the page, while other variables are located in the middle of the page.

```
<!--
/* You may give each page an identifying name, server, and channel on the
next lines. */
var s_pageName=""
var s_server=""
var s_channel=""
var s_pageType=""
var s_prop1=""
var s_prop2=""
var s_prop3=""
var s_prop4=""
var s_prop5=""
/* E-commerce Variables */
var s_campaign=""
var s_state=""
var s_zip=""
var s_events=""
var s_products=""
var s_purchaseID=""
var s_eVar1=""
var s_eVar2=""
var s_eVar3=""
var s_eVar4=""
var s_eVar5=""
/* Hierarchy Variables */
var s_hier1=""
```

Since the application server needs to interact only with the JavaScript variables, the majority of the JavaScript tag is placed into a JavaScript include file. The logic code is placed in this file so that, once cached, it will download only once and not need to be placed in full text on every page. By caching the file, load times are typically much faster.

```
/********* INSERT THE DOMAIN AND PATH TO YOUR CODE BELOW ************/
/********* DO NOT ALTER ANYTHING ELSE BELOW THIS LINE! *************/
var s_code=' ' //--></script>
<script language="JavaScript" src="http://INSERT-DOMAIN-AND-PATH-TO-CODE-
HERE/s_code.js"></script>
```

The following block of code writes the image request to send to the analytics application. This is how the information is passed to the analytics program, and has a very cryptic look.

```
http://stats.mysite.net/b/ss/mysiteID/1/G.6-Pd-R/
s45641272328490?purl=http%3A%2F%2Fwww.mysite.com%2F&pccr=true&&ndh=1 (etc.)
```

Some analytics vendors put this code inside of the JavaScript include file. However, by placing the code inside the include file, several browsers may be excluded from tracking.

```
<script language="JavaScript">
<!--
var s_wd=window,s_tm=new Date;
if(s_code!=' '){
    s_code=s_dc('pestana');
    if(s_code)document.write(s_code)} else document.write('<im'+'g
src="http://stats.mysite.net/b/ss/mysiteID/1/G.7--FB/s'+s_tm.getTime
  ()+'?[AQB]'+'&j=1.0&[AQE]" height="1" width="1" border="0" alt="" />')
//--></script>
<script language="JavaScript">
<!--
if(navigator.appVersion.indexOf('MSIE')>=0)document.write(unescape('%3C')+'\
!-'+'-')
//-->
</script>
<NOSCRIPT><img src=http://pestana.112.207.net/b/ss/pestana/1/G.7--NS/0
height="1" width="1" border="0" alt="" /></NOSCRIPT>
```

The final block of code is designed to capture information about the visitors who did not have JavaScript enabled or are using a browser that does not support JavaScript.

If you want to optimize data collection about your non-JavaScript users, you will also want to populate the <NOSCRIPT> image tag with the information you placed into the JavaScript variables. Keep in mind that if your visitor has JavaScript disabled, you will likely miss a lot of information that can be collected only with JavaScript.

Additionally, JavaScript plays a key role in cache busting [Hack #24], which is how JavaScript ensures that it tracks every page view even if it is reloaded from browser cache or a proxy server. It does this by generating a random number via JavaScript and then placing the number in the URL, which makes the browser believe it is requesting a new page every time.

 Many web measurement products do not collect information from browsers that do not support JavaScript.

By understanding how a JavaScript page tag works, we hope that you're able to develop an appreciation for the complexity involved. One thing to keep in mind is that you should *never* modify the functional component of a page tag unless directed by your vendor. Because vendors spend so much time optimizing their JavaScript, even the smallest change can break the tag (and in some cases, your entire web page). While it is possible to trim functional code [Hack #19] to further reduce download time and optimize performance, you should do so *only* with your vendor's assistance (or have them do it for you!).

—John Pestana and Eric T. Peterson

Understand Web Bugs

#29 A very important aspect of JavaScript page tagging is the use of a small image request to send information to the data collection device. Often referred to as a "web bug" or "web beacon," these images are usually one-by-one pixel image requests designed to carry data from place to place.

Many consumers are told to fear web bugs and web beacons as some type of spyware that will, if allowed, somehow ruin their computers (and potentially their entire lives!). Fortunately, when used in the context of web measurement, nothing could be further from the truth. Web bugs and beacons are simply a rather unsophisticated way to refer to the image request that many third-party web measurement and tracking systems make to collect data. Still, a Google search for "web bug" yields over 10 million documents, so it's worth understanding how consumers respond to the idea of a "bug" and, just in case someone accuses you of using web bugs, have a suitable response ready.

Really, What Is a "Web Bug"

Again, a "web bug" is a misunderstood term that addresses how third-party tracking applications work and what they're able to track. According to the Wikipedia:

> A web bug (also known as a tracking bug, pixel tag, web beacon, or clear gif) is a technique for determining who viewed an HTML-based email message or a web page, when they did so, how many times, how long they kept the message open, etc.

> Usually, a web bug is a transparent image or an image in the color of the background of what you are viewing. It is typically 1x1 pixels in size. But other techniques can also be used to track usage, such as IFRAMES.

> In effect, most people won't notice that what they are viewing is bugged. Web bugs are a favorite tool that spammers use to verify working email addresses.

It is perhaps the last sentence that highlights best why consumers have a negative attitude towards third-party tracking applications: they function much the same way as many of the nefarious tools used by spammers. As described in great length in the hack on JavaScript page tags [Hack #28], this type of request is a requirement, but one that is harmless at best, at least when used in the context of web measurement.

The Consumer Mindset About Web Bugs

Despite the fact that web bugs are harmless, third-party tracking systems have suffered from a spate of bad press over the years, increasing consumer concern. Coupled with the fact that few people actually understand the ins and outs of web measurement, the use of web bugs by spammers, and some particularly bad press that advertising tracking systems got in 2000 (try Googling the phrase "double-click abuse of cookies" for more information), the lack of accurate information has swayed the court of public opinion against third-party tracking.

Some consumers go so far as to use applications like Bugnosis (Figure 2-15) to warn them when web bugs are being used. You can View → Source on web pages and look for the presence of the third-party tracking code that actually generates these "bugs."

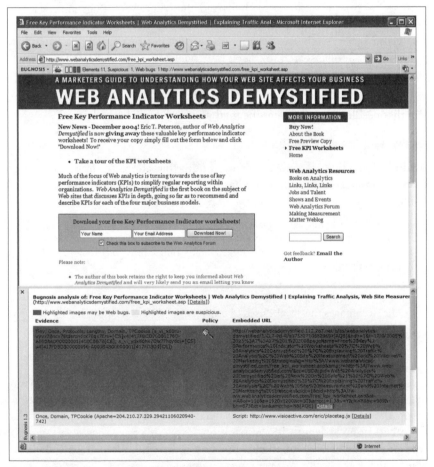

Figure 2-15. Bugnosis analysis for "web bugs"

If all of this has you concerned because you're using a third-party tracking system (or "hosted application," see [Hack #3] for a more complete list), fear not! You can stave off most if not all of the potential fallout by simply being direct and proactive about how you use tracking technology on your site.

Be Explicit About Your Use of Web Bugs and Beacons

If you're concerned that your site visitors are spooked by the idea of web bugs, here are a handful of things you should be doing.

Ensure that your privacy policy reflects your use of page tags. The worst mistake you can make is not proactively communicating to your visitors that you're using these so called "web bugs." Make sure you have a privacy policy in place and that your policy accurately describes how you use tracking technology [Hack #26].

Ensure that your P3P policy reflects your use of page tags. Potentially worse than not having a stated privacy policy that visitors can read is not having a P3P policy and P3P compact policy [Hack #27] that can be read by Internet Explorer. Failure to have these policies in place will generate the mysterious Z"red eye" in Internet Explorer that tells the consumer that "something is wrong"—a problem that needlessly perpetuates the myth that web bugs are bad news.

Have a good explanation ready if people complain. Regardless of how well you build privacy and P3P policies, the most important thing you can do regarding "web bugs" is have a really sound explanation ready for people who complain (and they will complain). If you already use a tag-based measurement solution, go ahead and ask your webmasters if they've had anyone complain about spyware. Chances are they get emails like that with some frequency, but are not exactly sure how to respond (since they're not setting any spyware, right?).

Often it is said that "the best defense is a good offense," and it's true in this case. When you get emails like this, you should immediately send a well-crafted email back to the writer explaining:

- Your commitment to their security and privacy online
- Your commitment to improving the user experience on your sites
- Your use of "modern web tracking" technology that is approved by international standards agencies as a strategy for improving the online experience via secure and private channels
- Provide a real person's email address for follow-up—don't hide behind an alias, or your response will ring hollow

You need to re-instill confidence in the consumer and make them question their original complaint without questioning your integrity or commitment to their privacy. When crafting this standard response, it's not a bad idea to consult your measurement vendor to see if they have any specific certifications worth mentioning.

HACK #30 Hack the JavaScript Document Object Model

Understand how the JavaScript Document Object Model is used by many, if not all, tag-based web measurement solutions.

Since most web measurement vendors use the JavaScript Document Object Model (DOM) extensively, you may be concerned about whether your provider's code interferes with your own JavaScript programming. More importantly, you should be concerned about whether your provider is taking advantage of all the possibilities for data collection the DOM makes available.

Some examples of information the DOM provides include the following.

- Browser version
- OS time
- OS language
- Monitor resolution
- Monitor color depth
- Browser height and width
- Form analysis

The Document Object Model is a framework used by web browsers and Java-Script to store and access information about a document and, in our case, a web page (Figure 2-16). JavaScript and the JavaScript programmer use the DOM to both gather and place information. From placing the web beacon to gathering information about site visitors, the DOM is central to web analytics.

While Figure 2-16 shows only a small selection of DOM components, it is useful in outlining the structure of the DOM. The window object is the root element and provides access to all other elements. Each object contains functions, properties, events, and/or other objects. JavaScript can be used to access or control each piece of the DOM, as described in the following sections.

Placing the Beacon

As you might expect, the most important piece of beacon-based web data collection is the beacon—the invisible GIF [Hack #29]. There are two main ways to place the beacon on the page: via server-side image tag generation

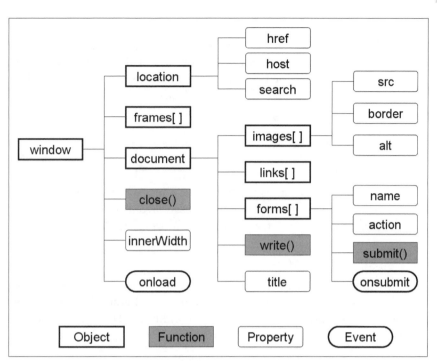

Figure 2-16. The JavaScript Document Object Model

and via client-side JavaScript. By using JavaScript to create the image tag, the web analytics provider allows itself to gather the most amount of information possible. When the web server creates the image tag, much of the information about the user is unavailable.

The document object's write function is used to write HTML or JavaScript into the HTML document. Here is how it is done:

```
<script language="JavaScript"><!--
window.document.write("<img src='http://omniture.com/images/1x1.gif' />");
//--></script>
```

This illustrates the ever-changeable nature of the DOM. We used the document object to add an element to the document. In this case, the element is an image. Now that the image is in place, it can be accessed via the DOM.

 An element within the JavaScript document model can change locations at any time.

Returning Document Information

While placing the image is essential, the reason for the image is to gather information about the page, browser, and visitor. This information is again available via the DOM. See how the DOM can be used to identify the URL of the page, and include that URL with the beacon:

```
<script language="JavaScript"><!--
var url=window.location.href;
window.document.write("<img src='http://omniture.com/images/1x1.
gif?url='"+url+" />");
//--></script>
```

Fortunately, the DOM can be used to gather a lot more than just the viewed URL. It can give you information about page layout, multimedia support, and form design, to name a few. Next, we'll address page layout.

Finding the Browser Width

If your entire web page fits in the left half of the browser window, you may be ignoring a valuable resource—empty real estate. Rather than having your developers ask their friends about browser width, the DOM can be used to ask your customers whether you're wasting real estate, for example:

```
window.document.documentElement.offsetWidth;
```

For recent versions of IE, this code returns the pixel width of the browser window. While this specific property is not available in all browsers, most browsers have a corresponding property offering the same information. If your web measurement provider does not make this information available in the report you need, you can get it yourself with the following code. Notice that the width is rounded to the nearest 50 pixels so that sorting through the resulting data isn't too cumbersome.

```
var width= window.document.documentElement.offsetWidth;
var width=Math.round(width/50)*50; // round width to the nearest 50 pixels
```

Track Form Entry Errors

So far, the DOM has been used to gather information about your web page and the browser. However, the DOM can also be used to watch the movements of the visitor to the page. For example, you can choose to monitor whether, and to what extent, a user interacts with a form. The DOM can be used to call a function when an event occurs. Many sites have JavaScript-based error checking for forms. What those sites often don't take advantage of is tracking which errors are occurring most often. The following example shows how to use your error checking function to record information about errors that occur in a form:

```
function checkError( ){
    // check that the credit card number contains 16 digits
    if( window.document.forms[0].creditcard.value.length!=16 ) {
        sendErrorInfo(window.document.forms[0].name,"Credit Card Error:
Length");
        return false;
    }
    // more error checking
    return true;
}
// call checkError when the form is submitted
window.document.forms[0].onsubmit=checkError;
```

After defining the checkError function, the JavaScript uses DOM to call that function as the form is submitted (the onsubmit event). Notice that the checkError function contains a call to a function named sendErrorInfo. A function like this, which should be available from your web analytics provider, writes an image to the page, thus sending information about the error to the data collection servers. The result is a report like the one in the next section, which shows the most common form errors on your site.

Form Analysis—Manna from the DOM

Now that you understand how the DOM is used to place an image, read browser information, and watch visitor interaction, we can combine these to create a valuable measurement tool. The DOM can provide valuable business information and a glimpse into the subtleties of the user experience. For example, which field in a form is the straw that breaks the camel's back? Is it too much to ask for a credit card number, hair color, mother's maiden name, or neighbor's phone number? At what point do potential customers give up?

JavaScript and the DOM can be used to send information (write an image to the page) as someone leaves that page. And before that person leaves the page, it can identify the last field touched by the user, the field that was quite possibly the last straw. The report in Figure 2-17 shows an example for the ShippingInfo form on the Checkout-Shipping page. Notice that the form was successfully submitted 154 times, but there were 202 instances when users left without touching the form. Notice also that users most often left the form after touching the PhoneNumber field.

For all analysts who have wished to be the proverbial fly on the wall of their customer's offices, the DOM is here to grant that wish. Like all web analytics tools, this method of gathering data won't capture 100 percent of visitors, but since well over 95 percent of the visitors to your site have JavaScript enabled, you get much more than a "statistically significant sample." There is a lot of information about your site that is waiting to be gathered. You just need to find someone who can unlock the information.

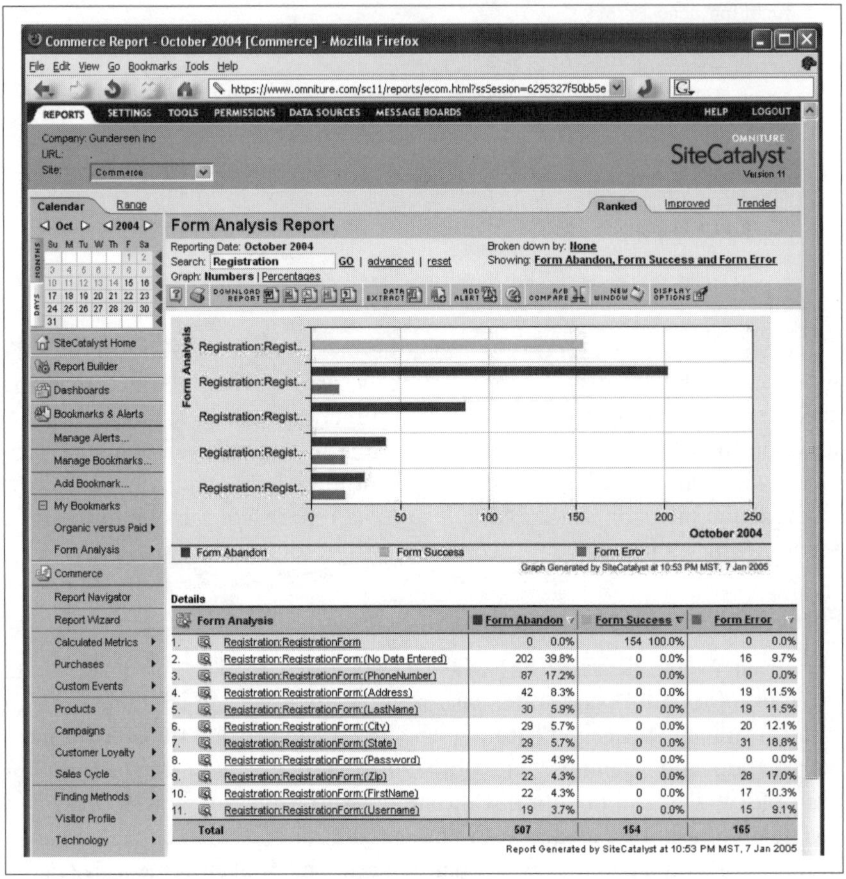

Figure 2-17. Sample form field analysis

—*Brett Error, John Pestana, and Eric T. Peterson*

HACK #31 Use Custom Variables Wisely

Use of custom variables to track data most relevant to your business, generating a more complete view of the visitor in the process.

While there is no industry standard definition, a custom variable is essentially an addition to your standard web site data collection strategy, commonly collected via a page tag or query string parameter and stored in a client-side cookie (Figure 2-18). You can have many custom variables per cookie, each containing a name=value pair such as "color=blue" or "rating=five stars". Custom variables can be used to count nontraditional data elements, but are ideally tied to a specific business objective.

```
var s_prop1=""
var s_prop2=""
var s_prop3=""
var s_prop4=""

        if (ConnectionSpeed != "undetermined") s_prop4=ConnectionSpeed;

var s_prop5=""
/* E-commerce Variables */
var s_campaign=""
var s_state=""
var s_zip=""
var s_events=""
var s_products=""
var s_purchaseID=""
var s_eVar1=""
var s_eVar2=""
var s_eVar3=""
var s_eVar4=""
var s_eVar5=""
/********* INSERT THE DOMAIN AND PATH TO YOUR CODE BELOW ************/
//-->
```

Figure 2-18. Custom variable deployment

When an objective tied to a custom variable is reached, the web measurement application records the event (and any quantifiable value of the event). Through this simple process, you can gain valuable insight into which initiatives are most successful.

Uses for Custom Variables

As long as your measurement application supports these custom variables, the opportunities are unlimited. Some examples of common uses for custom variables include:

- Internal search terms, so you'll be able to determine which searches are leading to conversion events **[Hack #64]**
- Split-path test participation **[Hack #63]**, so you can keep track of which test a visitor is participating in at any given time
- Registration status, so you can determine whether the visitor is known **[Hack #66]** to you or not
- Key event participation, so you can determine whether a visitor has seen an online presentation, looked at pricing, or downloaded a document
- Links clicked, if your particular web measurement application does not allow you to measure and assign value to links **[Hack #54]**
- Error messages, such as 404 (page not found) errors and client-side JavaScript errors **[Hack #34]**
- Demographic data, like age group or gender **[Hack #77]**

Finally, one of the most popular uses for custom variables is to measure use of "configurators" or product selection engines (Figure 2-19). To do this, simply capture the results of each feature selection set as a visitor moves through the process. The end result is a list of custom variables that will help you understand which features or configurations are most commonly selected and compare that list to the features that customers actually purchase.

Figure 2-19. The product "configurator" at store.apple.com

This specific use of custom variables is gaining a great deal of traction lately, and companies are using the information gained to make and save millions of dollars annually.

One-to-One Direct Marketing and Custom Variables

Those of you who live on the edge should consider using custom variables to support one-to-one direct marketing efforts by passing a unique user identifier [Hack #5] into a custom variable during your login authentication process. By correlating this user identifier with web behavior, you can market to an individual that has been authenticated on your web site, usually by using your measurement application to export the list of names into your email or customer relationship management application. A more sophisticated use of this strategy is to export email addresses only for visitors who completed a specific set of actions (such as downloaded a document or viewed a set of pages).

 Before you pass *any* personally identifiable information around in a custom variable, you *must* ensure your privacy policy and customer disclosures acknowledge this type of activity.

The use of custom variables and the collection of personally identifiable data require care and caution. This means having users opt-in to receive marketing communications, updating your compact privacy policy [Hack #27] to reflect these intentions, and updating your privacy statement [Hack #26]. This type of activity should not be undertaken lightly and should involve high-level decision makers. The legal folks should also be involved, along with officers of the company to ensure consensus.

Custom Variables in Action: An Example

Say your company is running a referral survey that asks customers how they heard about your business. You could ask this question during member registration, shopping cart checkout, or customer support. Using a custom variable to track these responses would easily show you which referral sources drive the greatest customer acquisition. Still, any basic survey system or database can tell you that, so what else can you learn using custom variables? Figure 2-20 illustrates why you'd want to use custom variables to gather survey data, helping to fill in the blanks between web measurement and survey data.

As you can see, "Radio Ads" (line 1) drove most customers—the most of any referral source. If you stopped your analysis there, you might recommend that your company invest more in radio advertising, and while logical, that would be a poor recommendation. Notice that while "Radio Ads" are the top customer acquisition *source*, they are not the leader in revenue conversion or lifetime value, which are your true performance indicators.

Now look at the "Billboard" referral source (line 4): at $18.64, initial revenues are the highest of any referral source. This valuable insight helps you evaluate where to focus your future customer acquisition efforts. However, using custom variables, you can take this one step further to examine lifetime customer value [Hack #84]. You may not be surprised to notice that customers referred by "Relatives" generate the most lifetime value, followed closely by "Friends."

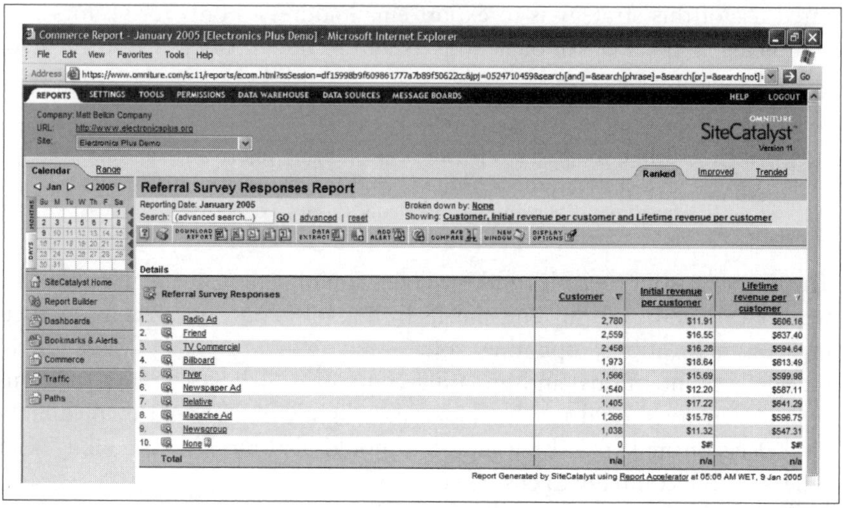

Figure 2-20. Using custom variables

Hopefully, you can see how custom variables are often the "missing link" between the data that measurement vendors want to provide and the information you may really need. Web measurement vendors have done a great job building out flexible data collection mechanisms, but stop short of being customized to your unique business needs. Custom variables let you do just that; capturing critical data and providing valuable insights that you really need to manage your business.

—Matt Belkin and Eric T. Peterson

HACK #32   Best Practices for Data Integration

Many companies, as they get more experience with web measurement, seek to integrate external data in an attempt to create a unified marketing interface.

Many web analytics reports are highly actionable, but usually the hidden power in web site measurement is the data itself. When combined with other data sources, web data can be used to analyze merchandising promotion gross margin contribution, campaign ROI, and how certain demographics behave on your web site. Web measurement data, when stored in a visitor-centric form, can be used to analyze the behavior of your survey respondents, target your email marketing campaigns, and even fuel your multichannel data warehouse.

Examples of Common Data Integrations

A number of common data integration projects have emerged over the past few years and are worth reviewing to develop an understanding of the value of combining disparate data sources.

Integrate cost data to calculate gross margin contribution. Many companies tie product cost data to their web measurement merchandising report to analyze product gross margin contribution driven by product category browsing, product real estate placement, on-site product search, and product site tool (such as "magnify") usage. The potential of this data is obvious. Merchandisers can, at a glance, see how their initiatives are driving bottom-line profit instead of gross sales. With this simple data import, all merchandising reports can be updated to show gross margin contribution in addition to gross sales.

Integrate marketing cost data to determine real campaign ROI. You may want to integrate campaign cost data into your web measurement marketing reports so you can more accurately determine the true return on investment for your campaigns. By tying campaign cost data and asking your vendor to customize their marketing reports to use that data, you will be able to analyze campaign ROI in addition to the typical metric of gross sales. With this combined view, you won't have to log into each campaign vendor's reports to see how much profit you are generating from each campaign investment. You will have a single campaign measurement source to report from and know that you are using the *same measurement methodology* to analyze the performance of all your online campaign sources.

Integrate customer registration data to drill into demographics. You may want to tie your customer registration data to your web measurement reports. If you collect household income, for example, and your vendor supports customer segmentation based on that type of data, you can analyze the behavior of customer groups by household income [Hack #77]. Imagine the power of analyzing how different customer demographics path through various parts of your site, what merchandise they abandon and purchase, and how they respond to email campaigns.

Integrate customer satisfaction data. Customer satisfaction is one aspect of data that most web measurement applications don't measure well. Because of the complexity of doing so, most companies use an outside vendor to collect satisfaction data; however, this data can be tremendously important to your understanding of your visitors and customers. Combining your web data with data collected by an outside vendor—say, BizRate or Foresee Results—can add valuable missing elements to your analysis (Figure 2-21).

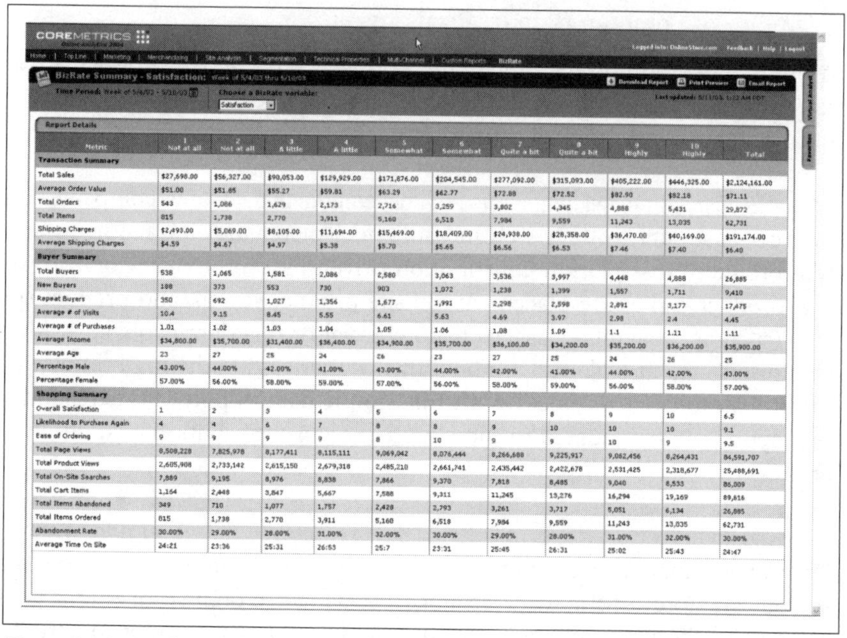

Metric	1 Not at all	2 Not at all	3 A little	4 A little	5 Somewhat	6 Somewhat	7 Quite a bit	8 Quite a bit	9 Highly	10 Highly	Total
Transaction Summary											
Total Sales	$27,698.00	$56,327.00	$90,053.00	$129,929.00	$171,876.00	$204,545.00	$277,092.00	$315,093.00	$405,222.00	$446,325.00	$2,124,161.00
Average Order Value	$51.00	$51.85	$55.27	$59.81	$63.29	$62.77	$72.88	$72.52	$82.90	$82.18	$71.11
Total Orders	543	1,086	1,629	2,173	2,716	3,259	3,802	4,345	4,888	5,431	29,872
Total Items	815	1,738	2,770	3,911	5,160	6,518	7,984	9,559	11,243	13,035	62,731
Shipping Charges	$2,493.00	$5,069.00	$8,105.00	$11,694.00	$15,469.00	$18,409.00	$24,938.00	$28,358.00	$36,470.00	$40,169.00	$191,174.00
Average Shipping Charges	$4.59	$4.67	$4.97	$5.38	$5.70	$5.65	$6.56	$6.53	$7.46	$7.40	$6.40
Buyer Summary											
Total Buyers	538	1,065	1,581	2,086	2,580	3,063	3,536	3,997	4,448	4,888	26,885
New Buyers	188	373	553	730	903	1,072	1,238	1,399	1,557	1,711	9,410
Repeat Buyers	350	692	1,027	1,356	1,677	1,991	2,298	2,598	2,891	3,177	17,475
Average # of Visits	10.4	9.15	8.45	5.55	6.61	5.63	4.69	3.97	2.98	2.4	4.45
Average # of Purchases	1.01	1.02	1.03	1.04	1.05	1.06	1.08	1.09	1.1	1.11	1.11
Average Income	$34,800.00	$35,700.00	$31,400.00	$36,400.00	$34,900.00	$35,700.00	$36,100.00	$34,200.00	$35,200.00	$36,200.00	$35,900.00
Average Age	23	27	25	24	26	23	27	25	24	26	25
Percentage Male	43.00%	44.00%	42.00%	41.00%	43.00%	44.00%	42.00%	41.00%	44.00%	42.00%	43.00%
Percentage Female	57.00%	56.00%	58.00%	59.00%	57.00%	56.00%	58.00%	59.00%	56.00%	58.00%	57.00%
Shopping Summary											
Overall Satisfaction	1	2	3	4	5	6	7	8	9	10	6.5
Likelihood to Purchase Again	4	4	6	7	8	8	9	10	10	10	9.1
Ease of Ordering	9	9	9	9	8	10	9	9	10	9	9.5
Total Page Views	8,508,228	7,825,978	8,177,411	8,115,111	9,069,042	8,076,444	8,266,688	9,225,917	9,082,456	8,264,431	84,591,707
Total Product Views	2,685,908	2,733,142	2,615,150	2,679,318	2,485,210	2,661,741	2,435,442	2,422,678	2,531,425	2,318,677	25,488,691
Total On-Site Searches	7,889	9,195	8,976	8,838	7,866	9,370	7,818	8,485	9,040	8,533	86,009
Total Cart Items	1,164	2,448	3,847	5,667	7,588	9,311	11,245	13,276	16,294	19,169	89,616
Total Items Abandoned	349	710	1,077	1,757	2,428	2,793	3,261	3,717	5,051	6,134	26,885
Total Items Ordered	815	1,738	2,770	3,911	5,160	6,518	7,984	9,559	11,243	13,035	62,731
Abandonment Rate	30.00%	29.00%	28.00%	31.00%	32.00%	30.00%	29.00%	28.00%	31.00%	32.00%	30.00%
Average Time On Site	24:21	23:36	25:31	26:53	25:7	23:31	25:45	26:31	25:02	25:43	24:47

Figure 2-21. Combining data using BizRate

Integrate data from targeted email campaigns. Another example is using web measurement data to drive targeted email marketing campaigns. With most web measurement solutions, you know what your product abandonment rate is. You also know how many customers are looking at products and not buying. Those measurements alone are helpful in changing your merchandise promotion and placement. But imagine the power of using that data to find the customers who are abandoned and target them with a special promotion. Many web measurement vendors in the last year have partnered with email delivery vendors to fuel their targeting engines with customer browsing and abandonment behavior.

Taking Action to Integrate Non-Web Data

The generalized steps to take to integrate non-web data are as follows:

1. Identify the problem you'd like to solve.
2. Identify the sources of web and non-web data that will be required.
3. Determine how you're going to tie the data sources together.
4. Integrate the data.
5. Generate reports and take action.

Obviously, none of these steps are trivial, and thus should be explored in greater depth.

Identify the problem you'd like to solve. Data integration is typically complex and very expensive. Consider the examples provided above; each is trying to create a more complete understanding of a common problem. Whether you're trying to determine "true" return on investment, better understand the customer, or improve your ability to drive loyalty, you're trying to solve a very concrete problem. Before you try and integrate data make sure you truly understand both the problem and how the combined data set will help you solve it.

Identify the sources of web and non-web data that will be required. Once you're sure you understand the problem you want to solve, you then need to determine which data you'll need for the job. Many companies make the mistake of trying to integrate all available data into a monster data warehouse, assuming that if all the data is in one place, any question can be asked and any problem solved. Unfortunately, this is never the case, and massive data combination projects nearly always fail. Instead, identify the minimum number of data sources you need to answer the question and integrate those; you can always go back and add appropriate data later as warranted.

Determine how you're going to tie the data sources together. Most data integration projects fail because of the difficulty tying multiple sources together in meaningful ways. In each of the cases listed above, there needs to be a unique identifier in each data set that relates the data together. Whether that ID is a product SKU, a marketing campaign ID, or a unique user identifier, your major challenge is determining how to associate the IDs in one data set with the IDs in another. It may sound trivial, but it's not, especially when you stop and consider that many data sources are incomplete or polluted (spelling errors, use of upper- and lowercase, etc.).

Integrate the data. Your first temptation may be to try and bring the data together in your web measurement application. Remember, however, that you can also use your company's existing analysis tools to analyze site activity data combined with additional in-house data. Web measurement data, if structured in an exportable format, can be analyzed in Microsoft Excel, Microsoft Access, Business Objects, Cognos, NCR Teradata, MicroStrategy, Oracle, and any number of analytical tools. It is important that you ask your web measurement vendor what export formats they support and what the exported data includes.

Generate reports and take action. If you took the time to form a good question in step one, taking action based on the data should not be a problem.

Once you get the data combined and you're taking action, you need to remember to maintain the combined data and forge a strategy for incrementally updating or cleaning the data from time to time. Again, one of the reasons many projects like these fail is the sheer size of the data sets involved. As long as you're realistic in your scope and are trying to answer well-defined questions, you're likely to be successful.

—*Brett Hurt and Eric T. Peterson*

HACK #33   Measure Your Intranet or Extranet

Companies collectively spend billions annually on intranet and extranet projects but often fail to take the extra step in justifying the expenditure and ensuring that employees and business partners are actually using available tools.

While public web sites get all the limelight, many enterprises have internal and business-customer facing sites that merit measurement as well. These can be intranets—sites for use by the organization's members that can be accessed from within the premises of the organization only—or extranets—secure web sites for the organization's members or its affiliates that can be accessed from anywhere on the Internet, but require password authentication. The essence of measuring traffic to your internal sites is to ensure that the right people are using the right resources the right way. Regardless of the type of site, there is significant value in measuring the use of these types of sites, mostly derived from cost justification and usage patterns.

Justifying Return on Investment

Intranets and extranets often require significant effort and expenditure to create and maintain. One approach you can use to justify these costs is to quantify the savings associated with having people self-serve information from your internal sites.

For example, you may wish to quantify the time and effort associated having to take phone calls instead of having your business partners self-serve through your extranet. To do this, you would run web measurement reports to count the basic transactions (find information, change a record, make a purchase, etc.) that your site delivers, assigning a non-web transactional cost to each. The sum of these costs would be the net savings associated with building and maintaining the extranet.

Perhaps an easier strategy, one anyone can do, is to determine how much it costs your average human resources person to answer a basic question like "What holidays do we get this year?" Multiply that cost by the number of visits to your corporate intranet's "vacation schedule" page, and you can begin to visualize cost savings.

Measuring Content and Application Adoption

If you're responsible for content or applications on your internal site, you want to know what is used versus what is not so that you can concentrate your development and maintenance effort on the important areas. Another benefit of deprecating underused content is that internal users will likely find what they are looking for more easily. Also, note that you may be able to determine that users *aren't* using content and applications they should. In this case, you may want to use this information to drive departmental leaders to reacquaint employees with the corporate intranet.

The easiest way to start is with a report covering the most frequently accessed pages and content on your internal site. Sorting the report ascending by visits will show you the least frequently accessed content. The next step is to group content on your web site into logical content groupings so that you can get an overview of which functional groups users are most interested in. You may also want to examine time spent on pages and groups to try and determine whether internal users are spending enough time to reasonably get any value from the content or the application.

Examining Internal Searches

Intranets and extranets that serve as content repositories or portals accumulate so much content over time that local search becomes the most important way visitors try to locate information. Many web measurement tools offer reports on the keywords that visitors enter into the local search box [Hack #64], provided that the keyword can be captured either from the query string in the URL of the search results page or via a page tag. Searches with no or few results can be identified if the aforementioned URL or page tag also includes a parameter with the number of search results that were found, often identifying gaps in the information content your users think you should have available.

Abandoned searches can be more difficult to measure, but provide greater insight into how you can improve the quality of your internal applications. In the easiest case, the visit's exit page will be the search results page, telling you that the user just didn't see compelling enough results to bother clicking on links. Usually users conduct additional searches before they resort to navigating the content hierarchy instead of using search. Next-click analysis from the search results page can provide valuable insight in this regard; any "next" click that opens a content folder instead of an individual document may be a click on the site's navigation options instead of the search results. Ideally, the next click after a search is on a document—one that hopefully contains the information the visitor is looking for.

Named User Analysis

As intranets and extranets are almost always secure sites, a username can be usually captured and associated with the visit. Some sophisticated web measurement tools can even look up the username in your company's user database and translate it into the user's demographic information, such as their name, role, department, branch or company location, or training certification levels (Figure 2-22).

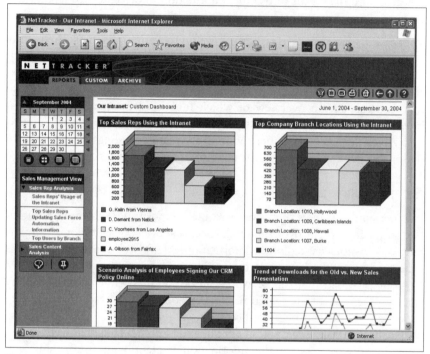

Figure 2-22. Tracking named users

If you want to get really sophisticated with measuring adoption rates, you can combine your organizational database with the web traffic database in suitable web measurement tools. Allowing you to measure beyond visitors, you can then calculate the percentage of persons in each department or branch that have adopted content on your site. Some enterprises also combine their web traffic database with their customer service call center logs to determine which customers are not using of their extranet and are instead calling into the hotline, incurring higher costs of service.

Tying It All Together

If you have a web measurement application with cycles to spare, here are five things you should do right away to make sure your intranets and extranets are being used:

- Generate a "Most Requested Pages" and "Most Requested Content" report to ensure that people are looking at information that actually makes sense.

- Generate a "Top Internal Searches" report and compare the results to your "Most Requested Pages" report, looking for inconsistencies in what people are searching for and what they're actually looking at.

- Generate a "Top Users" report by department (if you're able) and share it with departmental leaders, helping them understand which of their employees are perhaps not trained well enough on available resources.

- Compare your "Most Requested" reports with your deployment schedule to ensure that new functionality is actually being used.

- Compare your "Most Requested" reports to the volume of questions your human resources and support staffs are getting in an attempt to discover which user questions are not being answered by the intranet or extranet.

The last item is perhaps the most interesting since web measurement reports never really tell you that much about intent and satisfaction. By comparing the information you have available with the requests you get offline, you can hopefully see a trend, helping you identify additional content that needs to be added or made more visible.

—Akin Arikan and Eric T. Peterson

HACK #34 Measure Your Mistakes

One of the historical uses for web measurement tools that retain value is the ability to identify and diagnose error messages that your visitors may be seeing.

Nobody is perfect, they say, and web programmers are often less perfect than most. Constrained by tight deadlines, scope creep, and poorly defined standards for web page development, web programmers do the best they can. Unfortunately, the best is sometimes not good enough, and errors arise. One of the most valuable uses of your web measurement application is the identification of errors so any problems can be quickly corrected.

Types of Mistakes

There are many types of mistakes that can happen, but not all of them can be traced with typical web measurement tools alone. Here are a handful of the most common that can be tracked.

Web site is slow or fails to respond. There are services that specialize in web site monitoring designed to ping your web site regularly to ensure that it is accessible and that your web servers are handling page requests in acceptable amount of time. You can set up alerts for when something is wrong. Typical web measurement tools on the other hand do not provide adequate support for measuring these aspects, but it is possible to integrate response and availability into your web measurement application to provide a more holistic view of the situation [#Hack Measure Site Performance].

Broken hyperlinks. If a visitor requests a URL that is unavailable, the web server will return the classic HTTP 404 error (we suspect you've seen this error before). The most typical cause for this is that there is a broken hyperlink somewhere that points to an incorrect URL, one that does not exist. Web measurement tools can capture and report on this event after it happens.

> Monitoring your broken hyperlinks report is probably one of the most important things you can do with your web measurement application.

Run your broken link report every day looking for problems on your web site. Some of the time, the problem will be yours and easily corrected. Other times, the links will be coming from another site. In this case, you can either write the site asking them to correct the link or put a redirect in place of the broken link designed to push the visitor along to the right page.

Aborted page views and downloads. Tracking abandonment and interrupted downloads is more difficult than tracking HTTP errors, however. It requires using web server logfiles for your data collection because page tags can capture neither incomplete downloads nor the download time. The Microsoft IIS web server records a server status code of 64 when a request is terminated. Some web measurement tools supply such plug-ins and can report on page abandonment rates and incomplete downloads (Figure 2-23).

Client-side script errors. One of the most frustrating types of errors your visitors encounter are script errors—the type that prevent links from working, forms from being submitted, and otherwise result in a very poor user experience. While difficult to actively measure, creating a strategy for measuring this type of error can explain a great deal about why your visitors fail to move from page to page on your site.

How to Measure Your Mistakes

Depending on whether you are using web server logfiles or page tags for collecting traffic data, there are different methods to capture errors.

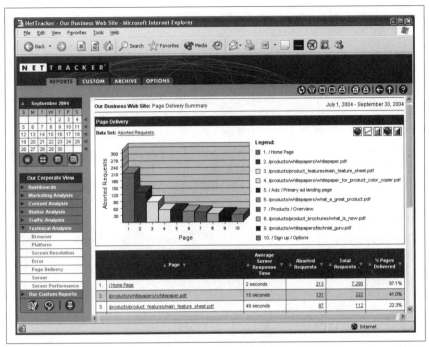

Figure 2-23. Report showing the percentage of pages and downloads delivered completely

Using logfiles as a data source. Web server logfiles record page requests with errors the same way they record successful page requests. The only difference is in the HTTP status code that is recorded along with the request in the logfile. Table 2-5 shows some of the most frequent HTTP protocol status codes:*

Table 2-5. Frequently encountered HTTP status codes

HTTP code	Interpretation
200	Successful hit; the request was fulfilled.
302	Redirection. The data requested actually resides under a different URL.
401	Unauthorized request. The request requires user authentication.
404	The server has not found anything matching the given URL.
503	Service unavailable. The server is currently unable to handle the request.

Using page tags as a data source. Many hosted application vendors have custom error page code that can be used to specifically capture errors, provided there is not a specific JavaScript error on the page. This strategy usually

---

* A complete listing can be obtained at *http://www.w3.org.*

requires that you have a custom error page (usually a 404 or "File Not Found" page) that can be coded.

Measuring client-side JavaScript errors. Page tags cannot detect many types of errors directly because the problem does not by default trigger an event. Placing a page tag on a custom error page and passing the error message in a custom variable [Hack #31] will record the incident for you and make the error information available to your reports.

One way to do this is to use page tags and error handlers in your scripts. For example, in JavaScript you can specify an onError handling function for your document. In onError, you can send additional information via the page tag to a custom variable [Hack #31]. The following code can be used to build list of client-side errors to pass to your web measurement page tag.

```
<SCRIPT>
' Tell JavaScript how to handle any client-side errors
window.onerror = myOnError
' Define arrays to capture the error messages
msgArray = new Array()
urlArray = new Array()
lnoArray = new Array()
' When an error is discovered, build an array of messages, urls and line
numbers
function myOnError(msg, url, lno) {
    msgArray[msgArray.length] = msg
    urlArray[urlArray.length] = url
    lnoArray[lnoArray.length] = lno
    return true
}
' Build a string that can be sent to the data collector
function sendErrors() {
    var errorList=""
    for (var i=0; i < msgArray.length; i++) {
       errorList = errorList + urlArray[i] + '|' + lnoArray[i] + '|' +
msgArray[i];
    }
    '
    ' CALL TO THE PAGE TAG/DATA COLLECTOR GOES HERE!
    '
}
</SCRIPT>
```

Depending then on how your particular web measurement application works, you'll replace the CALL TO THE PAGE TAG/DATA COLLECTOR GOES HERE line with an image request (or whichever strategy your vendor recommends) that will send the string generated in errorList to a custom variable that can be examined later.

Investigating Your Mistakes

Often, you'll see errors report and have no idea why they're being generated. Rather than sit and scratch your head, you should actually drill down into the problem and see what else you can learn about the source of the problem. By investigating your mistakes, you can both correct the short-term problem and prevent similar problems from arising in the future.

Investigate errors in relation to traffic loads. Segment the errors by time of day and day of week. If your web measurement tool can report on activity loads by time of day, see whether the error instances coincide with traffic rush hours. It may be that the system runs fine when idle but that errors arise with slower performance during times of heavy traffic.

Investigate errors in relation to web browsers. Segment the errors by the web browser and platform [Hack #71] that visitors used. You may find that the error is specific to certain web browsers. Browser version issues are the most common culprit when you're investigating script-related issues.

Investigate errors in relation to your servers. If you have a server farm and your web measurement tool can report on traffic segmented by each of your load balanced web servers, investigate whether one of your servers is responsible for errors while others may be running fine. A good indication of a problem would be significantly fewer pages being served from one machine relative to the volume of traffic distributed to the server (e.g., if a machine is served 50 percent of the traffic but only serves 30 percent of the page views, something is wrong).

Investigate errors in relation to dynamic URLs. If your web measurement tool can provide the necessary detail, investigate whether errors only occur with selected query strings among your dynamic URLs. If you're using a tag-based measurement solution, you may want to ask your vendor if it's possible to pass the full value of the requested URL along with the generated error message, perhaps in a custom variable, allowing you to complete this type of analysis.

Since you cannot watch people surf your site in appreciable numbers, it is essential to track your mistakes and act upon the data you generate. Nothing is more frustrating to a web visitor than error messages, especially when it is well within your power to prevent and correct problems.

—Akin Arikan and Eric T. Peterson

Build Your Own Web Measurement Application: The Core Code

One thing that every web measurement application needs to deal with, regardless of price or sophistication, is stitching together multiple page views into a visit and assigning that visit to a unique visitor.

In "Build Your Own Web Measurement Application: An Overview and Data Collection" [Hack #12], we saw how to write a small page tag script to record the visits to your web site. The program produced a logfile in this format:

```
1104772080 192.168.17.32  /index.html?from=google    http://www.google.com/
search?q=widgets    192.168.17.32.85261104772101338
1104772091 192.168.17.32  /products.html    http://www.example.com/index.
html?from=google    192.168.17.32.85261104772101338
```

In each line, the fields correspond to the time of the request, the client IP address, the page requested, the referring page, and the visitor's cookie.

Now that we have such a logfile, what should we do with it? One possibility is to analyze it by using one of the existing logfile analyzer programs, as long as the program can be configured to read data in our nonstandard format. For example, you can read the file by using the free web measurement application Analog (*www.analog.cx*) [Hack #10] and supplying the command:

```
LOGFORMAT %U\t%S\t%r\t%f\t%u
```

In this and subsequent "build your own" hacks we shall build a new program to read this logfile and produce a report. This will demonstrate the basics of what web analytics programs actually do under the hood. We will write our program in Perl. This may not be the best choice of language for high-traffic web sites, but it is adequate for smaller sites, and probably the clearest and most concise language.

Parsing the Data into Sessions

The first task you need to undertake in writing this application is to parse the data into visits and visitors [Hack #1], a task often referred to as *sessionization*. This is the bulk of the work: once the individual requests to the server are arranged into sessions, extracting data from the sessions is straightforward.

The traditional rule for carrying out this session parsing is to look for requests that appear to be from the same visitor. These requests are counted as one session, unless there is a half-hour gap between two requests, in which case, we start a new session.

We can see which requests are from the same visitor by looking at the cookies. A few visitors may block cookies, in which case, we use their IP addresses as an identifier. (This may cause us to combine two visitors from the same company who visit at about the same time, but that's likely to be a very small problem.)

There is one complication. The first time a visitor requests a file from a web server, a cookie is created and sent back to the visitor. It is only when requesting the second file that the visitor sends the cookie back to the web server and the cookie is recorded in the logfile. When our page tag script is on the same server as the pages, this is not a problem: the request for the page tag will be the second request to the server and will have a cookie. However, when the page tag is running on a separate server, the first page tag requested will not have a cookie (this is not the case if the tag is being served from the same server providing the web pages being tracked). In the example logfile at the start of this hack, the cookie will be missing on the request for /index.html?from=google, and appear only on the request for /products.html.

So our logfile reader must be able to connect sessions when the first line is missing a cookie. To achieve that, we apply the following rule. If the line has a cookie, look for a session from that cookie. If we can't find one, look for a session from that IP address. If that succeeds, re-label the session so that it becomes indexed by cookie instead of by IP address.

The Code

For this code to function properly, we recommend saving it in a file *readlog.pl* somewhere that has easy access to the files created by *readtag.pl* [Hack #12].

Here's the top level of the program:

```perl
# We start by declaring two classes, Request and Sessions.
#!perl -w
use strict;
use Request;
use Sessions;
# This variable determines how often we check for expired sessions.
my $purge_interval = 1000;
# Create an object to hold the sessions.
my $sessions = new Sessions;
# For each line in the logfile, check that the line can be parsed, and if not,
go on to the next line.
while (<>) {
    chomp;
    my $req = new Request($_) or next;
# Find or create the session into which this request falls, and add the
request to the session.
    my $sess = $sessions->FindSession($req);
    $sess->AddRequest($req);
# Every $purge_interval lines, clear up any expired sessions ($. is a Perl
variable holding the current input line number).
    if ($. % $purge_interval == 0) { $sessions->Purge($req->{time}); }
}
```

```
# After reading all the lines, clear up all remaining sessions, and write the
report.
$sessions->Purge();
WriteReport();
```

That's the end of the main program. Of course, it's the Request and Sessions classes that will do the real work. The Request class is very simple. It consists solely of a constructor, which constructs a Request object, given a line from the logfile. Save this file to a text file called *Request.pm*.

```
package Request;
use strict;
# Does the server on which the pages are stored use a case-insensitive
filesystem (e.g., Windows, not UNIX)?
my $case_insensitive = 0;
sub new {
# Take the string that was passed in. Attempt to parse it into its fields
using a regular expression, and return undef if failed.
my ($invocant, $str) = @_;
return undef
    unless (my ($time, $host, $file, $referrer, $cookie) =
        $str =~
        /^            # start of line
        (1\d{9})\t    # time: ten digits starting with 1
        ([^\t]+)\t    # host: non-empty string
        ([^\t]+)\t    # file: non-empty string
        ([^\t]*)\t    # referrer: possibly empty string
        ([^\t]*)      # cookie: possibly empty string
        $/x);         # end of line
# If the filesystem is case insensitive, convert the filename to lower case.
Then create and return the Request object.
$file = lc $file if $case_insensitive;
return bless {
    time => $time,
    host => $host,
    file => $file,
    referrer => $referrer,
    cookie => $cookie }
}
```

The Sessions class represents the collection of all the individual sessions. This class is in charge of defining the session. It also contains a class called Data, which stores all the statistics we shall report. Save this to a file called *Sessions.pm*.

```
package Sessions;
use strict;
use Session;
use Data;
```

A Sessions object will be a hash table of Session objects, indexed by cookie or client hostname. There will be one special hash key, DATA, to hold the statistics. This is a constructor to set up that hash table.

```
sub new {
  my $data = new Data;
  return bless {DATA => $data};
}
# Find or create a session containing a certain request.  As described above,
we first look for a session with this cookie. If that fails, look for a
session from this client address.
sub FindSession {
    my ($self, $req) = @_;
    my $key = $req->{cookie};
    my $sess = $self->{$key};
    if (!defined($sess)) {
        $key = $req->{host};
        $sess = $self->{$key};
}
# If we found a session, and it's not expired, return it.
# However, if we found the session by client address, and this request also
has a cookie, first move the session to be indexed by the cookie.
my $expired = 0;
if (defined($sess) && !($expired = $sess->IsExpired($req->{time}))) {
    if ($req->{cookie} && $key eq $req->{host}) {
        $self->{$req->{cookie}} = $sess;
        delete $self->{$req->{host}};
    }
return $sess;
}
# If we didn't find an unexpired session, create and return a new session.
$self->PurgeSession($key) if $expired;
$sess = new Session;
$key = $req->{cookie} || $req->{host};
$self->{$key} = $sess;
return $sess;
}
# The next function purges some expired sessions from memory.
# If a time is specified, purge all sessions up to that time.
# If not, purge all sessions.
sub Purge {
    my ($self, $time) = @_;
    while (my ($key, $sess) = each %$self) {
        next if ($key eq 'DATA');  # don't delete the special DATA key
        $self->PurgeSession($key) if (!defined($time) || $sess->
IsExpired($time));
    }
}
# Delete a single session, after saving its data in the Data object.
sub PurgeSession {
    my ($self, $key) = @_;
    $self->{DATA}->AddSession($self->{$key});
    delete $self->{$key};
}
```

Finally, for this hack, we shall describe the Session object. A Session will
just be an array of Request objects. First we need some variables to describe

when a session expires. It is considered stale if there is a gap of more than 1,800 seconds, or if it contains more than 250 requests. Save this to a file called *Sessions.pm.*

```perl
package Session;
use strict;
my $max_gap_in_session = 1800;
my $max_requests_in_session = 250;
# This is a minimal constructor setting up an empty Request array.
sub new { return bless []; }
# Add a request to the session.
sub AddRequest {
    my ($self, $req) = @_;
    push @$self, $req;
}
# The session has expired if the requests array is too large, or if it has
# been too long since the last request.
sub IsExpired {
    my ($self, $time) = @_;
    return (@$self > $max_requests_in_session ||
        $time > $$self[-1]->{time} + $max_gap_in_session);
}
```

Next Steps

In this hack, we've seen how to read a logfile, parse it to extract requests, and accumulate those requests into sessions. In "Build Your Own Web Measurement Application: Marketing Data" [Hack #53], we shall describe how to extract data from the session objects and create a report.

—Dr. Stephen Turner and Eric T. Peterson

HACK #36 Build Your Own RSS Tracking Application: The Core Code and Reporting

Syndicating content via RSS is similar to, but not the same as, building normal web pages. Because of this, the parsing of information collected is very similar to our "build your own" web measurement application, using a similar architecture. However, because RSS is designed to be presented in any number of applications and environments, the reporting is slightly different (but no less interesting).

Assuming you've already read how to collect data from within RSS feeds [Hack #12], you should have an RSS logfile. To learn anything meaningful from *RSS. log*, you need to parse the file and generate human-readable reports.

The reporting code is broken into five packages and driven by a single script called from the command line (*rss_report.pl*). The packages are:

RSS_Article.pm

> Holds the RSS_Event objects and provides methods for accessing events by type from the RSS_Request object

RSS_Articles.pm

> Holds articles by name from the RSS_Request and RSS_Data objects and provides methods for accessing information about the article

RSS_Data.pm

> Creates the summary data object and provides methods for processing and reporting

RSS_Event.pm

> Provides methods for accessing the RSS_Request objects for the event

RSS_Request.pm

> Parses the incoming log line to create an object containing data broken down by field name

Be sure to save each *.pm* file in your Perl */lib* directory.

RSS_Article.pm. The RSS_Article object is a container for the article that holds all of its RSS_Event objects by the type filed from the RSS_Request object. It provides methods for sending the request to the proper event, creating it if it doesn't exist, and access to the individual event objects. Type the following code into a file named *RSS_Article.pm*.

```
package RSS_Article;
use strict;
use RSS_Event;

# An Articles object will be a hash table of Events objects,
# indexed by type.
# This is a simple constructor for setting up an empty hash.
sub new {
  return bless {};
}

# Add the request to the article for the event
sub AddRequest {
  my ($self, $req) = @_;

  # Look for an event with this type.
  my $key = $req->{type};
  my $event = $self->{$key};

  # If we didn't find and event, create it.
  unless (defined($event)) {
    $event = new RSS_Event;
    $self->{$key} = $event;
  }
```

```
    # Add the Request to the Event
    $event->AddRequest($req);

}

# Find the event for the given type
sub FindEvent {
  my ($self, $type) = @_;

  # Look for the event by type
  my $event = $self->{$type};

  # Return the event if it exists and return undef if it doesn't
  if (defined($event)) {
    return $event;
  }
}
return 1;
```

RSS_Articles.pm. The RSS_Articles object is the container that holds all the
RSS_Article objects and a single instance of the RSS_Data object used to store
the statistical data. It provides methods for finding and creating the article
objects by the name field from the RSS_Request object, initiating the processing
of each article's data and initiating the writing of reports from *rss_report.pl*.
Type the following code into a file named *RSS_Articles.pm*.

```
package RSS_Articles;
use strict;
use RSS_Article;

# An Articles object will be a hash table of Article objects,
# indexed by article name.
# There will be one special hash key, DATA, to hold the statistics.
# This is a constructor to set up that hash table.

use RSS_Data;
sub new {
  my $data = new RSS_Data;
  return bless {DATA => $data};
}

# Find or create an article
sub FindArticle {
  my ($self, $req) = @_;

  # Look for an article with this name.
  my $key = $req->{name};
  my $arti = $self->{$key};

  # If we found an article, return it.
  if (defined($arti)) {
    return $arti;
  }
```

```perl
      # If we didn't find an article, create and return a new article.
      $arti = new RSS_Article;
      $key = $req->{name};
      $self->{$key} = $arti;
      return $arti;
}

# Process Articles Data into reporting data
sub Process {
   my ($self) = @_;

   while (my ($key, $arti) = each %$self) {
      next if ($key eq 'DATA');  # don't process the special DATA key
      $self->{DATA}->AddArticle($self->{$key},$key);
   }
}

# Write the report
sub WriteReport {
   my $self = shift;
   $self->{DATA}->WriteReport();
}
return 1;
```

RSS_Data.pm. The RSS_Data object creates the summary data object and provides the methods for processing the data from an RSS_Article object into summary data and writing the reports. One of the most important things to note about the RSS_Data package is the @events_to_sum and @events_to_list array declarations (in bold), which allow you to configure the reports that are generated. Type the following code in a file named *RSS_Data.pm*.

```perl
package RSS_Data;
use strict;

# The configuration of summary information to report
# The fields are event type and item name
my @events_to_sum = (
      [ 'v', 'Views' ],
      [ 'c', 'Clicks' ]
   );

# The configuration of article itemized information to report
# The fields are event type, report title, request field and # list items to
# display
my @events_to_list = (
         [ 'v', 'Top 10 Pages in which the Article was Viewed', 'url', 10 ],
         [ 'v', 'Top 10 referrers to the Page with the Article', 'ref', 10 ],
         [ 'c', 'Top 10 Links clicked within the Article', 'url', 10 ]
      );
```

```perl
# The constructor, with all the variables we will store
sub new {
  return bless {
    totals_events => {},
    totals_articles => {},
    article_reports => {}
  };
}

# Add Articles data to the totals
sub AddArticle {
  my ($self, $arti, $articlename) = @_;

  # Loop through each event type defined in %events_to_report
  # If the event type exits for the article collect and add
  # its summary data
  foreach my $event_sum (@events_to_sum) {
    my $type = @$event_sum[0];

    # Get the event
    my $event = $arti->FindEvent($type) or next;

    # Get a count of the Request for
    my $count = $event->NumRequests;
    if ($count) {
      $self->{totals_events}->{$type} += $count;
      $self->{totals_articles}->{$articlename}->{$type} += $count;
    }
  }

  # Loop through each defined report, process field values
  # and add report data
  foreach my $event_list (@events_to_list) {
    my $type = @$event_list[0];

    # Get the event
    my $event = $arti->FindEvent($type) or next;


    # Get the request field to count for this report
    my $field = @$event_list[2];
    my $title = @$event_list[1];


      # Get the values of that field from the event
      my $values = $event->GetFieldValues($field);

      # Process values if retuned
      if (@$values) {
```

```
      # Loop through each value and increment a count of that value
      foreach my $value (@$values) {
        #print $value . "\n";
        ++$self->{article_reports}->{$articlename}->{$title}->{$value} if
(defined($value));
      }
    }
  }
}


# Write all the reports we have collected
sub WriteReport {
  my $self = shift;

  # Write the Summary Report and then the Article Reports
  $self->WriteSummaryReport();
  $self->WriteArticleReports();
}

# Write Article Reports
sub WriteArticleReports {
  my ($self) = @_;

  my $hashref = $self->{totals_articles};
  foreach my $articlename (sort {$a cmp $b} keys %$hashref) {

  # Write the report title
  $self->WriteArticleReportTitle($articlename);

  # Write the summary statistics
  $self->WriteArticleSummaryStats($self->{totals_articles}->{$articlename});

  # Write the event reports
  $self->WriteEventReports($self->{article_reports}->{$articlename});
  }
}

# Write a report title, = underlined
sub WriteReportTitle {
  my ($self, $title) = @_;
  print "\n$title\n";
  print "=" for 1..(length $title);
  print "\n";
}

# Write an article report title, - underlined
sub WriteArticleReportTitle {
  my ($self, $title) = @_;
  print "\n$title\n";
  print "-" for 1..(length $title);
  print "\n";
}
```

```perl
# Write an event report title, - undelined and indented
sub WriteEventReportTitle {
  my ($self, $title) = @_;
  print "\n    $title\n    ";
  print "-" for 1..(length $title);
  print "\n";
}

# Write the summary report

sub WriteSummaryReport {
  my $self = shift;

  # Write the report title
  $self->WriteReportTitle('Summary Statistics');

  # Write the summary statistics
  $self->WriteSummaryStats($self->{totals_events});
}

# Write the summary statistics
sub WriteSummaryStats {
  my ($self, $hashref) = @_;

  # loop through each event type defined in %events_to_report
  # and write the summary statistics
  foreach my $event_sum (@events_to_sum) {
    my $type = @$event_sum[0];
    my $name = @$event_sum[1];
    printf "Total %s: %d\n",$name,$hashref->{$type} || 0;
  }
}

# Write the article summary statistics, indented
sub WriteArticleSummaryStats {
  my ($self, $hashref) = @_;

  # loop through each event type defined in %events_to_report
  # and write the summary statistics
  foreach my $event_sum (@events_to_sum) {
    my $type = @$event_sum[0];
    my $name = @$event_sum[1];
    printf "    Total %s: %d\n",$name,$hashref->{$type} || 0;
  }
}

# Write event reports by event type

sub WriteEventReports {
  my ($self, $hashref) = @_;

  #loop through each report defined for the event
  foreach my $event_list (@events_to_list) {
```

```
# Get the title of the report
  my $title = @$event_list[1];

  # Write event report title
  $self->WriteEventReportTitle($title);

  # Get the top items to print limit
  my $toplimit = @$event_list[3];

  # Test if event report data exists and write statistics if it does
  $self->WriteReportStats($hashref->{$title},$toplimit) if ($hashref->
    {$title});
  }
}

# Write the report stats list from most occurances to least limiting the
length to
# the incoming $toplimit
sub WriteReportStats {
  my ($self, $hashref, $toplimit) = @_;

  # Loop through sorted hash data and print until line numer matches
  # the top_items set for the report
  my $n = scalar keys %$hashref;
  if ($toplimit < $n) { $n = $toplimit; }
  for ((sort {$hashref->{$b} <=> $hashref->{$a}} keys %$hashref)[0..$n-1]) {
    printf "%9s: %s\n", $hashref->{$_}, $_;
  }
  print "\n";
}
return 1;
```

RSS_Event.pm. The RSS_Event object holds all RSS_Request objects for the event. It provides methods for getting a count of the requests it holds and getting the values from a specified field of the request, if they exist. Type the following code into a file named *RSS_Event.pm*.

```
package RSS_Event;
use strict;

# An Event will be an array of Requests.
# This is a minimal constructor setting up an empty array.
sub new { return bless []; }

# Add a request to the event
sub AddRequest {
  my ($self, $req) = @_;
  push @$self, $req;
}

# The number of requests the event contains is the length of the array
# of requests
```

```perl
sub NumRequests {
  my $self = shift;
  return scalar @$self;
}

# Return an array of values for a request field when it has a value
# If no requests for that field have a value return empty array
sub GetFieldValues {
  my ($self, $field) = @_;
  my @values = undef;
  foreach my $req (@$self) {
    my $value = $req->{$field};
    push @values, $value if ($value);
  }
  return \@values;
}
return 1;
```

RSS_Request.pm. The RSS_Request object parses the incoming *rss.log* line by line and creates an object that holds the data in individual fields. These fields are time, host, name, URL, ref (as in "referrer"), and cookie. There is an additional field (type) that captures whether the line was logging a page view (v) or a link click (c). Type the following code into a file named *RSS_Request.pm*.

```perl
package RSS_Request;
use strict;

# Construct a request hash from a string
sub new {

  # Take the string that was passed in. Attempt to parse it into its fields
  # using a regular expression, and return undef if failed.
  my ($invocant, $str) = @_;
  return undef
    unless (my ($type, $time, $host, $name, $url, $ref, $cookie, $revenue) =
      $str =~
        /^                # start of line
        ([cv])\t          # type: v for view or c for click
        (1\d{9})\t        # time: ten digits starting with 1
        ([^\t]+)\t        # host: non-empty string
        ([^\t]+)\t        # storyname: non-empty string
        ([^\t]+)\t        # url: non-empty string
        ([^\t]*)\t        # ref: possibly empty string
        ([^\t]*)          # cookie: possibly empty string
        $/x);             # end of line

  # If the parsing succeeded, create and return an object.
  return bless {
    type => $type,
    time => $time,
    host => $host,
    name => $name,
```

```
        url => $url,
        ref => $ref,
        cookie => $cookie }
  }
  return 1;
```

Bringing the packages together with rss_report.pl. The *rss_report.pl* script should be saved to the same directory as the *rss.log* file generated by *write_rss_tag.cgi*. Remember, the #!perl line may need to be adjusted to point to the location of Perl on your machine; for example, #!/usr/bin/perl. Type the following code into a file named *rss_report.pl*.

```
#!perl -w
use strict;

# The classes we're going to use
use RSS_Request;
use RSS_Articles;

# Create an object to hold the articles
my $articles = new RSS_Articles;

# For each line in the logfile
while (<>) {
  chomp;

  # Check that the line is parseable, and if not, go on to the next line
  my $req = new RSS_Request($_) or next;

  # Find or create the article into which this request falls
  my $arti = $articles->FindArticle($req);

  # Add the request to the article
  $arti->AddRequest($req);

}
# After reading all the lines, process them into the final data
$articles->Process();

# And write the report
$articles->WriteReport();
```

Now you're ready to generate your first RSS traffic report!

Running the Code

To run the program, you will need Perl installed on your computer. If you are using Unix or Linux, you almost certainly have Perl already, but if you are using Windows, you may not. You can download ActiveState's Perl for Windows from *http://www.activestate.com/Products/ActivePerl*.

All that remains now is to tell *rss_report.pl* where the *rss.log* file—generated by the *write_rss_tag.cgi* script—is located, and the rest is automatic!

From the command line (assuming that *rss.log* is in the same directory as *rss_report.pl*), all you need to do is type:

```
perl rss_report.pl rss.log
```

Figure 2-24 has sample output from the script showing summary statistics (total views and total clicks) for all tracked articles and a per-article break-down showing the total views, clicks, pages where the article was viewed, referrers to the article, and links clicked in the article, each of which are described below.

Figure 2-24. Sample output from the rss_report.pl script

The Results

Because RSS is a slightly different beastie than other types of web traffic, it is worthwhile to define each of the reports generated by *rss_report.pl*.

Total article views

Total article views are the count of all page views for all articles listed in your report.

Total article clicks

Total article clicks are the count of all clicks on links contained in the articles listed in your report. The clicks are limited to tracked RSS articles by the use of the <DIV> tag in the JavaScript [Hack #12].

Pages in which the article was viewed

The pages in which the article was viewed report reflects the key complexity of RSS—the fact that your content does not necessarily appear in your web pages. Other people are easily able to grab your XML feed and present your content in their web pages. This report will tell you who is doing that and which URLs you should be looking at to see how your content is reused.

Referrers to the page with the article

Referrers to the page with the article will tell you who is linking to your articles on the Internet. This is perhaps the single most powerful aspect of this application, allowing you to determine how readers respond to your content.

Links clicked in the article

Provided you have normal HREF based links in your articles, this list will tell you what people are clicking on. Remember, this report is limited to only the links in your post by the <DIV> wrapper around the post.

Hacking the Hack

Obviously, this hack provides only the bare essentials for measuring content syndicated via RSS, and there are a handful of things you could do to improve the quality of tracking, including:

- Adding the idea of "session" to the RSS_Event object, allowing you to generate both "visit" and "page view" counts for each article.

- Adding a NOSCRIPT tag, extending a lighter version of this tracking for applications that do not allow the use of JavaScript.

- Giving *rss_report.pl* the ability to accept a date range from the command line to limit the dates for which the report is generated.

- Giving *rss_report.pl* the ability to accept a text string from the command line to limit the names of the articles reported on.

While there is a small handful of other methods you can use to track the readership of you weblog (FeedBurner is one, at *http://www.feedburner.com*, Syndicate IQ is another, at *http://www.syndicateiq.com*), there are no major providers of this functionality who take such elegant advantage of then existing web measurement model. Until the rest of the measurement world comes around and provides this valuable functionality, enjoy, and remember you read it here first.

—Ian Houston and Eric T. Peterson

## CHAPTER THREE

Online Marketing Measurement
Hacks 37–53

One of the most immediate and practical things you can do with web measurement is understand and optimize your online marketing efforts. Assuming you're doing something to attract visitors to your web site—buying keywords at Google, running banner ads on MSN, sending email, or including your URL in your yellow pages ad—even the most basic web measurement applications provide the necessary tools to quantify the effect of this advertising. More importantly, the best web measurement tools provide you the ability to tie acquired visitors to critical events like a purchase, a lead, or a download, so that you can analyze both the quantity *and* the quality of visitors you're attracting.

It's Only Data

If you're not an experienced online marketer, this chapter has the potential to be somewhat overwhelming. You're going to be hit with a number of new and fairly specific terms and ideas and, depending on which application you're using, be required to jump through some hoops to implement and use these ideas.

Don't panic.

If you take the time to read each of these hacks, you'll begin to see the common, underlying framework used to measure marketing on the Internet. You'll see terms like "click-through rate" and "cost-per-acquisition" come up again and again, each in the context of the particular medium being measured. Try and see this pattern, and you'll be "hacking the hacks."

ROI

ROI is a complicated and often abused concept. If you follow the Internet software market at all, you've likely seen the abbreviation "ROI" dozens, if not hundreds, of times. Companies always talk about "achieving maximum ROI" and "rapid ROI," and "exponentially increasing the ROI for your ERP, SFA, and CRM systems." What they're talking about is *return on investment*: the money they're going to make because they've made the right decision in purchasing a product, solution, or service. While ROI is an overused term, calculating return on investment is central to online marketing and worth understanding.

While we'll cover the necessary calculations in [Hack #37], you should know that return on investment has two different meanings in web measurement and marketing. The return on investment you get for an individual campaign should be thought of as micro-ROI, whereas the return you get for your investment in a web measurement application and the team to support it should be thought of as macro-ROI.

Micro-ROI is fairly easy to calculate. The same cannot be said for macro-ROI. To calculate your macro-ROI, you have to add up all the costs associated with selecting, implementing, and maintaining a measurement solution, including opportunity costs associated with time spent looking for a solution, phone calls, implementation costs (both internal and external), hiring or training people to manage the application, and any associated hardware costs—the list of related costs is very long.

On the flip side, you need to keep very careful track of incremental gains made based on the data you're able to generate and use. If you're lucky and you find some nugget of gold that, when acted upon, generates a strong and noticeable increase in revenue, this calculation becomes slightly easier to make. Most companies use web measurement to achieve small, incremental gains that are hard to differentiate from the rest of their business.

Perhaps the best advice is to focus on micro-ROI and ignore the larger calculation. Vendors will try to sell you on "the strongest and fastest ROI in the market," but it's the way you use the data—not only the way you acquire it—that affects the bottom line. When you're successful in measuring your campaigns, identifying the top performers, and rolling gained insights into the continuous improvement process, you'll be achieving return on investment without effort.

HACK #37 Understand Marketing Terminology

Online marketers have their own language and lingo, always asking about your "CPA" and the "CPC" for a campaign.

Online marketing is a pretty well-established activity, but one full of sometimes vague and often confusing terminology. While you're already able to talk the talk [Hack #1] using web measurement lingo, here are a handful of marketing specific terms that you need to know.

Reach and Acquisition

The first terms we'll examine are the "big picture" measures and metrics for visitor reach and acquisition—the measurements that help you understand how well or poorly a campaign is doing in helping you find and attract prospects to your web site.

Click-though rate (CTR). Your campaign click-through rate is the ratio of impressions you serve to the number of clicks those impressions generate (clicks divided by impressions measured in page views). Click-through rate tells you whether the particular message you're using is well written, well presented, and well targeted to the particular audience you're trying to reach (Figure 3-1).

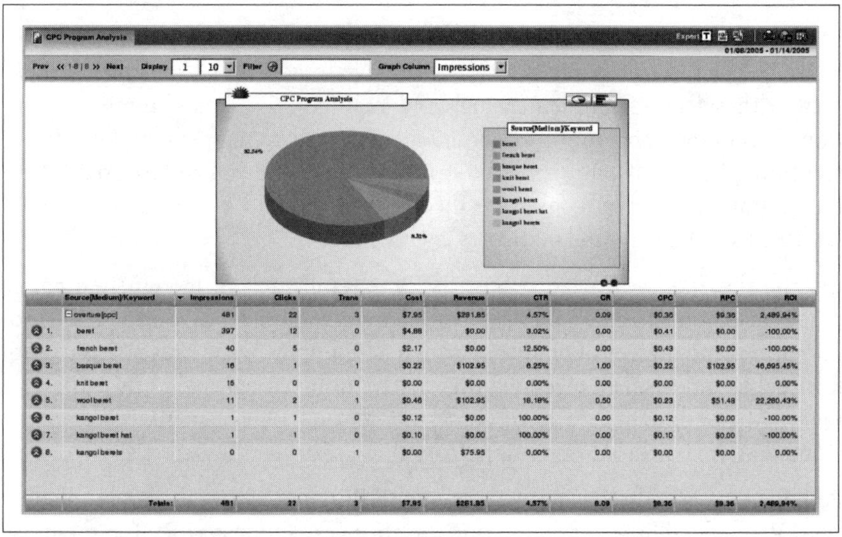

Figure 3-1. Paid keyword marketing dashboard

Your campaign click-through rates can be difficult to calculate because impressions are often served by external servers and usually require that data is imported into your measurement solution. Also, some advertising servers don't actually measure or report on clicks, forcing you to use responses as a proxy for clicks.

Cost-per-click (CPC). Campaign cost-per-click is a direct measure of how well your marketing dollars are spent. Literally, the total cost of the specific campaign divided by the number of clicks it generates, cost-per-click is the standard model for search engine marketing (often called the pay-per-click model).

Response rate. Your campaign response rate is the number of respondents (unique visitors) divided by the total number of impressions you serve or unique emails you send. This is similar to your click-through rate but based on real people, not actions. Don't be surprised if you have a much higher click-through rate than response rate [Hack #51].

Cost-per-acquisition (CPA). Campaign cost-per-acquisition is the total cost of the campaign divided by the number of respondents (unique visitors). Similar to cost-per-click, cost-per-acquisitions are a direct measure of how well your money is being spent.

As you can hopefully see, you're working for higher response rates and lower costs-per-click and acquisition. Maximizing inbound traffic while minimizing costs becomes important when you start to examine how well you're doing in actually converting the people you manage to acquire.

Conversion

All of your efforts in reaching and acquiring visitors are for naught unless you're able to somehow entice your respondents to complete some valuable action. Regardless of the type of site you have, there is always an act of conversion [Hack #39] you should be measuring.

Conversion rate. One of the most fundamental and valuable web site measurements, conversion rate is loosely defined as the number of completions divided by the number of potential completers. A number of hacks in this book discuss specific conversion rates, but in the context of online marketing, your campaign conversion rate is usually the number of conversions measured in visits divided by the number of visits the campaign drives to the web site.

Cost-per-conversion (CPC). Your campaign cost-per-conversion is simply defined as the total cost of the campaign divided by the number of conversions it drives. Another important measurement is the value-per-conversion or, if you're really good with numbers, margin-per-conversion. The value measurement is total sales divided by number of conversions; the margin measurement is total sales minus costs divided by conversions.

Revenue per visit or visitor. Very simply, revenue per visit or visitor is the amount of revenue a campaign drives divided by the number of visits or visitors from the campaign. Calculating revenue per visit or visitors allows you to look at the overall effect of your marketing efforts and provide a good comparator for specific marketing strategies like banner advertising [Hack #40] and search keyword marketing [Hack #42].

Order and buyer conversion rates. While a number of different conversion rates are described throughout this book, two are important and poorly understood enough to be defined explicitly here. If you sell anything online, your order conversion rate is the number of orders taken divided by the number of visits; your buyer conversion rate is the number of customers divided by the number of unique visitors. For example, say your site generates the following data in a week:

- 1,000 orders taken
- 100,000 visits
- 1.0% order conversion rate
- 800 customers
- 50,000 unique visitors
- 1.6% buyer conversion rate

By comparing our order and buyer conversion rates, we immediately realize that we're getting additional purchases from visitors who are coming back to the site (twice a month as a global average). To compare, say you generated the following data over a week:

- 100 orders taken
- 10,000 visits
- 1.0% order conversion rate
- 100 customers
- 10,000 unique visitors
- 1.0% buyer conversion rate

In this case, you can easily determine that visitors are visiting and purchasing only once during the week, which is fine except return customers are often much more valuable than one-time customers. As you can hopefully see, very reasonable numbers can generate fairly different conversion rates. The difference is subtle, but important and worth understanding. If someone tells you his conversion rate is 3% you should ask him if he means "order" or "buyer" conversion rate.

Return on investment (ROI). To make the micro-ROI calculation, you need only three numbers: the amount you spend on a marketing campaign, the amount of revenue (or value) the campaign drives, and the timeframe you're interested in. According to Jim Novo, web marketing guru, simple return on investment is calculated in the following way:

(Profit – Expenditures) / Expenditures = Return on Investment

For example, let's say that you spend $1,000 on a banner advertising campaign and that the visitors these banners attract end up generating $600 in value in the first week. Your ROI for the first week would be:

($600 − $1,000) / $1,000 = −0.40 (a 40% loss)

This demonstrates the importance of the third variable in the equation: time. You want to be cautious when making these calculations to consider the ebb and flow of different types of campaigns. Assuming, in the example above, the banner ads were scheduled to be delivered over the course of a month, and at the end of the month, you had generated $2,200 in revenue. Now your calculation would be:

($2,200 − $1,000) / $1,000 = 1.20 (a 120% gain)

Some people choose to calculate a rolling return on investment, breaking the costs up over time. Continuing our example, and again examining the first week of the four-week campaign (e.g., $250 per week), the rolling ROI calculation becomes:

($600 − $250) / $250 = 1.40 (a 140% gain in the first week)

The rolling ROI calculation is often helpful when you're examining your success for ongoing campaigns like pay-per-click search marketing where you'll have variable daily expenses based on the cost-per-click and number of clicks.

We recommend that you calculate both a rolling and simple return on investment for the campaigns you run. The rolling calculation will help you understand whether you're likely to be successful; the simple calculation will show you whether you were successful after the fact.

Retention

Retention metrics are among the most complicated concepts, since they depend on a variety of factors—any one of which can prevent making an accurate measurement if something goes wrong. Retention is most often measured by using a cookie [Hack #15], a small file stored on a visitor's computer that is easily deleted, preventing your measurement application from recognizing that a visitor has been "retained." Still, measuring retention and lifetime value driven by your campaigns is important to your online marketing efforts.

Visitor retention rate. Your visitor retention rate is the number of return or repeat visitors divided by the total number of visitors the campaign helped you acquire. Depending on your particular site, service, or offer, you may want to examine this rate over long periods of time (e.g., depending on what you sell, your visitors may not return for months after the initial campaign response).

Lifetime value of a campaign. The lifetime value of a campaign is a very complicated metric that describes the long-term value of a visitor, usually by original acquisition source (Figure 3-2). Covered in detail in the hack on lifetime value of a customer [Hack #84], lifetime value is usually defined as the total value of visitor actions (purchases, downloads, etc.) by original acquisition device (campaign, referring site, and search keyword or phrase).

To-date Lifetime Value - Source Conversion			
google[ppc]	**First Time**	**Prior**	**Total**
Absolute Unique Visitors	3,990	221	4,211
Goal 1 (Purchase)	0.23%	0.45%	0.24%
Goal 2 (Daily Special Purchase)	0.23%	0.45%	0.24%
Goal 3 (Sell Form Completed)	0.20%	0.90%	0.24%
Average Visitor Value	$16.96	$391.40	$36.62
Total Ecommerce Revenue	$67,690.00	$86,500.00	$154,190.00
Total # Transactions	10	3	13
Average Order Value	$6,769.00	$28,833.33	$11,860.77

Figure 3-2. Lifetime value report

While there are many other important metrics you'll read about in this book, the metrics in this hack form the framework for measuring the effect of your online campaigns.

—*Bryan Eisenberg and Eric T. Peterson*

Identify Your Business Objectives
HACK #38
To provide real business value, you must first know what to measure and why.

Fundamental to web site measurement is the question "Why do you even have a web site?" Defining your business objectives, literally, your site's *raison d'etre*, is tremendously important to identifying changes you should make now and which changes you should leave for later. There's nothing complicated about defining your business objectives. Usually, when you start to ask about your company's business objectives, everybody seems to understand exactly what they are. Still, if you're not sure, read the rest of this hack.

Every Site Has Business Objectives

No matter how few pages or meager your goals. If you've taken the time to write some HTML and FTP it up to a server, you've certainly done so with a goal in mind. Even the countless millions who built unattractive and poorly linked GeoCities pages had a goal in mind: for others to see their site. If you have an eBay store, a weblog, any site at all, you will undoubtedly be able to identify some type of objective.

Your business objectives are always the most basic things. If you're an online retailer your business objectives are to sell more products and support current customers. If you are growing a business selling software or services, your business objectives are to create interest and generate qualified leads. As you can see, brevity rules the day when you're defining your business objectives, helping you craft an elevator speech (a pitch concise enough to fit in the 30 seconds or so of an elevator ride). A handful of business models and their most common objectives are listed in Table 3-1.

Table 3-1. Example business objectives for common business models online

Business model	Business objectives	Sample companies
Retail	Sell products	Amazon
	Sell high-margin products	WalMart
	Support existing customers	Sears
	Increase revenues	O'Reilly
Non-packaged goods sales (e.g., services, software, durable goods)	Create product awareness	Toyota
	Generate leads	Bank of America
	Generate qualified leads	Mercedes Benz
	Sell products and services	Comcast
Customer support	Decrease phone support costs	Novel
	Increase self-service	Microsoft
	Deliver support content	PalmOne
Advertising/content	Increase advertising revenue	CBSNews
	Increase visitor loyalty	CNN.com
	Increase brand awareness	Google

Translate Business Objectives into Measurable Activities

As you can see, business objectives are very high-level, 100,000 feet and above. So how can something so theoretical have any real value to web measurement? Simple. Each business objective is tied to reality by a handful of activities that can be measured via clickstream analysis.

Let's take a closer look at perhaps the Internet's most popular business objective: sell products. How do you sell products online? Visitors click to your web site and find a product they want, they add the product to a shopping cart, and complete their transaction by checking out. Each of these individual activities (arrive, find, add, and complete) is relatively distinct and can be measured by even the most common measurement tools. Breaking the rather abstract "sell products" business objective into its constituent parts reveals what should be measured, as illustrated in Table 3-2.

Table 3-2. A handful of activities that define the "sell products" business model and associated metrics

Activity	Metrics used to measure activity
Visitors arrive at your site	Campaign responses
	Referring URLs
	Search terms
	Entry pages
Find products	Path analysis and fallout reporting
	Product and category page views
	Internal search terms
Add products to cart	Cart start rate
	Product add and removal rate
Complete checkout	Checkout start rate
	Checkout completion rate
	Order conversion rate
	Buyer conversion rate

Don't worry if the measurements in Table 3-2 are foreign to you, they'll be discussed the hacks throughout the rest of this book.

Once you've defined your business objectives and activities, you will know which reports to generate, which metrics to drill down into, which key performance indicators [Hack #94] to define and share, and even which hacks to read. It all starts with doing a good job of defining your business objectives.

HACK #39 Define Conversion Events

Measuring conversion events and conversion rates is one of the most popular uses of web measurement tools.

Loosely defined, a conversion rate measures the number of visitors who took the action you wanted on your site divided by the total number of visitors. Every end-goal conversion, like a purchase, is composed of many other conversion points, like the click-through path in a shopping cart. Before you can measure conversion rates and determine how to improve conversion on your site, the ultimate goal, you first need to establish a strategy for defining conversion events.

Identify Your Conversion Events

Most people don't really give the identification of conversion events enough thought. They simply think "Well, if a visitor makes a purchase or generates a lead, that is good enough for us," but while purchase is a very important conversion event, it is by no means the only one worth measuring. You should define *conversion events* as any activity visitors can engage in that is valuable to your organization. Here are some example conversion events you may want to measure once you recognize that the definition of conversion is broad.

- Makes a purchase
- Opts into a newsletter
- Submits some type of personal information
- Subscribes to an RSS feed
- Prints a page
- Uses "email this page to a friend" functionality
- Spends more than 10 minutes browsing the site
- Downloads a document or application
- Looks at a set of important pages
- Views a set number of pages during a visit
- Clicks a particular link to leave your site
- Searches for a specific product or piece of information

This list is far from exhaustive, but hopefully you get the idea. As visitors complete each of these types of events, they become more valuable to you and your company. Consider two visitors: the first makes a $100 purchase, and the second makes a $50 purchase but opts into your newsletter and sends product information to two friends. Which is more valuable? In the short-term, it is the former, but over the long run, it is very likely the latter, as she has expressed greater interest in your organization as a whole and was willing to tell her friends about you.

Here are some general guidelines for defining conversion events.

Be open-minded. Don't be so tied to getting revenue or leads that you forget about the bigger picture—in the long run, your business will be stronger if you're able to identify visitors and customers who are *truly interested* in what you have to offer. Consider the question "What does someone who is really interested look at on our web site?" and let the answers to this question define your conversion events.

Don't limit your definition to a single session. Provided you have the tools, consider conversion events like "visits three times in one week" and "spends more than 30 minutes per visit" or "visits more than one of our sites," if you have multiple web properties. Again, because conversion is more complicated than just "getting the sale," you need to think big picture. Fortunately, many web measurement tools are becoming sophisticated enough to allow you to define conversion as such.

If you're not sure how to set conversion events, consult your vendor. Since some of the conversion events are fairly complicated, you might need to call your vendor and explain to them what you're trying to do. You may need to write some additional JavaScript, track visitors using session cookies [Hack #15], or use visitor segmentation [Hack #48] to keep track of whether visitors are converting or not.

Make an attempt to assign a dollar value to non-revenue conversion events. Once you start thinking about conversion broadly, you'll see that many conversion events are not directly producing revenue. Still, you should make an attempt to assign a dollar value to every conversion event, at least in your key performance indicator reports [Hack #94] so you don't lose track of the fact that you're measuring conversion as a gauge of business success. Even if you have to approximate or assign a relatively low dollar value (for example, each search is worth five cents), what you'll see is that the combination of conversion events will help you understand where your *most "profitable"* visitors come from.

Measure Conversion

Once you've done a good job defining conversion events on your site, the next step is to figure out how you're going to measure successful completion of each event. In general, conversion events are measured using overall conversion and scenario analysis, the former being very high-level and the latter very granular.

Overall conversion. Overall conversion is basically a measurement of all the conversion events your visitors engage in during a period of time—basically the sum of conversion events divided by either the total number of visits or unique visitors to the site. The denominator you use will depend on whether you're trying to understand how people behave during visits or the people themselves. If you're interested in people, use unique visitors; if you're interested in behavior, use visits.

Say, for example, you define four conversion events, and 100,000 unique visitors complete those events 900 times during 125,000 different visits to the site. Your "visitor" overall conversion rate would be:

900 conversion events / 100,000 unique visitors = 0.9%

Your "visit" conversion rate for the same period of time would be:

900 conversion events / 125,000 visits = 0.72%

Neither number is particularly telling about the overall success of your site, but you want to trend that number over time and be ready to react to any significant changes in the number. Overall conversion rates are also good when trying to evaluate broad, sweeping changes. Use them to evaluate the results of a site redesign, a specific marketing campaign, or new site-search technology.

Two variations on overall conversion rates are order and buyer conversion rates for online retailers [Hack #37], which differ slightly from the previous definition because you would want to examine only actual purchase events, not all conversion events. The order conversion rate is the number of purchases divided by the number of visits; the buyer conversion rate is the number of customers divided by the number of unique visitors; and both measured for the same period of time. Each is valuable at a high level, and neither provides essential information necessary to make specific decisions, making them classic overall conversion rates.

Scenario conversion. Scenario conversion rates are more granular, designed to help you understand how successful visitors are in completing specific conversion events, and they are often measured using multi-step process measurement tools [Hack #59]. This type of measurement allows you to determine which marketing campaigns, affiliate relationships, or pay-per-click search engine keywords positively affect your business success. Everything on your site—new content, navigation, new link anchor text, promotions, calls to action, or merchandising—can be measured to determine if it contributes to or detracts from the scenario conversion rate.

One key thing to remember about scenario conversions is that there are two types: linear and nonlinear.

Linear

> Linear scenarios occur when visitors need to complete a registration process or checkout process. Your checkout conversion rate is the number of visits that complete the checkout process divided by the number of visits that start the process (e.g., click the "Checkout Now!" button). This one is easy to set up in most of the better web measurement tools.

Nonlinear

Nonlinear scenarios are created by visitor segments as they navigate your web site. These scenarios can be explicitly planned or implicit; occurring randomly since they were not planned. The key to measuring nonlinear scenarios is having the ability to keep track of which conversion events have been achieved.

The relationship between overall and scenario conversion is basically parent-child. You will have one or two overall conversion rates for your site that are ultimately defined by how successful visitors are in completing individual scenarios. The greater the completion rates in each scenario, the higher your overall conversion rate.

Bringing It All Together

Now that you're well-versed in conversion rates and how they're defined, the next step is to actually set up your web measurement application to report on conversion. Depending on the application you use, you may be able to define multi-step conversion funnels [Hack #59], define and track multiple conversion events, and track success through the variety of campaigns you're likely running—all good examples of scenario conversion. You'll also use conversion rates to understand whether internal campaigns [Hack #61] are successful and whether any split-path tests [Hack #63] you're running are generating positive results. If you're an online retailer, you're going to live and die by your conversion rates.

Because conversion rates are so important and such effective indicators of other more subtle changes occurring on your site and in your marketing acquisition programs, many companies use the best practice of generating key performance indicator reports [Hack #94] to distribute information about these events throughout their organizations [Hack #91].

The most important thing to recognize and remember is that, regardless of your business model, these rates and events are among the most important pieces of data you collect. By familiarizing yourself and your company with each of the measurements described in this hack, you significantly increase your chances of uncovering a wealth of information useful in your continuous improvement efforts.

—*Bryan Eisenberg and Eric T. Peterson*

Measure Banner Advertising

Knowing the impressions, response, success, and cost for each of your banner advertising campaigns can significantly improve the return on investment associated with this popular form of advertising.

Capable of reaching several hundred million people worldwide, banner ads have emerged as an essential tool for web marketers. As such, it is critical that you understand how best to measure banner advertising effectiveness and how to use this measurement to improve your business. To evaluate the effectiveness of any banner ad, there are three fundamental measurements: impressions, response, and conversion.

Impressions

Banner impressions are typically reported by an ad server solution, based on the number of image requests it receives. Impressions are usually broken out by the name of each creative element, but not necessarily by placement or timeframe. This can become a challenge if you run the same creative across multiple web sites and/or multiple periods. In this case, be sure to assign unique codes for each dimension you want to analyze—creative, web site placement, and timeframe (see Table 3-3). It is important to identify and carefully set these dimensions when you're making the placement. Backing into these dimensions can be difficult, time consuming, or impossible, depending on which web measurement system you use.

Table 3-3. Examples of banner elements you may want to track

Creative	Message
Medium	Web site placement
Sub-site placement	"Fly" dates (start and end dates)
Cost-per-impression (if known)	Cost-per-click (if known)
Ad identifier	Site identifier

Response

The measurement of response to a banner ad click is usually automatic in web measurement applications, provided you've told the application what to look for. Most vendors will want you to use either a standard identifier in the "click" URL or tell the system via some setup what to look for and what each of the variables maps to (Figure 3-3).

For example, you may use a URL like the following to identify campaigns:

http://www.oreilly.com/index.html?campaign=banner1&message=buynow

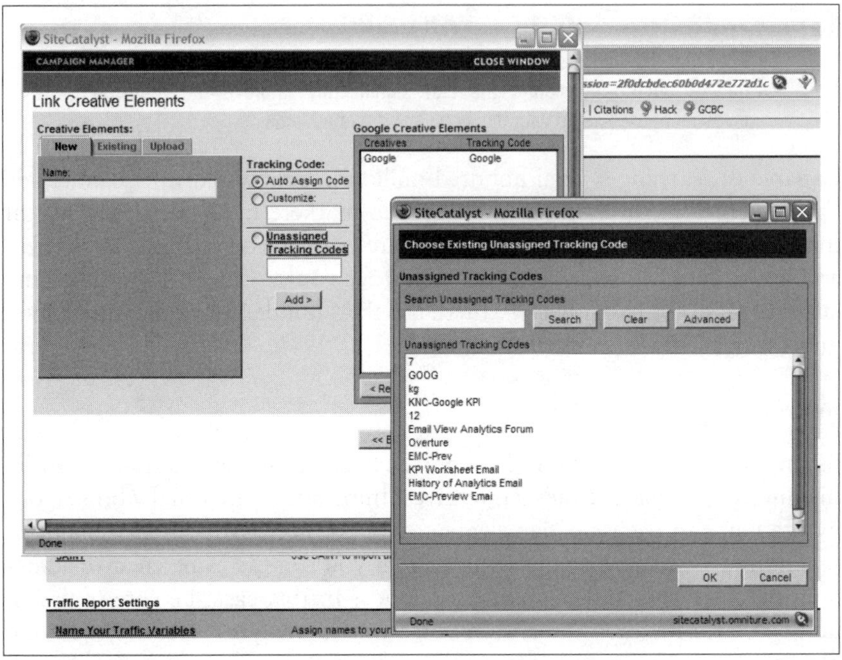

Figure 3-3. Identifying campaigns

When a user clicks to the web site with this link, the web measurement platform parses the URL, looks for the `campaign=banner1 name=value` pair, and if present, drops the campaign identifier in the user's cookie. When this happens, a "click" is recorded. But there is an added benefit. When the campaign identifier is added to the user's cookie, the application can now tie this to any subsequent action you are tracking with the platform.

> Sometimes the number of clicks reported by a banner advertising server doesn't match the number of responses you get to your site.
>
> This can occur because individuals bail out before a web page loads or because the URL is improperly coded. It's not uncommon to see up to 40% fewer clicks **[Hack #51]** reported by web measurement platforms when compared to ad servers.

The essence of measuring response is: make sure you correctly code each and every link you're using for your banner campaign. Any clicks that don't have the proper codes will not be recorded, and you're unlikely to be able to back and reconstruct those clicks. Get it right the first time, and you'll minimize frustration down the line. As always, if you have questions about exactly how to measure banner response, contact your vendor.

Conversion

Conversion events [Hack #39] are activities visitors engage in that have some inherent value to your organization. Purchase a product, book a flight, request more information, visit your web site—these are all conversion events. However, a word of caution: just because you've identified these events, it doesn't necessarily mean you can tie an event to your banner ad. Again, you want to make sure that you've defined conversion events correctly in your measurement application so they'll be tied to your banner ad response.

In the end, you should be able to generate a report that tells you (ideally) how many impressions each banner received, how many responses each generated, and how many conversions resulted (Figure 3-4). The best systems will then allow you to drill down into this information, exploring how individual dimensions (Table 3-3) performed and which conversion events each banner was most successful at driving. You may need to integrate data [Hack #32] to bring your impression data into the system, but if you use a unique identifier for each banner, this is actually less difficult than you'd think.

The Measurements You Need to Make

Once you've nailed down impressions, response, and conversion, you can calculate key performance indicators and improve your business (Figure 3-4).

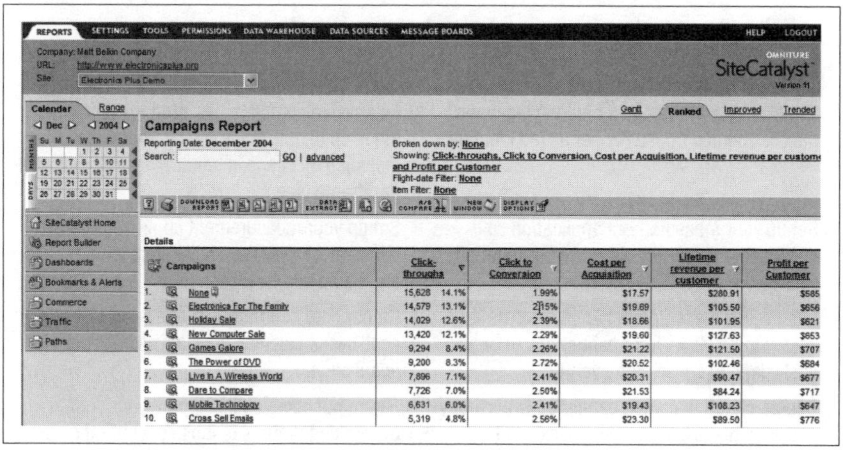

Figure 3-4. Key measurements for banner ads

Click-through rate (CTR). Calculated as total direct response divided by total impressions, the click-through rate tells you how effectively your banner ads elicit response. While industry average click-through rates are available, you're better off comparing your banner ads to one other [Hack #93]. Remember, poor click-through rates can be an early warning that your banner is poorly targeted or the call-to-action is unclear. Occasionally, exceptionally high CTR can mean unfiltered spider activity [Hack #23], which, if unchecked, can dramatically lower the conversion rate for the campaign.

Click-to-conversion rate (CTC). Calculated as total conversions divided by total response, the click-to-conversion rate provides insight into how well you are driving business success. High click-through rates and low click-to-conversion can indicate poorly designed landing pages or significant leaks in the conversion process—trouble spots that should be addressed immediately.

Cost per acquisition (CPA). Calculated as total conversions divided by total costs, cost per acquisition will indicate your average cost of customer acquisition for each banner ad. While this is a valuable metric to compare across different acquisition programs, it is most valuable when compared to revenue per customer, profit per customer, or lifetime value per customer. Obviously, any campaigns that cost more than the revenue they produce should be carefully scrutinized and perhaps discontinued.

Measuring Banner Advertising: A Checklist

To simplify the process, here is a checklist of things you *need to do* and things you *should do* when you set up a banner advertising campaign (Table 3-4).

Table 3-4. Banner advertising checklist

Things you need to do	Things you should do
Establish a URL strategy for identifying when the click comes from a banner ad (ad identifier).	Establish a complete URL strategy for recording each dimension of the ad impression, including message, medium, creative, site, and timeframe (see Table 3-3).
Set up your measurement application so it knows how to identify clicks from banner ads.	Set up your measurement application so you can capture every available dimension regarding the ad and its placement.
Set up your measurement application so it knows to tie clicks from banner ads to previously defined conversion events.	Gather cost information for each ad to make cost-based calculations such as cost-per-acquisition.
Double-check that each banner ad is correctly coded so the impression and click will be tracked properly.	Figure out how you'll compare your banner advertising metrics to those of your other marketing campaigns

In the end, if you follow this checklist and make the recommended measurements, you should be able to improve your banner campaigns with ease. The basic logic is "keep what works and cut the rest," and since you'll have great visibility, this will be a breeze.

—*Matt Belkin and Eric T. Peterson*

Measure Email Marketing

Email marketing is among the most popular methods for customer acquisition and retention, and a key factor driving conversion for many companies. Fortunately for you, email provides a plethora of interesting, easily measured data.

Email is one of the most important methods you have to communicate with your customers, but one often neglected nearly completely by the people sending the message. Regardless of whether you're prospecting or communicating valuable information to existing customers, the volume of email most people receive each day prevents us from spending enough time with any one message, unless the message is well timed and well crafted. Fortunately there are a number of things that can be measured that, when combined with fundamental marketing measurements, yield an incredibly powerful strategy for testing and measuring your email marketing efforts.

Things That Can Be Measured

By itself, email has a limited number of metrics you can track. Measuring the resulting web site visits, online and offline interaction, and purchases tells the whole story. In addition to *total sends*, the number of email addresses to which you send your message (and perhaps the most common email metric), there are a handful of other metrics you need to understand.

Hard bounces. A hard bounce is a message deemed undeliverable, usually because the address was mistyped or has been canceled. It's also likely to be an address that was entered by somebody who wanted to access content that required registration but didn't want to be in your database.

Tracked opens. Tracked opens are the number of recipients who opened the message using an HTML-capable email client. The inclusion of a nonresident graphic (a web bug [Hack #29]) or script can trigger a server call, indicating that the message has not only been received, but viewed.

> With the proliferation of spam, most email applications now reject scripts and nonresident images and warn recipients that something odd was included in the email. The use of scripts in email is a bad idea.

"Unique" opens help eliminate the confusion caused when one person opens the same message multiple times. This can be accomplished by relating the name of the called element to the email address.

Tracked click-through. Tracked click-through is the number of responses measured from an email message. This number may be greater than the number of opens or recipients if individuals click multiple times or if there are multiple links in your message.

Unsubscribes. The number of unsubscribes tell you how many people no longer want your messages. When measuring customer satisfaction, it is common to assume that one complaining customer might represent many unhappy customers who couldn't bother to complain. Given how easy it is to filter messages or simply delete them, unsubscribes are significant events.

Taken together, these metrics can tell you a lot about the quality of the email you're sending and provide the basis for testing your customer lists, the offers you make, and the way you represent those offers. Keep in mind that the aforementioned metrics are usually found in your email delivery and list management application. Once visitors successfully receive, read, and respond to your email by clicking to your web site, then the fun begins!

The Fundamental Email Response Metrics

Measuring the effectiveness of anything on the Internet begins with defining success. What is the desired outcome? Start there or you have no chance of success at all. A handful of reasonable measurements for success exist, including response rate, conversion rate, and a handful of relative value assignments.

Response rate and basic response metrics. Response rate is very similar to the click-through rate and is often a more practical calculation, since clicks can sometimes be difficult to measure accurately. Your email response rate is simply the number of responses divided by the number of total sends. In addition to measuring your response rate, you should look at the number of visits and unique visitors driven by the email message as a rough indicator of success.

Click-through rate. If you're able to import or input data about the number of total sends, you can use that value as the denominator to calculate your click-through rate. The calculation is simply the number of total clicks divided by the number of total sends. You should calculate click-through rate on a campaign-by-campaign basis and also for individual links contained in the email message, if there are more than one. Note that this calculation depends entirely on your ability to count the number of clicks generated, something that not every email delivery application and delivery strategy allows you to do.

Landing page "stickiness". Getting an email recipient to click is only half the battle. Once you get people to a web page, you then have to get them to keep moving into your site. Unless your landing page is the ultimate goal—and it almost *never* is—you need to get the recipient (who is now a visitor) to click more deeply into your site. An excellent KPI for keeping track of this on a landing page–by–landing page basis is the "stickiness" calculation: the number of single access page views divided by the number of respondents to the email campaign. A low "stick" from the campaign can mean that your landing page is poor, the message in the email is poorly matched to the landing page, or the page was slow to respond. If you're really ready to measure email, you might want to measure "stickiness" tied to different messages and links in each message, helping you better assess which variations work and which do not.

Conversion events and rates. Email conversion should be measured a variety of ways, looking at success on both a grand and granular scale (Figure 3-5). You should build an email conversion rate, defined as the total number of success events divided by the number of respondents, but you should also look at those conversion events on an individual basis. Put another way, you want to know that your email campaign had a 5 percent conversion rate but you also want to know that 85 percent of the conversions were purchases, 10 percent were downloads of some kind, and 5 percent were newsletter registrations.

You may also want to calculate a "relative respondent interest rate"—the percentage of email respondents who view more than five pages or reach a specific milestone page as a result of your message—thus relaxing the definition of "conversion" to include a variety of conversion events [Hack #39]. Each rate can be used to define key performance indicators, helping you understand how all your tests translate into improved visitor activity on your site.

Value metrics. When you attach costs and revenues to your email campaign measurements, you can begin to really explore the return on investment for your email marketing. Common KPIs include cost-per-email sent, cost-per-click, cost-per-respondent, cost-per-acquisition, revenue-per-click, revenue-per-respondent, and revenue-per-acquisition. Keep in mind that you don't have to be an online retailer to benefit from these calculations—there is always a cost associated with creating and sending an email, and you can also always assign some reasonable value to your conversion events.

Things That Should Be Tested

Assuming you're all set to measure the effect of each email you send through to a variety of conversion events, you should explore the following aspects of your email composition and delivery, looking for the "right" mix that speaks best to your particular recipients.

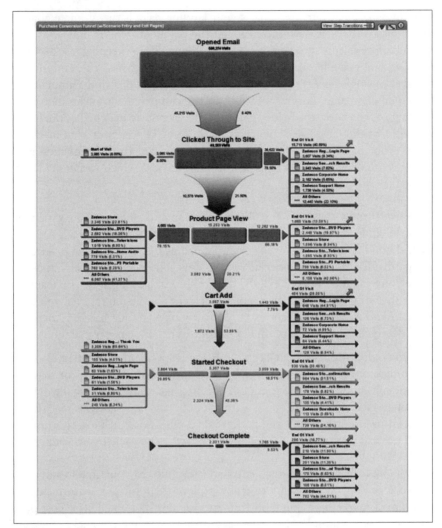

Figure 3-5. The visualization for email opens through to conversion

Format and layout. By mixing up the format and layout of the messages you send, you can look for differences in how recipients respond to changes in visual composition. You want to explore whether HTML, text, or rich media emails perform better, especially since the cost of producing and sending text-only emails is significantly lower.

Length and tone. Conventional wisdom states that short messages will perform better than long, rambling ones, but this is not always the case. By testing longer and shorter messages, you can experiment with your recipients' response. By varying the tone in your email, you can determine whether people respond to a more direct approach or a softer sell.

Date and time of delivery. Many marketers believe that Monday morning is a bad time to receive email offers—too much spam to sort through at the start of the week. Some suggest that Friday afternoon is also a bad time—people are trying to finish up their week, and your message may wait until that dreaded Monday morning before it is seen. But different audiences react differently.

Your subject matter might be just the thing your customers want before they begin their work week or just the thing before they start their weekend. So test time of day, day of week, and even the day of the month to see which helps you best reach your goals.

Return email address. The address from which your messages come may also have an impact on results. Emails could come from *Mail@Company.com*, *Marketing@Company.com*, or simply *Fred@Company.com*. This is especially important to explore so you're sure that recipients are not simply treating your email as unwanted spam.

The subject line. You'd be surprised at how much the subject line makes a difference in whether or not your email is opened. You should experiment with different subjects to determine the most effective for a particular offer and also the most effective' tone for your company. Some messages need loaded, direct subjects ("free if you respond NOW!"). Others 'benefit from a softer approach ("An update for Eric Peterson from Fred at Company.com").

The call to action. The call to action might be an invitation to see more information, enter a contest, or simply "Buy Now." Each different possibility fetches different results, but you need to test how your specific audience responds to different calls to action. Differ the means of response (click versus call versus email) and you increase the number of scenarios you need to test (but you still need to test them all!).

How to Put This Data to Work!

Now that you have the basic metrics, you can use them to measure the effectiveness of your email messages. In fact, you can use them to measure the effectiveness of all the elements of your email messages. When you sit down and compare results for different emails, you should keep the following in mind, going so far as to create a matrix of the "things that can be tested" juxtaposed against your tracked opens, tracked click-through, response, and conversion rates, and any relevant revenue or value metrics (Figure 3-6).

Test	Sends	Opens	Unsubscribes	CTR	Response Rate	Conversion Rate	Value
Format							
Text	1,000	532	12	12%	9%	2%	$8,000
HTML	1,000	877	32	18%	14%	4%	$16,000
Rich Media	1,000	212	41	2%	1%	0.25%	$1,000
Length							
Short							
Medium							
Long							
Date							
Weekday send	1,500	1,123	31	4%	3%	0.50%	$500
Weekend send	1,500	654	3	0.40%	0.15%	0.01%	$25
From							
Company email							
Personal email							
Landing Page							
Test landing page "A"							
Test landing page "B"							
Test landing page "C"							

Figure 3-6. Comparison matrix

To really take advantage of everything you've read in this hack, do the following every time you send a new email:

- Make sure you have access to the "things that can be measured," as they are important to making the rest of the calculations.

- Make sure you understand the "fundamental email response metrics" and that your web measurement application is set up to make them.

- Build a matrix like that shown in Figure 3-6, in which you identify which "things that should be tested" you're going to experiment with.

- Partition your potential audience into reasonably sized buckets based on the number of tests you're going to run. If you have enough recipients, plan on testing against only a subset of recipients, and then sending the "winning" message to the bulk of your audience.

- Send the different emails, being careful to tag each so that the "things that can be measured" and fundamental metrics can be partitioned easily for analysis.

- Fill in the appropriate fields in Figure 3-6, making the necessary calculations.

- Analyze carefully and send the balance of emails using the best strategy.

While following this strategy will obviously take more time than just throwing together an email and sending it out, the effort is definitely worth it. There are hundreds of examples of companies using this exact approach, called "digital Darwinism" by some (because only the strongest email strategy will survive), and this approach is widely credited with dramatically improving many companies' email communication efforts.

—Jim Sterne and Eric T. Peterson

Measure Paid Search Engine Marketing

Paid search marketing is one of the most popular marketing acquisition strategies in recent years, primarily because its effects are so easily measured. Taking the time to understand the "what" and "how" of search marketing can dramatically improve your return on investment for search keywords.

Paid search engine marketing can be measured and evaluated by simply modifying your click-through URLs to identify incoming paid traffic from popular pay-per-click engines like Google and Overture. Using your web measurement application, you can then segment those visitors for further analysis and profits—which, considering estimates that keyword costs will rise 30 percent between now and 2009, are worthy indeed.

How to Identify Paid Search Traffic

Different levels of tagging will yield small, medium, and large amounts of data. Whichever method you choose determines the amount of intelligence you can gather about your paid search marketing.

Low data gathering strategy. The overall big picture view of paid search is simply the identification of your traffic as originating from paid search. This can be done with a single query name/value pair on the end of all incoming paid search traffic. If there isn't already a query name/value pair, just add ?source=paid to your landing page URL:

http://www.mysite.com/landingpage.htm?source=paid

This segments your data into two distinct groups—paid versus organic. The amount of information that you gather from this approach is somewhat limited, is critical to differentiating paid from organic search [Hack #43]. If you can determine that people coming from organic search results are generating conversions, you can purchase that term for additional clicks and, hopefully, conversions.

Medium data gathering strategy. The next level of granularity comes with identifying which paid search engine generated the click. In this case, you will be appending information to the click-through URL that will include the name of the search engine from which you are buying the keyword. For example:

http://www.mysite.com/landingpage.htm?source=Google

Large data gathering strategy. The recommended method for measuring paid search engine marketing is to measure at the per-keyword level. While somewhat more time consuming to set-up, this level of granularity is most actionable and will help you best decide where your money is spent well and where it is wasted.

Each term, for each engine, would have its own unique query name/value pair. You can do this one of two ways—either by embedding all the information you want to track in the URL or by building a lookup table that associates the information after-the-fact. If you're going to embed information, you'll use URLs that look like the following in your paid search interface (when you set up the keyword campaigns):

> *http://www.mysite.com/landingpage.htm?source=Google&keyword= web+analytics&cpc=1.05*

Alternatively, the value can then be related back to your web measurement program with all of the related information in it, possibly through data integration [Hack #32]. An example of this is: *http://www.mysite.com/landingpage. htm?campaignID=112*, which, when combined with data from an external spreadsheet (Table 3-5) would tell you that campaignID 112 is related to Overture, the term "web analytics," and costs $1.05 per click.

Table 3-5. A sample spreadsheet that could be used to associate "campaignID=112" with other campaign information

Campaign ID	PPC engine	Term(s)	Cost-per-click
110	Google	"web analytics"	$1.02
111	Google	"web measurement"	$0.58
112	Overture	"web analytics"	$1.05
113	Overture	"web measurement"	$0.58

Obviously, despite the additional work, the "large data gathering" strategy should be used to ensure that you'll be able to accurately determine what is working and what is not. Once you've set up your strategy for identifying the clicks, the next step is to start collecting data.

Which Data Should You Be Collecting

The metrics that you'll want to consider when determining how your paid search marketing efforts are paying off include many of the standard marketing measurements.

Response rate (click-through rate). The response rate for each of your keywords is simply the number of generated visits divided by the number of impressions served at the search engines. You'll need to get the denominator from your paid search application, and again, don't be surprised if the number of clicks they report differs from the number of responses measured on your end [Hack #51].

Cost-per-click (CPC). Measure your cost-per-click simply by dividing the total cost of all of the clicks for that term in the time period by the number of requests in that time period. This should roughly match the per-click cost as reported by the advertising system that you are measuring. If not, then examine your system for possible points of loss [Hack #51].

Conversion rate by search engine and keyword. Measuring conversion rates on a per-engine and per-keyword basis is critical to understanding your success in paid search marketing. A keyword either drives success or it doesn't—it's that simple! You can compare the conversion rate across your paid search campaigns to see if similar terms across all of the search engines convert at the same rate. This is particularly useful when looking to see if a similar term on a new paid search campaign is going to be as profitable as it was in the past. To calculate this metric, divide the total number of clicks by the number of conversion events [Hack #39] for a particular time period.

Revenue (or loss) by search engine and keyword. Measuring the profit or loss per click is the ideal metric that all marketers should strive to measure. Especially if you're able to calculate profits based on margin, having this information will allow you to make truly actionable decisions about increasing or decreasing your bids for specific keywords and phrases. To calculate, simply subtract the total cost of your search campaigns from the total revenue driven directly by paid search, again being careful to differentiate paid from organic search [Hack #43].

Lifetime value of visitors from paid search marketing. Considering the amount that many companies spend on search marketing efforts, it is worthwhile to keep track of the lifetime value [Hack #84] of visitors who originate from paid search efforts. If you discover that paid search visitors are very profitable over the long run, you can feel that much better about your per-click costs.

What Do You Do with the Data?

So, in your web measurement tool, you know which search engine a visitor came from, which keyword he clicked on, how much you paid for that term, if that term converted, and what the value of that conversion was.

Let's run through an example with each type of data collection for a term that may be purchased to help sell this book—"web analytics," purchased on Overture. In the first small measurement example, you would know which clicks came from paid search and could track those from the referring URL to the conversion. You can then add that term to your Google AdWords account or other paid search engines.

Low data gathering strategy. If you're using the low data gathering strategy, you can measure the total paid search engine profits and determine your organic search term [Hack #43] profits:

> Total Revenue from Search – Revenue from Paid Search = Organic Search Profit
>
> Total Revenue from Paid Search – Cost of Paid Search = Paid Search Profit

Medium data gathering strategy. In the medium measurement example, you would know which paid–search engine generated every click. This is particularly useful for search engines that display results from multiple paid search publishers (like Dogpile.com or other meta-search engines). Also, it allows you to evaluate which search engine you should be spending your time and money on:

> Revenue from Paid Search Engine A – Cost of Paid Search for Engine A = Paid Search Engine A Profit
>
> Revenue from Paid Search Engine B – Cost of Paid Search for Engine B = Paid Search Engine B Profit

Large data gathering strategy. In the large measurement example, you would know for every click which paid search engine generated the click, how much you paid for the click, what the total cost is for all similar clicks on that engine, which clicks resulted in conversions, and what the value of each conversion is. This data can then be compared to the total profit/loss with the original click as the source to determine what the value per click is for that term (Table 3-6). (Note that keyword #1 is losing two cents per click (–$0.02) while keyword #2 is driving a profit of $0.75 per click.)

Table 3-6. Sample profit/loss calculation for two keywords

Keyword #1	Keyword #2
Per-click cost = $0.35	Per-click cost = $0.25
Number of clicks = 125	Number of clicks = 500
Total cost = $52.50	Total cost = $125.00
Total conversions = 1	Total conversions = 10
Total revenue = $50.00	Total revenue = $500.00
Profit/loss ($50 – $52.50) = –$2.50	Profit/loss ($500 – $125) = $375.00
Loss per click (–$2.50/125) = –$0.02	Profit per click ($375/500) = $0.75

Remember, for any individual search engine, the sum of revenues minus costs for each keyword you're buying is the profit (or loss) for that engine.

Analysis like this arms you with the knowledge that keyword #1 isn't profitable and should be examined to see if there is anything that can be done to make it profitable. Keyword #2 is a profitable term and should be purchased on all paid search engines for that price or lower to evaluate the term over a broader distribution network.

—Dylan Lewis and Eric T. Peterson

HACK #43 Measure Organic Search

Many people think that organic or natural search results are impossible to track. Fortunately, if you're careful with how you set up your paid search marketing, you often get organic search tracking for free.

Organic search results are those results from Google, Yahoo!, and the other major search engines that are not pay-per-click advertising. If you do any type of paid search marketing [Hack #42], your site will sometimes appear in both paid and organic result sets, obfuscating the effects of your paid marketing efforts. To resolve this problem and determine accurate return on investment for paid search and site optimization efforts, many marketers attempt to divide search results into distinct groups for paid and organic search. Even if you aren't investing in pay-per-click search, and therefore are certain your search traffic is organic, measuring the effects of that organic traffic is critical.

The Nature of the Problem

For traffic from a search engine, the key to understanding what terms brought visitors to your site is the referring URL information. The challenge when measuring organic search is telling your web measurement application how to differentiate between paid and unpaid placements.

For example, let's say you buy the phrase "fresh fruit" at Google and you're well-ranked in the organic results, so that both results appear on the first page. Regardless of the link a visitor clicks, she arrives at *www.bobsfruitsite.com*, and the referrer from Google is *www.google.com/search?q=fresh+fruit*.

"But wait!" you may be thinking to yourself, "I know for a fact that Google AdWords go through a redirect page that counts the click before going onward to the destination site. Surely we can exploit that data?" Tragically no, you cannot. It's correct that Google AdWords do go through a redirect, but the redirect never shows up in the referring URL. A referrer is, by definition [Hack #1], the previous page the user saw, not the previous page requested by the browser.

The Solution

Since the referrer is usually no help, the solution is found in the only other element we can control: the destination URL. By establishing different URLs for your paid listings you're able to differentiate paid from organic results. Changing URLs for organic results is very difficult; it usually requires complex search engine optimization technology and risks your incurring the wrath of the all-powerful search engines. Changing the paid destination URL, on the other hand, is a simple matter, something you're likely already adept at if you've bought any keywords at all.

If you've devised a unique system of landing pages for your paid advertising, you're not completely out of the woods. It is unfortunately difficult to be sure that search engines aren't indexing obscure pages, and therefore some organic clicks may end up on your "paid" landing pages. You need a method that *guarantees* identification of paid clicks so that your web measurement application can subtract these from the total searches to report on organic searches accurately.

Welcome to the World of Tracking URLs

The simplest solution is to append an identifier to the URLs in your paid listings, creating a tracking URL. You can add a simple parameter like source=google in *www.bobsfruitsite.com/index.html?source=google* to positively identify the paid placement to your web measurement solution.

URL parameters are usually synonymous with server-side scripting, but don't panic—the parameters you'll use require no web development and work fine on a static web page. The parameter becomes part of the request URL when the advertisement is clicked, but the server *simply ignores it*. You're only interested in getting something logged that differentiates paid and natural search listings. Furthermore, the parameter needs be present only on the first request—there is no need to pass it from page to page.

Tell Your Web Measurement Software to Ignore the Paid Search Traffic

All that remains is to tell your web measurement solution how to differentiate paid from unpaid search referrals, allowing the software to subtract the paid traffic from the total, leaving the organic results. Because the number of tracking URLs can be become quite large, the opportunity for user error exists, so many web measurement applications permit tracking URL data to be imported directly to improve accuracy (Figure 3-7).

The remaining task is to divide these referrals into two categories and view them side by side. Some applications perform this division and comparison using visitor segmentation or labeling, others simply make laundry lists of

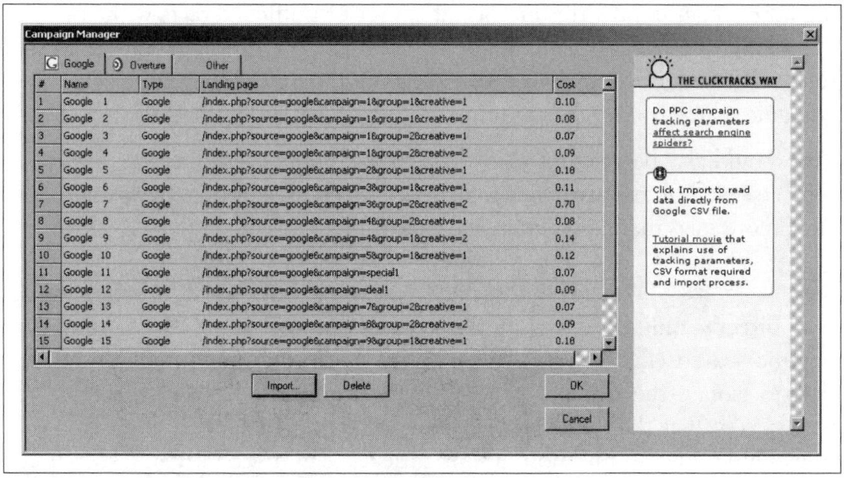

Figure 3-7. ClickTracks tool to import paid campaign data

each type of search term, and still others offer complex cross-tabulation associated with organic and paid search terms.

Now That I Can Tell Them Apart, What Do I Do?

Since paid search marketing is easy to experiment with, you should constantly optimize your keyword mix, isolate those clicks using this technique, and then add them to your organic efforts if they generate good returns. The metrics you'll want to consider when determining how your organic efforts are paying off include many of the standard marketing measurements.

Cost-per-click. In this context, cost-per-click is usually negligible, unless you're working with a search engine optimization (SEO) firm, in which case it becomes one of the key drivers to measure your return on investment. Divide the cost of your organic optimization efforts into the total number of organic clicks you're generating from all search engines to get a high-level cost-per-click. If you're optimizing around specific keywords, you may want to first divide the cost of the efforts by the total number of words you're optimizing for, and then divide by the number of clicks for those keywords (yielding a keyword-specific cost-per-click).

Examining your cost-per-click for organic search also provides a good comparison for your paid search marketing efforts [Hack #42]—an important comparison to ensure you're investing your marketing dollars wisely and effectively.

Conversion rate by engine and keyword. Regardless of your business model, you should be associating organic search traffic with conversion events, looking for changes in how this important source of traffic interacts with your site. Hopefully your measurement application supports the generation of this report automatically, allowing you drill down from "all organic search" to "organic search by search engine" to "organic keywords and phrases."

You should also be careful to look at which of your conversion events [Hack #39] organic search terms are driving. Searches for "web analytics newsletter" may yield more sales than newsletter sign-ups, for example.

Revenue (or loss) by search engine and keyword. If your goal is selling products directly online, you should calculate the revenue or loss from your organic search efforts. You'll need to use your web measurement application to isolate the number of visits or visitors arriving via organic search terms, as well as the total revenue these visits have generated. You may want to examine this number both at a high level (e.g., for all organic search and by search engine) and at the keyword level.

Lifetime value of visitors from organic search. While it can take a while to generate a good report on the lifetime value of visitors originally finding you via organic search, this report is important to generating a long-term view of your marketing efforts. Considering that companies spend significantly on paid search marketing, but the wide majority of clicks from search engines still come from organic results, understanding the long-term value of organic search visitors provides great insight into the relationship between paid and "unpaid" search marketing.

In addition to cost-per-click, you may want to build KPIs for cost-per-acquisition and cost-per-conversion [Hack #37] for organic search, again to help you determine the true return on investment for any money you spend optimizing your site.

—*John Marshall and Eric T. Peterson*

HACK #44 Contrast Paid Keywords Versus Actual Search Queries

One of the best kept secrets in paid search marketing is that you can save huge amounts of money simply by examining your paid search keywords in contrast to the actual search queries that visitors entered triggering your keyword advertisement.

You already know how to measure paid search engine marketing [Hack #42] and how to distinguish it from organic search [Hack #43]. There is an additional subtlety to know about paid search that can save you a lot of money. However, the terminology is confusing, which may throw you off. Therefore, let's start with a recap.

Paid Search Visits Versus Organic Search Visits

A paid search visit results from a visitor who clicks on your paid search ad. An organic search visit results from a visitor clicking on organic search results within the search engine. Interestingly, any one search query that a visitor enters into the search box can result in both organic as well as paid search visits to your site. Think of it. If in addition to organic search results from your web site there is also your paid ad appearing alongside, it just depends on where each visitor decides to click.

Paid Search Keywords Versus Actual Search Queries

For paid search visits, it helps to distinguish further between the paid search keyword on which you are bidding and the actual search query that visitors entered into the search box on the search engine. The paid search keyword is the specific keyword or phrase on which you have bid with popular pay-per-click engines like Google and Overture. The actual search queries do not have to exactly match your paid search keywords, but can be variations thereof.

When you bid on a paid search keyword, you can further control your listing by selecting how closely the actual search queries entered by the search engine visitors must match your keyword. For instance, various search engines allow you to designate "exact matching," "broad matching," and similar variations.

Exact Matching Versus Broad Matching

Exact matching tells the search engine to display your paid listing only when the exact keyword is entered, in order, and with no other phrases.

Broad matching allows the search engine to return your paid listing whenever a visitor to the search engine searches for a phrase containing your keyword. If your keyword is actually two words together, your listing will appear when a visitor enters both keywords in either order, even if there are other terms mixed in. Broad matching also includes "expanded matches," including plurals and common misspellings. Broad matching is typically the default setting for your listings with most major search engines.

Broad matching allows for your paid listing to be displayed to a larger audience, but also incurs the risk of attracting visitors who are searching for things that aren't actually relevant to your offerings. In these cases, the actual keyword used to find your web site will differ slightly from the paid keyword listing that referred the visitor.

Unfortunately, while pay-per-click search engines like Google and Overture provide you with reports on clicks by paid search keyword, they do not inform you on the actual search queries that these visitors used. If they did, you could verify whether those queries are really relevant to your web site.

Luckily, in your web site analytics, you can capture both—the paid keyword as well as the actual, broad-matched queries—and compare them (Figure 3-8). This is critical for ensuring that your pay-per-click budget is spent only on clicks from visitors within your target market. In the report example below, from a photocopy machine vendor, you can see that the actual, broad-matched query "history of color copiers" led to many paid keyword referrals, but not conversions. If you are selling color copiers, you likely do not wish to pay for visits from people interested in the history of color copiers. You may want to adjust your broad matching settings to exclude any key phrases that include the word "history." This can be achieved by configuring "history" as what is sometimes called a "negative" keyword.

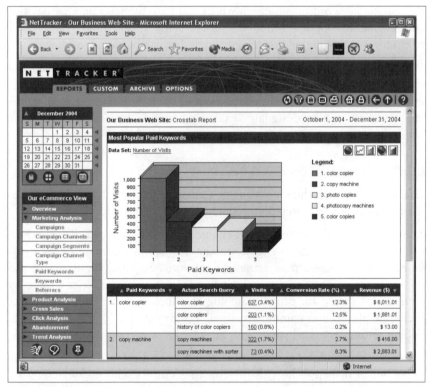

Figure 3-8. Paid search keywords and the broadly matched queries

You can also derive another very significant benefit from comparing paid keywords to the actual search queries that your visitors are employing. Like the above example, you may find that a large number of your visitors are actually entering the search phrase "copy machine with sorter" instead of just "copy machine." In that case, you can bid on "copy machine with sorter" and maybe even drop your bids on "copy machine." As your new paid keyword is more specific, competitors' bids will typically be lower on it, while your conversion rate from visitors clicking on your ad tends to be higher. This is one of the most common techniques employed by search engine optimization consultants to optimize your pay-per-click marketing.

How Can I Capture the Necessary Information and Create This Report?

For capturing and tracking paid search keywords, refer to the "large data gathering strategy" described in "Measure Paid Search Engine Marketing" [Hack #42]. You will see how to stuff your destination URLs with a parameter that reveals the paid search keyword responsible for each visit. The destination URL becomes the first page that the paid search visitor views on your web site after clicking on your ad. A web analytics tool capable of URL parameter analysis will allow you to extract the paid search keyword parameter from the entry page URL's query string.

Many pay-per-click search engines also offer shortcuts for specifying stuffed, unique destination URLs for each paid keyword. For example, in Overture, you can simply click to switch on Overture Tracking URLs, which automatically append a series of useful parameters for all your listings. In Google, you can use the placeholder {Keyword} when you specify destination URLs for each ad, as in the example below. When displaying your ad, Google will replace {Keyword} with the paid search keyword that triggered your ad:

> *http://www.mysite.com/landingpage.htm?source=Google&keyword
> ={Keyword}*

Actual search queries, on the other hand, are automatically captured and extracted from the referring URL of each visit by most standard web analytics tools today. If you look at the search results page on any major search engine, you will see that your search query that you had entered into the search box is coded into a parameter in the URL. This URL becomes the referring URL to any visitor who clicks on a search result to arrive on your web site. Web analytics tools are trained to look for this parameter and extract the query terms.

Finally, assuming that your web analytics tool allows you to combine multiple data elements to create custom cross-tabulation reports, you can reproduce a custom report similar to the one above that compares paid search keywords with the actual search queries. You could further filter this report to referrals from specific pay-per-click search engines to examine traffic from each of them.

—*Akin Arikan and Eric T. Peterson*

HACK #45 Measure Affiliate Marketing

Many online marketers take advantage of affiliates and affiliate programs to drive traffic to their sites without considering everything that can be measured.

Affiliate marketing is a very powerful customer acquisition strategy, essentially paying people a commission to evangelize your products or services and then sending traffic your way in hope that they'll complete the transaction. Your web measurement application should allow you to track affiliate campaigns, much like a banner ad or email message. Tracking your affiliate campaigns in as much depth as possible helps you learn from the creativity of others as you plan your own future marketing activities.

Pay for Clicks, Leads, or Revenue: Which Is Better?

Most affiliate management programs (Commission Junction, Linkshare, and Performics) require that you pay on either a per-click, per-lead, or commission basis (Table 3-7).

When you're paying for clicks, you might be paying for traffic that never actually visits your web site [Hack #51], or that never actually converts into a customer [Hack #39]. The best example of this type of affiliate relationship is the Google AdSense program. On a per-click basis, affiliate publishers are paid by the amount of traffic they generate. The more clicks generated, the more the affiliate gets paid. In this model, you want to be sure you're watching your affiliate conversion rate and the amount of revenue individual affiliates generate.

Where you're paying for leads, you want to be careful to watch out for poorly qualified leads—visitors who are unlikely to convert into revenue or other value for your business. If your affiliates send you poorly qualified traffic, the cost of all generated leads will be greater than the amount of revenue generated by those customers. In this model, you want to be sure you are tracking your profit or loss per lead to make sure this traffic maintains profitability.

The ideal financial relationship between your site and your affiliate network is pay-for-performance, for which you pay a commission per sale generated to your affiliates. This strategy can be measured only through value-based metrics, captured at the point of sale and tied back to the originating affiliate. With this type of relationship, there is no need for a loss column on any reports because the only payments that will be made will be to affiliates that generate revenue.

Table 3-7. Comparison of each type of affiliate marketing payment program

Type of program	Advantages	Disadvantages
Pay per click	Easiest to understand and monitor	Many clicks never make it to the site, and quality of clicks can vary greatly, driving up per-click and per-order costs.
Pay per lead	Guarantees that you gain more information about the prospect	The leads you get may not be "good" leads, thus driving up the cost of real leads.
Pay per performance	Guarantees that money goes in your pocket before any payment is made to the affiliate, and helps foster a mutually beneficial relationship	Usually the most expensive on a percentage of revenue basis, and sometimes difficult to create cost-effective partnerships.

Regardless of what you work out, there are a handful of standard measurements you should take to determine the success of your affiliate programs.

Use Web Measurement to Identify Affiliate Successes

Despite the fact that many affiliate programs come with some type of measurement tool built in, you owe it to yourself to validate those numbers using your web measurement application. Additionally, affiliate programs usually measure only what they pay on (clicks, acquisition, revenue), but the key insights you hope to gain about affiliate marketing will come from a deeper level of measurement, the kind nearly any web measurement tool provides.

The following are some of the key measurements you should be making on your affiliate traffic activity.

Paying for clicks? Determine your per-affiliate click-through rate. Your web measurement application should be able to quickly summarize the number of visits each affiliate sends your way, based on a unique URL string or query string parameters. For example, clicking a link on your affiliate's web site might bring direct visitors to *http://www.mysite.com/landingpage.htm?source=affiliate1*. The presence of the source=affiliate1 would allow you to identify that the visitors came from affiliate1 and track the visitors through to conversion.

While the number of respondents is often a poor proxy for clicks unless your affiliate management application provides you the necessary data, respondents and a visit-based measurement will have to do. Make sure you build a click-through rate using impression and click data reported from your affiliates or estimated impressions and respondent data. Even if someone else is managing the measurement and payments based on clicks, taking these measurements yourself will help you identify fraud and other activities you don't want to pay for.

Paying for leads? Measure lead generation rates. If you are paying your affiliates on a per-lead basis, you'll need to track when a form is successfully completed. The easiest way to do this is to identify the "thank you for your submission" page so that you see the original referrer of the traffic and the number of times that referrer produced traffic that landed on that page. Most web measurement applications allow you to set a goal page for analysis back to the referrer (Figure 3-9).

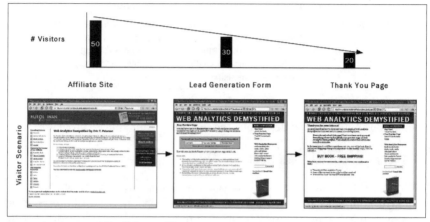

Figure 3-9. Visitor fall-off from affiliate to conversion

An even better strategy would be to create a conversion funnel [Hack #59] that lets you see on a per-affiliate basis how many visitors start and finish the lead generation process. Especially when yours is a more complicated process, identifying where abandonment occurs can help you improve the quality of your relationship with your affiliates. Remember, the best affiliates want to hear your suggestions for how to improve their message, since it increases their revenue stream at the same time!

Paying for performance? Paying commissions based on sales. Ideally, you are paying your affiliates a percentage of each sale they generate. This can vary depending on your model, but it is the recommended model for all affiliate relationships. This requires that your web measurement application be able to record the specific dollar amount that was given to you by the customer, the rate at which the affiliate earns their commission per sale, and the ability to tie the sale back to the original referrer. Table 3-8 shows an example of this information.

Plan on generating a report for "conversion and revenue by affiliate" for yourself—even if the affiliate management program you use generates one—for validation. If you're really sophisticated and are able to input the percentage you pay each affiliate, you're likely to be able to get any moderately sophisticated web measurement application to calculate your total affiliate sales and payments for you as well.

As you can see from Table 3-8, if you were paying per lead for the "Free Guide to Web Analytics," you would be losing money. By measuring all levels, you can determine the optimal structure for each affiliate relationship.

Table 3-8. Sample affiliate analysis showing the relationship between affiliate performance and profit

Affiliate name	Rate	Respon-ses	Leads	Conver-sions	Revenue	Cost	Profit
Web Measure-ment Blog	25%	435	400	10	$500	$125	$375
Analytics Bible	5%	34	14	0	$0	$0	$0
Librioteca de Web Analytics	10%	3,423	1,245	17	$849	$85	$764
Web Analytics Org	25%	3,404	1,789	56	$2,797	$699	$2,098
Association of Analytics Geeks	12.5%	4,543	58	58	$2,897	$362	$2,535
Free Guide to Web Analytics	15%	9,845	8,765	0	$0	$0	$0
Metrics Matter	20%	4,932	2,805	132	$6,593	$1,319	$5,275
TOTALS		26,616	15,076	273	$13,636	$2,590	$11,046

Other useful metrics used to measure affiliate marketing. In addition to the key metrics we describe above, you should be thinking about your affiliate traffic like any other valuable referring source and taking advantage of it. If you have robust visitor segmentation tools [Hack #48] in your measurement application, create a segment from affiliate visitors and see how their activity differs from other acquisition segments. Make sure you're looking at KPIs relevant to affiliate visitors—average time spent on site, average page views per visit, percentage new versus returning visitors, percent visits less than 90 seconds, and percent interested and committed visits (for a more complete list, consult Chapter 7)—as well as important measurements and lists like the top 25 pages viewed and top entry and exit pages.

Tying It All Together

Make sure you treat your affiliate partners like the valuable revenue stream they can be and the visitors they drive like the potential customers they are. Just because affiliate marketing is made easy by aggregators such as Commission Junction, Linkshare, and Performics doesn't mean you should take your affiliates for granted.

Finding beneficial affiliate relationships can be difficult to do if you aren't willing to meet halfway between their wants and your needs. You may need to try out relationships for a month to determine what the affiliates' expected revenue would be over the entire year. Don't be afraid to run a test rollout and then renegotiate the contract based on the metrics you collect. Let the affiliate know your sales expectations and their progress throughout the relationship. Constant communication about the resulting metrics can only benefit both parties.

Also, if possible, have the affiliate track their progress using their own measurement solution and compare notes about results. There will be differences between measurement systems, but this will help generate trust, and that is something that can't always be measured with a hack.

—*Dylan Lewis and Eric T. Peterson*

HACK #46   Use Unique Landing Pages

Many marketers make one critical mistake when attempting to lure visitors to their web sites—they use specific language, offers, and messages to drive visitors to the most generic landing page of all: the site's home page. The use of unique landing pages, while slightly more difficult to maintain, can dramatically improve key performance indicators like stickiness and conversion rates.

Did you ever wonder why marketing folks would spend so much money crafting banner ads, carefully writing emails and keyword ads at Google and Overture, and then simply dump all of the resulting clicks on the site's home page? The home page, by design, is a generic "catch all" for people stumbling on the site, a page designed to provide a shallow but broad view into what a company does. But visitors who are clicking on an ad, email, or search keyword have already expressed interest in a specific idea or goal—whatever the offer or message is in the advertisement they clicked upon. You should avoid this simple mistake and get in the habit of building unique landing pages for your marketing campaigns.

Unique Landing Pages Are Focused

Contrasted with your site's home page, unique landing pages should be designed to be about the very specific thing you were advertising or that your visitor was searching for. If people are searching on Google or Overture for "Arc'Teryx jackets" and they click on your ad, you already know something critical about them—they are looking for jackets and are specifically interested in the Arc'Teryx brand. If you sell jackets and just happen to sell the particular brand, why not deliver visitors to a page like the one seen in Figure 3-10?

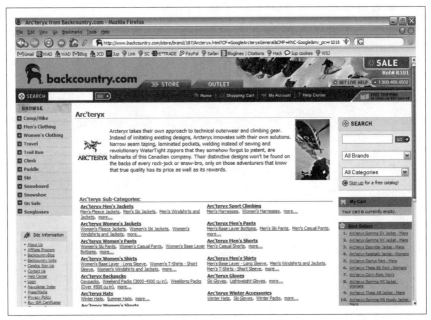

Figure 3-10. Unique landing page

As you can see, this entire page is about the Arc'Teryx brand. Backcountry. com is doing a very smart thing by presenting a complete picture of what they have to offer a visitor looking for Arc'Teryx, dramatically improving the visitor's chances of finding the specific product he's looking for.

Unique Landing Pages Are Not Always Unique

Funny as it may sound, you don't necessarily need to create a completely new page to take advantage of the idea of unique landing pages. As you can see in Figure 3-10, Backcountry.com is dropping searchers right on the Arc'Teryx brand page based on their search query. This page is not necessarily unique, and you can navigate to the exact same page by going to the site's home page and clicking on the appropriate links.

The reason some marketers make completely new pages for marketing campaigns is to better track the efficacy of the campaign, something easily done using the measurement strategies described throughout this chapter. In general, when using this hack, you want to ask yourself three questions:

- Do I have a way to track clicks to the landing page using some kind of tracking URL [Hack #43]?

- If people navigate to this page, rather than clicking on an advertising link, will I be able to differentiate "navigators" from "ad responders"?

- Do I have a content management system in place that will allow me to easily create and manage truly unique pages?

If you answer "yes," "yes," and "no" to these questions, you're much better off repurposing existing pages on your site rather than building new pages. The most important things you need to be able to do are measure and differentiate visitors to the page, identifying people who respond to ads and those who simply click around the site.

The exception to repurposing pages is when you're trying to drive people to your web site from some kind of offline advertisement—a television or radio ad, a billboard, or a print ad in a magazine or newspaper. In cases like this, you're almost always better off creating a unique page that can be managed as necessary, and that will ensure the most accurate count of visitors.

Hacking Unique Landings Pages: The Mini-Site Model

Some marketers take the concept of the unique landing page one step further and build complete mini-sites around marketing campaigns. Mini-sites usually present content that is very specifically focused around the marketing campaign or concept (Figure 3-11).

Mini-sites typically *do not* have all of the normal navigation elements you would find on the rest of the site, opting to present visitors with few choices that are all designed to focus their attention on the specific product, idea, or theme. While it isn't a bad idea to focus the navigation elements, you do want to provide visitors an out if they need one, allowing them to leave the mini-site without having to back up completely (the top line navigation elements in Figure 3-11 have links to Home, Products, Club, etc.).

Measuring Unique Landing Page Activity

Unique landing pages are measured just like any other type of campaign and are usually already captured as part of your reporting on email, banner advertising, or RSS. The most important measurements you can make using unique landing pages are their "stickiness" [Hack #58] and how likely visitors

Figure 3-11. The Star Wars mini-site at LEGO Shop at Home

are to click through to another page on the site once they arrive. You may want to use a browser overlay [Hack #62] to track clicks, especially if you build a mini-site.

Measure Content Syndicated via RSS

HACK #47

An emerging frontier in web measurement is the ability to track weblog readership, referrals, and link out clicks. No known vendors support weblog measurement directly, but this surprisingly simple hack will show you how to do it yourself!

Given the attention paid to weblogs and the blogosphere in general, it is surprising that no vendors have stepped up to provide a solution to measure content syndicated via really simple syndication (RSS). I personally have been blogging in the dark via my employer's web site for over a year, always wondering "Who reads this stuff and what do they say about it?" It turns out there are a few things you can do to measure reach and acquisition for your syndicated content, depending on how involved you want to get, your particular web measurement application, and the RSS publication platform you publish from.

Easy Things You Can Do to Measure RSS Readership

If you're only trying to figure out who is linking to your posts, not necessarily how many people are reading or which links they're clicking, Bloglines (*www.bloglines.com*) provides an excellent tool for doing exactly that. Their search for pages linking into a URL accepts the location of your weblog (for example, *http://weblogs.jupiterresearch.com/analysts/peterson/*) and tells you who is linking to you (Figure 3-12).

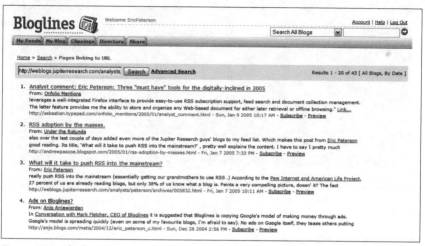

Figure 3-12. Bloglines citation search

Bloglines returns a list of other feeds indexed by their service that have a link to your site. Considering that at the time this book was written, Bloglines enjoyed a greater than 50 percent market share for RSS readers (an estimated four million people, based on data from the *Pew Internet and American Life Project*), the sample Bloglines provides is pretty good. Other resources for tracking how your posts are picked up around the Internet include:

Technorati (www.technorati.com)
> Here you can search for your content and see who is linking to you. You can also search for your feed URL, generate a report similar to Bloglines', and sort by recency and author.

Feedster (www.feedster.com)
> This site can be used much like Bloglines and Technorati, but has the added advantage of being able to generate an XML feed of the search results.

Blogdigger (www.blogdigger.com)
> This site is a variation on this same theme, but has a Firefox search extension so you can search Blogdigger right from your favorite web browser.

Still, you may be looking for more data than that, perhaps a simple count of which stories are being viewed when.

Hacking Your Web Measurement Tool to Track RSS

The nice thing about RSS is that it accepts normal HTML content and, for the most part, renders it correctly regardless of which reader application is used. This can be exploited by web measurement applications by using a simple IMG SRC request that will be tracked as a page view.

Simple RSS tracking using web server logfiles. The essence of this hack is the fact that web server logfiles process image requests just as readily as requests for normal web pages, and are nearly always able to parse information out of the query string. What this means is that if you drop a one-by-one pixel image somewhere on your web server, you can make a request for this image—including the name of the story in the query string—from inside your blog post.

In the following example, a file called *rss_blank_image.gif* resides in the site's */images* directory. When you paste this image request into your blog post, you would replace the RSS STORY NAME with the post's headline, converting spaces to plus-signs or %20s (whitespace characters):

```
<img src="http://www.yoursite.com/images/rss_blank_image.gif?n
=RSS+STORY+NAME" border='0' width='1' height='1'>
```

This will create a line in your web server logfile for the request and capture information about the date, time, user agent, and IP address of the requestor, along with the *n*=RSS+STORY+NAME information. You can then use your measurement application's query parsing capabilities to search for requests for the blank image and report back on the value of *n* as found in the query string.

> Consult your vendor directly about how to set up query string parsing.

Also, if you're lucky, your web measurement application will have the ability to set a server-side cookie, usually via an ISAPI filter of some kind. If this is the case, you will also likely be able to get visit and unique visitor counts from this simple image request.

Simple RSS Tracking Using JavaScript Page Tags. For tag-based solutions, which nearly always support a NOSCRIPT tag that allows for the collection of basic information (page name, content group, etc.), the strategy is nearly as simple.

All you're going to do in this case, using WebSideStory's NOSCRIPT tag as an example, is set the appropriate variables, including the story name, a content group where you'd like to track your syndicated content, and any other features the vendor allows you to leverage without JavaScript (a visitor segment, in this example):

```
<img src="http://ehg-companyname.hitbox.com/HG?hc=localagg&hb=
    DM12345678910&n=RSS STORY NAME&vcon=/CONTENT GROUP FOR RSS&seg=
    SEGMENT ID FOR RSS" border='0' width='1' height='1'>
```

The unfortunate problem with most hosted solutions is that you're less likely to get accurate visit and visitor counts using this method. The good news is that the reporting is automatic—all you need to do is open your content grouping report to whichever group you're tracking these posts in (CONTENT GROUP FOR RSS) and the data will be available.

The downside of the easy way of doing things is that you're not going to get any good information about who is referring traffic to your posts and which links people are clicking when they read them. To get this information, you'll need to work just a little bit harder [Hack #12].

Treat RSS Like Email or Banner Advertising

One important thing to keep in mind is that even if you don't do anything special to track the number of people reading your syndicated content, you still need to measure how that content drives visitors back to your web site. Put another way, the number one reason you should be syndicating content via RSS is to drive visitors back to your web site, an activity that can be measured in much the same way you measure email marketing [Hack #41] or banner advertising [Hack #40].

If you're syndicating regular content that you present on your web site (different than blogging), you should always do these two things:

- Provide only a summary view of the article, not the whole article.
- Embed tracking codes in any links in the summary to track the number of people who click to read the entire article.

Doing this will allow you to know how effective your RSS feeds are in terms of driving traffic back to the web site. But wait, you're not done there! Because you're embedding tracking codes and creating tracking URLs [Hack #43], you should be able to use your web measurement application to:

- Determine how many visitors and visits your feed is generating.
- Determine whether visitors from syndicated content are completing conversion events [Hack #39].

- Segment visitors [Hack #48] from syndicated content to determine whether their browsing habits differ from visitors acquired from other marketing channels.

If you get in the habit of treating content feeds just like any other marketing channel, you'll be able to take advantage of all the other learning you've done about how to best measure your marketing efforts. Content syndication and RSS are cutting-edge topics right now, generating tremendous excitement but getting very little attention in terms of how they're measured. Take advantage of this hack, and you'll be doing better than almost everyone else out there.

HACK #48 Segment Visitors to Understand Specific Group Activity

Web visitors are complex creatures, and each has slightly different behaviors and goals. Visitor segmentation is a popular strategy to differentiate these groups and develop a deeper understanding of your audience.

Different visitors come to your web site for different purposes. Some come to your web site to read your content, evaluate your offerings, or make purchases. Others come looking for employment opportunities or investment information. Still others may be looking for customer support. The behavior of these distinct groups will vary a great deal, as should your goals for their membership. For example, if a web measurement report told you that only one percent of your total visitors complete an important task, you may think that your web site is failing miserably. However, if you segment your visitors, focusing only on visitors who respond to a targeted email campaign, you may find that 30 percent of these visitors complete the task.

Given differences in browsing habits and ultimate goals, it certainly makes sense to leverage your measurement toolset to segment visitors in meaningful ways and create different sets of metrics for each. Fortunately, many of the top web measurement vendors offer some type of visitor segmentation tools that provide for differentiation of visitors (Figure 3-13).

Examples of Visitor Segments

No two web sites are likely to benefit from the exact same visitor segments; different analysts will use different criteria to examine the same behaviors, drawing different conclusions. It is likely that the segments you're interested in will change over time as your understanding of your audience evolves. Visitor segments are typically very specific to individual businesses.

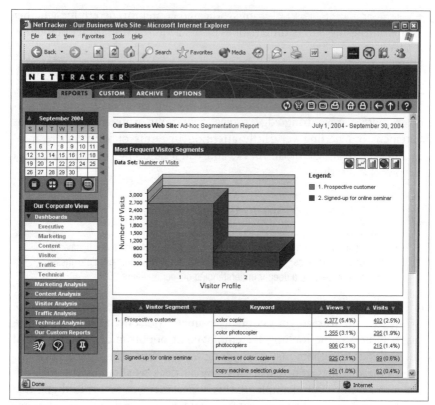

Figure 3-13. Visitor segmentation

That said, keep the following in mind as you brainstorm possible segments:

- Your site's varying constituencies (such as buyers, support customers, or tire kickers)

- The different information you offer to each of your constituencies (such as conversion reports, KPIs, lists of pages viewed, or referring domains)

- The various marketing campaigns you run to attract new visitors in each group (such as banner advertising, email, or RSS feeds)

- The particular role you have as a web data analyst and the aspect of the business you're responsible for (such as marketing, merchandising, site operations, or loyalty programs)

For example, as a marketing manager for a commercial web site, you may care about the visitors who are acquired via pay-per-click advertising. As a product or merchandise manager for the same web site, someone else may care about the smaller slice of visitors who clicked on the pay-per-click advertisement for a specific paid keyword, and performed a local search on the web site for related merchandise, but left the site without making a purchase. Your customer service manager may care about the segment of customers who searched the self-help content but finished their visit on the "contact us" page, apparently not finding what they were looking for.

General Requirements for Segmentation

Visitor segmentation is entirely driven by the abilities of your web measurement application. Put another way, if your particular solution doesn't support visitor segmentation, you can either get a new solution or not segment your visitors. Here are some general requirements that your measurement application needs in order to support to segment visitors:

- The ability to define a segment based on any applicable filtering criteria, such as pages or query strings viewed during visits, or the duration of visits
- The ability to customize any web measurement report by restricting it to a specific visitor segment or segments.
- The availability of detailed, historical web traffic data records that allow you to query historical data by slicing it into newly defined segments.

The last item is often considered a "nice to have" requirement, as many web measurement solutions provide only "move forward" segmentation—the ability to track segments from the time they're established, but not prior to that date—as opposed to *ad hoc* segmentation from any existing data. Ad *hoc* segmentation because it's very difficult to know in advance what you'll want to know later on. As usual, if you have any questions about your vendor's ability to segment your visitors in meaningful ways, the best advice is to pick up the phone and give them a call.

Defining Good Visitor Segments

The following are just a few basic examples of typical segments with hints on how you can define each segment based on the data available to you about your visitors.

New versus returning visitors
    Perhaps the most basic, but most valuable, visitor segment, you should definitely create a segmentation report for new versus returning visitors. By taking a closer look at the differences between which pages each type of visitor is looking at, you can hopefully learn how to convert more "new" visitors into "returning" visitors.

Conversion success
    Maybe the most frequent type of segmentation applied by web analysts is to distinguish between visitors who complete a critical action and

those who do not. Depending on the mission of your web site, that action may be completing a registration form, making a purchase, or finding a support document without dialing your call center. Here you would define the segment as the slice of visitors who have completed the success action, usually measured as a view of a specific page during their visit (for example, a thank you page).

Visitor acquisition source

To segment by visitor acquisition source, you would define segments by creating unique landing pages [Hack #46] for each of your marketing campaigns. Any visitor who starts her visit on one of these pages is assumed to have come from the related marketing campaign and should thus be assigned to the appropriate segment.

Purpose of visit

Without interviewing a visitor, it is not possible to know for sure what the purpose of his visit is. However, you can attempt to infer his purpose from the type of pages that the visitor is viewing or the order in which he views them. For example, you can define the segment of prospective customers as those visitors who view pages related to your offering. Similarly, you can define self-help visitors as those who spend time on your customer service section.

Product interest or purchase

A merchandise manager may wish to distinguish visitors by product interest in order to better understand how visitors research her line of products. This requires defining segments based on the products or product categories viewed or purchased during a visit. Make sure to differentiate "buyers" from "tire kickers" in this type of segmentation so that you have data to help identify why the tire kickers convert.

Value of the visitor

You probably want to focus some of your analysis on high-value customers to find out how they find your web site and navigate it. While the specific definition of "high value" differs greatly from site to site, in general:

- As a retailer, you may care about customers whose order value exceeds a certain amount. The order value is typically captured from a URL parameter or tag that you set aside on your order confirmation page.

- As a content web site owner, you may care about customers with more than five visits per week. You can track the number of repeat visits per visitor if you are using cookies or authenticated usernames to identify repeat visitors.

By segmenting high-value visitors, you will be able to mine their habits in an effort to create more high-value visitors. Look for clues in their referring sources (for example, do they come from a special set of sites?), their product interests (for example, do they browse and buy a certain set of products?), and their recency and frequency of visit (for example, do they visit more frequently than lower value customers?).

Tying It All Together

At the end of the day, visitor segments help you better understand your visitors as distinct groups. By culling customer support visitors out, you'll be able to generate more accurate buyer conversion rates. By removing non-customers from your support segment, you'll be able to better understand the challenges facing your paying customers. By segmenting visitors from a particularly expensive referring source, you'll be able to accurately determine the return for that investment.

While not easy, and often not inexpensive (several vendors charge extra for *ad hoc* visitor segmentation), visitor segmentation is an important component in your advanced web measurement toolset to help you better understand your visitors.

—Akin Arikan and Eric T. Peterson

HACK #49   Measure Conversion Through Multiple Goals

A particularly advanced use of your web measurement application is tracking visitors as they convert on multiple goals through your site. While easy to say, it can be much harder to do successfully unless you're careful in how you set up your conversion tracking.

Web sites have at least a primary goal: retail web sites sell products, financial services sites take applications for financial services, and travel sites allow the purchase and reservation of travel services. However, most sites have other primary or secondary goals. For instance, a site may enable its users to sign up for a newsletter, submit a customer service request, change a travel reservation, check an account balance, sign up for a loyalty program, request a government service, participate in a survey, sign up for a sweepstakes, download software, or read content that your company has published. In web measurement, each of these goals, when accomplished by a visitor to your site, is generally referred to as a value event.

How to Measure Conversion Through Multiple Goals

There are a number of important steps you must take to calculate conversion rates for the multiple goals of your site.

Understand the capabilities of your web measurement application. Some web analytics products and services require that all value events be designated in advance by physically placing a page tag on the page that indicates that such a value event has occurred. Others are able to identify certain requests that they collect as indicators that a value event has occurred; identification of the value event is accomplished "after the fact" and requires no page tagging. It is very important to know which of these capabilities your web analytics product or service employs. It is critical that you instrument all of your site's value events if your web analytics product cannot calculate conversion rates after the fac,t based on any event that occurs in your data.

Clearly identify your value events. Whether you are in the process of building a site or preparing to measure an existing one, it is very important to clearly define your value events. Many value events are identified with a "thank you" page that follows the completion of an event on your site.

For example, you could display a "thank you" page upon completion of a transaction (a "value event"). The request for *http://www.yoursite.com/thankyou.htm* can be defined as an indicator that a value event has occurred to your web analytics product. If a value event is not already clearly designated, it may be worthwhile to add a "thank you" page to your site that loads after a visitor submits an order or completes another type of transaction considered to be a value event.

Clearly delineate multiple value events. If your site has multiple value events, it is necessary to differentiate the site requests or page tag requests used to indicate the occurrence of value events. In this case, you may want to create multiple "thank you" pages, one for each type of value event.

For the first value event, you could display a page after the completion of your transaction called *http://www.yoursite.com/thankyouVE1.htm*. For the second value event, you could display a page after the completion of your transaction called *http://www.yoursite.com/thankyouVE2.htm*. Repeat for each value event in your site.

You could also delineate multiple value events by adding query-string parameters to the URL of the "thank you" page. For the first value event, you could display a "thank you" page after the completion of your transaction called *http://www.yoursite.com/thankyou.htm?valueevent=1*. For the second value event, you could display the same "thank you" page after the completion of your transaction but called *http://www.yoursite.com/thankyou.htm?valueevent=2*.

Decide what information is to be captured at each value event. In many cases, it is important that a value event measurement request carry additional information about the value event, such as the amount of the transaction (for example, price=19.99), the products sold (for example, productid=1967), the money saved (for example, `alternative_cost=7.00`), and/or any other information that your web analytics product might be able to use in analyzing your value events and the amount of value generated by your site.

If you want to capture transactional detail information along with a request indicating that a value event has occurred, you should do so in a way that is supported by your particular web analytics system. Some web analytics systems use a page tagging mechanism for this, while others use a server-side mechanism, such as the `AppendtoLog` method exposed through the response object in Microsoft's ASP or .NET environment. The method that you should use depends on your web analytics system. You should consult your web analytics vendor to select the right method for you.

After you have verified that your site is collecting data that identifies when each value event has occurred, you can begin calculating your conversion rates. Make sure that you define your conversion metrics to be calculated on data collected only after the time for which you have defined the value event in your page tags or in your web analytics system. If you include times in your calculation that start before your value events are measured, then you will skew your conversion rate metrics.

Types of Calculations for Visit Conversion

In general, there are three different types of conversion rate measurement: single event, multiple value events that can occur exclusively (termed *or* conversion events), and multiple value events that must be achieved to count as a conversion event (termed *and* conversion events).

Calculation of conversion to one value event. Your web analytics product probably allows the definition of at least one value event and the calculation of a conversion rate to that value event. If you have only one value event defined in your site, or you want to calculate the conversion rate for just one value event, then conversion rate may be calculated as follows: the count of visits in which value event #1 occurred, divided by the count of visits in that time period.

Calculation of conversion to one or more value events. Your web analytics product may allow for the definition of multiple value events and the calculation of a conversion rate to those value events. If this is the case, it will be important to determine what conversion rates you wish to calculate. The following examples show how conversion would be calculated for two value events though the same basic method may be expanded to cover many value events—for example, the count of visits in which value event #1 *or* value event #2 occurred, divided by the count of visits in that time period.

Figure 3-14 displays a set of value events and visit conversion. Every item on the screen is colored by the visit conversion rate where red is 100 percent conversion and blue is 0 percent conversion. Conversion is defined in this workspace as conversion to any of the value events listed in the table in the upper-left corner of the screen. The 3D map on the right side of the screen displays the visit conversion rate of sessions that visited the site sections displayed on the 3D site map.

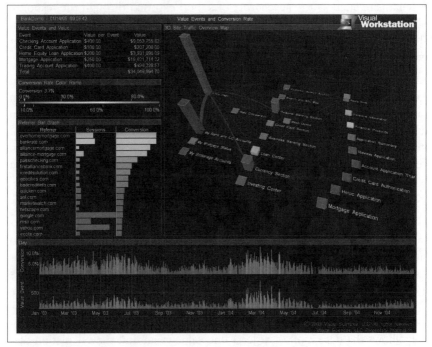

Figure 3-14. Measurement of conversion through multiple goals

Calculation of conversion through more than one value event. If in your site you want to consider conversion to have occurred for a visit only when value event #1 *and* value event #2 have occurred, then calculate conversion as: the count of visits in which value event 1 AND value event 2 occurred divided by the count of visits in that time period.

The same general methods used above may be modified to calculate visitor conversion instead of visit conversion. Depending on the capabilities of your web analytics system, you may also be able to dynamically select which value events to use in a calculation of conversion and calculate differently defined conversion rates on the fly as you do your analysis and set up your reports. Some web measurement systems even allow you to associate an average amount of value for each value event and produce a value metric that you can trend over time. With such systems, you can, for instance, trend conversion-related metrics such as value-per-day or value-by-referrer-by-day or value-by-marketing-campaign-by-week.

—Jim MacIntyre and Eric T. Peterson

HACK #50 Leverage Referring Domains and URLs

Knowing how visitors found you is as or more important than knowing what they do on your web site. Referring URLs are (usually) the source of this type of information.

A site or page's referrer is usually the URL a visitor was browsing when he clicked a link to your web site. Captured via the web server logfile [Hack #22] or reported by a JavaScript page tag [Hack #28], referring URLs are a powerful ally for the online marketer. Without referrers, you have no way to know who is talking about you, what they're saying, or how well your marketing dollars are being spent. While in a perfect world every request would contain a referrer that would help you understand a visitor's intent, the world is far from perfect.

How Referring URLs Are Typically Reported

Nearly all web measurement programs provide a basic top-level referring domains report as well as an option to drill down into the details of each referring URL. Data overload is a common problem when you're thinking about your referrers, and often it's best to simplify your referrers to show only the domain. However, in some cases you'll be forced to analyze the entire referring URL (Figure 3-15).

Figure 3-15. Referring URLs report

Common Problems with Referrers

Since the referrer exists only when a link is constructed from another site to yours, the referrer is one of the most exciting things to a marketer. The first time you see a list of referrers, you'll get very excited to see that people are linking to your site. Still, sometimes referrers get lost or dropped when they should be available for a variety of reasons, including:

- Redirects between the referrer and the landing page can cause problems and inconsistency. Sometimes the original referrer is reported properly, at other times the redirect shows up as the referrer, and occasionally the referrer is lost completely.

- Some browsers have bugs that prevent the referrer from being reported correctly (certain versions of Apple's Safari browser have this problem). At other times anti-spyware or privacy software strips the referrer or forcibly sets the referrer to null.

- When clicks are generated from within an email client such as Outlook, Outlook Express, or Eudora (for example, software-based email clients), there is no available referrer (the click is not coming from a web page). This is complicated by the fact that web-based email clients *do* provide a referring URL (for example, *gmail.com*, *hotmail.com*, or *yahoo.com*).

- Many rich media applications don't pass referring URLs correctly, and some don't pass referring URLs at all

- When a user directly enters the URL of your site directly into the browser or uses a bookmark to visit your site, no referrer is available.

Most often, when things in this list occur, your web measurement application will report a higher number of referrers from "No Referrer" than you expect.

How do you know how many "no referral" visits to expect? An excellent question! In general, the more offline and word-of-mouth advertising you do, the greater your expectation about people coming directly to your web site. Also, if you do a great deal of email marketing, or use of JavaScript-based links or rich media advertising, you may expect the number of "no referrer" visits to be higher (for reasons listed earlier). The converse is also true: if you do little or no email and offline marketing, any visits without referrers should be considered suspect.

Using Referrers to Your Advantage

Most of the value associated with referring URLs is associated with campaign-specific reporting like banner advertising [Hack #40], paid [Hack #42], organic search marketing [Hack #43], and affiliate marketing [Hack #45] for which the referring URL often contains the reference to the campaigns being examined. Still, the beauty of the Internet is that anyone can link to your site and you never really know how valuable referred visitors are until you can identify them and watch their interaction with your site.

The essence of leveraging your referring URLs is looking for referrers you *aren't expecting*. Use a "what's changed" report (Figure 3-16), get in the habit of looking for sites that have not previously sent you traffic, and work to determine why traffic volumes increase. Build a "top movers" or "top referrers" into your regular key performance indicator reports, and integrate an examination of your referring domains into your regular web measurement program. Who knows how the information you find will change your online business?

What's Changed Report

Comparing Mar 27 - Apr 2 with Apr 3 - Apr 9   Change dates

Referrers

Rising ⇧		Was	Now	Falling ⇩		Was	Now
Ask Jeeves		3	80	Google		705	700
www.figleaf.com		3	47	www.persimmonnews.com		205	183
www.fruitsuggestions.com		22	72				

Figure 3-16. "What's changed" report

Finally, since you always want to keep your business objectives squarely in mind when examining referrers, make sure that you're tying referrers to conversion goals whenever possible. Put another way, knowing who is sending you traffic is valuable, but knowing who is sending you customers is *invaluable*.

—*John Marshall and Eric T. Peterson*

HACK #51 Calculate Click-to-Visit Drop-off

Some advertising systems may report far more clicks than ever reach your web site, a frustrating proposition for anyone paying for clicks. Learn where those clicks might be going and how to bring them back.

A common challenge in Internet marketing is reconciling differences in reported numbers from system to system. This becomes especially obvious when you're trying to compare a system that measures "clicks"—such as Google and Overture—with a system that is designed to measure "responses." The essence of the problem is that Google will report that you had 1,000 clicks during a month, while your web measurement system reports only 750 paid visits from Google. The question then becomes "Where did they other 250 clicks go?"

If you're unable to find these clicks in the pay-per-click model, then you have to absorb the loss as a cost of doing business. Using the Google example where you lose 250 clicks, to calculate the true cost-per-click for the campaign, you need to add 25 percent to the cost of every click to absorb the missing traffic. Most marketers agree that click-based advertising is expensive enough already, and with keyword costs projected to increase by over 30 percent by 2009, wouldn't it be nice to figure out where those clicks are going?

Needless to say, there are a number of problems associated with counting clicks on the Internet, well beyond the scope of this hack (or even this book). To keep things practical and actionable, let's walk through the steps you should follow to determine if your tracking strategy is working properly and go over some possible causes for the loss.

Make Sure Your Measurement Strategy Is Working

The first step in determining where the clicks went is validating that your measurement and tracking strategy is working properly. We'll use Google AdWords as an example because it is so popular and easy to set up.

To ensure your measurement strategy is working properly, follow these steps:

1. Since every incoming advertisement should have its own unique tracking URL [Hack #42], create a URL like *test_page.html* that you can reference with a campaign ID (for example, *test_page.html?campaignid=114*). No other link should use this URL and campaign ID to ensure that the clicks from this test can be tracked in isolation.

2. Test the landing page to make sure it is tracking correctly by clicking on the link you created in step one. Does it record the page view, visit, and visitor properly? Check for JavaScript errors when the page renders, and make sure that the click is shown in your web measurement application. Because some applications process data in "real time" and others depend on batch processing, you may need to rerun your reports to make sure the click was reported. If your system depends on being rerun, follow these steps on a test server to cut down on processing time.

3. Test the same landing page again within 30 minutes. This may seem strange, but you want to ensure that your system records another click on that URL, but not another visit or visitor. If you don't see the second page view, there may be some sort of click defeating system so that if the same person clicks on a URL in a given time, they are not counted

twice—make note of this! It is not uncommon for marketing applications like Google to code rules that prevent fraudulent clicks from being recorded. If you have any questions about how the marketing application you're exploring treats successive clicks from the same visitor, ask!

4. Create an ad in Google using this test URL, search for the appropriate keyword or phrase, and click the advertisement when it is displayed by AdWords. Check to see if your click was recorded by your web measurement system, as evidenced by both a page view and a respondent to the campaign ID. If you don't see the click and response, clear your browser cookies and browser cache, restart your browser application, and click one more time.

 Sometimes cookies or the browser cache get in the way of tests like this. Plan on clearing your cookies and browser cache frequently.

At this point, you should ideally see three page views—one visit, one visitor associated with your *test_page.html* page, and one respondent to your test campaign ID. There may be more visits and visitors, depending on whether or not you had to clear your cookies and your specific system, but you should have three page views, letting you know that the system was getting the information.

Assuming you've set this all up properly, you're ready to deploy your pay-per-click tracking in the real world. However, the real world is not an elegant four-step test; the real world is an ugly place where clicks get lost for a variety of reasons.

The System Is Working, So Where Did the Clicks Go?

Once you deploy your campaign tracking and start getting clicks, if it still appears that you're still missing visits, based on the number of clicks reported, you'll need to take a long, hard look at your site and see if the problem is on your end. Here are a handful of questions you should ask yourself to further diagnose the problem.

Is your landing page a bandwidth hog? When you clicked your advertisement, were you able to make a steaming cup of espresso before your page fully loaded? Just because you have a broadband connection doesn't mean that everyone clicking to your site does. Some of these "missing" visits may simply be a result of users bailing out before your tracking system is able to measure them. Many industry analysts believe this to be the number-one source of loss in click-to-visit drop-off.

Especially when your visitors are coming from the search engines—web applications that spend millions of dollars to optimize their sites and information delivery—people develop an expectation for how quickly a page should load. If a user is happily and quickly searching along before she finds your link, but when she clicks your link she gets put on perpetual hold while your 127-KB home page loads, this click and many like it may back up before it's measured as a "visit."

A good site for checking your web page size is WebSiteOptimization.com (*www.websiteoptimization.com/services/analyze*, Figure 3-17). The service will tell you the total size in bytes of your landing page, along with number of objects, HTTP requests, and basic recommendations for making your site faster. You may also want to read *Web Performance Tuning* (O'Reilly) for more insight into how to optimize your web site architecture or leverage your web and performance measurement applications to create a unified view of your site's response [Hack #68].

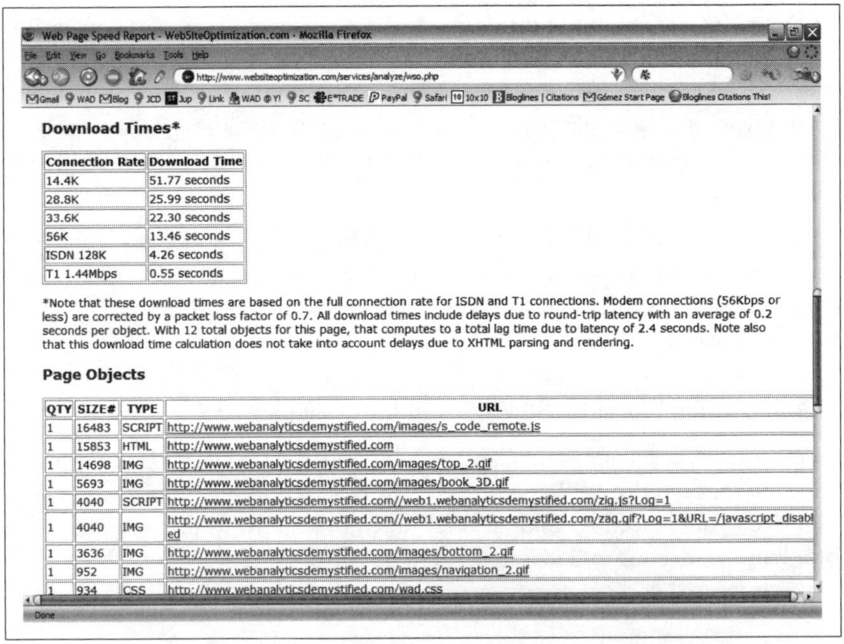
Web Page Speed Report - WebSiteOptimization.com - Mozilla Firefox

http://www.websiteoptimization.com/services/analyze/wso.php

Download Times*

Connection Rate	Download Time
14.4K	51.77 seconds
28.8K	25.99 seconds
33.6K	22.30 seconds
56K	13.46 seconds
ISDN 128K	4.26 seconds
T1 1.44Mbps	0.55 seconds

*Note that these download times are based on the full connection rate for ISDN and T1 connections. Modem connections (56Kbps or less) are corrected by a packet loss factor of 0.7. All download times include delays due to round-trip latency with an average of 0.2 seconds per object. With 12 total objects for this page, that computes to a total lag time due to latency of 2.4 seconds. Note also that this download time calculation does not take into account delays due to XHTML parsing and rendering.

Page Objects

QTY	SIZE#	TYPE	URL
1	16483	SCRIPT	http://www.webanalyticsdemystified.com/images/s_code_remote.js
1	15853	HTML	http://www.webanalyticsdemystified.com
1	14698	IMG	http://www.webanalyticsdemystified.com/images/top_2.gif
1	5693	IMG	http://www.webanalyticsdemystified.com/images/book_3D.gif
1	4040	SCRIPT	http://www.webanalyticsdemystified.com//web1.webanalyticsdemystified.com/zig.js?Log=1
1	4040	IMG	http://www.webanalyticsdemystified.com//web1.webanalyticsdemystified.com/zag.gif?Log=1&URL=/javascript_disabled
1	3636	IMG	http://www.webanalyticsdemystified.com/images/bottom_2.gif
1	952	IMG	http://www.webanalyticsdemystified.com/images/navigation_2.gif
1	934	CSS	http://www.webanalyticsdemystified.com/wad.css

Done

Figure 3-17. Report from WebSiteOptimization.com.

Is your tracking code in the optimal location (for tag-based solutions)? Even if your landing page isn't a true bandwidth hog, you might be missing visits from the clicks you're paying for because the visitor has moved on before your page tag can be executed [Hack #14]. If you currently have your tags deployed at the *bottom* of your web pages, move the script to the *top* and see if that reduces the percentage-wise loss. If it does help, perhaps your visitors are very fast readers and some are making it through without being counted (but there is nothing you can do about that).

Is your tracking code still deployed properly (tag-based solutions)? Sometimes changes get made to sites that affect the data collection capabilities, and measurement can get lost in the shuffle. Always verify that visits are being tracked on your landing page correctly. We recommend setting up a monthly reminder to audit your response tracking code. This will save you many headaches in the long run, especially with web sites in which many people are working on the code.

Are you tracking page views, visits, or visitors? If your web measurement solution reports on the number of page views, visits, and visitors from a referring URL or campaign, you are in luck. Clicks are page view analogs—one click at Google should result in one page view in your system, every time, in a perfect world. However, you want clicks to be a visit analogy—in which one click results in one visit to your web site—because if someone has to click two or three times to visit your site, you are paying extra for that visit—something you don't want to do!

Make sure you understand what both systems are reporting to you. Most pay-per-click systems are reporting exactly that, *clicks*; discrepancies are introduced at the measurement end. Call or write your measurement application vendor and ask them what the system is reporting, especially if the system refers to what it reports as "responses," a term that may be interpreted differently by different vendors.

Because the Internet and HTTP are not perfect, clicks will inevitably become lost. The best guidance is to work to minimize the number of lost clicks and, if large discrepancies continue, consider spending your hard-earned advertising dollars elsewhere.

—*Dylan Lewis and Eric T. Peterson*

HACK #52 Create Visitor Loyalty Segments

Merely watching your percentage of returning visitors rise and fall is not enough to understand visitor loyalty. You need to segment your visitors in profitable ways to truly understand and identify opportunity.

Converting more visitors into customers is absolutely essential to any successful business effort, but then what? You probably already know the answer: it's time to think about whether these customers will visit or purchase again. If they don't visit or purchase again, then your efforts to attract and convert them in the first place could be money losers.

Your particular web site may not need to create repeat visitor and customer behavior, but most web sites do. Customers who come back over and over generally have the highest value, and this value translates into profits for your business. Most web customer databases have from 80 percent to 90 percent one-time buyers or visitors. For an offline comparison, you could look to the catalog or TV shopping companies, where the one-time buyer rate is 40 to 50 percent. Why are web sites so ineffective at creating repeat visitors and buyers? Asked another way: why is the average value of a web customer so low when compared to offline customers?

Notice I said "average value." Some web visitors are, in fact, worth a lot. But there are so many that are worth very little that the average value of a visitor is quite low—that is, for most companies. Other companies seem to create visitors of much higher average value. For example, the online exotic pet store that generates $3.50 in sales per visit and has an 85 percent repeat buyer rate. Or the online specialty jewelry store that generates $25 in profits for every $1 spent on advertising. Or the content site with 5 million unique visitors, 90 percent of whom have visited at least once in the past 10 days. How do they do it? They understand the metrics of customer loyalty and value—the art and science also known as customer retention marketing—and apply these metrics every day in their analytics to drive higher marketing ROI. And they constantly test new ideas and measure the results based on the long-term value of their customers.

In short, they analyze visitor and customer behavior not just in the present, but also over time. And they use specialized time-based metrics to predict what visitors and customers will do in the future.

Use Visitor Segmentation to Measure Visitor Loyalty

You are probably already familiar with the simplest definition of web visitor retention—the repeat visit. A visitor who comes back to the site again and again is a generally good thing, especially if you bought ads to encourage the first visit. But are you using the real power behind this metric to drive increased profitability? Let's find out and, at the same time, learn how visitor segmentation [Hack #48] can be leveraged to understand visitor loyalty.

Many people track the *overall* percentage of repeat visitors. If this percentage is rising, that's good; if it is falling, that's bad. This metric makes intuitive sense to people and is at least a measure you can hang your hat on. But it's not terribly *actionable*; that is, standing by itself, repeat visit percentage doesn't provide any direction on what you might do to improve it.

To get more specific direction, you really need to segment your visitors to the repeat behavior of customers sharing some characteristic that allows you to make judgments about the value of the different customer groups and take some kind of marketing or design action based on this judgment. When you group visitors or customers by a common characteristic, any behaviors they share—like tendency to repeat visits—become amplified. By comparing your metrics across different visitor segments, you can more easily spot differences or trends and take action on them.

Profitable Loyalty Segmentation Strategies

How should you divide up or segment your traffic to analyze the percentage of visitors repeating? There are hundreds of ways to segment provided in most web measurement applications, and here's the hack: only five of them really affect the long-term behavior of visitors in a way that can make you more money.

By media source of the visitor. Segment based on search engines versus banner ads, or compare the repeat rate of visitors generated by different banner ads or keyword phrases. There can be huge differences in visitor behavior by source. Those of you already involved in pay-per-click marketing know what I'm talking about here, and the good news is if you are tracking source for your short-term conversions, you're already tracking what you need for longer-term loyalty and value metrics. Visitor source is the king of segmentation characteristics, and action taken in this area leads directly to bottom-line improvements.

By the "offer" you make to the visitor. For commerce sites, offer is pretty self-explanatory. For other types of sites, think about what you do to encourage visitors to do what you want them to do. This is your "offer." Whether it is a software download, white paper, game or interactive device, product sample, communications options, or newsletter, your "offer" has a significant effect on the retention of visitors. Test new offers regularly.

By the advertising copy you use. Ad copy is often closely tied to the issues in offer above. You can make the same offer in several different ways, and the way an offer is made will define the quality of the visitor segment it attracts.

By content area. Ask yourself, which areas of your site create the highest repeat visit percentage, and which create the lowest repeat visit percentage? Compare high and low scoring content areas to understand what might be causing the difference in repeat rate. Is it the content itself? The navigation? If you make a design change to a section of the site and the percentage of repeat visits drops, you should probably reconsider the changes.

If your web site is in the self-service category, you may have to look at this measurement in reverse—that is, there may be parts of your site where you would like to see repeat visit percentage *decrease*. For lead generation sites, it might go either way. For a long sales cycle or high-ticket product, repeats may be good because this behavior demonstrates ongoing interest. For a short sales cycle or low-ticket product, one might wonder why it takes repeat visits to convert the visitor and strive for decreasing repeat visits. For branding sites, repeats demonstrate loyalty and ongoing brand involvement, so high repeat rates would be desirable overall.

By category or item of purchase. Loyalty segmentation based on category of item purchased should be further segmented into first-time and repeat buyer segments. This will tell you which products are most profitable in the long term to feature or promote to new and current customers. It's not as important to understand *why* certain products generate repeat behavior. Simply understanding *which* products generate repeat behavior is a very powerful tool. As you can see in Figure 3-18, a typical report for understanding visitor loyalty segments for online retailers, this strategy can be used to examine relevant commerce metrics by "New Buyers" and "Repeat Buyers."

The power of this type of segmentation, however, really lies in being able to see differences in metrics, such as the average revenue per order for televisions: $1,475.56 for new buyers and only $524.95 for repeat buyers. Data like this should have you asking "What is it about new buyers that makes their television purchases so profitable?" and "How can we replicate this behavior throughout other product categories?" If you aren't segmenting loyal visitors, you won't have access to this type of data and will always be forced to deal with averages.

Bottom line, there really is no such thing as an "average visitor." By segmenting your visitors, you will begin to uncover powerful differences in their behavior, and taking action on this knowledge will lead you down the road to increased profitability.

—Jim Novo and Eric T. Peterson

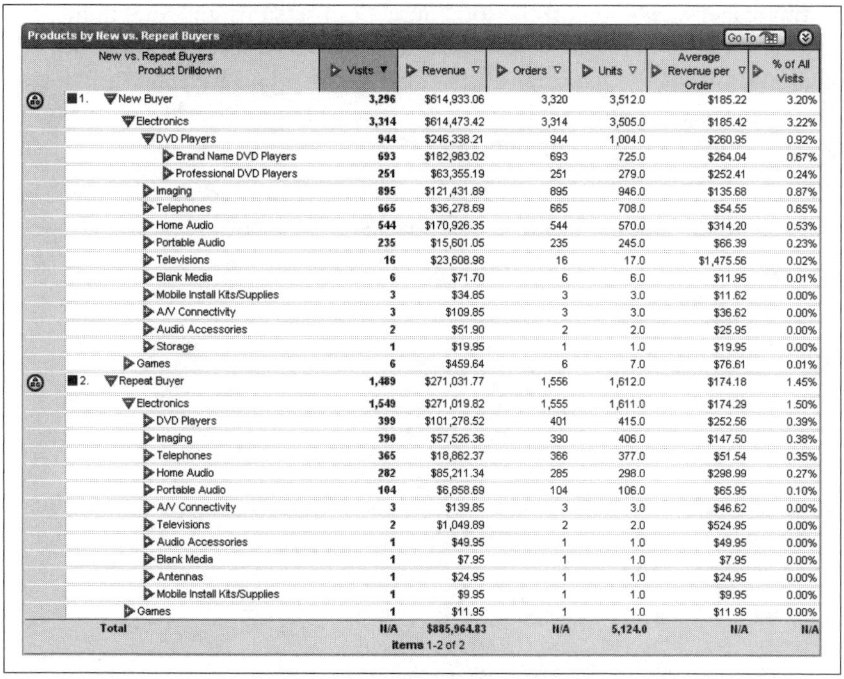

Products by New vs. Repeat Buyers

New vs. Repeat Buyers Product Drilldown	Visits	Revenue	Orders	Units	Average Revenue per Order	% of All Visits
1. New Buyer	**3,296**	$614,933.06	3,320	3,512.0	$185.22	3.20%
Electronics	**3,314**	$614,473.42	3,314	3,505.0	$185.42	3.22%
DVD Players	**944**	$246,338.21	944	1,004.0	$260.95	0.92%
Brand Name DVD Players	**693**	$182,983.02	693	725.0	$264.04	0.67%
Professional DVD Players	**251**	$63,355.19	251	279.0	$252.41	0.24%
Imaging	**895**	$121,431.89	895	946.0	$135.68	0.87%
Telephones	**665**	$36,278.69	665	708.0	$54.55	0.65%
Home Audio	**544**	$170,926.35	544	570.0	$314.20	0.53%
Portable Audio	**235**	$15,601.05	235	245.0	$66.39	0.23%
Televisions	**16**	$23,608.98	16	17.0	$1,475.56	0.02%
Blank Media	**6**	$71.70	6	6.0	$11.95	0.01%
Mobile Install Kits/Supplies	**3**	$34.85	3	3.0	$11.62	0.00%
A/V Connectivity	**3**	$109.85	3	3.0	$36.62	0.00%
Audio Accessories	**2**	$51.90	2	2.0	$25.95	0.00%
Storage	**1**	$19.95	1	1.0	$19.95	0.00%
Games	**6**	$459.64	6	7.0	$76.61	0.01%
2. Repeat Buyer	**1,489**	$271,031.77	1,556	1,612.0	$174.18	1.45%
Electronics	**1,549**	$271,019.82	1,555	1,611.0	$174.29	1.50%
DVD Players	**399**	$101,278.52	401	415.0	$252.56	0.39%
Imaging	**390**	$57,526.36	390	406.0	$147.50	0.38%
Telephones	**365**	$18,862.37	366	377.0	$51.54	0.35%
Home Audio	**282**	$85,211.34	285	298.0	$298.99	0.27%
Portable Audio	**104**	$6,858.69	104	106.0	$65.95	0.10%
A/V Connectivity	**3**	$139.85	3	3.0	$46.62	0.00%
Televisions	**2**	$1,049.89	2	2.0	$524.95	0.00%
Audio Accessories	**1**	$49.95	1	1.0	$49.95	0.00%
Blank Media	**1**	$7.95	1	1.0	$7.95	0.00%
Antennas	**1**	$24.95	1	1.0	$24.95	0.00%
Mobile Install Kits/Supplies	**1**	$9.95	1	1.0	$9.95	0.00%
Games	**1**	$11.95	1	1.0	$11.95	0.00%
Total	**N/A**	**$885,964.83**	**N/A**	**5,124.0**	**N/A**	**N/A**

items 1-2 of 2

Figure 3-18. Purchase categories segmented by visitor loyalty

HACK #53

Build Your Own Web Measurement Application: Marketing Data

At this point, we're sure you're itching to generate some real, useful data with your "build your own" application. In this hack, we attack common marketing measurements, including number of visits, page views per visit, referrers, search terms, and entry pages.

In this hack, we shall continue writing our miniature web analytics program. In [Hack #12], we parsed a logfile and collated the individual lines into visitor sessions. Now we shall report some actual results.

The Code

Previously, we used a class called `Data` to hold the statistics, but we didn't define that class. It's time to do that now. Save this code into a file called *Data.pm*.

```
package Data;
use strict;
The number of items to list in each report
my $top_n = 100;
```

At this stage, we will report the total number of sessions, the total number of requests, the list of referrers [Hack #1], and the list of search terms [Hack #43]. We shall also report the list of entry pages; assuming you have set up your ad campaigns to have different entry pages [Hack #58], this also tells you the number of visits from each campaign.

This constructor initializes all the variables we will need at this stage. We will add more variables in subsequent hacks.

```perl
sub new {
  return bless {
    total_sessions => 0,
    total_requests => 0,
    referrers => {},
    search_terms => {},
    entry_pages => {},
  };
}
# Just before deleting an old session, add its data to the totals.
sub AddSession {
  my ($self, $sess) = @_;
  ++$self->{total_sessions};
  my $reqs = $sess->NumRequests();
  $self->{total_requests} += $reqs;
  my $referrer = $sess->Referrer();
  ++$self->{referrers}->{$referrer} if ($referrer);
  my $search_term = $sess->SearchTerm();
  ++$self->{search_terms}->{$search_term} if ($search_term);
  ++$self->{entry_pages}->{$sess->EntryPage()};
}
```

The rest of the functions just output the data in a very simple (and not very beautiful) format.

```perl
sub WriteReport {
  my $self = shift;
  $self->WriteSummary();
  $self->WriteHash('Referrers', 'referrers');
  $self->WriteHash('Search Terms', 'search_terms');
  $self->WriteHash('Entry Pages', 'entry_pages');
}
# Write a report title, underlined.
sub ReportTitle {
  my ($self, $title) = @_;
  print "\n$title\n";
  print "-" for 1..(length $title);
  print "\n";
}
```

```
# Write the summary statistics.
sub WriteSummary {
  my $self = shift;
  $self->ReportTitle('Summary Statistics');
  printf "Total sessions: %d\n", $self->{total_sessions};
  printf "Total pages: %d\n", $self->{total_requests};
  printf "Pages per session: %.1f\n",
    $self->{total_sessions} == 0 ? 0:
    $self->{total_requests} / $self->{total_sessions};
}
# Sort and write one of the hash tables. This function will output a hash
table in this format:
#        13: web analytics demystified
#         5: web analytics
#         2: web analytics reviews
#         2: analytics demystified
sub WriteHash {
  my ($self, $report_name, $hashname) = @_;
  $self->ReportTitle($report_name);

# Sort the items in order of frequency, and print in columns.

  my $hashref = $self->{$hashname};
  my $n = scalar keys %$hashref;
  if ($top_n < $n) { $n = $top_n; }
  for ((sort {$hashref->{$b} <=> $hashref->{$a}} keys %$hashref)[0..$n-1]) {
    printf "%9s: %s\n", $hashref->{$_}, $_;
  }
}
```

Next, we need to enhance the Session (*Session.pm*) class we previously defined to report some statistics about the session.

```
# The number of requests the session contains is the length of the array of
requests.
package Session;
...
sub NumRequests {
  my $self = shift;
  return scalar @$self;
}
# The entry page and the referrer for the session are the URL and referrer
of the first request.
sub EntryPage {
  my $self = shift;
  return $self->[0]->{file};
}
sub Referrer {
  my $self = shift;
  return $self->[0]->{referrer};
}
```

The search term is more complicated. We need to extract the relevant part of the referrer. For this, we need a list of all the search engines and which parameters they use for the search term.

```perl
my %search_engines =
    (a9 => 'q', altavista => 'q', aol => 'query', ask => 'q',
     dmoz => 'search', google => 'q', kanoodle => 'query',
     msn => 'q', teoma => 'q', yahoo => 'p');
sub SearchTerm {
  my $self = shift;
  my $referrer = $self->[0]->{referrer};
  if (!$referrer) { return undef; }
# Check the search engines one by one.
# Is the referrer in the correct format?
# If so, return the found search term.
# If we fail to find a search term, return undef.
  keys %search_engines;  # resets the iterator for the following "each"
  while (my ($engine, $param) = each %search_engines) {
    if ($referrer =~
    m!^http://        # starts with http://
    (?:[\w\.]+\.)?    # e.g. "www." or "search." or ""
    $engine\.         # e.g. "google."
    .*\?              # the URL stem followed by "?"
    (?:.*&)?          # possibly some arguments ending in ampersand
    $param=([^&]*)!x) # the parameter=value we are looking for
    {
      return $1;
    }
  }
    return undef;
}
# Finally, the main program calls Sessions::WriteReport().
# We need to make that function devolve to Data::WriteReport().
package Sessions;
...
sub WriteReport {
  my $self = shift;
  $self->{DATA}->WriteReport();
}
```

Running the Code

To run the program, you will need Perl installed on your computer. If you are using Unix or Linux, you almost certainly have Perl already, but if you are using Windows, you may not. You can download ActiveState's Perl for Windows from *http://www.activestate.com/Products/ActivePerl*.

All that remains now is to tell *readlog.pl* where the *page.log* file—generated by the *readtag.pl* program and your JavaScript page tag [Hack #12]—is located, and the rest is automatic!

From the command line, assuming that *page.log* is in the same directory as *readlog.pl*, all you need to do is type:

```
perl readlog.pl page.log
```

Figure 3-19 has sample output showing summary statistics and the number of visits coming to your site from each measured referring URL [Hack #1].

Figure 3-19. Output from readlog.pl

The program is now self-contained, and can run and produce data. In subsequent hacks, we will add additional data collection and more reports to further increase the functionality of the basic system.

—Dr. Stephen Turner and Eric T. Peterson

## CHAPTER FOUR

Measuring Web Site Usability
Hacks 54–67

According to the Wikipedia, usability testing is "a means for measuring how well people can actually use something (such as a web page, a computer interface, a document, or a device) for its intended purpose." Testing generally measures how well a small group of subjects, recruited especially for the test, respond to four areas: time on task, accuracy, recall, and emotional response. Although web site measurement is not usability testing, it can often provide a great proxy for usability tests, allowing you to run simple usability tests on an ongoing basis over a much larger audience.

The essence of usability testing is to provide subjects a specific goal, watch them perform the task, and take notes along the way. One of the most powerful things you can do with usability tests is to gather developers and executives together (perhaps not at the same time) behind one-way glass and have them watch the test subjects in action. Regardless of your position in an organization, watching normal folks struggle with your beautiful creation can be heartbreaking.

Popularized by figures like Jakob Nielsen, Bruce Tognazzini, and Jared Spool, usability testing is a "must do" for any company building a new web site or web-based application. The problem with true usability testing is that it can be expensive and time consuming. Enter the relationship between usability testing and web measurement.

Because of the ongoing costs of true usability testing, most companies leverage their investment in web measurement applications in tandem with the continuous improvement process to run simple usability tests on very large audiences. Especially when run in conjunction with split-path testing, the measurement of multi-step processes, and the use of visitor segmentation to examine the behavior and success of different groups of visitors, exploring the usability of specific processes online can be very informative.

The biggest problem with using your web measurement tools to conduct faux usability tests is the inability to accurately determine the intent of the visitor. Without knowing intent, you can never really be sure if visitors are failing to complete a process because they are struggling or because they had no intention of completing the process in the first place. Especially in the shopping cart and checkout process so common in online retailing, often visitors are only exploring, daydreaming, or wishing as they add and remove products from the shopping cart or begin the checkout process. The fact that they never complete the process holds conversion rates down, but unless you know intent, it is impossible to cull those visitors out of the calculation.

Still, given that you probably already have a web measurement application that does some or all of the things described in this chapter, hopefully these hacks will give you a big push in the right direction.

HACK #54 Measure the Value of Pages and Clicks

Assigning value to your web pages and links will help you determine critical visitor paths to success.

When it comes to web page design, there are no shortages of opinions about what is best for your visitors. It's easily to slip into the "what works for me will work for everyone" mentality. Fortunately, web measurement helps remove this subjectivity with hard data on where your visitors click, where they do not, and the value of your web pages.

Measuring the Value of Clicks

Determining the value of a "click" on any link on your web site is a very powerful technique for examining the overall usability of your web site. While link tracking can be fairly cumbersome and difficult to implement [Hack #55], top vendors are now deploying applications that literally lay relevant data right on top of your web pages.

Link tracking. If your web site is like most, your home page probably contains multiple links to the same page. Perhaps one is a graphic image, while another is text in the global navigation bar. Which works better at driving traffic to the destination page? To answer this question, web measurement vendors first provided something called *link tracking* or *custom links*. To enable this feature, you would need to add an onClick JavaScript call to every link you want to track. You must also include unique names for each link so you can differentiate them by location and page in your reports. While this approach provides valuable insight, it obviously does not scale well and has recently given way to a newer technique called the *browser overlay*.

Browser overlays. Browser overlays [Hack #62] have quickly emerged as one of the most visible web measurement features in the marketplace. The overlay is a graphical representation of where visitors click on your web site. The data itself is superimposed over any page on your site. Links on the page are highlighted with color gradients: the greater the intensity of the color, the more frequently the link is clicked on.

Measuring the Value of Pages

While the use of link tracking and browser overlays has definitely increased the breadth of adoption of web measurement tools inside organizations, most data analysts consider link-level data too granular. Two more practical approaches to evaluating and assigning value to pages on your site are the page allocation and page participation models.

Page allocation. Page allocation attributes value to every page that a customer touches in a visit. For example, if a visitor sees 20 pages before purchasing a $100 product, the page allocation method would assign $5 to each of these pages ($100/20 pages = $5 per page). If you operate a lead generation web site, and a visitor sees 10 pages before submitting a lead, each page would receive credit for 1/10th of a lead. Again, the value is allocated across every page in a successful session.

In a practical sense, you can use page allocation to understand which pages contribute most to the success of your business (Figure 4-1). Similarly, you can eliminate pages that are least influential and help reduce your web site maintenance and resource burden. If you are running tests of different page flows, you can quickly assess which are most successful—a hack that doesn't require the implementation steps associated with custom variables and split-path testing.

Finally a word of advice: if your web site is not directly revenue focused, be sure to confirm that your vendor can support allocation to non-revenue events (such as page views, registrations, or leads).

Page participation. Page participation takes a slightly different approach. Full credit is given to every page the user touches in the success process. For example, if you touch 20 pages and purchase a $100 product, each page will receive $100 revenue credit. If you are lead-generation focused, and an individual traverses 10 pages to submit a lead, each of those pages will receive credit for one full lead.

Intuitively, this probably strikes you as odd, and possibly even wrong. You're counting one success event multiple times so if you total them, you'll get exponentially greater revenue or successes than actually occurred. How can this be helpful?

Details					
Page	Visits		Revenue Participation		Page Conversion
1. Home Page	68,840	63.9%	67.6% ($1,147,673)		0.31%
2. Buy Process - Shipping Information	11,692	10.8%	80.1% ($1,360,359)		1.87%
3. Popup Promotion Page	4,135	3.8%	2.6% ($43,322)		0.11%
4. Return Policy	3,415	3.2%	2.8% ($47,870)		0.16%
5. Buy Process - Order Confirmation	2,932	2.7%	100.0% ($1,697,401)		9.56%
6. Halo by Microsoft	1,163	1.1%	2.1% ($35,514)		0.47%
7. Shipping Policy	886	0.8%	10.3% ($174,377)		2.82%
8. Buy Process - Receipt	154	0.1%	6.3% ($106,969)		9.72%
Total	107,794	100.0%	$1,697,412		n/a

Report Generated by SiteCatalyst using Report Accelerator at 01:41 AM WET, 1 Jan 2005

Add Your Notes
Add your notes to help explain this report or how your organization uses the information.

Quick Help
This report lists all of the pages of your web site that are being tracked by SiteCatalyst, and tells you which pages are being visited the most.

Use this report to:
- Identify important pages that are getting missed, so you can highlight them more prominently.
- Measure page views to promotional, sign up, or order pages for marketing effectiveness.
- Monitor all traffic to all pages in one easy-to-read report.
- Learn which pages/products your visitors are most interested in.

SiteCatalyst
© 1997-2004 by Omniture, Inc. Patents Pending.

Omniture Headquarters:
550 East Timpanogos Circle
Orem, Utah 84097
801.722.7000 Tel

Omniture Client Services
877.722.7088 [toll-free]
801.722.7088 [direct]
SiteCatalyst Support
Omniture Privacy Policy

Figure 4-1. Page valuation and conversion report

By taking an additive approach to page valuation, the page participation model allows you to easily determine which of your web pages should be most closely protected or scrutinized. Use this strategy in tandem with the relative page allocation model, and you're able to paint a fairly complete picture of your site's most valuable pages.

Tying It All Together

Most companies that are successful with browser overlays integrate them into regular weekly meetings, encouraging managers to explore usage patterns within their sections of the site. It turns out that this visual presentation dramatically increases people's ability to relate to web measurement data, motivating them to make improvements that will be observed in subsequent meetings.

Organizations successfully using page allocation and page participation models have integrated these measurement techniques into their ongoing data analysis and key performance indicators. By carefully monitoring for pages that "shift rank" in allocation and participation reports, analysts can determine changes in visitor browsing habits as they're occurring, without having to mine extensive clickstream reports.

Despite which approach you take, the most important thing is that you're making data-driven decisions. Web measurement can significantly contribute to your business success, but only if you use and act on the data. Measuring the value of clicks and pages is an excellent start.

—*Matt Belkin and Eric T. Peterson*

Measuring Clicks the Old-Fashioned Way

HACK #55

If your particular web measurement application doesn't provide you the ability to measure which links your visitors are clicking, use this simple JavaScript hack to track them yourself.

Before browser overlays, many vendors used JavaScript to track clicks on pages. Since the script is not very complicated and is used in other contexts in this book [Hack #13], it is also worth presenting as a standalone hack.

The Code

To track clicks the old-fashioned way, you simply hijack JavaScript's onClick event handler, instructing it to fire off a message to a custom variable [Hack #31] in your measurement application right before the click is processed. The JavaScript for this is pretty straightforward; simply include this JavaScript in any page you want to track clicks on.

```
<script language="JavaScript">
' Use random numbers to ensure that the link doesn't get caught in
' the browser cache
'
rnum = Math.random( ) * 1000000;
rnum = Math.round(rnum);
d=document.location;
r=document.referrer;
i.onload = SetClickTracking;
'
' After the click is processed, pass the click along as usual
'
function ClickTrackRedirect(url){
  window.location.href=url;
}
'
' When a link is clicked, send a new image request to the measurement
application
' NOTE: Your string in the "c.src=" line will differ depending on your
particular
' application.  Consult your vendor for the specific string you'll need to
use
'
function ClickAlert( ){
  c=new Image( );
  c.src="http://www.yourtrackingapplication.com/
    tracking_code.cgi?link_href="+escape(this.href)+"&rn='+rnums;
  c.onload=ClickTrackRedirect(this.href);
}
'
' This function sets up the link array and calls ClickAlert when a link is
clicked
'
```

```
function SetClickTracking( ){
for(i=0;(link=document.links[i]); i++){
  link.onclick=ClickAlert;
};
}
</script>
```

The most important things to note about this code are:

- You need to replace http://www.yourtrackingapplication.com/tracking_code.cgi with the URL you use to identify a page request to your tracking application. Be sure to include any necessary page and account identification to ensure that the click is tracked.

- You need to replace the link_href= with the necessary code to pass a data to a custom variable [Hack #31].

- In most instances, calling this script will increase the page view count for the page at the same time the click is recorded. Consult with your vendor for a workaround to this problem, if necessary

And perhaps most importantly, most modern web measurement applications are able to measure clicks with relatively little setup and will present the results in a more elegant fashion than this code.

—Ian Houston and Eric T. Peterson

HACK #56 Use Language to Drive Action

The use of language on your web site is a critical usability element, one that has a tremendous amount of control over whether or not your visitors are satisfied.

Roy H. Williams once said:

> You study pivotal people and the events of history, searching for a common denominator. You hope to identify the recurrent elements of greatness, the keys to phenomenal success. You search for the secret of miracles. After several hundred hours of reading, you reach an utterly inescapable conclusion: Words are the most powerful force there has ever been.

So if words pack enough muscle to change something insignificant like world history, they are certainly powerful enough to motivate a visitor through your web site.

You have goals for your business. You want customers to come to your site and complete the action you want them to take. You want them to buy, register, or become a lead. You want your visitors to engage with your web site, your marketing, and your brand, and proceed down the path of your sales process.

However, visitors come to a web site with their own goals in mind. They are engaged in their own process—their buying process, regardless of whether the ultimate goal is making a purchase. To be successful in your conversion efforts, you must interweave the "sales" process with the "buying" process: to help the company convert more visitors while assisting those visitors to accomplish their goals.

Know Your Visitors Motivations and Create Scent Trails

Do the research to reveal and learn everything possible about your site's customers and their goals.

- Study the topographics: the competitive environment as a whole and the users behavior within the environment
- Study the psychographics: what do customers do psychologically as part of their buying processes?
- Study demographics: what are the customer's attributes and how do they affect their buying processes?
- Study your site's traffic patterns—specifically keyword referrals

Now you are equipped with the tools needed to use this information to build information scent trails that will lead visitors down the road to conversion.

- Prospect your visitor by using her language.
- Build rapport by keeping copy relevant and addressing her issues.
- Qualify your visitor by leading her down the path she's most interested in.
- Present only the solution she's qualified herself as interested in.
- Close for the action you want her to take only after demonstrating that you understand her problem and have her solution.

Put yourself in the shoes of one of those typical visitors. Can you imagine arriving at your landing page and clicking through your buying process's hyperlinks (which mirror your selling process)? Does every click feel completely relevant and made just for you? If you answered no, why should your visitor feel differently?

Each time visitors click and take an action, they make the decision to take that action. Your job is to motivate and persuade them to take each of those actions as they proceed down our sales process; to convert that click. But, again, the visitor's buying process sometimes gets in the way.

How do we deal with that? One thing you need to recognize is that successful visitors move through the buying process using two types of links.

Use Two Types of Hyperlinks

You must understand Internet linking and these two types of hyperlinks:

Calls to action

The links people are most familiar with, which deal with the sales process.

Points of resolution

The links most sites don't seem to use often enough—those that help visitors in *their* buying process.

Links that move visitors along the sales process are traditionally more linear, moving people forward to a close. Call to action hyperlinks are typically well constructed by using an imperative verb and an implied benefit, such as Buy Now, Add To Cart, Subscribe, and Contact Us.

Point-of-resolution links are often nouns. Imagine a young accountant, David Commonsense, who's fallen in love. He wants to propose marriage to his girlfriend. David is methodical in his decision making: he likes to conduct lots of research and feel confident about any action he takes. David is about to purchase an engagement ring, so he wants to understand everything he can about diamonds. He recognizes he needs to do an information search.

He heads to Google and lands on the "Learn About Diamonds" page of Leo Schachter's web site (Figure 4-2).

Figure 4-2. An informational web site about diamonds

Leo Schachter's goal for David is to run a search for a retailer. David will spend time reading the page and getting an overview about diamonds. He needs all the facts and details. Notice there are quite a few links on the page. Most are points of resolution for David. He may want to dig deeper and learn about the 4 Cs of diamonds, diamond certification, or diamond shapes.

None of these links are actually related to the sales process Leo Schachter wants David to partake in. Yet these links, and the information on the pages, are intended to give David confidence and move him closer to a purchase decision in the buying process.

Many point-of-resolution pages seem circular, linking to one another. If at any time, on any of these pages, David's ready to exit, he'll find carefully worded hyperlinks that bring him to a call-to-action or sales-process page. These links have nothing to do with hierarchy. David is never required to enter point-of-resolution links; they simply allow him to collect the data he needs and desires, while always providing him with an opportunity to convert.

In this way, Leo Schachter is using language to drive action. He's allowing David to traverse a nonlinear path—conducting research, but ensuring at every point that the right call to action is present. The essence of this linguistic strategy, often referred to as persuasion architecture, is careful consideration of how words and links are used to create calls to action and points of resolution.

Put More Effort into Copy

If visitors arrive on your site and don't read what you've written or take a desired action, your marketing and web development dollars are wasted. Your copy can make a big difference. Here is how most copy on the web reads:

> Bath & Body Oils
>
> Pure natural oils blended with essential oil scents. Soothing for all skin types. These oils can be used in the shower or after your shower for all day fresh and supple skin that is softly scented.

Snooze. But check this copy from Philosophy.com

> Amazing Grade Shampoo, Bath & Shower Gel
>
> How you climb up the mountain is just as important as how you get down the mountain. And, so it is with life, which for many of us becomes one gigantic test followed by one gigantic lesson. In the end, it all comes down to one word. Grace. It's how you accept winning and losing, good luck and bad luck, the darkness and the light.
>
> Amazing Grace shampoo, bath, and shower gel is our best-selling, uniquely feminine, moisturizing shower gel for gracious bodies.

Who do you think sells more bath and shower gel?

What Matters to People Matters to Search Engines. Words and hyperlinks matter to people and search engines [Hack #43], and who doesn't want to improve their organic search results? By using language to drive action and by leveraging well-formed hyperlinks and the use of keywords in your content, you can both drive search traffic and delight your visitors!

Here are a few very specific things you can and should do to use language to drive action on your web site:

- Don't use single word or generic *click here* hyperlinks.

- Link specific phrases that matter to your visitors; simply use the search referral keywords they used to get to your site.

- Since keywords can reveal intent of your visitor, they should be used to create scent trails. What is a better hyperlink, "Click Here to Download" or "Get Your Diamond Buying Guide"?

Because search engines are always laboring to deliver the most relevant content to searchers, pages that actually deliver relevant content will always rank well. Pages on the Leo site typically rank well (some rank #1 in Google), because the content on each page is relevant and the internal links are keyword-rich.

—Bryan Eisenberg and Eric T. Peterson

HACK #57   Deconstruct Time Spent on Site

Your measurement of time spent on site and on pages is one you may end up struggling with from time to time. Still, knowing how much time visitors spend browsing information on your site can help you begin to understand some of the most common usability issues all sites face.

It's ironic that the exquisitely exact, to-the-second statistics on time spent on a web site are, in fact, quite soft and anything but exquisite. When you scratch their surface, you usually find them to be a little flawed. Still, it's possible to learn from them, especially if you improve their accuracy, examine page-to-page variations, and establish meaningful comparison points.

The Basic Terms and Concepts

To understand the problems that arise when calculating time spent on site, it's best to start with some descriptions of how these statistics are usually calculated and brief descriptions of commonly observed patterns.

Time spent per page. Time spent per page is obtained by subtracting the time of one page request from the time of the next page request. The variation from page to page is usually marked, and can be tapped for insight into page design and content.

Time spent on site. Time spent on the site is the time of the visit's first request subtracted from the time of the final request during the visit. The length of an "average" visit is remarkably consistent over time, often varying by only a few seconds from month to month, with most variation happening after major site events such as redesigns. The greatest variability in visit time is sometimes between workday browsing and after-work visits. On some retail sites, for example, after-work visits tend to be longer, in terms of numbers of pages as well as time spent per average page.

Visit expiration. After 30 minutes of inactivity during a visit [Hack #1], most web measurement programs consider the visit finished, and the last request before the pause marks the visit termination time. Even if the visitor hasn't left the site and starts clicking again, the new activity will be counted as a new visit (and will baffle us by appearing in referrer reports [Hack #58] as having a referrer from our own site because the new visit's referrer is the last page clicked before the pause).

Sources of Inaccuracy When Calculating Time Spent on Site

The preceding three measurements work fairly well in most instances and appear precise on the surface. Unfortunately, the Internet is far from perfect, and so we commonly see three factors that introduce inaccuracy.

Delays due to download and rendering time. The first source of inaccuracy is simply that the reported viewing time of a page is different from the time the page spends fully displayed on the visitor's screen. This is because an unknown and highly variable component of "read time" is actually the transmission and rendering of the page in the web browser. If your site's visitors tend to use dial-up, for example, the viewing time may represent some viewing time and a lot of waiting time.

To get an idea of page transmission and load time, visit a site such as *www.websiteoptimization.com* to get an estimate of transmission time at various connection speeds, or see the hack in this book on [Hack #69].

Variability in treatment of the final page in a visit. Another source of inaccuracy happens because the view time of the last page of a visit isn't reported at all. This is because, by definition, an exit page has no "next request" to mark the end of its viewing. The last request is, however, included in page count reports. If a web measurement program doesn't account for this missing information, some time statistics can be skewed. As a very simple example, consider a visit with only two page views, reported as a five minute visit measured by the "subtract the first request time from the last request time" method. How long was the "average page view"? Some web analysis programs will report 2.5 minutes (the reported visit length divided by the number of pages requested). But since the last page's view time is completely unknown, the truth is that the first page was viewed for five minutes, and a better estimate of "average page viewing time" would be five minutes.

If you want to know which method your web measurement program uses, do the following:

1. Choose a page that appears high on the exit pages report and jot down four statistics for it: number of times it was an exit page, the number of times it was viewed, its total viewing time in seconds or minutes, and its average viewing time.

2. Divide the total viewing time by the number of times it was viewed, and also divide it (separately) by the number of times it was viewed minus the number of times it was an exit page.

3. Compare the two quotients to the reported average viewing time. If the reported average viewing time resembles the first quotient more than the second, your web measurement program is using the less-accurate calculation method.

The randomness of human behavior. The final big source of inaccuracy is perhaps the most obvious: the reported "viewing time" for a page will sometimes be quite different from the time the typical visitor really spends looking at it. It's inevitable that some visitors leave their browsers open for long periods when they aren't actively engaged with the site. Even a few of these can greatly distort basic viewing time statistics. For example, Figure 4-3 shows how only two very long page view events out of 50 page views can pull the calculated average quite far from the number most of us would call the typical visit length—namely, the tall bar to the left.

One way to get a more accurate idea of a "typical" visit in a skewed distribution is to use a statistic called a *median*, which is calculated differently from the average. The median, despite being the more accurate measurement in this context (see Figure 4-3), is available in a few web measurement packages; consult your vendor to see if median is available to you.

Hacking Time Spent on Site

It would be nice to lop off all really long page times that involve relatively little visitor attention, wouldn't it? It's possible to do it if your measurement program allows you to change the visit expiration time from 30 minutes. Simply decide on the page view time that you want to ignore (for example, eight minutes and up) and change the analysis program's visit expiration time correspondingly. In the resulting report, all page views that are followed by eight-or-more minute periods of inactivity will be treated as final pages of visits, which

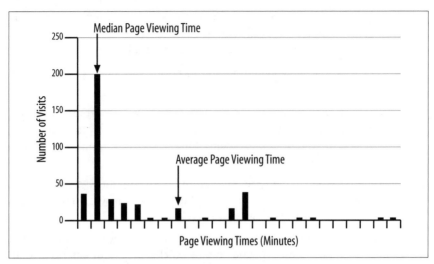

Figure 4-3. *"Time spent on site" report*

means they will not be counted at all in view time calculations. The average viewing time per page will drop dramatically to something more realistic. Expect a decrease of as much as 70 percent for some pages.

 If you try this, it's best to do it as a separate analysis, because an eight-minute timeout can wreak havoc on your other numbers.

Not all vendors support changing the visit expiration time, and keep in mind that if you make this change, *all* of your visit-based calculations will change as well, which can have a dramatic effect on your overall analysis.

Assessing Page View Times

If and when you think you've obtained fairly accurate viewing times for individual pages, you can start learning from them. Here's where the rubber hits the road: answering questions like "What's a 'good' page view time?" If you've been working toward more accurate time estimates, your terrific numbers can suddenly seem mushy and obscure when you start thinking about evaluating them. Short page viewing times may be interpreted as pages where visitors move quickly because the pages are overwhelming, uninteresting, unimportant, or, paradoxically crystal clear and quickly understood. Long viewing times may correspond to difficulty reading or understanding content.

Think about your pages in context. Develop an estimate of a normal viewing time for a particular page. It's actually not too difficult to obtain an approximate ideal viewing time using a bit of your own expertise and bit of systematic evaluation. Just go over the page with fresh eyes, a stopwatch, and a mindset approximating that of a site visitor. Have other people do the same. After you do this three or four times, you should have a pretty good idea of what people are trying to do on that page and how long it should take.

With this simple approach, you can come up with a reasonable minimum and maximum viewing time range that you feel pretty good about. The minimum should roughly correspond to "got just enough information to proceed," and the maximum should correspond to "got most of the information without being slowed down by usability issues." You'll almost certainly be surprised by these objective numbers because most people over- or underestimate page view times. And it's also likely that you'll see more consistency in your stopwatch times from person to person than you expected.

Compare page times to ideal ranges. Of course, the next step is to compare the times in your reports to your quasi-objective ideal ranges for each page. Look for reported times that lurk at the edges of your range or outside it. The greater the number of visits where that page is viewed longer or shorter than your ideal range, the higher the likelihood the page is a problem.

Identify why problems occur. The last step is simply to go back to those pages with the lurking times. Take a close look and do some hard thinking about possible reasons for discrepancies. Did we say last step? We didn't mean that.

As an astute web analyst, you will inevitably want to leverage insights about time spent on site as part of the continuous improvement process [Hack #2]. You may start to think about segmenting your data into first-time and returning visitors because you'd expect repeat visitors to get through pages more quickly. You can watch for longer viewing times when deeper in a site, because you think the commitment is greater. You can find the time of day or night when your visitors have longer page view times and wonder whether your marketing can capitalize on diurnal patterns. You're limited only by the amount of time you have!

—Chris Grant and Eric T. Peterson

Use the Entry, Exit, and Single-Access Page Report

#58
When you boil it down, your ability to understand visitor interaction with individual pages is one of the most important things you'll do with your web measurement application. Knowing where visitors enter and exit your site, and which pages are least engaging, is fundamental to this knowledge.

Depending on your site goals, there are a number of different metrics and reports you will want to review. It is however extremely unlikely that you won't take a close interest in your entry pages, exit pages, and single-access pages. No online marketing program is complete without taking a close look at one or all of these page reports, as the information they provide about leakage, slippage, and stickiness in your site is absolutely invaluable. Fortunately, no matter what web measurement tool you are using, these three reports are part of the standard report set.

Entry Pages

An entry pages report displays the most commonly used pages for entering the site. This is the first page that visitors see when they come to your site. Upon reviewing this report, you may be surprised to learn that 100 percent of your site visitors don't enter the site through the home page. In fact, they may not even see the home page at all during their visit.

There are a number of reasons why people enter the site through pages other than the home page, including:

- Search engine results that point to internal pages
- Campaign landing pages of all types, including offline promotions
- Bookmarks
- URL passing among friends or colleagues or designed viral marketing efforts
- False entries

From this list, the final entry ("false entries") is the one element that should be of concern to Internet marketers and is worth a deeper look. False entries are usually caused by cached pages, missing tracking (for tag-based solutions), and the technical expiration of a visit when the visitor was still engaged.

Page caching. This is a more common problem when analyzing logfiles rather than tracking tags placed on the pages. If a page is not served from the server and you are relying on traditional logfiles, you won't see that first page in the logfiles or web analytics reports. But if the second page is pulled from the web server (not cached), it would look like the second page viewed was the entry page to the site according to your tracking tool. You can avoid this problem by using tracking tags.

Missing page tracking tags. There are unique problems when relying on tracking tags to track visitor behavior if they aren't implemented correctly. Often, new pages are launched without the necessary tracking tags. If a site visitor enters the site on a page that is missing tracking tags, the first page he views that does have the tracking tag will show up as his entry page.

Expiration of visit session. All tracking tools have a time limit when they end a visit session after no behavior. If you leave your a computer in the middle of a visit, your measurement tool will likely consider your visit over after a certain period of inactivity [Hack #1]. When you return and click a link on the site you were on before, it will consider you as starting a new visit and record you as a new entry. That can help explain why sometimes you see entries behind secure portions of the site that require login. Your tracking tool considers it a new visit, while the web site knows you are still logged in.

It is important to understand entries to the site to ensure you are providing the right content and calls to action to the right people based on the top entries. You may also find that people convert on your desired behaviors (sales, leads, etc.) at higher or lower rates, depending on where they enter the site. This can help you identify some of the drivers to those conversion behaviors.

Exit Pages

Exit pages are the last pages people view before they leave the site. The same principles apply to "false exits," which we described above as "false entries." It is important to understand that all visitors to your site ultimately leave your site, and they have to leave from some page. Also, there are good places and poor places for people to exit the site, based on your overall site goals.

It can be misleading to look only at the top few pages listed in the entry and exit page reports. Take a few minutes and compare the top 20 pages viewed on your site and the top 20 exit pages on your site. In many cases, the pages that receive the most traffic also record the highest number of exits. The better way to look at it is to create an exit ratio report—a comparison of page visits to page exits (Figure 4-4).

	A	B	C	D	E
1					
2	◢◤ ZAAZ TOP EXIT PAGE RATIOS				
3			Visits	Exits	Exit Ratio
4	Homepage		1,109,026	716,748	64.63%
5	/employement.asp		8,641	5,359	62.02%
6	/products.asp		24,767	15,206	61.40%
7	/contact.htm		9,142	3,996	43.71%
8	/press.htm		5,091	2,167	42.57%
9	/about.asp		5,089	2,076	40.79%
10	/basket.asp		18,865	7,468	39.59%
11	/checkout.asp		5,799	2,020	34.83%
12	/productdetail_A.asp		859,286	244,993	28.51%
13	/myAccount		5,303	1,447	27.29%
14					

Figure 4-4. Exit page ratio report

You can create this report within Excel as part of your normal key performance indicators [Hack #94] and sort the pages on the site from those with the highest exit ratio to the lowest.

When looking at the exit ratios, it is helpful to break the pages into different categories. The most common categories include:

Home page
> From an exit standpoint, your home page should be considered unique from all other pages on the site. Typically, a home page exit rate of less than 20 percent is desirable, indicating that the majority of visitors are clicking deeper into the site.

> Be aware that many sites that offer private login sections drop people to the home page when they select "log out," driving up the home page exit rate significantly.

Destination pages
> These content pages provide the information that users seek.

Transition pages
> The only purpose of these pages is to provide options for people who are looking for deeper content on the site. Consider a banking site that has a main product page that lists all the products—it does not really provide any information, but it helps direct people to the specific product pages.

Within each of these, we are looking for:

Natural exit pages
> This is where we expect people to leave. It may be the confirmation page of a shopping cart or the page with a completed lead conversion form.

"Unnatural" exit pages
> These are key conversion or transitional pages where you don't want to lose visitors.

Look through the important conversion pages recording high exit ratios and for pages that influence the most site visitors. Focus on improving these pages to reduce the exit ratio. You can strengthen calls to action, improve navigation, and cross sell other content on the site.

Single-Access Pages

Single-access pages are really just a combination of an entry and an exit without viewing any other pages on the site. A page is recorded as a single-access page if a visitor comes to a site, views only one page, and then exits. It is recorded as an entry to the site, an exit from the site, and a single-access page visit. These types of pages are almost always recorded by your measurement application and reported in a "single-access page" report (Figure 4-5).

Figure 4-5. Single-access pages report

These can be a real problem: you have done all the things you need to do to drive people to your site: they come, view one page, and then leave. It is difficult to come up with a scenario when viewing a single page on a site can be considered a positive for the site owner—no matter what your business model. When calculating exit ratios, look at what percentage are single-access pages.

You can work to improve these pages the same way you address pages with high exit ratios. You need to move people from those pages recording high single page visits to other pages on your site. We aren't going to eliminate single-access pages all together—that is not our intent—rather, we are just trying to drive more people further into the site so we have a better chance of convincing them to convert.

Unfortunately, many single-access page visits come through search engines, campaigns, and pay-per-click campaigns. And guess what—you may pay top dollar for those campaign visits that click over once and instantly bail. This is another good reason to track campaign ROI through to conversion rather than just clicks.

It is easy to see how these three metrics are related, and the importance of understanding them on their own as well as together. Depending on your site and overall site goals, there are a number of ways you can use this information to improve site performance.

Using All Three Reports Together

While each report is powerful on its own, two very important ratios can be generated on a per-page basis that form useful key performance indicators.

Page "stickiness." It is tremendously important to your marketing initiatives that visitors see more than just a single page when they arrive at your site. While looking at your single-access page report is valuable, as is looking at your entry page report, the concept of "stickiness" of a page is another useful way to examine the likelihood that a page is a strong positive contributor to your marketing programs. Calculate page "stickiness" on a page-by-page basis using the following:

1.00 – (Single-Access Page Visits / Entry Page Visits)

For example, you would determine how many times your home page was the entry page for a visit and the home page was the only page in a visit, and use the above formula to calculate your home page stickiness.

Needless to say, the more sticky the page, the more valuable it is. Any landing pages that have a stickiness of less than 40 percent should be closely examined for usability and performance issues.

Ratio of page entries to exits. The ratio of entries to exits for a page provides you a rough proxy for the popularity and value of a page. The calculation will yield a ratio between 0.0 and, well, a very large number, depending on the page in question. The lower the number, the less popular the page (e.g., people leave from it more frequently than they arrive at it); the higher the number, the more popular the page.

This calculation should be used in the context of the page—ask yourself "Does that make sense, given what I hope that visitors do on that page?" If you're looking at your shopping cart "Thank You" page, a very low number would be appropriate (for example, most people will exit the site after making a purchase, and nobody should be entering at that page). Conversely, the higher the better for your home page, although you rarely see exceptionally large numbers on your most generic of all landing pages.

While few web measurement applications calculate page stickiness and the ratio of page entries to exits, these views of your page activity are too important to ignore. You should add each of these ratios to your key performance indicators and monitor them frequently.

—*Jason Burby and Eric T. Peterson*

Measure Multi-Step Processes

Reducing abandonment through multi-step processes is a tried and true method for making your investment in web measurement pay off.

Multi-step processes are flows of two or more pages on your site that, when successfully completed, somehow contribute to the success of your business. Processes you encounter online every day include shopping cart checkout, new member registration, search, and the simple act of moving from more general to more specific information in any type of site.

Measuring multi-step processes is important, because with every successive click, you lose visitors; this is often called *abandonment* because the visitor is "abandoning" the process. Regardless of the reason, any impediment will prevent visitors from successfully completing the process, making your web site less successful. Your job is to identify these leaks using the right data and experiment with changes that can reduce abandonment.

When measuring and analyzing multi-step processes, there are several key metrics you should be familiar with:

Retention rate
> This metric is calculated as the percentage of visitors that successfully continue to the next step of your funnel. This rate highlights how many visitors are retained.

Attrition rate
> This metric is calculated as the number of visitors lost at any specific step of the funnel. It is effectively the inverse of the retention rate.

Conversion rate
> This metric is calculated by dividing the number of visitors that complete the process by the number of total visitors that began the process. For example, if 100 visitors start at your home page, and 5 of them complete the expected process, your conversion rate is 5 percent.

Abandonment rate
> This metric is the inverse of the conversion rate. It describes how many total visitors are lost in a given process. Following the previous example, your abandonment rate would be 95 percent.

Identify the Leaks

When web measurement tools were first deployed, analysts began using clickstream data to understand where people were abandoning a given process. Applied to multi-step processes, clickstream data provides useful insight into the specific paths visitors are navigating.

However, clickstream analysis has a significant drawback in generally assuming that people navigate in a linear, task-oriented fashion. Unfortunately, countless analyses and usability studies have demonstrated that users navigate web sites in a *nonlinear* fashion, browsing multiple site sections and pages before zeroing in on a specific task.

Despite erratic behavior, the fundamental question remains: where are users bailing out of a process? To address this need, some web measurement vendors now provide functionality to measure multi-step processes (sometimes called "fall-out reports").

Process reports allow you to select several "checkpoints" that users must pass through before successfully completing a given process. The process report doesn't care if it took 3 or 30 clicks to get from A to B to C, just that the user made it from A to C and passed through B at some point along the way.

Analyzing Multi-Step Processes

When used properly, fallout reports can provide powerful insight into where your most significant leaks are occurring. Figure 4-6 highlights a typical online purchase process.

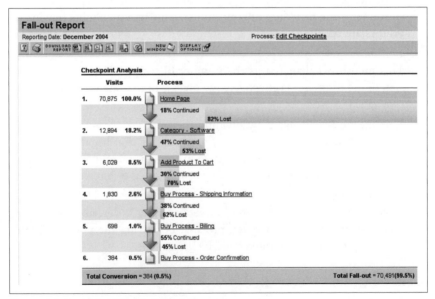

Figure 4-6. Typical online purchase path

Users begin by entering the site on the "Home Page" and have successfully completed an order when they reach "Buy Process – Order Confirmation." You'll notice that between steps one and two, 82 percent of the visits are lost (for example, only 18 percent of home page visitors reach the "Category – Software" page). While this looks pretty bad, you cannot reasonably expect every visitor to be interested in software products. You should be less concerned about abandonment early on in the process, especially when visitors have a large number of choices available to them early on.

You can see that between steps two and three, only 47 percent of the visits are adding a product to the shopping cart. This is where the red flags start to go up in my mind and I start asking myself, "Is it something about the way the page is laid out or the language that we use that is preventing people from clicking the 'add to cart' button?"

Further down, between steps three and four, you'll notice 70 percent of visitors exit after the "Add Product to Cart" page; this is significant. These prospective customers have sent a clear signal that they are considering a purchase but, for some reason do not enter the checkout process. The central question you need to ask yourself is "why?" and this page should be flagged for additional study.

Between steps four and five, 62 percent of prospects are leaving after viewing the "Buy Process – Shipping Information" page. This means 1,830 people have clicked from your home page, added a product to cart, and read about shipping information, but chosen not to proceed further. Again, this should be flagged for additional study. Often this area of attrition is associated with poorly displayed shipping rate information, creating an opportunity to test shipping charges using A/B testing.

Even more fascinating, 45 percent of prospects have made it to the next-to-last step in the process, the "Buy Process – Billing" page but, for some reason, abandoned the process. Why? Often abandonment at a step where you're asking for money is simply driven by people's unwillingness to commit. That said, frequently companies forget to post privacy and security information on pages like this, causing visitors to abandon because they're not sure they can trust the site. In this case, double-check the page to make sure everything looks professional, the language is clear, and privacy and security policies are clearly described (or at least links to these policies exist). You should also augment these theories by apply clickstream analysis to understand what content visitors are clicking away to access (for example, are they visiting the "Help" section, and never returning to purchase?).

The net result of this multi-step process and significant attrition is that the site is left with a 0.5 percent conversion rate, and we've identified at least four pages that need to be checked and tested. Fortunately, since you have established attrition and abandonment baselines, you can experiment with design ideas at the page and process levels.

The Payoff

The payoff of improved conversion is usually significant. Using the example above, this site attracted 70,875 visitors in the month of December, 0.5 percent of which you convert generating $38,400 in sales based on an average order value of $100.00.

Now let's assume this site somehow reduced abandonment from the "Add Product to Cart" page by 10 percent, meaning 40 percent of prospects continue to the "Buy Process – Shipping Information" page instead of the current 30 percent. If all other attrition levels stay the same, this site would generate 122 additional orders (506 total orders, up from the original 384) yielding an additional $12,200 in sales—a 32 percent increase.

Now imagine that the site was able to decrease abandonment in other steps in their checkout process.

Hopefully you can see the power of multi-step process analysis. Most of the significant financial gains that companies make using web measurement applications are tied to this type of analysis. Because top vendors make this type of analysis fairly easy to implement and understand, you'll be able to take advantage of process reporting somewhere on your web site as well!

—Matt Belkin and Eric T. Peterson

HACK #60   Measure Usability in the Checkout Process

For online retailers, one of the single greatest opportunities for improvement exists in the checkout or purchase process. Exploring the usability in this part of your site using web measurement often provides significant return on the time invested.

Your web site could present customers with the exact product(s) that they want to buy, but if they are unable to navigate your checkout process, all the personalization in the world won't matter. The checkout process is arguably the most critical step in the conversion funnel and for sites with considerable scale, moving the conversion needle even slightly will lead to significant incremental sales.

A "usable" checkout process is simply one that makes it easy for your customers to buy from you. The process is intuitive as well as efficient, and customers do not question the security of their information or the impending fulfillment of their order. So how do you know if your checkout process is usable? Let's explore the most common steps in a checkout process and focus on key usability concepts.

Stylized Checkout Process

Most retail checkouts work the same way: you add products to the cart, click "Check Out," identify yourself somehow, provide shipping and billing information, pay, and you're done. Because so many checkouts are similar, a handful of time-proven strategies are worth discussing.

Step one: Adding a product to the shopping cart. Imagine you are at your favorite retail store. How would you like to walk to the checkout counter with each product you wish to purchase, one by one? More often than not, this is exactly what consumers encounter at retail sites. For sites that average more than one item per order, this usually creates a situation in which customers hit the famed "Continue Shopping" button and find themselves back at the home page. To determine if this is a potential problem for your site, there are a few data points that are important to consider.

In addition to items per order, data such as the following may indicate that you should consider either improving the intelligence of the "Continue Shopping" button or modifying the add-to-cart process so that customers are not forced out of their shopping experience and are simply informed that their product has been added to cart:

- Customers frequently purchase more than one color/size of the same SKU.

- There are natural product pairings within your product mix (e.g., printers and printer paper).

- Your "may we also suggest" program on the product detail page is fairly successful.

- The conversion rate for customers who use the "Continue Shopping" button is lower than those who proceed directly through the checkout process after adding their first product.

Step two: Logging in. This step is an important bridge between the shopping and buying processes, and can make the difference between a pleasant and a frustrating customer experience. Two concepts to focus on here are making it easy for customers to create or retrieve their account information, while also providing the option to proceed anonymously.

Determining how usable your login process is can be quite simple. First, make sure that each of the three visitor segments (new account, logged in, and anonymous) can be tracked separately. Overall checkout process completion rates for each segment will provide a baseline and will likely point toward the low-hanging fruit. For existing customers, you should also assess the impact of interacting with the "forgot password" and/or the "forgot username" links. If these interactions significantly reduce the probability of completion, the retrieval functionality employed should be revisited.

Step three: Billing and shipping. The more onerous this step appears, the more likely a customer is to depart entirely. Attrition is likely high on this step, particularly for those customers who arrive at a blank form, so a critical measurement to look at here is direct site departure. These customers probably don't even start to fill out the form. If your analytics solution provides information on form field interactions for completers as well as abandoners, this is a key usability metric for this step. In addition, you should test the impact of side-by-side forms to avoid scrolling. And, if you aren't providing customers the option to easily use the same address for both billing and shipping (for example, by checking a box), by all means, do it!

Form field validation errors are another driver of site departure at this step. Again, your analytics solution may provide information about which errors are received as well as the impact these errors have on form completion rates. In the absence of this data, one proxy for determining whether errors are a problem is the average number of times this page is refreshed (ratio of page views to visits). This would likely indicate a customer was attempting to fix errors and resubmit the form. Improving the messaging around how to format answers as well as the error messages themselves will reduce the frequency and impact of these errors.

Step four: Payment and confirmation. There are many substantial opportunities to identify potential usability improvements at this final step in the checkout process. This step is also a significant attrition point, often because it is the first time customers are seeing their order total. While providing estimates of taxes and shipping earlier in the process (for example, at the "shopping cart") will definitely shift attrition, it will also lower it because customers' expectations will be more effectively managed. The higher conversion rates should come from fewer direct site departures as well as fewer steps backward in the process to lower shipping costs (for example, choosing a different shipping method, removing expensive items, or removing heavier items).

Data indicating that customers are moving backward to edit shipping or billing information may provide insight into further opportunities for improving usability at the "Billing and Shipping" step. In many cases, customers miss the option to use the same or different addresses the first time around. Likewise, the form field concepts discussed in the previous section also applies to the payment method component of this step.

In summary, by analyzing the behavior of customers who are not moving forward in the process, you will uncover your usability challenges. Very simple modifications to your checkout process will likely result in significant gains, so before you engage in strategies to increase the volume of orders moving into the checkout process first, make sure it is easy to navigate.

—Brett Hurt, Marianne Llewellyn, and Eric T. Peterson

HACK #61 Measure "Internal Campaigns"

Don't forget about your internal campaigns—efforts to up-sell and cross-sell your visitors on other products, solutions, or ideas—which are also easily tracked using your web measurement solution.

Frequently, marketers overlook the tracking of internal campaigns run on a web site. Since most commerce sites have a conversion rate of about two percent of all site visitors, internal marketing should be a central focus. Internal campaigns consist of many different elements on your web site, including promotional text links and images, product placements on category pages, and cross-sell product promotions

To measure internal campaigns, you need to make sure you tag your site appropriately so you understand how each element on a page drives success on your web site. There is no difference between tracking internal and external campaigns. For both internal and external campaigns, you must understand impressions, clicks, fallout, orders, revenue, and other metrics about each campaign or promotion you run on your web site.

There are several ways to track your campaign element.

- Add a simple URL parameter or tracking code [Hack #43] to each link URL. The code can be captured via your application server, JavaScript, or from the URL via the web measurement service or software.

- If you are not able to tag each campaign with an ID, you can track them by sending each campaign to a landing page [Hack #46].

- Several advanced analytic solutions allow automatic link detection [Hack #54] via JavaScript.

- Use a server-side redirect to capture the click [Hack #55].

Figure 4-7 shows how to track a campaign by adding a tracking code to the URL.

A web site has a promotion on its home page promoting their "Winter Holiday Sale." The standard link for this promotion would look like this:

http://www.yoururl.com/store.cgi?PAGE=342553

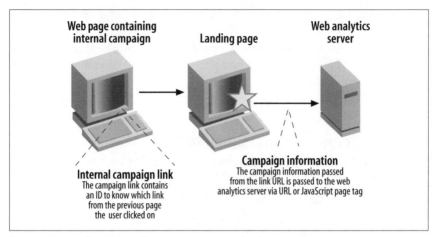

Figure 4-7. Tracking internal campaigns

With the tracking code added, the internal campaign link would look like this:

> *http://www.yoururl.com/store.cgi?PAGE=342553&internal_campaign=Winter_Holiday_Sale*

When someone clicks the holiday sale page element, the landing page knows that the visitor clicked the campaign on the previous page, because the tracking code is passed to the landing page. The tracking code is collected into the web measurement server via the JavaScript page tag or web server logfile. You cannot look at the page referrer to know where the visitor came from, because the page referrer tells you which page the visitor came from and not which link on the page. Frequently, there are multiple links from one page to another.

Several web measurement vendors use a technology that overlays a visual map [Hack #62] onto a web page to display click information. This click technology is another great way to track internal campaigns placed on a page; however, be sure that it provides conversion reporting for each link and not just click-through.

When you place internal promotions on your web site, you may want your content server to populate the link URL with not only your campaign ID, but also other information you have about the location of the banner. If you pass in the internal campaign ID and placement information, your URL would look something like this.

> *http://www.YOURURL.com/store.cgi? PAGE=fallpromo&internal_campaign=fall_sale_05&placement=Left_Menu*

It is a common practice today for most web measurement systems to give credit only to the last value passed into the internal campaign variable. In addition to understanding the last campaign viewed by a visitor, you may want to track internal campaign participation. Participation is a metric that distributes credit to all campaigns that participated in the success of a visitor. For example, a visitor to a financial services web site clicks the "refinance your home special" link on the home page. This link takes her to the home loans page that features a "special fixed rates" link. The visitor clicks that link and applies for a loan. Which promotion contributed the most to the visitor's success? The fact is that both internal campaigns played a vital role in getting the visitor to apply for a loan. It is important to track both the last campaign a visitor clicked and also all promotions that contributed to the success of that visitor.

The metrics you want to track for your internal campaigns are similar if not the same as those for banner campaigns [Hack #40], including impressions, click-through rate, conversion rate, and conversion events, as well as order and revenue data if your site is an online retail model (Figure 4-8).

	Internal Promotions	Click-throughs	Orders	Orders Participation	Ord Conv.	Revenue	Revenue Participation	Avg. Order Size
1.	Free Shipping on orders over $99	4,383	122 24.2%	24.2% (122)	2.7%	$75,176 21.8%	21.8% ($75,178)	$616.22
2.	Liquidation Center	3,491	79 15.7%	15.7% (79)	2.2%	$53,326 15.4%	15.4% ($53,326)	$675.02
3.	This weekend only specials	2,808	63 12.5%	12.5% (63)	2.2%	$47,914 13.8%	13.8% ($47,914)	$760.54
4.	New Product!	2,224	44 8.7%	8.7% (44)	2.0%	$38,019 10.9%	10.9% ($38,019)	$864.07
5.	Internet specials	2,323	60 11.9%	11.9% (60)	2.6%	$31,668 9.1%	9.1% ($31,668)	$527.81
6.	Deal of the day	1,951	34 6.7%	6.7% (34)	1.7%	$24,877 7.2%	7.2% ($24,677)	$731.69
7.	Spotlight Specials	1,266	28 5.6%	5.6% (28)	2.2%	$16,625 4.8%	4.8% ($16,625)	$593.78
8.	None	0	20 4.0%	4.0% (20)	2.3%	$16,345 4.7%	4.7% ($16,345)	$817.23
9.	Blowout Clearance Items	868	25 5.0%	5.0% (25)	2.8%	$16,279 4.7%	4.7% ($16,279)	$651.16
10.	Free Case with Digital camera	701	17 3.4%	3.4% (17)	2.4%	$13,099 3.8%	3.8% ($13,099)	$770.50
11.	Weekly Web Specials	434	6 1.2%	1.2% (6)	1.4%	$8,230 2.4%	2.4% ($8,230)	$1,371.64
12.	Free Printer with Intel Pentium 4	251	6 1.2%	1.2% (6)	2.4%	$5,790 1.7%	1.7% ($5,790)	$964.98
	Total	n/a	504	504	n/a	$347,351	$347,351	n/a

Report Generated by SiteCatalyst using Report Accelerator at 11:10 PM WET, 7 Jan 2006

Figure 4-8. Internal campaign report

Understanding your internal promotions and how visitors interact with them allows you to improve your web site.

—John Pestana and Eric T. Peterson

Use Browser Overlays

Browser overlay applications have rapidly become a popular tool for sharing web measurement data outside of analysis teams and exploring data using more natural visual models. There are a handful of best practice uses for these tools that can help you be more productive.

A handful of web measurement vendors now offer tools for visualizing reports directly on the pages of the site. Such tools are often described as browser overlays—they allow marketers, merchandisers, and site designers to superimpose metrics such as click-through rates for each of the page links. In general, browser overlays are a complement to classic path analysis tools; they are installed as a browser plug-in to Internet Explorer and use ActiveX to display statistics on a given page, usually in a left-side column and by placing metrics and percentages on top of links and images (Figure 4-9).

Figure 4-9. Browser overlays

Optimize Site Design

One great strategy is to use browser overlays to optimize navigation, as well as the structure of some of the key pages of your site. With click-through rates superimposed over links, you can quickly understand which menus, links, and sections of your web pages are getting the most clicks. Use this information to determine what your users most frequently do, and optimize your navigation accordingly. For example, you may have a variety of category links on your home page but find that most of your users are going directly to your product search page. Try featuring your search box more prominently on the home page so it will be easy for users to find.

Identify and Minimize Page Abandonment

Your goal should be to minimize your exit rate for key pages on your site. This can be accomplished by intelligently positioning links on those pages to make them easier to navigate or by changing their appearance. For example, avoid leaving popular links below the browser fold because not all site users will think about using the scroll bar. Likewise, some users have their screen resolution [Hack #70] set to 800 by 600 pixels—which limits their ability to see links that would be too far right. The classic mistake is to put a "Help" or "Contact Us" link too far right on the page. Browser overlays also tell you how effectively you are using your screen real estate. The promotion on your home page may be consuming most of the real estate above the browser fold, but if the click-through rate on this promotion is low, you may be better off featuring top-selling products instead.

Optimize Multi-Step and Transactional Processes

Take a close look at your transactional pages like checkout pages for retail sites or any kind of multi-step process for general sites (for example, newsletter sign ups or registration processes). On those specific pages, most clicks, if not all, should be on the Next, Place Order, or Sign Up buttons. Play with browser overlays to analyze how changes to the color of such buttons, their shape, or their placement affect click-through rates. You can accomplish these comparisons using a split-path test [Hack #63] and comparing side by side the page flow using browser overlays.

Engage the Previously Unengaged

One of the best and perhaps least obvious things you can do with tools like these are drive adoption and interest in web site measurement. Many companies that have adopted these tools at the urging of their data teams have come to realize that managers and "dataphobic" types appreciate the available visualizations as much or more than the "core geeks." The next time you need to explain some aspect of your web measurement to a group of the uninformed or uninitiated try this:

1. Start your presentation by simply showing your site's home page (or the most relevant page).
2. Set the stage, tell people what you're going to tell them, and why it's a problem, but be brief.
3. Open the browser overlay and show people the top-level metrics. Be animated and try to highlight the fact that it is a super easy-to-use tool.
4. After about two minutes, go into the core presentation, referring back to the overlay once or twice if possible.
5. End the presentation by going back to the overlay and highlighting the relevant link/page/content using the tool, leaving your audience with that visual element to mull over.

If you play your cards right, you'll do two things: first, get positive feedback for giving a presentation about data that was actually, gasp, engaging, and second, get phone calls from people wanting to use the application themselves, thus creating interest in web measurement in general.

—*Xavier Casanova and Eric T. Peterson*

HACK #63 Run Your Own Split-Path Tests

While there are a number of vendors providing split-path testing tools, relatively simple code will let you run your own tests.

While there are a handful of vendors that provide solutions and services for split-path testing—the practice of randomly showing visitors alternative pages or content to improve conversion—most charge between $25,000 and $100,000 annually for their services. However, if you have a reasonable amount of control over your web application platform, it's not unreasonable to simply build the ability to distribute and track visitors right into your existing site.

Regardless of how you choose to implement split-path testing, the essence of a good strategy is as follows:

1. Check for test participation.
2. Assign the visitor to a test or control group.
3. Tag the visitor.
4. Redirect test subjects to the appropriate page.
5. Monitor for completion of goals.

Perhaps the most important is step 5: monitoring for the completion of goals. Keep in mind that split-path testing is a lightweight adaptation of the scientific method—you have a control group and one or more tests, and you're looking for the differences between the two sets. In the case of a web site, the differences should be measured by an increase in leads collected, sales generated, pages viewed, etc., depending on your particular business objectives **[Hack #38]**.

The Code

The following code is written in VBScript for Microsoft's Active Server Pages, although it could be quite easily adapted to PHP, Perl, or Java. You should save the following code as *split-path_testing.inc* and plan to include it in your header files (ideally, via a server-side include).

```
<%
'****************************************************************
' Define the tests to be performed.
' Tests are stored in an array. Be sure to dimension the
' array to the number of tests minus 1!@
'****************************************************************
```

```
Dim Test(1) ' SET TO MAXIMUM NUMBER OF TESTS MINUS ONE
Test(0) = "Home_Page_Test,index.asp,index_test.asp,12/1/2004,12/31/2004"
Test(1) = "Buy_Now_Test,buy_now.asp,buy_now_test.asp,12/1/2004,12/11/2004"

Dim SplitArray
Dim TestName(20), TestFile(20), DefaultFile(20), TestStart(20), TestEnd(20)
For i=0 to Ubound(Test)
SplitArray = split(Test(i), ",")
  TestName(i) = SplitArray(0)
  DefaultFile(i) = SplitArray(1)
  TestFile(i) = SplitArray(2)
  TestStart(i) = SplitArray(3)
  TestEnd(i) = SplitArray(4)
Next

' Define a function called RandomNumber that will be used
' to assign visitors to the test or control group
Function RandomNumber(intHighestNumber)
Randomize
RandomNumber = Int(Rnd * intHighestNumber) + 1
End Function
```

' The bulk of the code first sets a few variables including the current date and the name of the || script currently being loaded in the visitor's browser (ScriptName):

```
Response.Buffer = True
ScriptName = Request.ServerVariables("SCRIPT_NAME")
ThisDate = FormatDateTime(now(), vbShortDate)
```

' The rest of the code simply iterates through the tests already loaded into arrays to see if the page is one included in a test, if the visitor is already in a test group and if not, which
' test group they should be assigned to. As soon as the test assignment is made, the visitor is
' then redirected (if they've been determined to be part of a test) or nothing happens and the
' rest of the page is loaded

```
For i = 0 to Ubound(Test)
if InStr(ScriptName, DefaultFile(i)) then
  if (CDate(ThisDate) >= CDate(TestStart(i)) AND CDate(ThisDate) =<
CDate(TestEnd(i))) then
    if IsDate(Request.Cookies("TestCookie")(TestName(i))) then
      Response.Redirect("./" & TestFile(i) & "?TestGroup=" & TestName(i))
    elseif Request.Cookies("TestCookie")(TestName(i)) <> "CONTROL" then
      Response.Cookies("TestCookie").Domain = "www.webanalyticsdemystified.com"
      Response.Cookies("TestCookie").Expires = now() + 365
```

```
' Here is where we assign the visitor to the test or control group.
' Note the TestGroup=[TestName] in the redirect–the critical piece to
' allow us to tag the visitor:

if RandomNumber(100) > 50 then
    Response.Cookies("TestCookie")(TestName(i)) = ThisDate
    Response.Redirect("./" & TestFile(i) & "?TestGroup=" & TestName(i))
else
    Response.Cookies("TestCookie")(TestName(i)) = "CONTROL"
    end if
  end if
  ' If the end date for the test has expired, clean out the cookie so that
the test name can be reused if necessary:
  elseif CDate(ThisDate) > CDate(TestEnd(i)) then
    Response.Cookies("TestCookie")(TestName(i)) = ""
  end if
end if
next
%>
```

Check for Test Participation: Pages and People

You need a way to keep track of whether the viewed page is part of a test or not. To do, use a simple array to keep track of the name of the test (for your measurement application, a nice, readable name), the default and test filenames (physical script names), and the start and end dates for the test. Each element in the array holds information about an individual test.

```
<%
Dim Test(1) ' SET TO MAXIMUM NUMBER OF TESTS MINUS ONE
Test(0) = "Home_Page_Test,index.asp,index_test.asp,12/1/2004,12/31/2004"
Test(1) = "Buy_Now_Test,buy_now.asp,buy_now_test.asp,12/1/2004,12/11/2004"
```

For the most part, all you really need to know is that the format for the test definitions is important: you have to have the name of the test, followed by a comma, followed by the default filename (e.g., the control group), followed by a comma, the name of the test file, comma, the start date in MM/DD/YYYY format, comma, and then the end date in MM/DD/YYYY format.

You also want to set a cookie in the visitor's browser that lets you track his participation in your tests. The code to do this is very simple:

```
Response.Cookies("TestCookie")(TestName(i)) = ThisDate
```

You create a cookie called TestCookie with a name/value pair where the name of the test (TestName(i)) equals today's date (ThisDate). Then you'll be able to check the cookie for a valid date to see if the visitor is participating in the test.

```
if IsDate(Request.Cookies("TestCookie")(TestName(i))) then
```

Assign to a Test or Control Group

Assuming the visitor is not already participating in a test, the next step is to randomly assign him to the test group (so that he will see the test pages) or the control group (so that he will see the control pages). While there are many ways to do this, I like to use the simple "heads you're in, tails you're out" strategy:

```
If RandomNumber(100) > 50 then
```

Basically, using a random-number generating function in VBScript, you generate a number between 1 and 100; 1 through 50 are in the control group and 51 to 100 are in the test group. Visitors are assigned to test or control groups on every tested page, in order to preserve random distribution throughout your site.

Tag the Visitor

If a visitor is going to be part of a test, you need to let your measurement application know this. The easiest way to do this is to modify the URL making the request for the test file so that either your logfile can be mined for the presence of a name/value pair like ?TestGroup=[TestName] or you can use this information to load a variable for your JavaScript page tag, e.g.:

```
var _abTestGroup="TestName";
```

We do this by appending to the end of the test filename, contained in the TestFile(i) array variable.

```
Response.Redirect("./" & TestFile(i) & "?TestGroup=" & TestName(i))
```

Note that if your test filename already has parameters in the query string, you'll need to convert the "?" to an "&" for this redirection to work properly.

Keep in mind that the method you use to identify the test visitor will be defined based on which data source you're using [Hack #3] and specific to the application you're using.

Redirect Test Subjects to the Appropriate Page

As long as the TestFile(i) variable is properly set, the visitor is going to be redirected along to the test page and assigned membership to the appropriate group. One thing you want to keep track of is whether the distribution of visitors is roughly 50/50, based on our simple test assignment strategy. Monitor the traffic to both the control and test pages to make sure they're receiving roughly the same number of page views; if they're not, something may have gone wrong with the code.

Monitor for Completion of Goals

This is the single more important thing you'll do with this code, though it has little or nothing to do with the code itself. You need to make sure that you're using the ?TestGroup=TestName in the query string to let your measurement application know that this visitor has to be tracked as a separate visitor segment [Hack #48] or member of an A/B test. Again, how you make this assignment really depends on which data source and type of application you're using, but a phone call to your vendor should yield a pretty simple explanation about how to do this.

Ideally, if you're using a moderately powerful measurement application, you'll then be able to see whether members of the test group are completing goals more frequently than those in the control group. This is important since it's the only reason you would use the following code.

Running the Hack

The best way to run this hack is to make sure that *split-path_testing.inc* is included in your common header file using a server-side include.

```
<!--#include file="split-path_testing.inc"-->
```

If you don't have a common header file, I recommend you create one rather than adding this code to every page on your site. This is the most efficient way to make global changes to the array that defines the tests, including ending all of the tests if you need to.

Don't forget, the most important thing I'm not explicitly showing you in the code is making sure that your measurement system knows about the tests. Getting test subjects into appropriate visitor segments and tracking those segments through the completion of goals is far and away the most important piece in split-path testing. Be sure and consult with your application vendor when you're setting this up to capture as much useful information as possible.

Hacking the Hack

When you get really good at split-path testing, keep in mind that the code is already set up to let you test multiple pages at once. Because you're building an array of tests, you can add as many as you'd like and really work hard to optimize your web site. The most important thing to keep in mind is that because arrays start at 0 rather than 1, you need to redimension the Test array to one less than the total number of tests you're running or you'll get a nasty ASP error.

For example, if you had 100 different tests, you would redimension the Test array to 99, and then add additional elements for each new test:

```
Dim Test(99) ' SET TO MAXIMUM NUMBER OF TESTS MINUS ONE
Test(0) = "Home_Page_Test,index.asp,index_test.asp,12/1/2004,12/31/2004"
Test(1) = "Buy_Now_Test,buy_now.asp,buy_now_test.asp,12/1/2004,12/11/2004"
Test(2) = "Splash_Test,splash.asp,splash_test.asp,12/1/2004,12/11/2004"
...
Test(99) = "Recommendation_Test,rec.asp,rec_test.asp,12/1/2004,12/11/2004"
```

Finally, know that there is such a thing as "test overkill" and if too many visitors pass through too many tests, you won't know for sure which tests were working. I recommend running only three or four tests at a time, trying to isolate them in the site if possible. This strategy allows you to quickly test your ideas while not creating too much data to be analyzed reasonably.

HACK #64 Measure Internal Searches

Sites that have deployed an internal or on-site search application have a great opportunity to leverage their web measurement application to learn a great deal about their visitors.

Think about the last time you went to a site and had trouble finding what you wanted. Did you try to locate the product or information by navigating through the site, or did you go straight to the on-site search? If you tried the on-site search, did you get the results you were expecting immediately, or did you have to search more than once?

Far too often, both the navigation and the on-site search fail to deliver, resulting in frustrated visitors who bail out–clearly not a desired behavior. They may even leave for a competitor's site and feel that you have wasted their time, neither of which benefits your business or your brand. This is unfortunate because if you've deployed internal search technology, you have a powerful ally that, properly maintained, can help you delight and convert web visitors.

Understanding How Visitors Search Your Site

The following are a set of metrics to evaluate the performance of on-site search tools. Understanding these measurements will help you improve the effectiveness of your search functionality, which can improve overall conversion rates and the success of the site.

Percentage of visits using search. Do people automatically start with the on-site search when they land at the site, or do they move through the site and rely on search when they can't find what they want? Some sites will record only a small percentage of search use, while others see a vast majority of visitors relying on search. Calculated as the number of visits seeing at least one "search results" page divided by the total number of visits, this percentage can help determine how high of a priority optimizing your on-site search should be. Once you review the other metrics below and see how your search is reporting, it may become a high priority to optimize it.

Searches per search visit. This is a measure of the number of distinct searches an average visitor conducts. The ideal is one search per search visit, meaning people search once and find what they want immediately. Unfortunately, many sites record much more than one, often three or more searches per search visit. This is calculated by dividing the number of distinct searches by the number of search visits.

In general, the greater the number of searches executed in a visit, the greater the confusion on the part of the visitor. If you have to keep changing the words you search for because you're not getting the results you're looking for, eventually frustration sets in and you leave unsatisfied.

If you are using page tagging to track pages through your web measurement tool, each time someone explores one of the links on the results page and then returns to that results page, it may look like another search. In this case, you want to be careful that you're measuring distinct search terms, not just additional page views for the same search term.

Percentage of exits from the search return page. One indication of a failed search is when a visitor exits the site from the search return page, the page that lists the search results. Ineffective searches can be frustrating if visitors follow a number of links and still don't find what they want. They may simply exit the site from the results page. If visitors find what they want, they'll link off the results page and continue the visit. This can often be an alarming metric to view if you have not reviewed it before. Think of how those people feel about your site as they move on to a competitor.

Conversion of search visits to sales, leads, or other desired conversion. It's important to understand how your search visitors convert on key metrics, such as sales and lead generation [Hack #39], compared to non-search users. Depending on the difference, you may want to point more or fewer people to the on-site search. If search visits convert at a higher rate, it may be worth analyzing the content that visitors see when coming through search pages. You can then use that information to drive the non-searchers to that content. You may have hidden the content that really drives conversion.

Average items per order for search visits versus non-search visits. Like the conversion above, you may see a difference in the average number of items per order or the average order value. Again, you can adjust how and where the content is being presented to either group.

Percentage of searches with no results ("zero results" searches). What percentage of visitors use on-site search and get no results? What are they looking for? What do they do when they don't get any results on the search return page? This is another big one, and obviously has a significant impact on those search return exits.

The recommended strategy to deal with zero results searches [Hack #65] is to carefully examine the search terms in question. Often you'll realize that you *should* have returned results and that something is wrong with your search index. At other times, you'll learn that searchers are using different language to look for information than you use. In the latter case, you should be able to modify your search index or pages to generate results for those searches, taking advantage of the information your visitors are freely giving you.

Percentage of searches that generate no clicked links ("zero yield" searches). Often, searchers will get a list of results that may or may not be correct, but for whatever reason, the list doesn't look right. In this case, it is not uncommon that a visitor will not click any link and either back up and search again—driving up your searches per search visit metric—exit your site, or otherwise use your navigation. In this case, the search has failed your visitor, so the list of zero yield searches should be carefully examined looking for patterns or problems.

Top search terms. What do people search for? Understanding the most common search terms can help you determine why visitors come to your site. With this information, you can improve navigation or call-outs so people don't need to rely as heavily on the search. Make it easier for visitors to find what they're looking for on your site. Keep in mind that how and what visitors are searching for on your site will change over time and even seasonally. It is imperative to monitor this on an on-going basis. This also gives you a good indication of what people are most interested in when they come to the site. This offers more opportunities to improve not just your on-search, but also the site overall.

As you can see, these metrics can tell you a great deal about not only the search portion of the site, but the entire site. You can gain insight into the priorities and desires of your site visitors and learn more about the motivators that get them to perform your desired behaviors.

—*Jason Burby and Eric T. Peterson*

HACK
#65
Take Advantage of "Zero Results" Internal Search Results

On-site search, also known as internal search, can make or break a site. Often, many small things can be done to greatly improve an on-site search, and this can ultimately improve site performance.

When visitors are searching for something they *think* you have, or should have, it can be especially frustrating to them when you return no results (e.g., a "zero" or "no results" set) as a response. When your start thinking about your internal search engine, start with the low-hanging fruit, attempting to gain an understanding of the top terms visitors search for on the site and take special note of the terms that return the frustrating "Sorry, No Results" page. Typically, the exit rate from those "no results" pages are alarmingly high.

On the other hand, getting 2,000 results can be just as frustrating. Hopefully, the first two or three of those numerous results offer accurate descriptions and links that lead visitors to the content they seek. Otherwise, you'll often see "zero yield" searches [Hack #64]: searches that return a set of results but none of those results get clicked on.

Measuring "Zero Results" Searches

There are a number of ways to measure the "no results" terms. While many of the search technologies and tools have their own reporting, often it makes sense to do much of the reporting with a well-trusted web measurement tool. This can help you understand the impact of the search function on conversion, exit rates, and other metrics across the entire site. Depending on the application, there are a number of ways to design a report that will provide the information you need. In most cases, you need to pass the information related to the search term through a parameter.

How to track "zero results" searches. If the search page is *www.zaaz.com/search.asp* and the search results page shows results on *www.zaaz.com/search-results.asp*, passing this information on the search terms and results in the URL will allow the measurement application to track searches. For example:

```
www.zaaz.com/search-results.asp?search-term=websites&results=14
```

In this case, websites is the term that visitors are searching for and 14 means that 14 results were presented for the search term.

A "no results" page URL would look like this:

```
www.zaaz.com/search-results.asp?search-term=Napoleon%20Dynamite&results=0
```

In this case, Napoleon Dynamite is the term that visitors are searching for, and zero results were found and returned.

Similarly, if you're using a page tag, you would populate the search term number of results into the tag itself. Some vendors provide precustomized tags for tracking search terms and results, similar to WebSideStory's HBX code that has .keywords and .results variables (example below). Other vendors will require you to use custom variables [Hack #31].

```
//INSERT CUSTOM EVENTS
var ev1 = new _hbEvent("search");
ev1.keywords = "oakley sunglasses";
ev1.results = "117";
ev1.attr1 = "";
ev1.attr2 = "";
ev1.attr3 = "";
ev1.attr4 = "";
```

Using the values in the parameters, you can look at all the top searches by just focusing on the "search-term" parameter. Or, you can see the breakdown of the "no results" responses by looking at the "results" parameter. Next, look at the terms by "yes" and "no" results, and combine both parameters in one report.

It can also be helpful to determine what is driving the traffic to the "no results" searches. Are they common pages that people are coming from when they then receive "no results" post-search? Are certain campaigns or referring sites driving this type of traffic?

Decreasing Search Failure

There are a few primary reasons that no results are returned. They include:

The content does not exist on the site.
> This is OK if people are searching for something outside of your business model for which you do not intend to provide information. More often, the case is that users are searching for information on your site that they are not able to find.

The search tool is not able to find the relevant information.
> This is very common and can be based on the tool, the way it is configured, or the way the site is indexed. Technology can also get in the way of finding the right information. Terms embedded in flash animations, dynamic content, and PDFs are overlooked by most search tools.

The search terms are misspelled.
> The most common source of frustration for searchers is not finding any information when they accidentally misspell something. Fortunately, most search applications provide tools to map misspellings to the right content or, even better, automatically correct or suggest the right spelling for the searcher.

Take Advantage of "Zero Results" Internal Search Results

Strategies to resolve these common issues are slightly more involved and depend somewhat on the search application you use.

Point your search index to the "right" information. The most common strategy used is to fix the search tool so it finds the content that exists on the site. Leverage your search application's relevance controls or explicitly tell the application that "when a visitor searches for 'X,' we want to show them document 'Y.'"

Improve site navigation. The usual suspect when you have content that is just not being indexed properly is your navigation structure—something is preventing your search application from finding the relevant pages and indexing them properly. Consult with your search application provider to determine whether your linking strategy is preventing indexing.

Loosen spelling requirements. Some search applications allow you to address common misspellings and point people to the right content on the site, despite how well they spell in the search box (Figure 4-10). If your search application provides spelling correction, enabling this feature will greatly improve the search results.

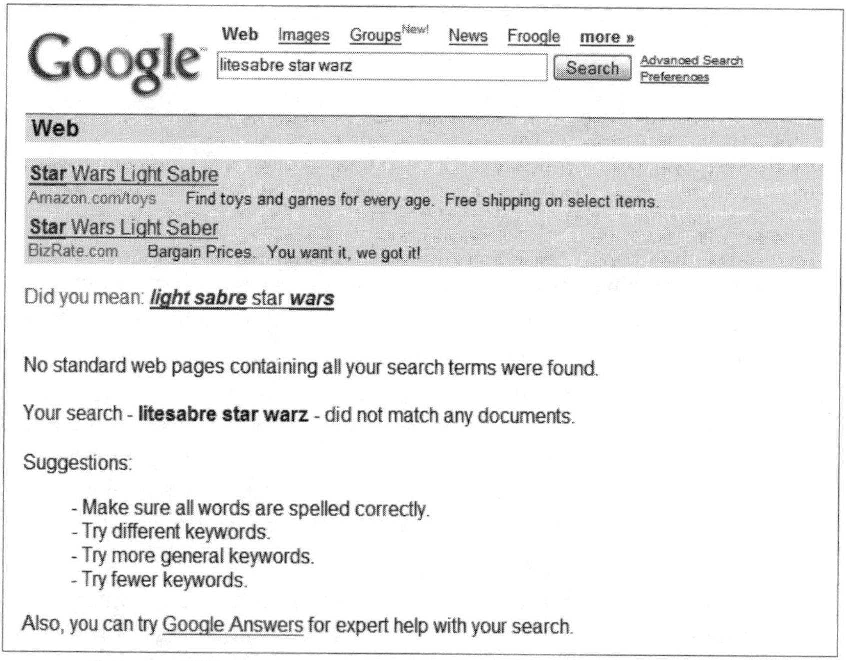

Figure 4-10. Handling misspellings

Provide an outline of categories to point people to content that most people are searching for when people search for "no results" terms. Also, a list of FAQs can often help move people to the content they seek. Some sites go so far as to provide a complete site map when searches fail (Figure 4-11).

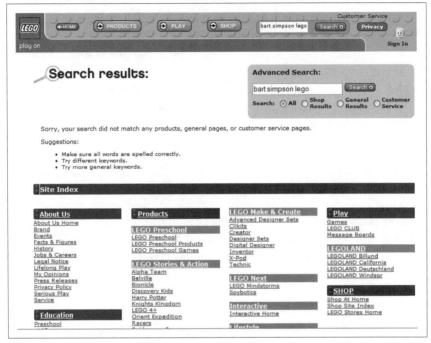

Figure 4-11. Response to a failed search

Make sure new pages are indexed correctly. This may seem like a "duh, yeah!" statement to make, but you would be surprised at how many times a new page is added to a site but doesn't make it into the search index. Whenever you make any additions to your web site, make sure you rerun the indexing engine and double check that new pages are properly indexed.

Take Advantage of "Zero Results" Searches

Dealing with the "no results" search issue is not a one-time thing. Most likely, you will experience the most significant gains the first time you analyze these terms and make changes. It is important to continually review the terms that are yielding "no results" so you can continually optimize your search tool. This can help visitors find, get, and act on the content they seek and, in turn, motivate them to take the desired behaviors designed to help you reach your overall business goals.

The most effective thing you can do with these types of searches on an ongoing basis is develop your understanding of how your visitors think about your products and services. Often your visitors will use lingo or colloquialisms to search for products. Unfortunately, if these terms aren't in your content, they won't appear in your search results. By mining failed searches for terms that "make sense in a weird way," you'll be able to better understand your visitors' mindset and thus respond to their needs.

—Jason Burby and Eric T. Peterson

HACK #66 Effectively Measure the "Known" Visitor

Sometimes it makes sense to track individual visitors to your site and create a feedback loop.

There are three kinds of unique visitors coming to your web site—truly anonymous, mostly anonymous, and known visitors [Hack #5]—and each category affords you more or less detail about the individual behind the clicks. The latter category, "known" visitors, has a great deal of potential for some business models to use web measurement to impact both the online and the offline relationship with the visitor. Smart web data analysts will go the extra mile to report about these visitors and create action plans based on their usage patterns.

Identify Known Visitors

Briefly, the known visitor is someone you can positively identify in the offline world, either by virtue of a unique login or some other authentication scheme. The common log format (CLF) has a field for authenticated usernames:

```
127.0.0.1 - frank [10/Oct/2000:13:55:36 -0700] "GET /index.html HTTP/1.0"
200 2326 - "Mozilla/4.08 [en] (Win98; I ;Nav)"
```

The frank in the preceding server logfile entry indicates that someone has successfully logged into a domain requiring authentication as "frank" and then made a request for the file *index.html*. Solutions based on JavaScript page tags also commonly accept a unique user or customer identifier:

```
hbx.hcv="";//CONVERSION VALUE
hbx.cp="null";//LEGACY CAMPAIGN
hbx.cpd="";//CAMPAIGN DOMAIN
//CUSTOM VARIABLES
hbx.ci="epeterson93111";//CUSTOMER ID
hbx.hc1="";//CUSTOM 1
hbx.hc2="";//CUSTOM 2
```

In this example, the JavaScript declaration hbx.ci="epeterson93111"; identifies a visitor in real time as epeterson93111 to WebSideStory's HBX code. The critical aspect in identifying a known visitor, one outside of the scope of this hack, is connecting the unique user identifier (UUID) to a database of personal information about the users. The most common personal information connected to web measurement data are things like name, company, title, department, phone number, and email address. As you can see in Figure 4-12, this type of information can then be used to build useful reports about the individual (but don't forget to read [Hack #26] before you do *anything* like this!)

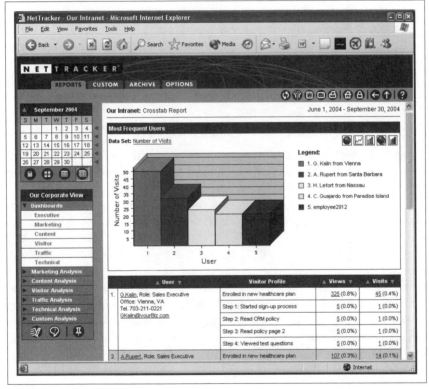

Figure 4-12. Known visitor report

Types of Known Visitors

Remember, the known visitor is someone who is identifying herself to you, either because she's required to do so to use your system or because you've provided her a significant incentive to do so. The former group is often composed of intranet/internal users or business partners logging into a secure extranet, the latter group is often made up of customers of some kind. Table 4-1 provides a handful of examples of internal/business-to-business (B2B) and external/business-to-consumer (B2C) visitors that are easily identified.

Table 4-1. Examples of know visitors that you may want to measure

Internal/B2B visitors	External/B2C visitors
• Sales and support staff	• Registered customers
• Executives	• Forum/moderated discussion participants
• Business partners	• Identified leads and prospects
• PR and marketing agencies	• Auction participants (e.g., eBay buyers and sellers)
• Outside graphic design agencies	• Newsletter subscribers
• Business-to-business customers	• Registered visitors

While this list is far from exhaustive, hopefully you get the idea. Once you identify the known visitors you want to track, the next step is to figure out which reports you'll generate and what you'll do with those reports!

Reports That Help Build Relationships with Known Visitors

In general, there are four categories of reports useful to helping you better understand your known visitors: activity reports, content consumption reports, customer support reports, and sales analysis reports. Each of these types of reports is designed to provide you with a wealth of information to understand customer needs or proactively market.

Application usage/activity reports. The most common report type for intranet users, activity and application usage reports, can help you understand who within your organization has adopted the tools you've built for your intranet and who is likely using the wrong resources (for example, bugging other people when they could be self-servicing via the intranet). A great strategy for increasing intranet adoption in organizations is to sort departmental usage by employees and have the top 10 percent of users offer intranet training to the bottom 25 percent of users!

Content consumption reports. Content consumption reports are similar to activity reports, but generally focused more on external known users in an attempt to identify preferences for products or content. Once identified, these visitors can be segmented and directly marketed to in an effort to increase loyalty and future conversion. A useful strategy is to generate a list of visitors who spend more than 10 minutes browsing information on a weekly basis and communicate to them differently than you would a less engaged visitor.

Customer support reports. Usually, a report describing how visitors interact with your customer support content will help make your customer support agents smarter and more helpful. If you're able to generate this information, why wouldn't you show your support agents the list of articles and pages the customer was looking at prior to picking up the phone so that he can better assess the likely problem? A must-generate report for any company dedicated to providing highest-quality support to their customers!

Sales analysis reports. When retailers get really good at outbound marketing and up-selling to existing customers, a sales analysis report can help you mine for likely prospects. The best example is probably customers who have purchased a particular product and who have looked at but not purchased ancillary products. Sending those folks a "We know you already have product X and we're having a sale on widgets for product X this week only" often generates incremental sales.

Hacking Known Visitor Reporting Using Content Groups

Some web measurement application vendors, especially those providing hosted solutions, don't include anything but the most rudimentary "who visited" reports for known visitors. Still, you may want to understand activity for these visitors and get you own metrics like page views, visits, and unique visitor counts. A clever hack for doing this is repurposing your content group variable to include the known visitor's UUID. For example, use the following code to identify my page names and content groups via a JavaScript page tag:

```
... ' ALREADY IN A JAVASCRIPT BLOCK FOR THE PAGE TAG
var _pn=document.title; ' SET PAGE NAME (_pn) TO THE HTML <TITLE>
var _mlc="/" + "CATEGORY" + "/" + "SUBCATEGORY";
... ' JAVASCRIPT CONTINUES
```

To this code you can simply add a userID variable before the content group to capture high-level information about individual users:

```
... ' ALREADY IN A JAVASCRIPT BLOCK FOR THE PAGE TAG
var _pn=document.title; ' SET PAGE NAME (_pn) TO THE HTML <TITLE>
var _UUID="USER_IDENTIFIER_IF_KNOWN";
if (_UUID != '') {
   _userID = "/" + _UUID;
} else {
   _userID = "/anonymous_visitor"; }
var _mlc=_userID + "/" + "CATEGORY" + "/" + "SUBCATEGORY";
... ' JAVASCRIPT CONTINUES
```

This way, you'll end up with a report that has, at the top level, a list of usernames (or user identifiers) and a group for anonymous_visitor with the appropriate metrics associated with each. Ideally you'll then be able to drill down into any of the users and see what pages and content they viewed.

While this is a pretty good hack for tracking known visitors, never do this in your main traffic measurement account. Doing so will hamper the normal reporting process significantly. Instead, ask your vendor for an extra account for this kind of tracking and get their help setting it up if necessary.

Tying It All Together

While this may seem like a lot of extra work, it's important to consider the easiest person to sell to or connect with is somebody you already know. Every successful business person knows this, so don't be afraid to measure the known visitor and take advantage of the relationships you already have. Be respectful and don't be intrusive, but take advantage of this powerful strategy.

—*Akin Arikan and Eric T. Peterson*

HACK #67 Build Your Own Web Measurement Application: Usability Data

Now that you've read up on usability data, it's time to add average time spent on site and a report on the number of single-page visits to the mix in your homegrown web measurement application.

In this hack, we'll continue our example logfile analyzer by adding statistics for the time on site [Hack #57] and the number of single-page visits [Hack #58]. With the infrastructure we've already built up, adding new reports is now easy. We just need to expand the Session and Data classes to include some new statistics.

The Code

The Session class needs to know how many seconds the session lasted. This is just the time between the initial and final requests. However, it's worth noting that this doesn't include the time the visitor spent on the final page of the session. It is possible to write a second piece of JavaScript that makes a request to the server when the visitor leaves the page, in which case you can measure the time spent on the final page. But we won't cover that here. To add the code, you will need to append the code into the appropriate spot in each file.

Append the following lines to the Sessions class in *Sessions.pm*.

```
package Session;
...
sub NumSecs {
  my $self = shift;
  if ($self->NumRequests() == 0) { return 0; }
  else { return ($self->[-1]->{time} - $self->[0]->{time}); }
}
```

Three new variables are added to the constructor and measured in Data::AddSession. Append these lines to the end of the Data class in *Data.pm*.

```perl
package Data;
...
sub new {
  return bless {
    ...
    total_seconds => 0,
    atomic_sessions => 0,
    atomic_pages => {},
  };
}
sub AddSession {
  ...
  $self->{total_seconds} += $sess->NumSecs();
  if ($reqs == 1) {
    ++$self->{atomic_sessions};
    ++$self->{atomic_pages}->{$sess->EntryPage()};
  }
}
# Data::WriteSummary will report the average time on site, and
# the number of sessions with only one page.
sub WriteSummary {
  ...
  printf "Average time on site: %.1fs\n",
    $self->{total_sessions} == 0 ? 0:
    $self->{total_seconds} / $self->{total_sessions};
  printf "Sessions with only one page: %d (%.0f%%)\n",
    $self->{atomic_sessions},
    $self->{total_sessions} == 0 ? 0:
    $self->{atomic_sessions} / $self->{total_sessions} * 100;
}
# And Data::WriteReport will write a list of the pages which
# people arrived at but didn't progress any further through the site.
sub WriteReport {
  ...
  $self->WriteHash('Pages in single-page sessions', 'atomic_pages');
}
```

Running the Code

Just as you learned in [Hack #53], all you need to do to run this program from the command line (again, assuming that *page.log* is in the same directory as *readlog.pl*) is type:

```
perl readlog.pl page.log
```

This time you will be treated to some additional summary metrics (average page views per visit, average time spent on site, and single page view visits) and a report showing the number of visits by entry page and single access pages (Figure 4-13).

Figure 4-13. Output of readlog.pl

The next additions to *readlog.pl* and your "build your own" web measurement application will be relevant technographic data, covered in Chapter 5.

—Dr. Stephen Turner and Eric T. Peterson

Technographics and "Demographics"
Hacks 68–80

There was a time when most web data analysis was done simply to understand the technographics of web site visitors: which browsers and operating systems they used, how much bandwidth they were consuming, which load-balanced servers pages were being served from—really pretty boring stuff. Fortunately the fields of web measurement and web data analysis have progressed sufficiently that we're now able to ask truly interesting questions of the data in an effort to continuously refine the user experience online. Still, one should not forget one's roots, and so, inevitably, there are still a handful of good reasons to turn to technographic data from time to time.

Demographic data, on the other hand, is cutting edge—the idea that you can know not only what your visitors are looking at but *who they are*, where they live, etc. Many of the recent advances in web measurement have revolved around attempts to tie web and CRM (customer relationship management) data together to create a more "holistic" view of Internet visitors. In fact, there is an often abused notion that the combination of web and CRM data will help companies create a "360-degree view" of their customers, detailing everything about how they interact with your organization, enabling you to better serve and sell to them.

This notion has yet to be convincingly proven. Some companies are able to integrate data [Hack #32] and create a "180-degree view" of the customer and others simply say they do—but when the rubber hits the road, the data is usually almost meaningless.

In this chapter, we'll deal with practical uses for technographic and demographic data, leaving the fantasy of a complete view of the customer to analysts and other dreamers.

Technographic data is often referred to as the "ugly details" underlying a visitor's visit to your web site. This includes data points such as the type of browser visitors use, the operating system they're browsing from, the level of

JavaScript they support, their acceptance or denial of cookies, and so on. Some of this data is actually pretty useful, and some clearly is not [Hack #74]. The trick is figuring out what data is useful to you and how to put it to work.

The best uses for technographic data almost always revolve around your web development and quality assurance programs. Regardless of whether you're responsible for a simple web site or a complex web-based application, you have roughly the same commitment to quality—a page error is a page error, and no web visitor looks kindly on page errors. The essential elements of using technographic data are:

1. Determining what technographic data has potential to influence how your site or application functions
2. Determining the level of granularity you're able to get reporting on from your measurement application
3. Agreeing on the level of traffic or visitation that will cause technographic elements (for example, browser versions) to be included in the testing list
4. Building a list of technographic elements you'll be testing against and populating a testing lab with appropriate combinations of browsers and operating systems
5. Testing and repeating

While any good web QA manager will likely scoff and say, "duh, of course!" the reality is that most companies completely botch step 3, either drawing the line too low, too high, or not at all. You don't want to test everything, and you don't want to test nothing; the challenge is to determine your tolerance for visitor complaints and work backward from that. If every visit that fails because of a JavaScript error costs $30, then you should be more aggressive than when the same error costs only $0.03.

Why the "Quotes" on Demographics?

I say "demographics" in the context of web site measurement because Wikipedia has this to say about demographics:

> Demographics comprises selected characteristics of a population (age and income distribution and trends, mobility, educational attainment, home ownership, and employment status, for instance) for purposes of social studies.

This is a fairly pure definition of demographics, covering the standard characteristics that marketers are interested in when they're trying to target an audience. It is not unheard of that companies will purchase advertising opportunities in an effort to target, for example, "18- to 25-year-old men with annual incomes over $32,000 and at least a bachelor's degree who are either homeowners or in the process of buying their first home"—which is pretty specific targeting when you think about it.

Because the level of targeting for web visitors is rarely as granular as the most basic offline targeting efforts, I prefer to refer to "demographics" in an effort to convey that what we're trying to do is similar but not same. Demographics in the web measurement world will usually be confined to relatively simple and binary demographic segments—for example, male versus female, geography, or age groups. The one exception is designated marketing area (DMA) [Hack #78], which is a traditional demographic element that is making its way into some measurement applications.

Because the data is difficult at best to get, and even more difficult to meaningfully integrate, our treatment in this chapter will remain both light and practical; for a more complete treatment of how demographic data can meaningfully be combined with your web data, I recommend contacting your measurement vendor.

HACK #68 Measure Site Performance

Combining site performance and visitation data can provide valuable insight into visitor behavior.

Because it is so critical to a visitor's perception of one's site, web site performance has been discussed at great length by a multitude of authors. For example, *Web Performance Tuning* by Patrick Killelea (O'Reilly) is an excellent resource for this information. In this hack, I discuss site performance in the context of web site measurement. If you're interested in a more complete treatment, I encourage you to grab a copy of Patrick's book.

The elements of site performance you need to know in the context of web measurement are the basics of performance measurement and how performance and visitation data can be meaningfully combined in a "one plus one equals three" data integration model.

Web Performance Measurement: The Basics

Web performance management applications measure response time and availability. Response time, or the amount of time a page or process [Hack #69] takes to load, is usually measured from a variety of geographic locations and ideally over both modem and broadband connections. Usually what you end up with is a report similar to Figure 5-1.

The essence of these reports is the average, maximum, and minimum response times and corresponding availability from as many geographic locations as you wish to test (read: "pay for"). The nice thing performance measurement vendors do, at least regarding web site measurement, is provide this data in easily transformed spreadsheets suitable for import into your web measurement application.

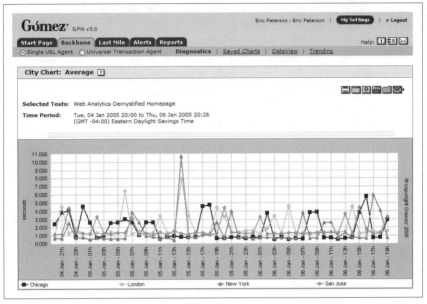

Figure 5-1. Site performance report

Integrating Performance and Visitor Data Meaningfully

Provided that your web measurement application has the ability to import data from external sources, you may be able to build a side-by-side comparison of your traffic and site performance data (Figure 5-2). There are three basic strategies you may want to consider for combining these types of data, depending on your measurement application's abilities and your particular data needs.

Basic aggregate performance and availability integration. The simplest model involves doing little more than importing the average download time and availability for all measured locations and reporting side by side with relevant traffic metrics. While this is the easiest integration possible, it is also the least interesting, not providing minimum or maximum response times or geographically based measurements.

Detailed performance and availability integration. A slightly more complex model involves importing the minimum, maximum, and average response times for your aggregate performance measurement. This data, visualized with basic traffic data, will help you better understand whether there were any significant performance events during the time period (identified by high maximum response times).

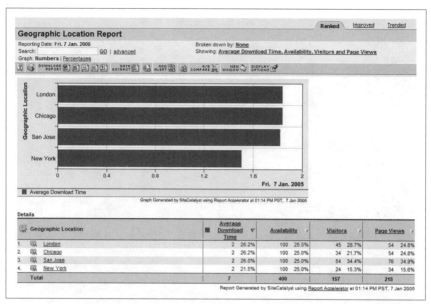

Figure 5-2. Geographically correlated performance and availability

Geographically correlated performance and availability integration. If you're really motivated and you're using a flexible enough web measurement application, you can geographically correlate your performance and traffic data. In this view, you're able to see your performance and availability data, measured from specific geographic regions, correlated with measured traffic from those locales. Figure 5-3 shows a sample report.

If you're interested in integrating performance data into your web measurement programs, it's probably best to contact your web measurement vendor. Given the large number of vendors able to measure site performance (Keynote Systems, Gomez, Mercury Interactive, ProactiveNet, AlertSite, and Symphoniq, for example) and the relative commoditization in the space, you're best off to choose a performance measurement application that your measurement vendor has previously integrated.

Measure Connection Type

H A C K
#69

Determine whether your visitors use modems or broadband connections, and support critical site design decisions.

One of the most common questions asked of web measurement applications regarding site performance is, "How can I tell how my visitors connect to the Internet when they're coming to my site?" This question gets asked most often when companies are trying to make design decisions about page size, use of multimedia and Flash, and whether or not to deploy weighty tracking code.

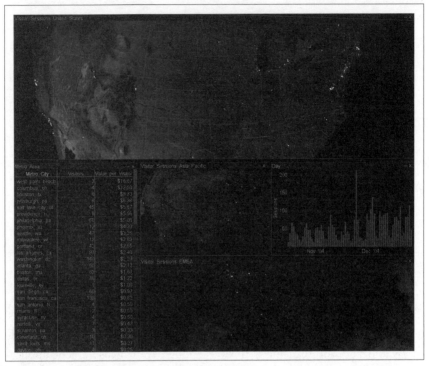

Figure 5-3. High-end geographic reporting

Many web measurement vendors attempt to provide this information using an obscure hack, the fact that IE users self-report how they connect to the Internet, and that this information is available via the JavaScript document object model. You'll commonly see reports called "Connection Type" that provide percentage of visitors using "LAN," "modem," and "unknown" or "other" types of connections (Figure 5-4).

While these reports are moderately useful, especially considering they come with no additional setup hassles, you can use some relatively simple JavaScript to build a much more complete report using custom variables.

The Code

The following code has been written in JavaScript, which is pretty much your only option since it needs to run in the visitor's web browser to test how long it takes to download an image.

The essence of this hack is as follows:

1. Download the sample image from *http://www.webanalyticsdemystified.com/sample/speedtest_28629B.gif* and save on your local server in the */images* directory. The size of this file is the basis for the cstImageSize variable; if

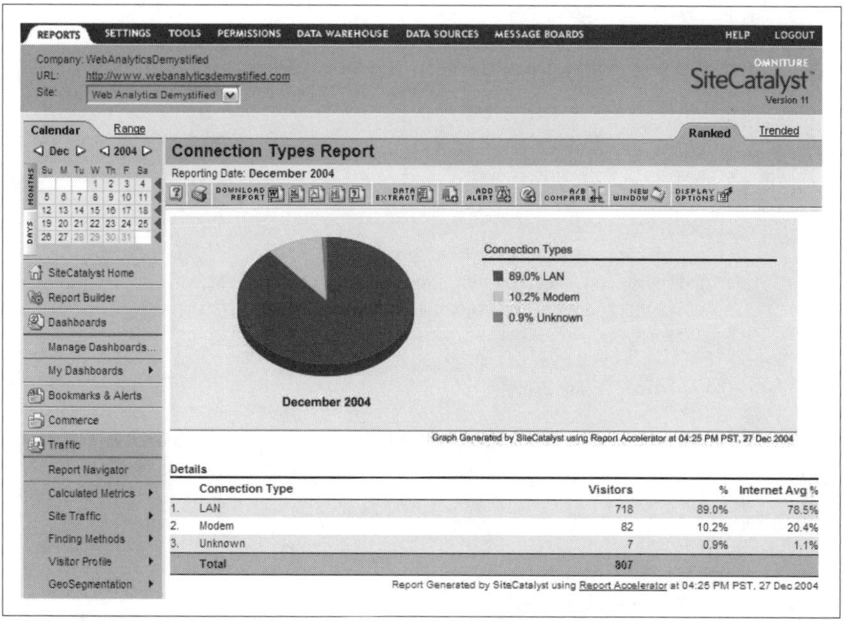

Figure 5-4. Connection type report

you use a different image, be sure to change the value of that and the cstImageURL variables.

2. You add the JavaScript code to your home page (ideally, via a server-side include called *visitor_connection_type.inc*).

3. You pass the value of the script's variable connectionType to your client-side page tag.

The imageSRC variable references a sample image you can use, thanks to Ian Houston of VisioActive. Go to *http://www. webanalyticsdemystified.com/sample/ speedtest_28629B.gif*, download the image, and save the file on your local server in the */images* directory. If you change the image, be sure to change the imageSize variable to the size of the image in bits.

Set the URL of the image to use for the test, the size of the image in bytes, and the name of the cookie you'll be using to store the information. Save the code into a file called *visitor_connection_type.inc* and plan on including it on your site's home page via a server-side include.

```
<script language="JavaScript">
var cstImageURL = "speedtest_28629B.gif";
// Specify the size of the test image in Bytes
var cstImageSize = "28629";
// Specify the name of the cookie to use
var cstCookieName = "ConnectionSpeed";
```

```
//Specify ConnectionSpeed Default Value
var ConnectionSpeed = "undetermined";
// If the cookie exists, pull the value from the Cookie.
// Otherwise set window.onload to run the test after the page has finished
loading.
 // Initialize the Test
 var cstCookies = document.cookie;
 var cstCookieStart = cstCookies.indexOf(cstCookieName + "=");
 if (cstCookieStart != -1) {
     cstCookieStart += cstCookieName.length + 1;
     var cstCookieEnd = cstCookies.indexOf(";", cstCookieStart);
     if (cstCookieEnd == -1) cstCookieEnd = cstCookies.length;
     ConnectionSpeed = cstCookies.substring(cstCookieStart, cstCookieEnd);
 } else {
     window.onload = RunCST;
 }
// Start the test by setting the start time, declaring a new image object by
// calling the calculating function and telling the new image object to
// begin the download.
// Run the Test
function RunCST() {
    cstStartTime = new Date();
    var cstImageTest = new Image(0,0);
    cstImageTest.onload = CalcCST;
    cstImageTest.src = cstImageURL + "?" + cstStartTime.getTime();
}
// Finish the test by getting the end time and calulating the speed of the
// download in kbps. # Wrap it up by passing that value to a function that
// will interpret and output the results.
// Calculate the Results to kbps

function CalcCST() {
    cstEndTime = new Date();
    var cstDownloadTime = (cstEndTime.getTime() - cstStartTime.getTime())/1000;
    if (cstDownloadTime == 0) cstDownloadTime = .001;
    var cstKBytes = cstImageSize/1000;
    var cstLineSpeed = cstKBytes/cstDownloadTime;
    var cstKbps = (Math.round((cstLineSpeed*8)*10*1.02))/10;
    OutputCST(cstKbps);
}
// Read in the speed of the download and translate into manageable groupings
related to
// connection types. Output the new value to a cookie to make it available
going forward
// without running the test with every subsequent every page view.
// Output the Test Results function OutputCST(cstKbps) {
if (cstKbps <= 14.4) {
    ConnectionSpeed = "14.4 modem";
} else if (cstKbps <= 28.8) {
    ConnectionSpeed = "28.8 modem";
} else if (cstKbps <= 33.6) {
    ConnectionSpeed = "33.6 modem";
} else if (cstKbps <= 53.4) {
    ConnectionSpeed = "56.6 modem";
```

```
} else if (cstKbps <= 64) {
    ConnectionSpeed = "ISDN";
} else if (cstKbps <= 128) {
    ConnectionSpeed = "Dual ISDN or cable modem or dsl";
} else if (cstKbps < 1500) {
    ConnectionSpeed = "fractional T1 or cable modem or dsl";
} else if (cstKbps >= 1500) {
    ConnectionSpeed = "T1 or faster";
}
var cstExpiration = new Date();
cstExpiration.setTime(cstExpiration.getTime() + 86400000);
document.cookie = cstCookieName + "=" + ConnectionSpeed + "; expires=" +
cstExpiration.toGMTString() + ";path=/";
}
```

The code basically checks to see if the test has already been run by checking for a cookie that expires in 24 hours. If the cookie exists, the connection information is available via the ConnectionSpeed JavaScript variable, which can be passed to your web measurement application.

The code is written this way since most page tag–based measurement applications won't wait for the test to run before passing information back to their servers. You're only going to get connection information for visitors who view more than one page, but this is a benefit really, helping you to better understand the connection type for people who are at least nominally engaged.

Running the Code

The code is self-sufficient and will run on its own based on the window. onload = RunCST command. When all is said and done, the variable ConnectionSpeed has a string value that describes the visitor's connection to the Internet. All that remains is to load that value into a custom variable supplied by your web measurement vendor. Using Omniture's SiteCatalyst, the code to do this is simply:

```
var s_prop3=ConnectionSpeed;
```

If you are using a web server log-based measurement application, you may want to consider appending the ConnectionSpeed variable's value to subsequent page requests in the URL. For example, if you have a link to *index.asp* you would modify that link dynamically to index.asp?ConnectionSpeed=56. 6+modem. Doing this will allow your application to mine for the particular name/value pair you provide and report on the connection speeds provided without affecting the link being clicked.

The Results

As you can see in Figure 5-5, as this information is passed into your web measurement application, you're able to see the distribution of connection types, ideally over both unique visitors and page views.

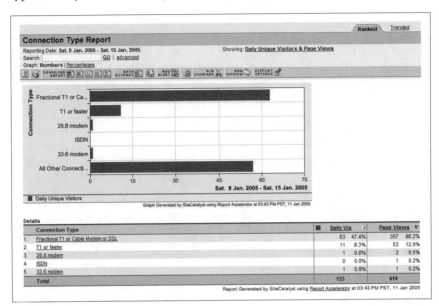

Figure 5-5. Connection type report

Whatever level of granularity you choose to report on, this information should be trended over time and, depending on the flexibility of your web measurement application and its ability to correlate custom variables, allow you to segment visitors or otherwise examine browsing habits by connection type. This data provides high-level insight into your visitors' needs that will impact design and development decisions over time.

—*Ian Houston and Eric T. Peterson*

HACK #70 Know How to Use Screen Resolution Data

Answer the question "Should we build pages for 1024×768 or 800×600 screen resolution?" using the data you already have.

One of the most common questions people ask when building web sites is whether designers should build for higher or lower screen resolutions. On one hand, we have professional web designers who want to build brilliant-looking designs unconstrained by low-resolution (e.g., 800×600) monitors. On the other hand, usability guidelines state unequivocally, "Thou shall not force the user to scroll horizontally!" What is a web designer to do?

Use Your Screen Resolutions Report

Any web measurement application worth its salt will have a screen resolution report similar to the one shown in Figure 5-6.

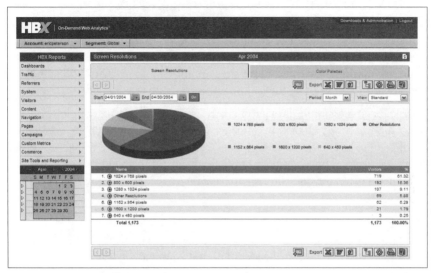

Figure 5-6. Screen resolution report

Any decision you make about your web site should be data-driven, right? So why not use screen resolution data to decide when to move to a 1024 pixel screen width! As you can see in Figure 5-6, less than 17 percent of the visitors used lower-resolution monitors; while this helps answer the question, you should also consider trending the data over time to develop a more complete view of when to make changes, based on historical and emerging trends.

So When Do We Switch Over?

Worldwide, the 800×600 browser share is still hovering around 30 percent. Unfortunately, you should never do anything that will negatively affect 30 percent of your audience. This would be like running a store where you were rude to every third person who asked you a question; you might get away with it at first, but before long, people would know you for being rude and would eventually shop elsewhere.

So there are no easy answers, but fortunately, we've already highlighted the important view of the data—your specific visitor trends compared to the Internet-wide average. If your screen resolution report indicates that your visitors' use of lower-resolution monitors is roughly half the Internet average, you can begin to make a case for up-sizing. My gut feeling is that you as long as you're seeing a downward trend for lower resolutions and your current 800×600 share is 20 percent or less, you can switch.

There, I said it. Never anger a third of your audience, but go ahead and mess around with a fifth of them.

Sounds arbitrary (and perhaps it is), but you have to make the switch at some point, and you're not going to see 800×600 monitors disappear anytime soon with inexpensive desktop and notebook machines beginning to flood the market. More and more sites are moving to a 1024×768 standard, and you don't want to be the last business to make the change.

Thanks to some simple JavaScript, there is an intermediate solution, a hack that supports nearly all of your audience (provided you're willing to add a little bit of code to your pages and templates). The following hack will allow you to query the visitor's browser in real time then substitute an alternative cascading style sheets (CSS) file for visitors who have lower-resolution browsers.

The Code

The JavaScript to test for screen width and switch to a different CSS file simply needs to be inserted into the header of each document you want to modify:

```
<link href="pageStyle1024.css" rel="stylesheet" type="text/css">
<script type="text/javascript">
    if (screen.width < 1024)
        link = document.getElementsByTagName( "link" )[ 0 ];
        link.href = "pageStyle800.css";
</script>
<!-- NORMAL DOCUMENT HEADERS INCLUDING TITLE AND META TAGS GO HERE -->
```

This code assumes that you have two CSS files, one called *pageStyle1024.css* and another called *pageStyle800.css*, residing in your root directory. The page will default to the larger CSS style by default, dropping down to the smaller style if the visitor is using a lower resolution browser.

This strategy works because you'll use smaller fonts or make some other significant change to your styles that will better accommodate visitors using lower-resolution browsers. Likely, you'll need to experiment to get the right combination of styles for the lower-resolution browser. For a very complete treatment of CSS, I recommend the *CSS Cookbook* by Christopher Schmidt (O'Reilly).

Running the Code

To run the code, simply include the JavaScript code in the <HEAD> section of any page you want dynamically modified. You will also need to ensure that the CSS files are properly defined.

If you really want to be sophisticated from a web measurement perspective, create a custom variable [Hack #31] that tracks the version of the screen the visitor was shown (e.g., smaller or larger), using any of the various techniques described in the other hacks. This way, you can then begin to determine whether changing the style sheet for lower-resolution browsers has any impact on their likelihood of success.

HACK #71 Know How to Use Browser Version Information

Make sure you're performing application quality assurance testing for the browser versions that your visitors are actually using.

Web application developers have learned to fear final-stage application testing for multiple browser versions and platforms. The basic fear is that you spend a great deal of time writing complex code, usually JavaScript and dynamic HTML, for a single browser—usually the dominant version of Internet Explorer at the time—but when all is said and done, the code won't run in Netscape, Opera, Macintosh's Safari, or Firefox.

Smart web quality assurance managers know that your web measurement application already reports on the information you need to build a browser plan. Like other technographic reports, browser type and browser version reports are pretty much standard (Figure 5-7).

Unfortunately, these reports often go unused, but it doesn't have to be this way. Three things you can do to take advantage of your browser versions report include build for your top five browsers, pay attention to emerging trends, and monitor the Internet averages (if possible).

Build for Your Top Five Browsers

Notice the word "your" in the sentence above—you should focus your quality testing on the browsers that your visitors actually use when they visit your web site. Until recently people's browser choice had been pretty much made for them—Windows people used Internet Explorer, Macintosh people used Safari, and Unix people, well, they were probably using some version of Netscape or Mozilla. While people would upgrade browser versions, few switched browser platforms completely, at least until recently

You want to closely examine your browser versions report to make sure your testing plan is built around the top five browsers people use when they visit your site. For my site (Figure 5-7), I will be focusing on Internet Explorer 6.0, Firefox 1.0, Safari 1.2.1, Internet Explorer 5.5, and Mozilla Gecko. Despite the fact that the last three browser versions add up to only five percent of my visiting traffic, I want to pay close attention to these

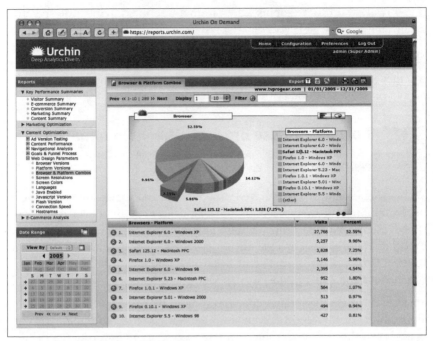

Figure 5-7. Browser version by operating system report

applications to be sure that they don't create any complications so that if I attract more visitors using these platforms, or if they magically surge in Internet-wide popularity, I'll be set.

Why? Because the worst thing you can possibly do to a visitor or loyal customer is show them a message like the one in Figure 5-8 when they try and update a 401K plan.

If, by chance, you still have a browser version that is being used by more than five percent of your visitors after you consider the top five, make sure and add those browsers to the test plan as well.

When examining browser versions, look at data from the last 90 days: that's enough time to gather meaningful data but not enough to dilute emerging trends.

Pay Attention to Emerging Trends

To reinforce the assertion that you should examine the last 90 days and consider the top five browser versions even if your traffic volume is low for some of those browsers, you should also get in the habit of looking at a trended view of the data (Figure 5-9).

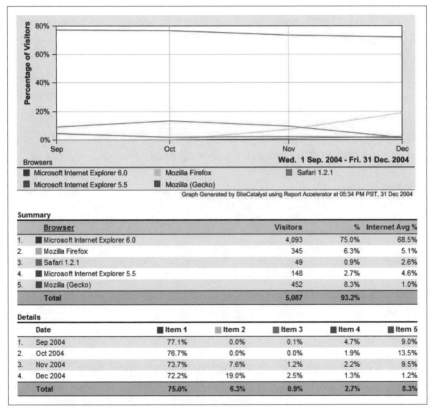

Browser Requirements

This site is optimized for use with Internet Explorer 5.5 or greater and Netscape 7.1. You are using a browser that is not supported by this Web site. Please take a moment to upgrade your browser or install one of the versions below.

More than 98% of our audience uses one of the browsers listed below. We want to help you update your browser so that you have a better experience on   and other Web sites. We recommend you use a browser with 128-bit encryption for security purposes. If you do not have 128-bit encryption, or cannot obtain same due to export restrictions, this site can be accessed using 40-bit encryption.

Click one of the download links below to upgrade your browser for free:

Internet Explorer 5.5 or greater

Netscape 7.1

☐ Do not show this message again

Continue

Figure 5-8. Annoying browser requirements error message

Figure 5-9. Browser versions over time

The trended view of the data will help you better plan for the future. In the case of Figure 5-9, it is clear that it makes more sense to pay closer attention to Firefox, and less to Mozilla Gecko (or possibly even consider dropping Mozilla Gecko from the test plan entirely). While it's rare that a new browser will emerge and create a situation in which 0.0 percent of visitors are using Firefox in October 2004, 7.6 percent in November 2004, and 19.0 percent in December 2004, this is the exact data and presentation that will save your QA team time and effort in the long run.

Monitor Internet Averages

Finally, you want to keep an eye on an Internet-wide report of browser version use if possible. Offered by companies like Holland's OneStat (*www.onestat.com*) and WebSideStory's StatMarket (*www.websidestory.com*) and occasionally embedded in web measurement applications (see the "Internet Average Percentage" column from Omniture's SiteCatalyst 11 in Figure 5-4 and Figure 5-7), this data can help you understand how your visitor audience differs from the teeming masses of Internet users.

> Monitor Internet-wide distribution of browsers *only* to watch for emerging trends—don't bother building a test plan for browsers that nobody uses when they visit your web site.

This statement is bound to be controversial, and your QA manager may argue this point until she is red in the face, so here's a caveat.

> If your quality assurance team is fully staffed with qualified individuals and has all the time in the world to test against obscure browser platforms, test away. Conversely, if they're already too busy and you constantly risk missing deployment deadlines because test plans are overreaching, take my advice.

There you have it: a reasonable and easy-to-follow plan for taking advantage of the browser version information already reported by your web measurement applications.

Know if People Are Bookmarking Your Site
HACK #72

One fairly strong indicator of audience loyalty is whether or not people have 'saved your site in their bookmarks folder; use this hack to track this behavior.

One of the surest signs of loyalty to a web site is whether visitors are bookmarking your site or saving it in their "favorites" folder for easy access. Because of the addition of a browser feature in Internet Explorer 5.0 and above that attempts to associate an icon with bookmarks, it is relatively easy to get a rough feel for how many people are actively bookmarking your site by monitoring the "favicon."

The "favicon" is a 16×16-pixel image that, when saved into your document root directory on your web server, is picked up by Internet Explorer and Firefox and presented in bookmark folders and browser toolbars (Figure 5-10).

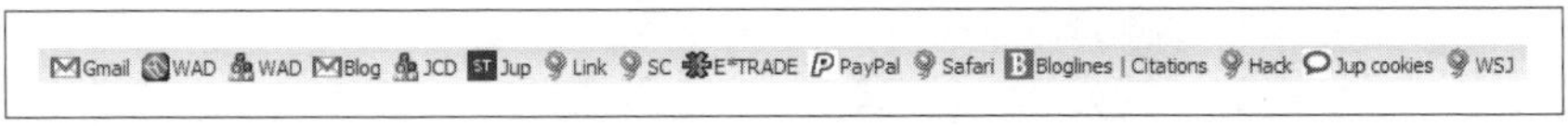

Figure 5-10. A handful of "favicon.ico" images

To let web browsers know you have a *favicon.ico* file, all you need to do is add a little bit of code to your web pages:

```
<link rel="icon" href="/favicon.ico" type="image/x-icon" />
<link rel="shortcut icon" href="/favicon.ico" type="image/x-icon" />
```

More information about *favicon.ico* is available at the Microsoft web site (*msdn.microsoft.com/workshop/Author/dhtml/howto/ShortcutIcon.asp*).

How to Measure Bookmarking with favicon.ico

Provided you have a *favicon.ico* created and deployed in your document root directory, simply ask your web analytics application to tell you how many times the file was requested. You'll need to use a logfile-based measurement tool to make this measurement, but any of the free log analyzer applications [Hack #10] or Stephen Turner's Analog [Hack #11] will suit your purposes just fine.

If you haven't created the *favicon.ico* file, you can also look in your 404 (Page Not Found) [Hack #34] report for presence of this file (Figure 5-11).

One important thing to keep in mind is that most applications are going to report requests for *favicon.ico* on a per-hit [Hack #1] basis. As you'll hopefully recall, "hit" is not a particularly useful term, but in this context, it is worth understanding. The reports are telling you that the file was requested a certain number of times. For example, in Figure 5-11, we can see that the *favicon.ico* file was requested 2,310 times in the reporting period. This tells you nothing about the number of unique visitors making the request.

Because you're unable to determine how many people are actually book-marking your site based on the number of hits observed, there are two recommendations to improve the usefulness of the data:

- Consult with your application vendor and see if they're able to report this data on a per-visitor basis.

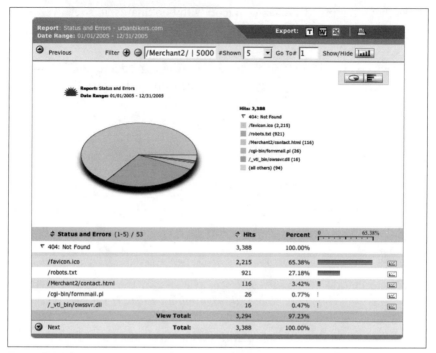

Figure 5-11. favicon.ico in a typical 404 (Page Not Found) error report

- Treat the hit-based report as directional, using the data to explore whether it appears that more people are bookmarking your site and how quickly this activity is increasing.

Hacking the Hack: Differentiate IE from Firefox Requests

Because the behavior of Internet Explorer and non-Explorer browsers is slightly different, you may want to use different icon files (or at least different icon filenames) to allow you to differentiate requests. If you use Apache, you can leverage the mod_rewrite module and modify your *httpd.conf* file, adding the following code:

```
RewriteEngine on
RewriteCond %{HTTP_USER_AGENT} !.+MSIE.+
RewriteRule ^/favicon.ico$ /bookmark.ico
```

For this to work, you'll have to have a copy of your *favicon.ico* file called *bookmark.ico* in your document root directory. Non–Internet Explorer browsers will be directed to the *bookmark.ico* file, allowing you to get a count for IE and non-IE browsers separately.

More information about Apache's mod_rewrite module is available at *httpd.apache.org/docs/misc/rewriteguide.html*.

Measure Browser Plug-ins

HACK
#73

If you're developing any advanced functionality that requires external plug-ins, you should use your web measurement application to make sure your visitors have the right plug-ins installed.

Understanding the plug-ins your visitors use helps guide web site technology decisions. For example, if only 20 percent of your visitors have Real-Player support, you may consider offering videos in other formats such as QuickTime or Windows Media. You may be looking at research data to understand plug-in penetration. Research data is a starting point, but you will want to check your own web site visitors. For example, a software company web site may have a much higher concentration of advanced plug-ins than a generic search portal.

Determining which plug-ins are installed on a visitor's browser is difficult, because each browser works differently. Before Internet Explorer became so popular, you could easily get a list of plug-ins by accessing the `navigator.plug-ins` array, which contains all of the installed plug-ins for Netscape and Mozilla-based browsers. The problem with Internet Explorer is that it does not provide a list of plug-ins. Instead, you basically ask the browser about each plug-in.

Ask the Browser

To detect and track a plug-in with Internet Explorer, you will need to add some code to your page—usually JavaScript, but in some cases VBScript—and pass in the information to a variable or URL of your web measurement application (note that some vendors have this functionality by default).

Tracking plug-ins is not an exact science and does not work in all versions of Internet Explorer; however, it should work with the majority of your visitors.

Since it is not feasible to check all plug-ins at once with Internet Explorer, we will add some JavaScript code to our web pages to test three media plug-ins. The code example below checks each of our site visitors to see if they have QuickTime, Macromedia Flash, and/or Windows Media Player installed.

The Code

If you use the following code with your web measurement application you will need to pass the results into JavaScript variables, which will be collected by the web measurement application. With some additional modifications to this code, you can even display the plug-in version in your web measurement application.

```
<script language="JavaScript">
<!--
    function ie_plugin_check(id) {
        document.body.addBehavior("#default#clientCaps");
        if (id.substring(0,1) != '{') {
            id = '{' + id + '}';
        }
        if (document.body.isComponentInstalled(id,'ComponentID')) {
            return true;
        }
        return false;
    }
    var plugin_list = new Array;
    plugin_list[0]      = new Object;
    plugin_list[0].id   = 'D27CDB6E-AE6D-11CF-96B8-444553540000';
    plugin_list[0].name = 'Macromedia Flash';
    plugin_list[1]      = new Object;
    plugin_list[1].id   = '22D6F312-B0F6-11D0-94AB-0080C74C7E95';
    plugin_list[1].name = 'Windows Media Player';
    plugin_list[2]      = new Object;
    plugin_list[2].id   = '23064720-C4F8-11D1-994D-00C04F98BBC9';
    plugin_list[2].name = 'Windows Media Player RealNetwork Support';

    var s_prop1 = "";
    for (var plugin_num = 0;plugin_num < plugin_list.length;plugin_num++) {
        if (1 || ie_plugin_check(plugin_list[plugin_num].id)) {
            s_prop1 += (s_prop1 ? ',' : '') + plugin_list[plugin_num].name;
        }
    }
//-->
</script>
```

Once your analytics application collects the data, you can run reports to determine plug-in usage. You should be able to view a report that shows you the page views, visits, visitors, and even success events by plug-in. This helps you determine how critical plug-ins may be to the success of your web site.

Hacking the Hack

Another way to understand your visitors is to segment them based on a plug-in and then measure how they interact with it. For example, if you're running a clothing web site with a three-dimensional model, does the model increase sales versus a two-dimensional image?

On the product pages in which the visitors used the 3D model plug-in, we would pass in to a JavaScript variable something like "3D Image Used," and for the visitors that used the standard 2D image, we would pass in to a Java-Script variable "2D Image Used." From within your web measurement application, you would see a report that looks something like Figure 5-12.

3D Plug-in Usage		Visitors		Orders		Revenue		Conv-Rate	
1.	3D Image Used	19,965	59.7%	486	61.1%	$360,442	64.8%	2.43%	
2.	2D Image Used	13,462	40.3%	309	38.9%	$195,511	35.2%	2.30%	
	Total	33,427		795		$555,953		n/a	

Report Generated by SiteCatalyst using Report Accelerator at 07:10 PM WET, 11 Jan 2005

Figure 5-12. Browser plug-in report

By looking at simple reports, you can understand the usefulness of plug-in technologies and how they can help create a better web site experience.

—*John Pestana and Eric T. Peterson*

Know Which Technographic Data to Ignore

HACK #74

Not all technical data is as useful as it looks at first glance. Knowing what to pay attention to and what to ignore can save you time and prevent frustration.

As you've certainly surmised by now in reading this book, web measurement applications provide a wealth of information about your visitors, most of it good! While the vendors certainly mean well, often they provide information because they can—not because there is a great business reason for doing so. Unfortunately, not all the available information is useful, especially when you're talking about technographic reports (Figure 5-13).

Since most vendors provide the same technographic data, it is worth reviewing which of this information you should use and which you should ignore.

Technographic Data to Use

The following are technographic data points and reports that are generally useful to web data analysts.

Browser type
    Your web developers and quality assurance group will benefit from a complete list of visitor browser types. Use recent (last 90 days) samples to ensure QA efforts map well to current browser trends.

Browser width
    A central concern for web developers is how much screen real estate to use, and the schism between 800×600 and 1024×768 screen

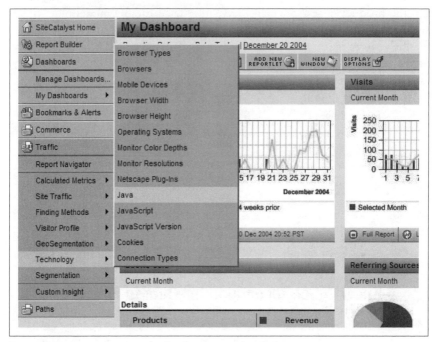

Figure 5-13. Representative sample of technographic data

resolutions. Keep a close eye on how these numbers evolve; looking for the opportunity to use more screen real estate [Hack #70] will help you make more effective design decisions.

Cookies

The cookies report provides a partial glimpse into the accuracy [Hack #15] of your data if you're using a page tag or augmenting your web server logfiles with a cookie. While not the final word on cookie acceptance by your visitors, I recommend checking this report on a monthly basis to look for any large decreases in cookie acceptance.

Connection type

While this report is almost always built from an obscure setting available via the JavaScript DOM for Internet Explorer users, as long as your IE browser share is high, this report can help you understand whether most of your visitors are broadband or modem users, helping you refine your page design and development strategy.

Technographic Data to Ignore

The following are technographic data points and elements that are unlikely to provide valuable insight into your visitors, either because they're too granular, not granular enough, or because they're otherwise useless.

Browsers
> While the specifics of browser type are useful from a development stand-point, watching the browser wars play out is interesting, but not useful.

Browser height
> Simply put, if you do a good job presenting content, your visitors will scroll. Alternatively, the "fold" (bottom-most point in a browser's initial load without any scrolling) is well-defined by the browser's width using a standard calculation.

Monitor color depth
> You should build well-designed web pages that use web-friendly colors.

Monitor resolutions
> The screen width report provides relevant and useful information.

Netscape plug-ins
> Depending on the breakdown of browser versions at your web site, it is very likely that this report will not paint a useful picture of plug-in usage [Hack #73] on the part of your visitors. I recommend avoiding all but the most standard plug-ins (Adobe PDF, RealPlayer, Windows Media Player, Macromedia Flash) and always building to the *last* version released (when relevant).

Java
> Unless you do something particularly complex on your web site, you should avoid using Java. If you need Java, know that over 90 percent of Internet users have Java enabled and use it carefully.

JavaScript
> Same as Java, but over 95 percent of Internet users allow JavaScript to run in their browsers.

Technographic Data that Depends on Your Specific Needs

As you might expect, some data points are either useful or not, depending on your particular needs at the time. The following data points are classified in an "it depends" category and are worth understanding, just in case.

Mobile devices
> If you're actively working to provide content to mobile users, use this report the same way you would the browser types report. If you're not concerned about mobile users, ignore.

Operating systems

Since you'll be able to get the important information about which browsers are being used by OS from the browser version report, you may be able to ignore operating systems. However, if you develop downloadable applications, you should use this report to make sure you're providing for less-popular operating systems.

JavaScript versions

Since over 95 percent of Internet users allow JavaScript 1.3, unless a new version of JavaScript is released, this report is only nominally useful. If a new version of JavaScript is released, you should still consider building only for Version 1.3 until 90 percent of the Internet supports the new version.

In general, technographic metrics are for web design and development teams and have little direct impact on your overall business success.

HACK #75   Know How to Use Visitor Language Reports

Knowing which languages your visitors speak will help you improve your message and improving your message will help your conversion rates.

While tracking your visitor's specific geographic distribution **[Hack #78]** is important, consider the primary and secondary languages of you visitors.

Online, you should strive to be helpful, courteous, and friendly—at least when you can determine that you have enough foreign traffic to benefit from your benevolence. But how do you know when you should consider translation? Easy—use your visitor language reports!

Visitor Language Reporting

Most web measurement applications provide language reporting based on information gleaned from the visitor's web browser, most often generating a report similar to that seen in Figure 5-14.

The languages reported are picked up from the web visitor's browser and controlled by a setting you can easily change in your browser if you'd like. Want to try this out? In Firefox simply click Tools → Options → General and then click the "Languages" button to add any number of International languages you'd like the browser to support. Piece of cake!

The information reported in a visitor languages report is particularly good, because users are telling you which language they prefer to communicate in. If I understand English but I read, speak, and write Spanish, I am very likely to change my primary language setting to "Spanish" in the hope that your web site will speak to me in Spanish. Again, if you stop to think about this, you'll see the power in using this information.

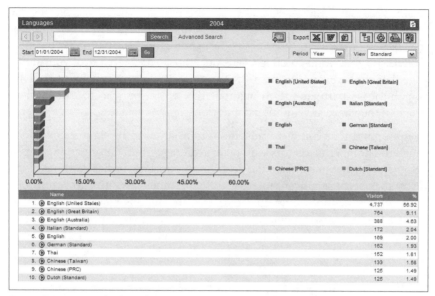

Figure 5-14. Visitor languages report

How to Use Language Information

To leverage your visitor language report, you're looking for larger-than-expected segments of visitors browsing your site in languages other than the one(s) you currently support. Using the data from Figure 5-14, you can see that 1.5 percent of the visitors in 2004 prefer Dutch as their primary language. Cross-referencing this with the Internet averages for languages, you find that the site has nearly three times the Internet average for Dutch speakers.

Armed with this data, you might consider translating part of the site into Dutch in an effort to better connect with those visitors, increasing their likelihood to convert. Still, translation can be very expensive, so be cautious when deciding when and how much to translate.

Knowing When and How Much to Translate

Translating your site into multiple languages shouldn't be attempted on a whim; it can be an arduous and expensive task. The major reason you should keep track of your visitor languages report is to help determine if or when it is necessary to translate. As a rule of thumb, any time you see more than 10 percent of visitors browsing in a language other than English (assuming your site is already in English), you should start to explore translating your site.

Again, because of the associated costs, the best way to start exploring the value of translation is to convert a small number of pages and then monitor the volume of traffic to those pages. Depending on your particular business model, you may want to offer a series of translated pages off of your home page that explain your business's commitment to international visitors, who your business partners are throughout the world, or who to call (by language) if they have any additional questions.

Keep in mind that you want this initial translation to be simple so you can gauge the number of visitors who take advantage of the information. This is designed to help you validate the decision to translate further, nothing more. If you then see a significant increase in the number of visitors to your translated pages and (hopefully) an increase in the actions you present on that page, consider translating more of your site. Conversely, if you build a translated page and make it clear that the page is available but then nobody visits the page—well, perhaps the need for translation is not so great.

HACK #76 Hacking into Page-Level Details for Language

Generate a page-by-language text file that can be mined for deep and rich information.

While most web measurement applications do a pretty good job reporting on the percentage distribution of languages used to browse your site, very few go so far as to let you segment your visitor activity [Hack #48] by language. Fortunately, if you have a nominal amount of control over your web site, you can write a relatively simple hack to provide this information.

The Code

The following code is written in VBScript for Microsoft's Active Server Pages, but could quite easily be adapted to PHP, Perl, or Java. You should save the following code as *language_by_page.inc* and include it in your header files.

```
<%
Dim fso, lf
df = "en" ' Default language for site is English (en)

' Test to see if current visitor is using other than the default language
(df)
if (Left(REQUEST.SERVERVARIABLES("HTTP_ACCEPT_LANGUAGE"), 2) <> df AND
REQUEST.SERVERVARIABLES("HTTP_ACCEPT_LANGUAGE") <> "") then

    ' If so, open the language_by_page.txt file for appending
    Set fso = CreateObject("Scripting.FileSystemObject")
    Set lf = fso.OpenTextFile("c:\websites\webanalytics\cgi-data\
      language_by_page.txt", 8, True)
```

```
' Append the name of the script, the language and the time stamp
lf.WriteLine( REQUEST.SERVERVARIABLES("SCRIPT_NAME") & "|" &
   REQUEST.SERVERVARIABLES("HTTP_ACCEPT_LANGUAGE") & "|"  & now())

' Don't forget to close the "lf" object
lf.Close
end if
%>
```

Running the Code

Here is what you need to do to have *language_by_page.inc* track the pages your non-English visitors are viewing:

1. Create a file called *language_by_page.txt* in a writeable directory (*/cgi-data* is a good place).
2. Change the permissions on the *language_by_page.txt* file to be writable.
3. Make sure you change the **c:\websites\webanalytics\cgi-data** reference to the physical location of the *language_by_page.txt* file on your file-system (otherwise, the script will crash).
4. Save *language_by_page.inc* in the same directory as your header file(s).
5. Make sure you have server-side includes activated for your web site.
6. Have your common header file(s) include this page using the following directive:

   ```
   <!--#include file="/language_by_page.inc"-->
   ```

That's it. As soon as visitors who have their browser language set to something other than English (which can be changed by changing the df variable; consult *http://www.w3.org/WAI/ER/IG/ert/iso639.htm* for a complete list of ISO 639 language codes and two-letter abbreviations used by HTTP_ACCEPT_LANGUAGE), the request is saved for future analysis in the *language_by_page.txt* file.

> Be warned: because this script opens a file on the filesystem every time it executes, it can have a slowing effect on the rendered pages if used in high-volume situations. You should consult with your IT staff before deploying this (or any) script designed to modify files on your filesystem.

The Results

What you'll end up with is a text file looking something like Figure 5-15. that contains a list of filenames, language codes, and times all separated by a pipe character.

```
/add_link.asp|es-es,en-us;q=0.7,en;q=0.3|12/26/2004 7:34:03 PM
/free_preview.asp|es-es,en-us;q=0.7,en;q=0.3|12/26/2004 7:34:06 PM
/index.asp|es-es,en-us;q=0.7,en;q=0.3|12/26/2004 7:34:07 PM
/free_kpi_worksheet.asp|es-es,en-us;q=0.7,en;q=0.3|12/26/2004 7:34:08 PM
/link_list.asp|sw,en-us;q=0.7,en;q=0.3|12/26/2004 7:34:40 PM
/link_list.asp|sw,en-us;q=0.7,en;q=0.3|12/26/2004 7:34:41 PM
/index.asp|sw,en-us;q=0.7,en;q=0.3|12/26/2004 7:34:43 PM
/free_kpi_worksheet.asp|sw,en-us;q=0.7,en;q=0.3|12/26/2004 7:34:45 PM
/free_preview.asp|sw,en-us;q=0.7,en;q=0.3|12/26/2004 7:34:46 PM
```

Figure 5-15. The language_by_page.txt file

If you import this list into Microsoft Excel or any reasonable database, you can then begin to take a closer look at which pages your non-English speaking visitors are most interested in. These pages are good candidates for translation!

An Alternative to Hacking for Page-Level Details

If you're shy about writing code or you get a funny look from your system administrator when you show him this hack, don't despair. Some web measurement vendors provide the ability to segment visitors by browser language. While this functionality is far from ubiquitous, all you need to ask your vendor is, "Can you show me a report of all activity—including page views, referrals, and conversion events—by visitor browser language?" If you get a blank stare (or silence on the phone) you may want to point them toward this hack and have them do their homework!

Regardless of how you get the data, knowing what your non-English reading visitors are most interested in on your web site and in what numbers they are visiting will help you to define a future plan for having a truly global Internet presence.

HACK #77 Track Demographic Data Using Custom Variables and Visitor Segmentation

If you're collecting any type of demographic data from your visitors using forms, you can easily pass this information along to your measurement application and do some light demographic analysis.

It is very common for sites that require registration to ask a few questions about demographics in the process of signing a visitor up for a service (Figure 5-16).

The most typical questions are, "What is your gender?" and, "When were you born?" but occasionally sites ask for other information, such as annual income, marital status, or whether you have children. Fortunately for you,

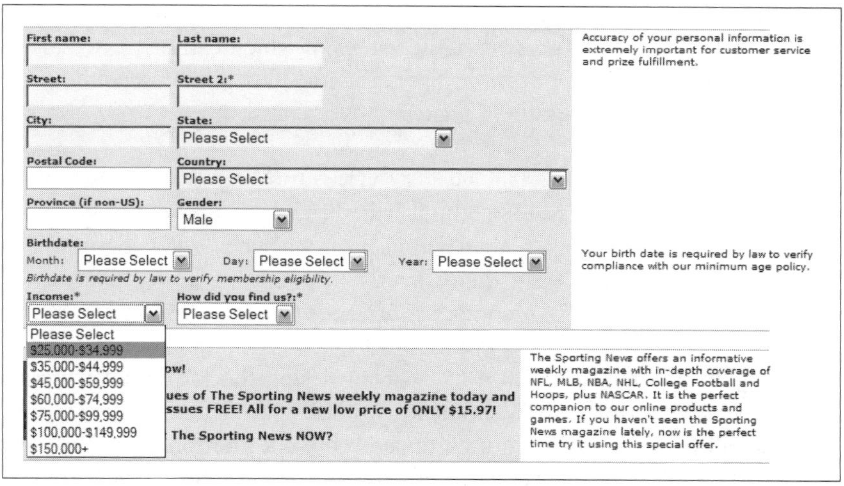

Figure 5-16. Subscription form with demographic data

since this information is nearly always collected via an HTML form, the results can easily be passed to your web measurement system and collected into custom variables [Hack #31] or used to create visitor segments [Hack #48].

How to Pass Demographic Data to Your Measurement Application

For the most part, forms like the one in Figure 5-16 use the form POST method in HTTP to hide the fields and values from prying eyes, a good idea when you're asking for personal information. If this is the case, you'll have to use some server-side code to grab the information from the form processing script and pass it to your measurement application.

For example, the following form uses the POST method to collect three pieces of useful demographic data:

```
<FORM ACTION="formprocessor.asp" METHOD="POST">
Your gender:
    <SELECT NAME="gender" size="1">
    <OPTION>Male</OPTION>
    <OPTION>Female</OPTION>
    </SELECT><br>
Your year of birth: <INPUT TYPE="TEXT" SIZE="4" NAME="year_of_birth"><br>
Your marital status:
    <SELECT NAME="marital_status" size="1">
    <OPTION>Married</OPTION>
    <OPTION>Single</OPTION>
    </SELECT><
<INPUT TYPE="SUBMIT">
</FORM>
```

The script *formprocessor.asp* will have access to three variables—gender, year_of_birth, and marital_status–the values of which can be passed along to your measurement application. Specific strategies differ, depending on whether you're using a logfiles or page tags as a data source.

Pass demographic data to a server log analyzer. Unfortunately, unless your forms are set up to use a GET method, it is difficult to provide this type of information to your measurement application via web server logfiles. The GET will post all of the form data directly into the logfile for analysis. If you're required to use a POST, contact your vendor directly for ideas.

Pass demographic data to a client-side page tag. Using the form above, Active Server Pages/VBScript, and WebSideStory's HBX JavaScript page tag as an example, all that would be required to send this information using the page tag would be to use Active Server Page's REQUEST object to drop the form values into JavaScript.

```
//CUSTOM VARIABLES
hbx.ci="";//CUSTOMER ID
hbx.hc1="<%= REQUEST.FORM("gender") %>";//CUSTOM 1 = GENDER
hbx.hc2="<%= REQUEST.FORM("year_of_birth") %>";//CUSTOM 2 = YEAR OF BIRTH
hbx.hc3="<%= REQUEST.FORM("marital_status") %>";//CUSTOM 3 = MARITAL STATUS
hbx.hc4="";//CUSTOM 4
hbx.hrf="";//CUSTOM REFERRER
hbx.pec="";//ERROR CODES
```

When the *formprocessor.asp* script is rendered at the server prior to being passed back to the web browser, the ASP code is processed and, assuming the visitor answered "Male," "1970," and "Married," the rendered Java-Script will look like this when it arrives in the browser:

```
//CUSTOM VARIABLES
hbx.ci="";//CUSTOMER ID
hbx.hc1="Male";//CUSTOM 1 = GENDER
hbx.hc2="1970";//CUSTOM 2 = YEAR OF BIRTH
hbx.hc3="Married";//CUSTOM 3 = MARITAL STATUS
hbx.hc4="";//CUSTOM 4
hbx.hrf="";//CUSTOM REFERRER
hbx.pec="";//ERROR CODES
```

When the JavaScript is then executed in the web browser, the page tag sends this data along and it is collected in custom variables one through three.

What to Do with Demographic Data Once You Get It

There are two basic things you can do with this type of data, one fairly benign and one tremendously powerful. The simple strategy is to simply use the measurement application to count the number of members of each demographic group. While benign, even this type of data can be very help-ful to your web marketing group, allowing them to better understand the demographic makeup of your typical visitor or subscriber (whatever the impetus for completing the form is). Simple data such as this can be very useful in helping companies challenge their assumptions. Imagine:

- You believe your offer appeals mostly to males, but when you collect demographic data, 30 percent of the respondents are female.
- Your service is aimed mainly at people with children, but mostly single people and couples without children are using your web site.
- You are working to target a high-income demographic but 70 percent of your respondents report earning less than $25,000 a year.

Just having this type of information can be very telling, occasionally forcing companies to substantially change their marketing acquisition strategy.

A tremendously powerful use for demographic data collected in this fashion is to build demographic visitor segments from the data. Given the recent rapid maturation of visitor segmentation tools in some of the best web mea-surement applications [Hack #3] and depending on which application you use, you may be able to:

- Create a segment of "males" and one of "females" to examine how browsing habits differ by gender
- Create age segments to determine whether different content or informa-tion is consumed by different aged visitors
- Create economic segments to explore how different products you offer appeal to people who likely have more or less disposable income

What's more, the best applications will allow you to easily combine demo-graphic data with more traditional web data and create very complex visitor segments. Depending on your applications ability, you may want to:

- Create combined "gender" and "age" (or "age group") segments to explore how the different genders at different stages in life may be responding to your content
- Create segments of ages by referring sources (e.g., search engines, ban-ner ads, outbound email) to examine whether different aged groups are preferentially responding to different marketing vehicles
- Create complex multi-dimensional segments that combine age, gender, and economic status in a matrix to attempt to identify the most valu-able demographic group to your company

The fundamental value in creating these segments is that, usually, once you add a visitor to a specific segment, she *remains* in that segment from visit to visit (at least as long as her cookie doesn't get reset [Hack #17]). This means that once you're able to establish that a particular visitor is "female, 18 to 25, single with annual income from $25,000 to $34,999," you'll be able to track her habits as she returns to the site and continues her interaction.

> Consult your web measurement application vendor for specifics regarding establishment of visitor segments. Some vendors charge extra for advanced segmentation.

Again, depending on your particular measurement application's sophistication and ability to create and manage complex segments, this type of analysis may provide the single greatest benefit from your investment in web analytics.

Things to Keep in Mind

There is a handful of things you'll want to keep in mind when attempting advanced segmentation and analysis.

It is usually not easy to do. While it's pretty easy to describe, and it sounds easy enough to gather the data and build segments, the reality is that most vendors' abilities to collect custom data and convert that data into useful visitor segments are relatively immature. Either one of these needs in isolation is complex enough; the combination is sometimes impossible.

It requires tremendous planning to pull off properly. The recommendation is to carefully define which demographic data you're going to collect and which demographic segments you're interested in well in advance of doing any coding. You should then contact your vendor and share this plan, asking them to explain where they see risks and which reports you'll be able to generate for the segments in question.

Most often your sample size will not be significant. Depending on what you're doing to get visitors to complete the form in which you ask the demographic questions, you may never get enough visitors through the form to segment a statistically relevant sample of your population. Keep this in mind when you're setting up segmentation as a critical factor influencing the return you'll get for the work you do. You may want to consider offering some incentive to visitors to complete the form, driving more segmentation.

Some consumers are liars when filling out forms. Depending on what you're offering people to complete forms like the one shown in Figure 5-16, you may or may not get truthful responses. Companies that collect this type of data online often report a tremendous number of 18- to 25-year-olds who make in excess of $100,000 annually, data that does not match known populations. You may want to consult with a trained statistician to make sure you have statistically relevant populations before you start making business decisions based on this data.

Not every report is always available for every segment. Imagine that you've gone through all of the trouble of creating useful demographic segments to learn that the reports you're most interested in aren't available to visitor segments? Because of the cost and complexity associated with segmentation, it is very common for vendors to provide only a subset of their reports to visitor segments. The only way to know for sure is to ask.

Occasionally the payback is hardly worth the effort. Keep in mind that sometimes the great insight you'll get from this type of analysis—and sometimes web measurement in general—is nothing more than "yeah, we knew that." Be prepared to not be blown away by the data once you get it. If you end up in a situation like this after having spent hours on planning and implementation chalk it up to experience that you'll use down the road and feel good in knowing you were right in the first place.

The fundamental recommendation when trying to build these types of segments is to *start small*. Instead of collecting *every piece* of demographic data possible and building 50 segments, slicing and dicing your visitors every way possible, consider collecting simple demographic data (gender is a good example) and segmenting from that. Starting small helps you develop the technical skills necessary to build more complex segments and explore whether the information is truly valuable to your organization.

Simple Demographic Segmentation

Some of the currently available web measurement applications are unable to build complex, *ad hoc* visitor segments and are instead limited to creating simple "move forward" segments. If this is the case for you, don't despair! You can still take advantage of the type of segmentation described with a little more work.

The usual strategy for simple visitor segmentation is to require you to create segments in advance. These segments are then assigned numerical IDs that are added to page tags or server requests when a visitor is determined to have joined a group. The extra work is that you need to figure out which demographic elements are assigned to which IDs in advance. For example, if you wanted to track gender and marital status, you might create a segment matrix such as this:

Demographic data	Visitor state	Segment ID
Gender	Male	1
	Female	2
Marital status	Single	3
	Married	4
	Divorced	5
	Widowed	6

As you can see, you simply make a list of demographic data points and possible states of each, then use your analytics application to assign an ID to each. While this is simple for relatively binary demographic data, consider if you want to keep track of visitors by gender *and* marital status:

Demographic data	Visitor state	Segment ID
Gender and marital status	Male, single	1
	Male, married	2
	Male, divorced	3
	Male, widowed	4
	Female, single	5
	Female, married	6
	Female, divorced	7
	Female, widowed	8

Now imagine that you want to add age groups to the mix! Hopefully, you can see that this strategy is slightly more limited and requires additional thought and planning to pull off. Fortunately, sometimes rigorous planning makes you appreciate the problem more deeply and encourages you to collect only data you're prepared and able to actually use.

Fraught with complexity, dependent on visitors who may or may not lie about their demographic grouping, and reliant on vendors who may charge exorbitantly for the chance to learn more about your audience, perhaps this segmentation strategy hardly sounds worth it. Still, given the opportunity to learn more about an anonymous audience, especially the demographic details that can be mapped back to the offline world, and a tremendous body of learning about how different types of people shop and interact with their environment, most marketers simply ask, "Who do I make the check out to?" when offered this type of information.

Track Your Geographic Visitor Distribution

Knowing where your visitors reside can help focus online and offline marketing efforts.

The Internet is great, because it completely breaks down geographic boundaries. Need information about the price of tea in China? Visit a Chinese web site to get the latest quotes! Need authentic Italian leather shoes? Visit *http://www.rossetti.it* for authentic Fratelli Rossetti shoes from Italy! Wherever you are in the world, you're only a click away on the Internet.

Unfortunately, this works against marketers trying to connect more deeply with their online visitors. We live in a multichannel world—you use the Internet but you also watch local television, read magazines and newspapers, and listen to the radio—and the ideal marketing program will connect with you through as many channels as possible, thus increasing your brand awareness and likelihood to convert. Fortunately, many of the best measurement applications provide facilities to help you track the geographic distribution of your visitors.

Geographic Distribution Reports

While few vendors do quite as elaborate a job presenting the data as does Visual Sciences (Figure 5-17), geographic distribution reports are nearly ubiquitous in web measurement applications.

These reports are usually limited to the number and percentage of visitors from each locale. The granularity of information is usually country, state, and city, but some vendors offer reporting at the area code, Zip Code, and Nielsen Media Research Designated Marketing Area (DMA; for more information about DMAs, see *http://www.nielsenmedia.com/DMAs.html*)

How Do They Do That?

A visitor's geographic location can be inferred from her IP address. A number of "geo-targeting" services maintain databases of IP addresses that allow vendors to feed the IP address gleaned from either a server logfile or page tag to an API, which returns whatever geographic information they request. Some of the most popular services are:

- Digital Envoy (*www.digitalenvoy.com*)
- Quova (*www.quova.com*)
- Akamai (*www.akamai.com*)
- IP2Location (*www.ip2region.com/*)
- MaxMind (*www.maxmind.com/*)

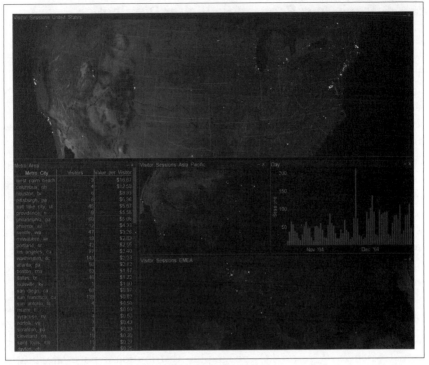

Figure 5-17. High-end geographic reporting

The most sophisticated solutions for geo-targeting have distributed networks of computers that probe IP addresses around the Internet using common network tools like PING, TRACEROUTE, and NSLOOKUP in tandem with complex algorithms for spatial comparison. Sounds ugly, huh? The end result is still a database of IP addresses mapped to physical locations, only now vendors can claim accuracy levels like 99 percent at the country level and 94 percent at the city level. Solutions like these are also able to resolve the observation that many web data analysts mistakenly make—the inference that the majority of their web visitors live in Vienna, Virginia, USA.

Simply put, they don't.

Vienna, Virginia is a bucolic suburb near Tyson's Corner, Virginia, only 15 miles from Dulles, VA, and as of the 2000 U.S. Census, Vienna was home to just over 14,000 residents. So how is a report like the one presented in Figure 5-18 even possible?

The answer has to do with Vienna's proximity to Dulles, the corporate home of America Online, one of the world's largest dial-up Internet service providers, boasting 22.7 million subscribers in late 2004. A substantial majority of these folks use dial-up numbers that essentially route them through an AOL proxy server farm in, you guessed it, Vienna, Virginia.

Most Active Cities	
City, State	User Sessions
1 Vienna, Virginia, United States	75,293
2 Medofrd, Oregon, United States	5,242
3 San Francisco, California, United States	4,320
4 Atlanta, Georgia, United States	3,186
5 Nashville, Tennessee, United States	2,557
6 Denver, Colorado, United States	1,643
7 Palo Alto, California, United States	1,147
8 Falls Church, Virginia, United States	1,103
9 Waltham, Massachusetts, United States	1,041
10 Hoffman Estates, Illinois, United States	886
Total For the Cities Above	96,418

Figure 5-18. Sample WebTrends report

If you're still seeing results like those in Figure 5-18, you should definitely call your measurement vendor and ask them how you can get better geographic data, data you can really use!

How to Really Use Geographic Distribution Data

Here are some actions you can take based on your geographic distribution data:

Decide where to spend your offline advertising budget
 If you have a strong offline presence, you should consider using city, Zip Code, and DMA information to decide where to purchase newspaper inserts, buy television advertising, or put up roadside billboards to build the awareness you have already generated among online visitors.

Quantify how your regional advertising dollars were spent
 You can use the relatively data-rich online channel to help quantify the effect of local and regional advertising investment, looking for an increase in value per visitor from those areas where more money is being spent; especially if you're embedding your URL in the offline message (highly recommended), you can use KPIs like revenue or value per visitor in specific geographic regions to build a return on investment model.

Look for new opportunities
 If you have physical presence (e.g., stores or catalogs), you can use online data to look for new markets to build stores, establish partnerships, or buy catalog distribution lists. Look for cities or states that generate significant online sales but don't currently have any physical stores, and conduct deeper feasibility studies on those markets.

Explore international interest
 Always remember: the Internet is a global presence, creating global opportunities! Geographic information can help you identify international interest in your products or services. Look for countries in your

geographic distribution report that are home to a disproportional number of visitors, and pay close attention to the activity of these visitors, using segmentation tools.

Explore investment in local search offerings
>   As search engines such as Google (*http://local.google.com/*) and Yahoo! (*http://local.yahoo.com/*) offer more local search features, including local advertising opportunities, geographic information can help you determine where to target your local search efforts. Don't forget to use geographic data to then calculate the return on investment for local search!

This list is by no means exhaustive, but hopefully you get the idea. Keeping track of your visitors' geographic distribution is one of most powerful things you can do to really begin to know your visitors!

If you have a significant offline presence (or are working to establish one), you may want to consider building a key performance indicator that tracks percentage-wise distribution of visitors from your target markets.

HACK #79 Accurately Measure Downloads

Many sites need to know not just who has requested a downloadable file but whether that file was successfully delivered. Fortunately, in many instances, you can use your web measurement application and server logfiles to make this determination.

Measuring downloads can be crucial for many types of web sites, including those belonging to software vendors, content publishers, and computer gaming companies. Accurately measuring downloads from such sites can be challenging. Many common approaches to web analytics do not allow downloads to be measured at all. Page-tagging data collection methods are oriented toward measuring web page views only, not the download of the thousands of other files types that may be distributed through web sites. If tracking downloads is important for your site, then you will need to take this into special consideration when selecting a web analytics product or service. In addition, tracking downloads has become more complicated by the proliferation of "download managers" that are used to speed download times for users.

Multiple Levels of Measurement Can Be Used to Track Downloads

Downloads can be tracked to a lesser or greater degree of granularity and accuracy, depending on how involved you want to get. The first level of granularity includes determining that a visitor requested a download and that the particular download began. The second level of granularity includes determining that a download began and was actually completed, and the third includes determining that a download was completed in multiple parts by a download manager.

Mine basic HTTP requests. The first level of measurement of downloads requires that you use a web analytics product that collects the HTTP request data directly from your web and application servers, either into logfiles or into a database. For example, if a web site is distributing trial versions of multiple software products, then you must meet the following minimum requirements to measure "that a download was started by a visitor to the site."

- You must have a web analytics product that allows you to define downloads as a metric separate from your page views metrics. Many web analytics products do not have a construct for downloads; they require that you look at a download as if it were a page view. Though you will be able to see how many downloads were started, your page view counts will be skewed.

- Make sure your web analytics product is set up to extract requests for the types of files that you publish for download. Different web analytics products require that this be done in different ways, but almost all of them require that you do this proactively. For instance, define *.zip*, *.pdf*, *.exe*, and other file types as "downloads." You may also need to configure your web analytics product so that it does not filter out requests made for these files types. Some products will filter out these requests by default.

Understand that this first level of download measurement is not "accurate" with regard to the completion of a download. It will tell you only that a visitor requested and started a download.

Mine basic HTTP requests for download completion. The second level of downloads measurement has the same requirements as the first leve,l plus a few additional requirements. The objective of the second level of download measurement is to determine whether the download was completed. The following steps can be taken to make this determination.

- Create a delimited file listing all of the URIs corresponding to each of the downloadable files you host for distribution through your web site. In this list, you will need to add information about each of these downloadable files: the URI stem to the downloadable files and the actual byte count of each of these files. The following is an example of such a delimited file:

```
Product1TrialVersion|downloads/product1.zip|48947000
Product2TrialVersion|downloads/product1.zip|59936897
Product1Docs|downloads/product1docs.pdf|7893457
Product2Docs|downloads/product2docs.pdf|7864509
```

- Configure your web server to capture the actual bytes sent when a request for a particular download is made. This configuration varies by web server. In Microsoft Internet Information Server, this configuration is called bytes sent or sc-bytes and may be checkboxed in the extended logging properties dialog box within the Microsoft IIS web site properties.

- When you process your log data, have your web measurement product look for the URI stem, as defined within your delimited file, corresponding to the downloads in the logs as they are processed. When you see one that matches your list, look up the actual byte count of that download in your list of downloadable files. Then compare that actual byte count with the bytes sent for that download. If the bytes sent equals or is greater than the actual byte count for that particular downloadable file, then increment your count for successful downloads of that file by one. If bytes sent are less than the actual byte count for that downloadable file, then increment the unsuccessful downloads count for that downloadable file by one.

Compensate for download managers. The third level of accurate download measurement compensates for the use of download managers. Your site visitors may use one of the many available download managers to speed the downloading of files. FlashGet, GetRight, Go!Zilla, Fresh Download, and Internet Download Manager are among the commonly used download management applications. While these applications ease the process of downloading files for your visitors, they may add complexity to the measurement of downloads from your site.

Consider an example in which FlashGet was used to download a large *.zip* file (48947000 bytes). Here are the relevant log records (FlashGet shows up in the logs as cs(User-Agent) (Mozilla/4.0+(compatible;+MSIE+5.00;+Windows+98)):

```
date time c-ip cs-username s-sitename s-computername s-ip s-port cs-method
cs-uri-stem cs-uri-query sc-status sc-bytes cs-bytes time-taken cs(User-
Agent)cs(Cookie)cs(Referer)

2004-11-22 12:49:16 192.168.10.38 - W3SVC1 VS 10.2.1.90 80 GET /product1.zip
-200 10420488 249 32000 Mozilla/4.0+(compatible;+MSIE+5.00;+Windows+98)
c=419389F68E854973 Download+Test
2004-11-22 12:49:16 192.168.10.38 - W3SVC1 VS 10.2.1.90 80 GET /product1.zip
- 206 9961776 273 30703 Mozilla/4.0+(compatible;+MSIE+5.00;+Windows+98)
c=419389F68E854973 Download+Test
2004-11-22 12:49:16 192.168.10.38 - W3SVC1 VS 10.2.1.90 80 GET /product1.zip
- 206 9961776 273 30968 Mozilla/4.0+(compatible;+MSIE+5.00;+Windows+98)
c=419389F68E854973 Download+Test
2004-11-22 12:49:16 192.168.10.38 - W3SVC1 VS 10.2.1.90 80 GET /product1.zip
- 206 9929568 273 31031 Mozilla/4.0+(compatible;+MSIE+5.00;+Windows+98)
c=419389F68E854973 Download+Test
```

```
2004-11-22 12:49:17 192.168.10.38 - W3SVC1 VS 10.2.1.90 80 GET /product1.zip
- 206 10027312 273 31656 Mozilla/4.0+(compatible;+MSIE+5.00;+Windows+98)
c=419389F68E854973 Download+Test
```

The log records show that FlashGet made five GET requests for *product1.zip*, and the sc-bytes for the five requests add up to 50,300,920. The first request has HTTP status code 200 (successful request by the client), and the second through fifth requests have status code 206 (partial content; the partial GET request has been successful). FlashGet accepted a persistent cookie and let the user set cs(referrer); most often you will find cs(referrer) to be null.

To track a successful download for a particular download manager user with a particular cookie (cs(cookie)), you must add up the sc-bytes from an initial 200 status record for the download file and the multiple subsequent 206 records from the same cs(cookie) until the number of sc-bytes exceeds the downloadable file's actual byte count (i.e., the sum of the 200 and 206 requests' sc-bytes counts will generally exceed the download file's actual byte count; most download managers download more than a proportional part of the file with each request as an intentional overlap to allow correct concatenation at the download manager). In an unsuccessful multi-part download, the sum of the sc-bytes counts for the 200 requests and 206 requests would be less than the actual byte count of the file.

> Different download managers other than the one used here may behave differently, and different but similar rules would need to be applied.

It is highly unlikely that you will want to invest time and resources to investigate your log data in this manner for all of the download attempts that occur from your web site. Certain web measurement products can automate this process for you, as long they can consider multiple log records that come in over time and operate on them together to determine whether a download was successful or unsuccessful. Your vendor's solution may define a "rule" to produce a list of cookies or IP and user agent combinations that make multiple GET requests for the same object (starting with a 200 record followed by multiple 206 records) within some time span. With this information, you could assess the behavior of various download managers and set your web analytics products' rules appropriately for tracking successful and unsuccessful downloads attempted by download managers.

—Jim MacIntyre and Eric T. Peterson

#80 Build Your Own Web Measurement Application: Technographic Data

> One of the more interesting things that web measurement applications are able to do is help you understand the geographic distribution of your visitors. In this hack, we leverage a freely available geo-targeting database and add IP-based visitor geography reporting to the build your own application.

In this hack, we show how to extend our example program to report the number of visitors from each country [Hack #78]. This is often known as *geo-location*, *geo-targeting*, or *geographic segmentation*. The way it works is that certain companies sell large databases mapping numerical IP addresses to countries, or even to regions and cities. The databases can never be 100% accurate because the way ISPs route data through their internal networks is unpredictable. But, at least at the country level, they give a reasonably good idea.

Installing IP::Country and Geography::Countries

One advantage of using Perl is that when you want to do something like this, someone's probably already done it for you and built it into a Perl module. In this case, we'll use MaxMind's Geo::IP module. MaxMind's basic country database is free, although they do sell more accurate and more detailed databases.

To download and install the Geo::IP module, you need to follow the instructions at *http://www.maxmind.com/app/perl*. Under Unix or Linux, you have to download and install the GeoIP C library and the Geo::IP Perl modules from that page. Under Windows, provided you have Perl and the Perl Package Manager (PPM) installed, all you need to do is issue the following command from your Perl directory:

```
ppm install http://theoryx5.uwinnipeg.ca/ppms/Geo-IP.ppd
```

When you're prompted to fetch and install the *GeoIP.dat* database, make sure you say "yes" to both questions you're asked; otherwise, the database won't be properly installed (Figure 5-19).

The Code

We have to extend our Session class to report the country of the session. With the Geo::IP module installed, this is easy. Append the following code snippet to the Session class in the *Session.pm* file:

```
package Session;
...
use Geo::IP;
my $geoip = new Geo::IP;
```

Figure 5-19. Installation of MaxMind's Geo-IP module

```
sub Country {
  my $self = shift;
  return $geoip->country_name_by_addr($self->[0]->{host});
}
```

We also have to extend our Data class to save and report this data. Append the following code snippet into the appropriate points in the Data class in the *Data.pm* file:

```
package Data;
...
sub new {
  return bless {
    ...
    countries => {},
  };
}
sub AddSession {
  ...
  my $country = $sess->Country();
  if (!$country) { $country = "Unknown"; }
  ++$self->{countries}->{$country};
}
sub WriteReport {
  ...
  $self->WriteHash('Countries', 'countries');
}
```

And that's it. The module handles all the work for us.

Running the Code

This time, when you execute the `perl readlog.pl page.log` command (see [Hack #53] for details about running the script), you'll be treated to a report showing where your visitors were coming from geographically (Figure 5-20).

Figure 5-20. The "Countries" report

Next up is a focus on collecting data relevant to online retailers for your own analysis.

—*Dr. Stephen Turner and Eric T. Peterson*

## CHAPTER SIX

Web Measurement and the Online Retail Model

Hacks 81–90

The online retail model is fascinating from a web measurement standpoint, if for no other reason than because it is so easily measured. The ability to correlate marketing expenditure and revenue acquisition in near–real time is both satisfying and useful, allowing online marketers to rapidly optimize their strategies to provide the greatest return on investment. Plus, since online retailers have so much invested in web site measurement, many vendors have built out their applications to specifically support the business model, some deploying whole modules for merchandising, others tightly integrating commercial aspects into their non-commerce reporting.

Billions of dollars are spent each year online; estimates put online retail sales in the U.S. at $66 billion in 2004, growing to $130 billion by 2009—six percent of total U.S. retail sales. With this much money changing hands, it's no surprise that online retailers are intensely focused on understanding how their marketing dollars are being spent and where their sites can be optimized to increase sales. Additionally, it is estimated that by 2009, nearly 70% of Internet users will be making purchases online, highlighting the need to ensure that the buying process is not just "OK" or "good enough" but instead "delightful"—processes that will encourage people to come back again and again.

Given the amount of investment in web measurement applications that online retailers have made in the last few years, it's not surprising that many of the published best practices and case studies revolve around selling online. Each of the top vendors has at least one description of how they've helped an online retailer improve the quality of their marketing or merchandising, literally paying for the application time and time again. A few examples of initiatives in which web measurement played a key role include:

- CompUSA optimized its shopping tools critical to high-value customers, returning an annualized $2.2 million in increased revenues.

- LAMPS PLUS optimized their online marketing and advertising efforts, lowering their customer acquisition costs by 30 percent.

- Royal Appliance (makers of the Dirt Devil) increased their shopping cart conversion rate to personal best of 18 percent.

The important thing to keep in mind is the continuous improvement process and the idea that many small gains eventually add up. Put another way, if you read and run the hacks in this chapter and aren't immediately able to make changes that yield a six-figure return on your investment, persevere. Often it's a function of trying the right combination of changes, balanced against the proper insight, and managed over time. Still, you can rest assured that your investment in web measurement—provided that you treat it as a serious investment—will pay off for both you and your customers.

HACK #81 Know How to Use Retail Analytics

While not exactly a class of its own, web measurement for online retailers entails fairly specific uses of the tools and hacks described in this book; knowing how and when to leverage these tools can significantly increase your ability to market, merchandise, and sell.

Learning how to use retail web measurement applications may equip you to sustain the double-digit growth you have become accustomed to as an online retailer. Pouring additional dollars into your marketing budget might also do the trick, but web measurement offers an inexpensive and easy way to achieve quick wins that can translate into additional sales, more active customers, and marketing cost savings.

Retail web measurement applications leverage most of the web measurement concepts, tools, and hacks you already know; extend a few of these items to better address specific retail scenarios; and apply the resulting measurement approaches and nomenclature to a fairly straightforward set of objectives:

- Attract highly qualified visitors
- Convert these visitors into repeat customers
- Generate more sales
- Do all of the above with less (fewer marketing dollars, less time, etc.)

Start with a simple retail web measurement framework that includes the following analyses. Even if you have already performed an analysis of your checkout funnel and managed to increase completion rate by a few percentage points, this hack introduces two additional exercises you can quickly perform to improve your site's ability to attract, convert, and retain customers.

Optimize Your Marketing Spend

Optimizing your online marketing spend is an almost failsafe way to drive additional visitor acquisition and site revenue by reallocating marketing dollars to the most efficient marketing channels and programs. If cost savings is your primary goal, you can use this same exercise to identify laggard marketing programs that you no longer need to invest in.

You need to optimize your marketing expenditures via tracking and analysis of key data:

- Track individual marketing elements (such as search keywords, banners, affiliates, and emails)

- Analyze the performance of these elements in terms of visitor loyalty, conversion and sales, and other descriptive retail metrics, such as shopping cart abandonment rate and average order value

Many web measurement vendors generate a report that describes all marketing activity using multiple fields: vendor, channel, campaign, message type, creative format, and URL, for example (Figure 6-1). You can sort the report by each of the retail metrics mentioned above or by a combination of them.

 Be careful not to combine more than two or three different sorts, or your resulting analysis may suffer.

You'd be surprised at how much additional information you can glean simply by sorting columns:

- If your primary goal is to drive traffic to your site, pure and simple, sort by visitors or visits.

- If your primary goal is to attract big spenders, sort by average order value.

Optimize your marketing spend by aligning your investments with your business goals. By reallocating 30 percent of your online marketing budget to the relationships that drive the most traffic by volume, the most valuable traffic, the highest sales, or the largest order values, you can quickly recover marketing losses and better achieve the specific goals of your retail site.

Analyze Product Placement and Look to Book

On a retail web site, shoppers make a series of decisions before purchasing online. They look for products of interest in the places they most expect to find them. If they find them, they make a near instant judgment of whether the product is presented, described, and priced in a compelling way.

Vendor / Category / Placement / Marketing Item	Cost	Estimated Conversion Rate	Sales	Orders	Average Order Value	Buyers
Email	$13,551.08	7.41%	$505,464.79	4,956	$101.99	31,455
Overture	$7,876.66	5.18%	$337,176.06	2,999	$112.44	13,227
Women's	$2,315.06	5.85%	$95,710.40	896	$106.84	4,344
Keywords	$2,315.06	5.86%	$95,710.40	896	$106.84	4,344
Blouse	$311.64	9.50%	$21,024.80	226	$93.24	1,060
Dress	$294.90	7.38%	$17,498.80	156	$112.32	742
Sandals	$270.48	6.73%	$16,096.60	133	$120.80	633
Skirt	$406.06	6.51%	$14,606.25	125	$116.80	601
Belts	$273.86	6.51%	$14,050.70	125	$112.36	598
Purse	$242.45	3.71%	$4,799.05	55	$86.70	280
Gloves	$198.47	3.51%	$4,376.75	43	$101.67	225
Bathing Suit	$146.72	2.95%	$3,257.45	33	$99.31	179
Hats	$110.39	0.50%	$450.00	6	$75.00	15
Jewelry	$60.10	0.50%	$425.00	5	$85.00	11
Men's	$2,415.53	5.56%	$86,130.56	761	$113.26	5,702
Home	$1,677.00	5.41%	$77,525.42	674	$114.98	3,596
Garden	$1,471.84	5.40%	$69,732.66	609	$116.56	1,929
Google	$6,630.82	5.18%	$303,458.46	2,699	$112.44	11,913
Shop at AOL	$6,111.71	4.99%	$294,537.60	2,100	$140.26	9,280
LookSmart	$9,807.82	3.97%	$278,163.90	1,499	$185.82	6,661
MSN	$6,908.46	2.44%	$219,865.80	760	$289.22	3,433
NextTag	$2,478.60	2.21%	$197,879.22	684	$289.22	2,793
Linkshare	$5,621.70	2.00%	$170,091.30	616	$289.22	2,274

Figure 6-1. Breakdown of marketing programs

You should leverage your web measurement tool to explore how shoppers make decisions, using the following steps:

1. Generate reports that list all products viewed for a specific time period.

2. Start by looking at a time period of a week or longer.

3. Examine product metrics by product category or site location to get the "big picture" view of how shoppers are browsing your products.

4. Drill down, reviewing key merchandising metrics like product views, abandonment rate, orders, and sales for each product.

5. Analyze product placement by looking at abandonment rate and look-to-book ratios (product views divided by orders for a particular product) aggregated at the category level.

Categories with high values for product views but low look-to-book ratios may be attracting shoppers in search of products that they wrongly expect to find. Solve this problem by recategorizing products, placing products in multiple categories, and enhancing site navigation or search. Whatever the root cause, unresolved problems with product placement lead to lost sales and lost potential customers.

Analyze specific product performance by looking at abandonment rate and look-to-book ratio at the product level. Products with high abandonment rates may have excessive shipping and handling charges that are revealed only after the product is placed in the shopping cart. Products with high look-to-book ratios may be poorly presented, unattractively priced, or labeled as out of stock. Address problems with poor look-to-book ratios by enhancing site navigation, site search, product imaging and presentation, price, and shipping options.

Streamline the Checkout Funnel

A typical checkout sequence includes steps for:

- Shopping cart
- Login or registration
- Shipping and billing address entry
- Payment information
- Coupon or promotion code entry
- Order review

You need to measure each of these attrition points not only in terms of completion or defection, but also by shopping cart value, time to complete, and new versus repeat buyer status [Hack #52]. You can remedy many defection problems by applying web interface usability best practices to key information entry pages, such as registration and address entry. Fortunately, many of these best practices are well understood:

- Observing the differences between new and repeat buyer checkout behavior may expose an opportunity to redesign the checkout sequence to incorporate passive site registration.
- Steps with high time to complete values may be too laden with heavy graphics, excessively long (in the case of an information entry page), or text-heavy, or they may lack necessary security precautions and messaging.
- High abandonment at the login or registration steps may indicate that you haven't done enough to demonstrate reasons that new shoppers would want to spend the time to do this.
- Abandonment during coupon or promotion-code entry steps may indicate discontinuity in how you're presenting and accepting these codes— for example, you tell them the code is "123-XYZ-PDQ-2" but the form does not accept the dash (-) character.
- Higher-than-expected abandonment of shopping carts may indicate that your proceed-to-checkout button is not visible enough or is buried on

the page somehow. All checkout buttons should be highly visible on the page, even if they look ugly.

- High abandonment from your shipping and billing address pages may indicate that you're asking for too much, you're not clearly indicating which fields are *required*, or there is a problem with how you're processing the form. The standard recommendation is to ask only for the *minimum* amount of data needed to complete the order.

- High abandonment from the payment information and order review steps may indicate that you're not doing enough to convey your commitment to the shopper's security and privacy. Make sure you have TRUSTe and BBB logos [Hack #26] on pages where you're collecting personal or financial information.

Combined with effective marketing and merchandising analyses, regular optimization of the checkout and registration funnels is the foundation of retail web analytics.

—Brett Hurt and Eric T. Peterson

HACK #82   Measure the Shopping Cart

For online retailers, there is perhaps nothing more important than measuring visitor flow and abandonment through the shopping cart. Your use of metrics and measurement in these pages can make or break your business.

In retail web analytics, measuring the shopping cart is analogous to gazing into a crystal ball. Each visitor interaction with the shopping cart is a measurable activity that generates data useful for sales and demand forecasting, promotion planning, and shopper behavior analysis. This hack introduces measurement approaches for key shopping cart interactions and also discusses factors that can degrade the accuracy of shopping cart measurement.

Measuring Products Being Added to the Cart

Think of this interaction in terms of distinct products (line items or SKUs), item quantities, and visits or visitors. More importantly, think of each of these metrics in relative terms to arrive at meaningful conversion rates for the add-to-cart action, often termed *shop action* and expressed as a percentage:

- Item-Based Shop Action Conversion = Items Added to Cart / Total Item Views (for a specific product)

- Visit-Based Shop Action Conversion = Visit Adding Items to Cart / Total Visits

- Visitor-Based Shop Action Conversion = Visitors Adding Items to Cart / Total Visitors

As an online retailer, one of your primary objectives is to drive shop action conversion through effective product selection, presentation, pricing, and messaging on availability, shipping costs, and other handling and delivery options. Shop action conversion rates express the performance of your site at achieving these objectives, so it is essential to actively monitor them.

Measuring Products Being Abandoned in the Cart

Removing items from the shopping cart results in changes to item quantities or complete abandonment of the cart—neither outcome is welcome! But when measuring *abandonment*, it is important to distinguish between two related abandonment metrics: item and cart.

- *Item abandonment* measures the number of times a specific product or SKU is left in an abandoned cart and not purchased.

- *Cart abandonment* is the overall measurement of abandonment for all carts during a time period.

Misusing these metrics can make the abandonment issue seem to be a much bigger or much smaller problem than it really is. Table 6-1 illustrates the importance of both abandonment metrics.

Table 6-1. Illustration of how item and cart abandonment can affect your aggregate conversion rates

	Cart A	Cart B	Aggregate
Items added to cart	6	4	10
Items purchased from cart	3	0	3
Item abandonment	50%	100%	70%
Cart abandonment	0%	100%	50%
Cart conversion	100%	0%	50%

Cart A does convert but not at a *true* 100 percent. Over half the items placed in Cart A were not purchased, so a significant sales opportunity was lost. Cart B failed to convert, as a total of four items were added but none were purchased. Item abandonment and cart abandonment for Cart B were 100 percent, resulting in both a lost sales and customer acquisition opportunity.

In general, when we talk about "shopping cart abandonment," we're talking about *cart abandonment* and when we're exploring look-to-book ratios [Hack #81], we're exploring the nuances of *item abandonment*. The interesting thing in the previous example is that only 50 percent of the carts completed and in the one cart that did convert, three products had been removed from the cart prior to purchase, lowering their individual look-to-book ratios.

Measuring Maximum Shopping Cart Value

Given the misleading signals that a single shop action or abandonment metric can send, it is important to consider all of the metrics that may be used to describe the state and performance of your site's shopping cart.

Maximum shopping cart value (the maximum dollar value of items added to the cart during a specific time period) is a useful metric to trend, as it may expose spikes and lulls in online demand as a result of the launch or decay of a recent marketing campaign, such as an email blast or major keyword buy.

Trending maximum shopping cart value against online sales (Figure 6-2) enables you to instantly gauge the size of the abandonment problem in dollars, the most useful measure of all for a web retailer. The area between the two trended lines represents an enormous sales and customer acquisition opportunity.

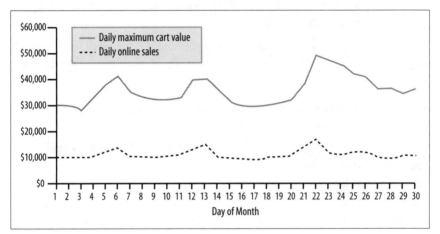

Figure 6-2. Online sales (bottom line) versus total maximum cart value (top line) report

Measuring What Matters in Shopping Carts

To summarize the hack so far, the list of measurements you need to make to accurately understand how shoppers are using your shopping cart includes:

- Total number of items added to the cart
- Item-by-item list of products and SKUs added to the shopping cart
- Dollar value of all items added to the shopping cart, even if they're abandoned or removed

You then want to be able to follow each of these measurements through each step in the checkout process [Hack #83]. Again, you're gathering this information to calculate the following:

- Item-Based Shop Action Conversion = Items Added to Cart / Total Item Views (for a specific product)

- Visit-Based Shop Action Conversion = Visit Adding Items to Cart / Total Visits (similar to order conversion)

- Visitor-Based Shop Action Conversion = Visitors Adding Items to Cart / Total Visitors (similar to buyer conversion)

- Shopping Cart Potential = Total Dollar Value of All Items Added to the Cart

Because of the complexity involved, you're much better off if your measurement or commerce application will make these calculations for you, but getting a good handle on these metrics now will save you time and trouble when you get deep into diagnosing problems with your merchandising and your checkout process.

When Is a Shopping Cart Not a Shopping Cart?

Sometimes a shopping cart is not used as you intend. For example, visitors might use a shopping cart as a wish list, or the shopping cart may simply persist over time, yet never complete a sale. These two factors, which can obfuscate your analysis of the shopping cart, are worth understanding.

The cart as a shopping list. Sometimes visitors use the shopping cart as a shopping list, such as a personal wish list or gift list for an upcoming birthday or holiday. This activity may significantly skew same-session shop action rates by artificially inflating the number of items added to the cart (because there was no real intention to purchase the items in the "wishing" session).

It is difficult to know when this activity is happening without analyzing shopper cross-session behavior, but you should be aware of it, particularly if you sell products that potential buyers prefer to research extensively before purchasing. High-ticket items that may require a spouse's or parent's approval before being purchased are also often repeatedly added to the shopping cart and revisited over multiple sessions prior to purchase, which may take place offline.

Persistent shopping carts. Many online retailers implement persistent shopping carts, a move that often exacerbates the skewing effects of using the cart as a shopping list. However, persistent carts do present an opportunity to extend the definition of shopping cart conversion (and abandonment) to include activities that occur across multiple sessions. In-depth analysis of cross-session activity often yields valuable insights into the online research and buying patterns of your customers.

If your site uses a persistent cart, be aware of its impact on your web analytics solution's measurement of abandonment. Most solutions define shopping cart conversion and abandonment in same-session terms, which may overstate the size of the abandonment problem for retailers using persistent carts.

—Brett Hurt and Eric T. Peterson

HACK #83   Measure the Checkout Process

Improvements in the online checkout processes have yielded more incremental revenue than almost any other aspect of web site measurement.

The checkout process is the most important process for any retail site to optimize. Luckily, it is also the easiest to analyze, and the improvement opportunities uncovered through analysis are extremely tangible. Following this simple framework will allow you to identify changes that have allowed retailers to make up their investment in these enhancements during the first day post implementation!

Step One: Establish a Baseline

The first step is establishing a baseline, as well as a method for monitoring the checkout process performance efficiently and on a periodic basis. There are two high-level metrics that should be trended and provide an excellent baseline:

- Same-session checkout completion over a given analysis period (for example, the fiscal month), defined as the number of visits (including receipt page) divided by the number of visits (including first step in checkout process)

- Cross-session checkout completion over a period representative of the average amount of time it takes a shopper to purchase, defined as the number of visitors reaching receipt page divided by the number of visitors starting the checkout process

In terms of monitoring the checkout process itself, you should go one level deeper and look at what is happening at each step. The metrics you need to pay attention to at each step in the checkout process include:

- The number of visits reaching each subsequent step

- The total potential sales at each step (based on the number of items remaining in the shopping cart compared to abandoned carts [Hack #82])

- The number of visits continuing to the next step in the process

- The abandonment rate from step to step (often expressed as a percentage of visits continuing or percent of visits still engaged in the process)

- The percentage of visits that leave the checkout process but remain on the site
- The percentage of visits that leave the checkout process *and* the site altogether
- The dollar amount of sales departing the checkout process
- The dollar amount of sales continuing in the checkout process

Keep in mind that measuring the checkout process is really just a specific variation on measuring multi-step processes [Hack #59]. Vendors will often provide each of these metrics in a single report, detailing the checkout process step by step (Figure 6-3).

Step Number	Step Name	Sessions Reaching This Step	Potential Sales	Sessions Continuing to Next Step	% Completing Funnel	Sessions Departing Funnel	Sessions Leaving Immediately	Departing Potential Sales
1	View Cart	423,242	$72,895,060.11	227,327 (53.7%)	38.0%	195,915 (46.3%)	28,667 (6.8%)	$30,640,863.97
2	Sign-In	227,327	$34,254,176.14	187,844 (82.6%)	70.8%	39,483 (17.4%)	7,859 (3.5%)	$11,316,785.22
3	Shipping	187,844	$22,937,390.92	184,056 (98.0%)	85.7%	3,788 (2.0%)	1,817 (1.0%)	$397,171.40
4	Payment	184,056	$22,540,219.52	166,343 (90.4%)	87.5%	17,713 (9.6%)	4,762 (2.6%)	$4,023,430.98
5	Display Order	166,343	$18,516,788.54	161,040 (96.8%)	96.8%	5,303 (3.2%)	2,280 (1.4%)	$689,134.76
6	Complete Order	161,040	$17,827,653.78	-	100.0%	-	117,669 (73.1%)	-

Figure 6-3. Checkout funnel analysis report

For each step, you now know the likelihood of a customer moving forward in the process versus leaving the process or, even worse, leaving the site altogether. In addition, you immediately see the financial impact of losing these customers. Hopefully, most of you are saying, "That's great, but how can I stop this mass exodus from my checkout process?"

Step Two: Diagnose Problems

Next you need to diagnose the problems that are causing the attrition described above. The key to this diagnostic analysis is to uncover where people are going when they are not moving forward. In many cases, this will allow you to form some hypotheses around the root cause of these movements.

The ultimate diagnostic data source for this analysis is clickstream data, which lays out the exact path customers are taking from each step in the process. It is useful to characterize these movements into the following buckets:

- Direct site departure
- Forward to any subsequent step in the process; if there are no optional steps, this is the next step
- Backward to any previous steps in the process

We recommend that you generate a flow chart of the checkout process with the metrics above included for each step. You'll already know where the big attrition points are, but now you can get closer to what is driving the attrition and see whether it is backward or non-process movements that are causing the problem. The next question you should ask is "Which is worse?"

Most web measurement vendors provide some type of clickstream analysis designed to provide you with the data you need to fully diagnose abandonment in your checkout process in a visual way (Figure 6-4). These reports are variations on the table of information described above and presented in Figure 6-3, designed to highlight problems around a single page in the process—in this case, exploring how many sales and orders are driven by people clicking from the "Checkout1: Sign In" page.

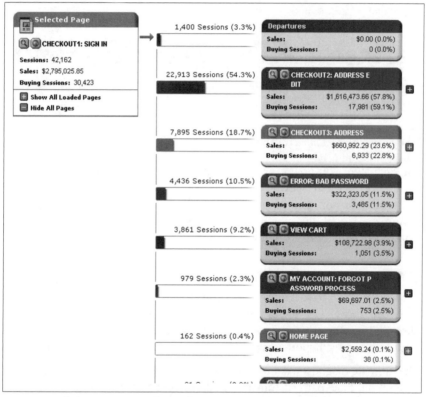

Figure 6-4. Clickstream report of page flow on a per-session (visit) basis

Reports and visualizations like this one can help you better diagnose problems that are highlighted by tables like the one in Figure 6-3. You'd be surprised at how valuable the ability to visually explore this information can be, yielding key insights like:

- Discrepancies in the number of visits moving forward and the total number of orders taken, similar to the 9.2 percent of sessions that go from step 1 to "View Cart" although only 3.5 percent of these yield orders

- Movement in unexpected directions, such as the 1,400 visits that leave the site and the 162 visits that return to the home page (resulting in only 0.1 percent of all orders)

- Errors in the process, like the 4,436 visits to the bad-password page and the 979 visits to the forgotten-password page.

Bringing It All Together

In summary, the methodology for measuring the checkout process is quite straightforward:

1. Establish a baseline and monitor high-level trends.

2. Monitor what action customers are taking at each step in the process in order to identify key areas of focus.

3. Dig a little deeper and determine where customers are going if they are not moving forward and create some hypotheses around why they exhibit this behavior; characterize the magnitude of these "leaks" in terms of volume.

4. It often makes sense to analyze individual customer segments [Hack #48] separately to provide further insight into customer behavior as well as to ensure that any changes that are made won't adversely impact one segment for the benefit of another. Typical segments include new versus repeat customers, most valuable customers, customers driven by marketing campaigns, customers of a particularly high price point category, etc.

5. Assess the revenue impact of customers taking a given path, using both conversion rate and dollars per buying session.

6. Prioritize opportunities for improvement based on potential return and cost of enhancement.

7. Test any changes that will help to plug the leaks.

8. Measure the impact of your changes and start all over again!

Assuming you become adept at using the continuous improvement process [Hack #2], you should be making small but important incremental improvements in your checkout process before long.

—*Brett Hurt and Eric T. Peterson*

Understand Frequency and Lifetime Value

Not all customers are created equal, nor are all customer acquisition strategies. Frequency and lifetime value are powerful metrics to help you differentiate customers and the content they engage in most profitably.

Repeat visit behavior metrics are a good place to start understanding customer retention. The idea is simple, and measurement is very straightforward. But many ideas that are "simple" are not "the best way," and this is true with using the repeat visit metric to determine visitor value. When you are just starting to look at visitor behavior, it's a fine tool—certainly better than not paying any attention to retention or visitor value at all. But once you start learning about the profitability implications of managing visitor retention, you will most certainly ask, "What's next? How can we do this even better?" When you get to that point, you'll need a better toolset that provides a more meaningful picture of visitor behavior.

The Limits of the "Percent Returning Visitors" Metric

So what's wrong with using repeat visits? For one thing, the repeat visit metric is bipolar—a repeat either happened or did not, and there are certainly more types of visitors than two. For example, the repeat visit metric doesn't take into account the difference in value between a 200-time visitor and a 2-time visitor, and you probably would agree the difference in value here could be significant. So we will need to account for these differences in value in our visitor retention management thinking.

In addition, some web sites, particularly commerce sites, have access to very specific measures of customer value—actual sales. So for these sites, we want a retention model allowing the flexibility to be more specific about visitor value.

Use Frequency and Lifetime Value to Better Understand Your Visitors and Customers

There are two additional measures of visitor value we can use on the Web that address the shortcomings of the repeat visitor metric: frequency and lifetime value.

Frequency. Frequency is a more accurate measure of visitor value than repeat visits, and if the site doesn't sell anything, may be the most accurate visitor value metric you can use. Frequency goes beyond "repeat visitor" status to count *how many times* a visit has occurred during the tracking period. Most companies would like visitors to come back to a site. Some sites depend on it because visits are tied to revenue. When trying to allocate resources towards various projects on the web site, it might make sense to allocate more resources towards the areas generating visitors who come back to the site more than twice. Low-frequency visitor segments are often "accidental" or can be "noise" and may not be worth spending money on; the example of the 200-time versus 2-time visitors comes to mind here. High-frequency visitor segments can be the most valuable and loyal, especially if the site is ad supported and relies on this activity to generate page views.

When trying to decide how to group number of visits into "low" and "high" frequency, a good rule of thumb is to draw the line based on the average number of visits the "average visitor" makes before he engages in a conversion event. For example, if you're an online retailer and you know that most of your customers visit the site at least three times before they purchase, you can define "low" frequency as less than three visits and "high" frequency as more than six visits (double the minimum number of visits to convert). Keep in mind that you will always have fewer high-frequency visitors than low-frequency visitors and that your definition of these groups should reflect this rule of thumb.

Lifetime value. Lifetime value in this context is the total sales generated since tracking of the visitor or customer began. This metric is self-explanatory; more sales are normally a good thing for a web site. When you are just starting out with retention management, tracking sales to put a monetary value on a segment is technically probably the easiest thing to do. Later on, you may decide to use a different measure of monetary value, such as "gross margin" or "gross margin net of acquisition costs." It really doesn't matter when examining behavior (it does when looking at profits though) as long as you are consistent in the way to determine "value" across all the visitor segments.

Use Frequency and Lifetime Value to Segment Your Customers

Frequency and lifetime value are used in visitor segmentation in the same way as the repeat visit metric. Segment visitors by some characteristic and then compare the value of the segments to determine where the greatest value is generated. How should you divide or segment your customers to analyze repeat rates? How about using these characteristics:

- Media used to acquire the visitor or customer, including the specific search engine and keyword phrases used to find the site
- Offer you made on the initial visit
- Ad copy used to present the offer
- Content areas visited
- Products or categories purchased from

When you segment your visitors by these characteristics, you discover significant differences in current value by source or experience with the site, just as you found with repeat visits. There is one slight difference, however, and that is the way the metric is calculated. When you are using repeat visit percentage, you are looking at the *percentage* of visitors who completed more than one visit. When you are using frequency or lifetime value, you are looking at the *average* across all the visitors in the segment.

It is very useful to examine frequency in the context of the average lifetime value of visitors. Consider the following data, where we see the frequency and lifetime value metrics by content area of the site visited:

Content area visited	Average frequency	Average lifetime value
News	66	$83
Sports	10	$33

In this case, it doesn't matter whether frequency or lifetime value is more important to your web site; visitors viewing news have much higher value than visitors viewing sports. It would make financial sense to reallocate resources away from sports coverage towards news coverage to attract and retain high-value visitors.

With this in mind, different types of sites will use frequency or lifetime value preferentially:

- If you can directly assign a dollar value to a visitor segment, as with commerce and most lead-generation sites, lifetime value is probably the measure to use, because it relates directly to the bottom line.

- Content, branding, and self-service sites lacking direct revenue-generating components should use frequency.

- For some self-service sites, segments with low frequency might be seen as "best," since a visit to the site is evidence of a "problem" that needs to be solved.

Use Lifetime Value per Visit to Drive Action

What if the table above looked like this, with low frequency and high lifetime value for news and the opposite for sports?

Content area visited	Average frequency	Average lifetime value
News	10	$83
Sports	66	$33

Well, you just have to decide which is more important to your business model; I'm betting it's probably lifetime value. But think about what else this table is saying to you: on average, news delivers $83/10 visits, or $8.30 in lifetime value per visit; sport delivers $33/66 visits, or $0.50 per visit. This discrepancy strongly suggests that you should compare these two content areas and find out if there is something being done in news that could be ported over to sports. Why is news so much more *productive* than sports on a per visit basis? Is it the way the content is displayed? Navigation? The use of engagement devices?

Suffice it to say, by understanding the frequency and lifetime value of your customers, you should be able to begin making better decisions about how to interact with them. By examining the lifetime value per visit on a per-page, product, or category basis, you can start to identify differences in how customers bond with you over time. By using this information in tandem with the continuous improvement process [Hack #2], you can take advantage of this extremely valuable data about your "best" customers.

—Jim Novo and Eric T. Peterson

HACK #85 Measure Potential Customer Value Using Recency and Latency

The most powerful predictor of future purchases is the measurement of how recently the last purchase was made. Recency and latency are two very powerful metrics for predicting future customer behavior and business success.

As with current value, the repeat visit percentage of a segment is an OK predictor of potential value, but it's kind of a blunt instrument. When you want to start really homing in on defection behavior and potential value, and taking specific action to increase profits, there are special metrics you should use.

Recency is a potential value metric commonly used for predicting customer defection in a business where the customer is in control, which probably includes all the free content and branding models, most commerce models, and some self-service models. A special form of recency called *latency* is often used in businesses where orders and contacts have a defined "cycle," including those with a defined sales process, subscription-based businesses, and for businesses selling durable goods or high-ticket items. This would include many of the lead-generation and paid subscription content models, as well as some commerce models. We're going to look at both of these retention metrics and how you can use them to rank the likelihood of visitor segments to defect.

Recency

Let's say I offer you a bet. I want you to choose from two customers the one most likely to continue purchasing in the future. The customers are very similar to each other, and each has a lifetime value [Hack #84] of $3,000. There is one difference though: the last purchase of one was over a year ago and the last purchase of the other was in the past 30 days.

Which would you bet is the most likely to buy in the future, and therefore, has the higher potential value?

Most people would select the one that has purchased most recently, hands down. Who knows what happened to the other one? At least the one purchasing more recently has demonstrated they are still in the game.

Customer defection in consumer businesses is usually measured in terms of how long it has been since the customer has had contact with the company, because the longer it has been since you had contact with the customer, the less likely it is that the customer is still a customer. The span of time since last contact is called *recency*.

Think about your own behavior—hobbies you used to have, restaurants you used to go to, and video games you used to play. How did it happen that you "defected" from those activities? The time between instances of engaging in them grew longer and longer until you stopped completely. That's a *defection*. And you can predict defection by looking at patterns of recency.

Use Recency to Drive Revenue

A good place to start with recency is to simply determine the "average recency" of your visitor or customer base by following these steps:

1. Determine, on average, how long your visitors wait between making purchases.

2. Once you have an average, create two groups: those with last visit or purchase at the average or more recent than average, and those with last visit or purchase less recent than average.

Customers with last contact dates at the average or more recent than average are the most likely to still be customers. Customers with last contact dates less recent than average are the most likely to be in the process of defecting or are already defected customers.

Don't take my word for this; you can prove it to yourself. You probably have a newsletter or special offer you send to customers and visitors. Flag visitor segments as more recent than average or less recent than average and send out the email. When you look at responses or visits back to the site, you will find that those who are more recent than average have a response rate 3 to 10 times higher than those less recent than average. Why? Because those less recent than average are in the process of defecting; they are your future "former" customers or visitors.

And because they are more likely to defect, they have *lower potential value.* For example, consider the following table of average visit recency:

Visitor or customer source	Average visit recency
Average for all visitors	8 days
From search engines	3 days
From banner ads	14 days

Here we have the average visit recency of the overall web site and two specific sources of traffic: search engines and banner ads. Search visitors are more recent than visitors coming from banner ads, and are more recent than visitors to the site as a whole.

What does the info in this table mean? Let's say search engines and banner ads generate visitors of equal *current value*; you believe a dollar spent on either ad medium is equally profitable in terms of the value of the visitors generated. But the reality is every dollar you spend on search marketing works much harder than every dollar you spend on banner ads, because search generates visitors with higher than average recency. In other words, the *potential value* of search visitors is higher than that of banner ads.

You can make these kinds of visitor segment comparisons using a slew of characteristics. The ones listed below are generally the most significant for differentiating potential value segments:

- Media used to acquire the visitor/customer, including the specific search engine and keyword phrases use to find the site
- Offer you made on the initial visit
- Ad copy used to present the offer
- Content areas visited
- Products or categories purchased from

This list might look familiar to you: it's the same list of characteristics we used to look at *current value.* The same characteristics responsible for creating *current value* are often strong predictors of *potential value.* Hopefully, now are you are beginning to understand how powerful these particular characteristics are?

Latency

The basic recency model above works best when there is completely free will on the part of the customer to make decisions. In some businesses, there are external forces or cycles affecting customer behavior. For example, in many business-to-business sales, there are a lot of process-defined sequential steps that have to take place. Many high-ticket sales in general tend to be for items considered "durable goods," which are replaced when they wear out or on some "cycle." In these cases, a related metric, *latency*, may make more sense to use than recency to determine potential value.

Latency uses the time *between* customer contacts as a reference point, rather than the time *since* last contact as recency does. You can calculate latency two ways:

- Look at the average time *between* visits or purchases instead of the date of last visit or purchase
- Determine the number of days *between* first visit and first purchase or conversion

Like recency, the longer a visitor or customer does not fulfill the expected behavior, the less likely it is she ever will. If the average visitor segment converts to a lead 10 days after first visit, and you are looking at a visitor segment that has diverged from average, taking an average of 15 days to convert to lead, the segment with 15-day latency has lower *potential value* than the average visitor segment with 10-day latency.

When you see the behavior of a particular segment diverge from the average behavior of other segments, you get a "tripwire" event. Visitors in the segment are not behaving as expected given the behavior of visitors in the other segments; this likely means a challenge or opportunity with the visitors in the segment. This divergence is like an alarm or flag; it is telling you to pay attention and find out what might be going wrong (or right). Since the calculation of latency is very simple, and the diverging behavior is easy to spot, this type of tripwire is an ideal candidate for "lights-out" or automated rules-based visitor retention/value improvement campaigns.

Use Latency to Drive Revenue

Latency is used much the same way as recency: use the average time between events as a guide, and look for segments with higher-than-average and lower-than-average latency for a particular cycle or step. The average time between actions is the tripwire; any segment taking longer than average to progress to the next step or cycle is likely beginning the defection process. The longer the segment postpones completing the step, the more likely defection becomes.

As with recency, certain sources, offers, copy, content, and products will create visitor segments with average latency either above or below the seven day tripwire, and you should take action to adjust marketing or content appropriately. If your subscription offering is expensive, it might be worth it to be proactive in finding out why somebody who pays a lot of money for the service accesses it less regularly than the average subscriber, and take action to retain the segment. Latency is highly predictive of defection in cases where a regular cycle is expected.

—Jim Novo and Eric T. Peterson

HACK #86 Manage Lifetime Value Using the Visitor Segment Value Matrix

Combine the measurements of current value and potential value to refine your business's customer marketing and retention strategy.

What happens if you look at both the current *and* potential value of visitor or customer segments at the same time? You get the four groups shown in Figure 6-5.

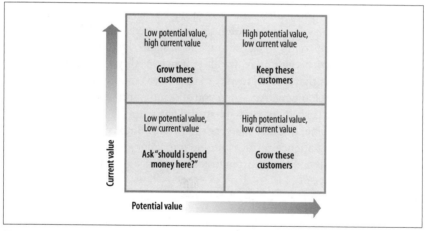

Figure 6-5. Visitor segment value matrix (courtesy of Jim Novo)

How do you create your own visitor segment value matrix? Easy:

1. Take your customer segments and rank them by potential value (recency or latency [Hack #85]), and then split them into two groups: above average and below average.

2. Take all of these potential value groups and rank them by current value (frequency or lifetime value [Hack #84]), then split them into two groups: above average and below average.

You will end up with the four classifications above, each containing unique visitor segments.

3. Do an analysis like this every month so you can compare the results with your financial statements.

Consider how powerful it would be to know the ranking of visitor segments based on this model. The segments in the upper-right box are the rocket fuel of the company. They are the 10 percent of the segments that create 90 percent of the profits—now, and in the future. This is where you should focus customer retention efforts [Hack #52]. The segments in the lower-left box are a drag on the company; they are the result of poorly targeted customer acquisition programs, for example. You should stop spending incremental marketing or service money on these segments—don't "fire" them, but don't spend a bunch of money on them either.

The upper-left and lower-right boxes in the matrix represent the best targets for customer value enhancement programs. This is where the majority of money is made in loyalty programs, for example. The bulk of the marketing budget should be spent in trying to move these segments toward the upper-right box.

If you have created the matrix above, you have hacked the equation of lifetime value (current value plus potential value equals lifetime value). Why spend all your time trying to figure out the *absolute* lifetime value of a customer when a *relative* value is really all you need? All you need to know to allocate spending is that this segment or customer is more valuable, less valuable, or its value is changing. And then you allocate resources based on the *relative value* of the customers or segments. That's not to say you shouldn't measure lifetime value, because it's very important. But if you are a new business or don't have patience to measure lifetime value, relative value as determined by the visitor value segment matrix is a useful substitute.

Use the Matrix to Drive Content Decisions

Now, think about the fact that certain media, offers, copy, content, and products are *responsible* for customers being in each of the four groups above. Those in the top group can easily generate many, many times the profit of those in the bottom group for a company. If you are choosing which media, offers, copy, content, and products to offer to visitors, you are choosing how many visitors end up in each of the four groups above. As you can see, the most profitable retention program you can probably execute *in the short-term* is to engage in some fine-tuning on your acquisition efforts.

Figure 6-6, a report using frequency and latency, will help provide an example of how to peg visitors segmented by campaign to the matrix.

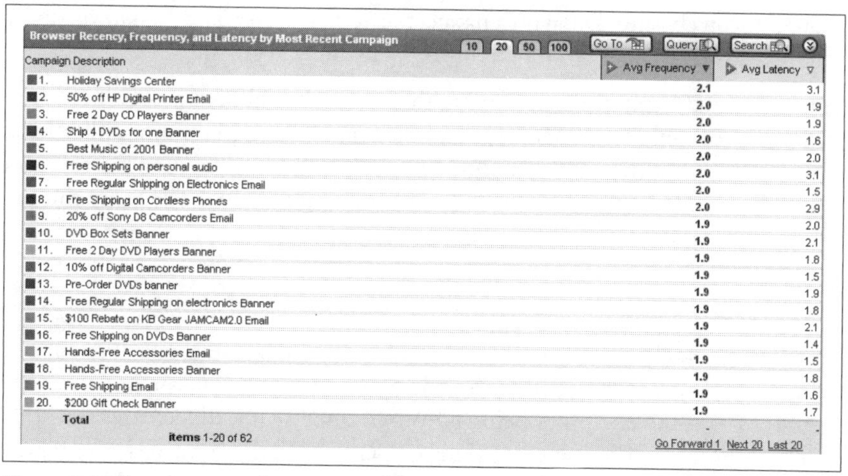

Browser Recency, Frequency, and Latency by Most Recent Campaign

Campaign Description	Avg Frequency	Avg Latency
1. Holiday Savings Center	2.1	3.1
2. 50% off HP Digital Printer Email	2.0	1.9
3. Free 2 Day CD Players Banner	2.0	1.9
4. Ship 4 DVDs for one Banner	2.0	1.6
5. Best Music of 2001 Banner	2.0	2.0
6. Free Shipping on personal audio	2.0	3.1
7. Free Regular Shipping on Electronics Email	2.0	1.5
8. Free Shipping on Cordless Phones	2.0	2.9
9. 20% off Sony D8 Camcorders Email	1.9	2.0
10. DVD Box Sets Banner	1.9	2.1
11. Free 2 Day DVD Players Banner	1.9	1.8
12. 10% off Digital Camcorders Banner	1.9	1.5
13. Pre-Order DVDs banner	1.9	1.9
14. Free Regular Shipping on electronics Banner	1.9	1.8
15. $100 Rebate on KB Gear JAMCAM2.0 Email	1.9	2.1
16. Free Shipping on DVDs Banner	1.9	1.4
17. Hands-Free Accessories Email	1.9	1.5
18. Hands-Free Accessories Banner	1.9	1.8
19. Free Shipping Email	1.9	1.6
20. $200 Gift Check Banner	1.9	1.7
Total	-	-

items 1-20 of 62 — Go Forward 1 Next 20 Last 20

Figure 6-6. Use of average frequency and latency to understand how campaigns segment into the visitor value matrix

Item 7, the "Free Regular Shipping on Electronics Email" campaign is delivering visitors who come back more often—high average frequency—and have the lowest likelihood of defection—low average latency. This campaign is generating a "rocket fuel" visitor segment when compared with all the other campaigns.

Very often, when designing retention programs, people worry about the dangers of allocating marketing budgets like this—what if a segment in the lower-left box suddenly has the potential to become an upper-right box segment, and you have been ignoring them? Well, in the first place, it doesn't happen very often, and the amount of money you will waste trying to make it happen will far exceed any benefit you might get. Retention marketing techniques are all about allocating precious budgets to the highest return on investment (ROI) activities, and the ROI is more likely to be lowest in the lower-left box. So as long as you are comfortable with not driving the highest profitability possible, by all means, spend money marketing to them.

Besides, this kind of model does not operate in a vacuum; there are built-in checks and balances. Because this is a *ranking model*, as the "status" of a segment changes, so does its place in the matrix. If a segment in the lower-left box were to show up in the next analysis in the lower-right box, you could still do something about it: this segment has newly defined potential and deserves some kind of marketing program to encourage that potential. Similarly, a segment in the "rocket fuel" box that shows up in the next analysis in the upper-left box is a best customer segment in the process of defecting and needs attention right away. Something has happened to this segment—did you change the web site? Did you change the terms of service? Whatever it is, action needs to be taken to retain this best customer segment.

You can waste a ton of money trying to change the value of a customer. It is far more profitable to recognize when change is taking place and either help it accelerate, as in the case of a segment increasing in value, or slow it down, as in the case of a segment defecting or decreasing in value. These are the situations where the ROI is the highest.

Hacking the Hack

To hack the hack, don't just *report* on the customer value matrix, create a field in each customer record for a code representing the customer value segment to which the customer belongs. Why? Once again, this creates the ability to automate marketing campaigns or personalization of a web site based on current and potential visitor value. Reps in a call center could also use the code, giving them a heads-up on the value of the customer to the company. As part of a customer retention plan, this code could determine how a rep responds to a customer request or problem.

The bottom line on visitor and customer retention is this: identifying the *current value* of visitor and customer segments is moving from "best practice" to "no-brainer" status. The next leg up over your competition will be to use *potential value* metrics to make more profitable customer investment decisions for your company

—*Jim Novo and Eric T. Peterson*

HACK   Use Cross-Sell Data to Sell More Products
#87
One proven strategy for increasing your average order value is cross-selling products when a visitor is committing to a purchase. Your web measurement application can provide great insight into who best to cross-sell to, provided you know where to look.

The actions that visitors take on your site represent the most valuable data available for determining product offerings and pairing. For example, on an apparel site, certain sweater/shirt combinations may sell particularly well together. By presenting these articles side by side, visitors will be more likely to purchase both, streamlining the shopping process and increasing average order size. By being able to intelligently recommend items that go together, brand owners can provide customers with valuable information at the moment when they are making their purchase decisions, while at the same time working to improve their bottom line.

Before examining the uses of product affinity data, however, it is worthwhile to define the difference between a cross-sell and an up-sell.

Cross-sell item

A complementary product that is purchased at the same time or immediately after a sale. For example, if a customer were buying a video game platform, a good cross-sell would be a few video games, even though he intended to buy only the game console.

Up-sell item

A product that a vendor persuades a customer to purchase in addition to the products that they are already interested in. For example, if a customer were planning to buy a video game platform, a great up-sell would be a plasma television to enhance his new gaming console.

The two definitions are similar, but there are important differences. With a cross-sell item, a customer is showing an interest in two naturally related items and the web site must be able to help them easily find both. With up-sell, however, the customer has shown an interest in a single product, but can be influenced to purchase more based on recommendations he sees on the site.

Quantify the Value of Product Recommendations

Before investing in a product recommendation initiative, it is important to first be able to quantify the value of cross-selling and up-selling products on your site. This not only ensures that you prioritize your projects appropriately, but also provides you with a baseline for understanding where to make future improvements.

Step one: Track cross-sell links separately. The first step to understanding the value of cross-sell begins with tracking. Do you provide cross-sell recommendations on product pages? What about special cross-sell categories or checkout cart links? For each of these different types of recommendation, you should look to track the behavior of visitors that view and purchase product as a result of clicking on cross-sell links. By isolating these behaviors, you can understand the impact of cross-sell and identify areas for improvement.

Step two: Measure cross-sell performance. There are two basic types of measurement to understand for cross-sell: link usage and sales. Link usage measures how easily visitors are able to find a cross-sell link on a page. One way to measure this is by calculating the frequency of link click-through relative to total site visits. Cross-sell sales measures how much your investment in cross-sell is paying off, providing insight into the relevancy of your recommendations.

Step three: Take action. Is your cross-sell usage low? Change the location on the page where cross-sell offers are located to be above the fold, or label cross-sell links more intuitively. Which of our cross-sell categories are delivering the best sales? For underperforming categories, it may be useful to reevaluate the product pairings to ensure that you are providing the right recommendations.

Now that we have defined a basic process for tracking and managing cross-sell results, we can take a look at how to use web data to improve our recommendation capabilities.

Data-Driven Analysis: Find the Low-Hanging Fruit

Cross-sell and up-sell are two of the most data-driven applications for web analytics. Given the sheer volume of data available, companies must begin by focusing their efforts. The best way to do this is to start with the most popular products sold on the site. By matching these products with appropriate cross-sell recommendations, you can quickly increase site sales for a large population of shoppers. To do so requires an understanding of exactly which products are relevant to recommend. The data that can be captured for this type of analysis falls roughly into two categories: cart overlap data and common buyer data.

Tracking cart overlap. When a customer creates an order, the items that she purchases are all available for capture directly from the order confirmation page. By simply taking the top products sold on a site and matching those with items with which they were most frequently sold, data analysts can quickly understand which products are "cross-sold" effectively. These represent items where customers are interested in a bundle, since they are purchasing both products in a single session. Placing these items pairings on product pages can be an easy way to improve cross-sell effectiveness.

Tracking common buyers. Tracking product purchases over multiple sessions provides even more insight into customer affinities. By tracking the top items sold and then tying them to the top products those buyers have purchased over time, data analysts can understand the propensity for "up-selling" a customer who is purchasing a given item. By placing these product pairings on the checkout page or in targeted emails, brand owners can easily increase up-sell performance for a site.

An example of cart overlap and common buyer overlap is depicted in Figure 6-7, which shows that 39 percent of customers who bought a basic dress shirt also bought a reversible belt. From this we can infer that the belt is a good candidate for cross-sell with the shirt.

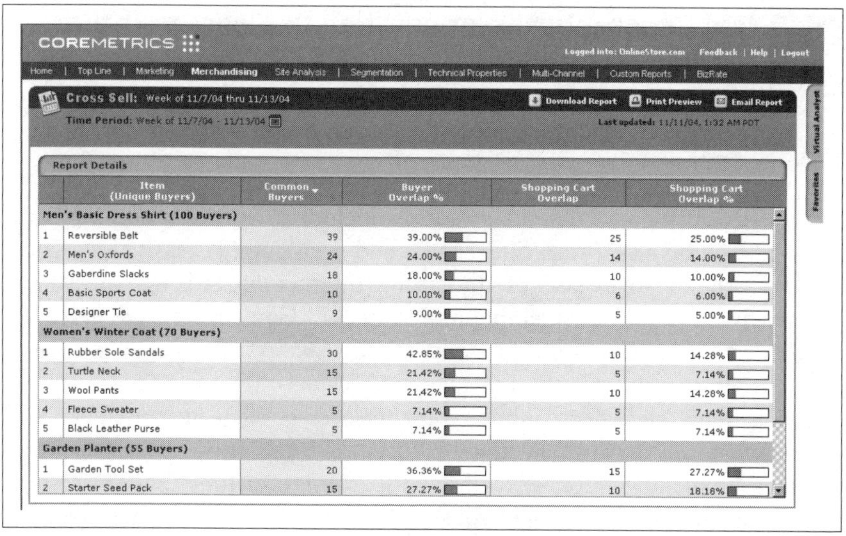

Figure 6-7. Cart and common buyer overlap

Leverage Cross-Sell Data

Populating cross-sell recommendations for the hundreds or thousands of products would be a daunting task even for a large team of analysts. As a result, extending the value of cross-sell data requires more than just analysis. To deliver intelligent up-sell in a timely and cost-effective manner requires automation. By using a data warehouse to capture and store product purchases and export this information in a structured format to your online retail, call center, or email systems, you can do just that.

To enable automated, intelligent cross-sell, you must begin by thinking about the types of recommendations you are making. Will you be populating recommendations on the product page? Fueling email campaigns to recent buyers? The uses of the data will drive the type of information that is required. During this analysis, it is important to keep in mind the difference between cross-sell and up-sell. For example, when populating product page pairings, the focus should be on items that sell well together in-session (cross-sell), ensuring that all results returned are immediately relevant. With email, however, you may want to focus on non-obvious products that the customer is likely to desire, based on his historical purchase behavior (up-sell).

—*Brett Hurt and Eric T. Peterson*

Use Geographic Segmentation to Measure Offline Marketing

With the growing adoption of multi-channel retailing strategies, Geo-segmentation can now provide valuable insight into offline advertising effectiveness.

Offline advertising can take many forms, including television commercials, radio ads, billboards, print, direct mail, and even guerilla marketing. Compared to the relative ease of measuring Internet advertising, measuring offline advertising is considerably more difficult. Companies have relied on coupon codes, purchase and brand awareness surveys, dedicated 800 numbers, and other costly tactics. Fortunately, because offline advertising is now directing many audiences online, you can leverage web measurement and geo-segmentation to evaluate the effectiveness these efforts [Hack #78]. Most top measurement vendors provide geo-segmentation tools either as standard or as an add-on package; consult your particular vendor for specifics regarding how to get geo-segmentation added for your analysis.

To begin, you must decide which regions you are advertising in. Then decide which regions will serve as control; that is, regions that you are *explicitly not* advertising in. The control regions are important, because they will be used to remove bias that may occur in your target regions from other, unrelated marketing activities. Once you pick your targets and controls, establish precampaign baselines for traffic, revenue, leads—whatever key performance indicators best highlight campaign success. Without diving deep into statistics, you should at least draw on as much history as the actual advertising campaign will run. For example, if you are running the ad for two weeks, you should have at least two weeks of historical baselines to reflect on.

Once your promotion launches, be sure to keep a close eye on changes in these KPI baselines. If you identify a poor performer early in the campaign, you can save significant costs and increase ROI by reallocating those funds and resources to better-performing regions or initiatives. Of course the response time will vary greatly depending on which marketing tactic you choose (i.e., a catalog or direct mail piece could take six weeks, while a television or radio ad may occur in the same day), so be sure not to cut the strings too early without understanding the particulars of your market and marketing tactics.

Key Measurements

As with other marketing initiatives, standard measurements like response, conversion, revenue per acquisition, lifetime value, profit per customer, and campaign ROI are all relevant.

However, there are also some unique metrics you need to be aware of:

Response lift

This metric is calculated by taking visits from your target regions during the promotion, and subtracting visits from before the promotion. Then compare your control regions in the same way, such that you have net visits from your target regions and net visits from your control regions. Now subtract the two numbers, and you will be left with the response lift for your regions.

Success lift

Similar to response lift, you simply compare success events (such as revenue) for each target region and each control region. By taking the net difference of the two, you can calculate success lift, which in turn will allow you to determine campaign ROI.

An Example

Assume you run a series of radio advertisements in California in November 2004 that directs listeners to your web site. The primary call to action is submitting a lead form, so the most important KPIs are visitors, leads, and leads per visitor.

You decide to run the ads in Northern California—namely San Francisco, San Jose, Palo Alto, Sunnyvale, and Santa Clara. Furthermore, you decide to use Los Angeles, San Diego, Orange County, and Santa Monica as control cities—regions where you will specifically *not* run these ads. The first step is to establish traffic baselines from October 2004 data. (For the sake of simplicity, the example excludes lead and leads per visitor baselines in this hack. In a practical setting, this would naturally be a key focus.)

The next step is to track changes in key KPIs over time in response to the campaign. Figure 6-8 illustrates the highlights, and shows how many of the target regions demonstrated strong visitor growth.

Palo Alto jumped 61.7 percent, Santa Clara was up 61.7 percent, and San Francisco was up 11.2 percent. But look at the control cities, where there was also some strong growth there: Los Angeles jumped 10.7 percent, San Diego jumped 43.4 percent, and Santa Monica jumped 69.7 percent. Perhaps those frigid California winters kept more people inside and on the Web in November. Perhaps a competitor in San Diego went out of business; perhaps the marketing group improved local advertising efforts in Santa Monica—there are numerous possibilities.

If you do not reduce the chance of bias from these possible influences, you could overstate or understate your true advertising effectiveness. This is

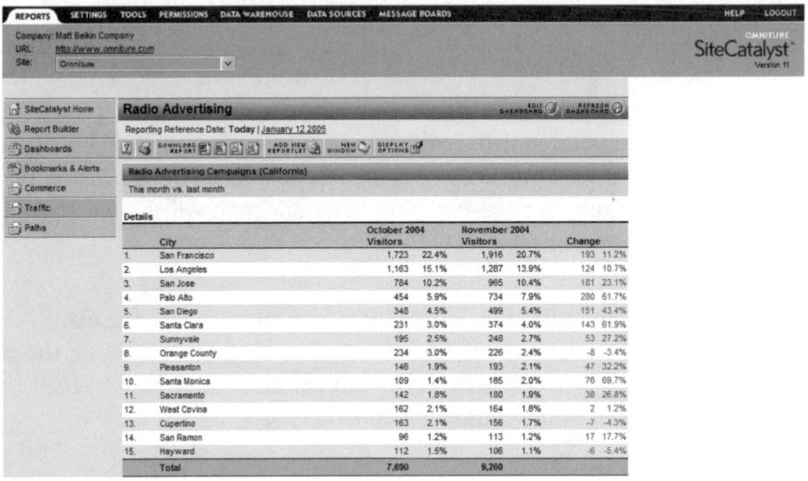

Figure 6-8. Custom measurement of offline data

where your control groups come into play. First, sum up visitor traffic for the target cities in October. In the example, this is 3,387 visitors. Do the same for November; the 4,237 for this period in the example suggests a 25 percent *gross* increase over October. Then perform the same analysis for the control regions, arriving at 1,854 visitors in October and 2,197 visitors in November. This suggests an 18 percent increase.

Subtracting the 18 percent control growth from the 25 percent target growth yields a 7 percent *net* increase in visitor traffic from the radio promotion. In other words, the response lift is 7 percent, and it is reasonable to attribute this to the radio promotion.

Depending on the average visitor value, a 7 percent increase in visitors could translate to significant revenues. For example, assuming the average lead conversion rate is 5 percent and the average deal size is $100,000, this 7 percent increase in visitors would yield over $1 million in campaign-driven revenue.

—*Matt Belkin and Eric T. Peterson*

HACK #89   Measure New and Returning Customers

One of the keys to successful web optimization lies in effective segmentation of your visitor population. One of the most obvious areas of segmentation is simply evaluating behavioral and conversion differences between new and returning customers.

New customers are exploring. Returning customers often know what they are looking for. Does your site make it easy for both groups to find what they need? Or by optimizing *in aggregate*, have you made it ideal for nobody? The only way to know for sure is to effectively differentiate between these groups, and then explore page-by-page differences in click and conversion behavior between the two segments.

So, how can you optimize your chances for accurate differentiation of new and returning customers?

At least for now, the best option is to ensure that the persistent cookies set on your visitors' machines are set in your domain (in other words, first party), even if you're using an ASP analytics provider. There are several options for making this happen.

Serve Your Own First-Party Cookie

The first and best approach to implement a first-party cookie via an ASP script is to simply serve the cookie from your own web site. The cookie must contain a unique visitor identification code, typically a random number or alphanumeric string that is passed back to you with each page viewed on your site. To then pass that ID value to your ASP as a parameter with the image request, simply make a small modification to your tagging script. Something like this (where MYFIRSTPARTYCOOKIENAME is the cookie you'll set and MYSESSIONPARAMETER is the parameter that you'll use for sessionization):

```
function fpc(MYFIRSTPARTYCOOKIENAME){
        var cookies = document.cookie;
        var pos = cookies.indexOf(MYFIRSTPARTYCOOKIENAME + "=");
        if (pos != -1){
                var start = pos + MYFIRSTPARTYCOOKIENAME.length + 1;
                var end = cookies.indexOf(";", start);
                if (end == -1) end = cookies.length;
                var cookievalue = cookies.substring(start,end);
                cookievalue = unescape(cookievalue);
                MYSESSIONPARAMETER = cookievalue;
        }
}
```

Finally, identify the new parameter as the tracking method with your analytics application.

Of course, before you make any changes to the tracking script of your analytics vendor, you might want to double-check with them to ensure that it will work. It's probably also important to note that not all analytics solutions allow you to specify backup sessionization techniques, so ensure that yours will.

Because the cookie is now being served by your own domain, it is less likely to be subject to removal by anti-spyware programs, and returning visitors will be accurately identified. Note, though, that anti-spyware programs that prevent 1×1 GIF image [Hack #29] requests to specific domains (such as those of the ASP analytics vendors) may still prevent visitor tracking. If eliminating this problem is important to you, you must use one of the two following techniques, whether or not you also implement your own tracking cookie.

- Use web server logfiles and, if using an ASP, talk to them about the ability to upload those logs for analysis
- Implement your own client-side data collection point, served from your own domain, and then upload that data to the service for analysis

Under these scenarios, you maintain the interaction with your customers and you serve your customers a legitimate first-party tracking cookie, while still maintaining the flexibility of using a hosted analytics solution.

Have Your Application Provider Serve a First-Party Cookie for You

As an alternative to managing your own cookie, hosted service providers can generally serve a first-party cookie instead of the default third-party cookie for unencrypted (non-SSL) traffic. This solution requires you to select a hostname, configure this hostname in your DNS servers as an alias to another host provided to you by your analytics vendor, and modify the tracking code on your web pages to reference the new hostname within your domain. The result is a first-party cookie in your domain that is served by your hosted analytics vendor.

This process involves creating a CNAME record that would look something like this:

```
my.internal.network.name. IN CNAME  my.vendors.network.name
```

Sites that have secure pages, such as shopping cart checkout procedures, require additional procedures. Because secure pages are generally encrypted using SSL (secure sockets layer), an SSL certificate must be present for each fully qualified domain name object referenced on the page. For a hosted service to properly serve the tracking image for these SSL pages, you must acquire an appropriate SSL certificate and provide it to them. However, the potential security implications of this approach require serious consideration.

Now that we've maximized our collection through the use of first-party cookies, we need to be sure that we have a place to store that visitor information so that it can be put to good use. Ensure that your vendor employs a visitor history database that will track key events like visits, campaign responses, conversions or purchases, segment IDs, and, of course, a unique customer identifier. Ideally, you'll be able to access the data in this database directly, as you may simply want to mine in an ad hoc way—for example, you may think, "Give me a list of all of the customers who have spent more than $500 with me, in key segments, who haven't visited the site in more than three months."

Using the Information

Combining new versus repeat buyer segmentation with behavioral information on your web site can yield valuable information that you can put to very tactical use. For example, generate a report that shows a product drill-down by new versus repeat buyers that will tell you your most popular, highest-revenue-producing products for each segment (Figure 6-9).

New vs. Repeat Buyers Product Drilldown	Visits ▼	Revenue ▽	Orders ▽	Units ▽	Average Revenue per Order ▽	% of All Visits
■1. ▼New Buyer	3,296	$614,933.06	3,320	3,512.0	$185.22	3.20%
▼Electronics	3,314	$614,473.42	3,314	3,505.0	$185.42	3.22%
▼DVD Players	944	$246,338.21	944	1,004.0	$260.95	0.92%
▷Brand Name DVD Players	693	$182,983.02	693	725.0	$264.04	0.67%
▷Professional DVD Players	251	$63,355.19	251	279.0	$252.41	0.24%
▷Imaging	895	$121,431.89	895	946.0	$135.68	0.87%
▷Telephones	665	$36,278.69	665	708.0	$54.55	0.65%
▷Home Audio	544	$170,926.35	544	570.0	$314.20	0.53%
▷Portable Audio	235	$15,601.05	235	245.0	$66.39	0.23%
▷Televisions	16	$23,608.98	16	17.0	$1,475.56	0.02%
▷Blank Media	6	$71.70	6	6.0	$11.95	0.01%
▷Mobile Install Kits/Supplies	3	$34.85	3	3.0	$11.62	0.00%
▷A/V Connectivity	3	$109.85	3	3.0	$36.62	0.00%
▷Audio Accessories	2	$51.90	2	2.0	$25.95	0.00%
▷Storage	1	$19.95	1	1.0	$19.95	0.00%
▷Games	6	$459.64	6	7.0	$76.61	0.01%
■2. ▼Repeat Buyer	1,489	$271,031.77	1,556	1,612.0	$174.18	1.45%
▼Electronics	1,549	$271,019.82	1,555	1,611.0	$174.29	1.50%
▷DVD Players	399	$101,278.52	401	415.0	$252.56	0.39%
▷Imaging	390	$57,526.36	390	406.0	$147.50	0.38%
▷Telephones	365	$18,862.37	366	377.0	$51.54	0.35%
▷Home Audio	282	$85,211.34	285	298.0	$298.99	0.27%
▷Portable Audio	104	$6,858.69	104	106.0	$65.95	0.10%
▷A/V Connectivity	3	$139.85	3	3.0	$46.62	0.00%
▷Televisions	2	$1,049.89	2	2.0	$524.95	0.00%
▷Audio Accessories	1	$49.95	1	1.0	$49.95	0.00%
▷Blank Media	1	$7.95	1	1.0	$7.95	0.00%
▷Antennas	1	$24.95	1	1.0	$24.95	0.00%
▷Mobile Install Kits/Supplies	1	$9.95	1	1.0	$9.95	0.00%
▷Games	1	$11.95	1	1.0	$11.95	0.00%
Total	N/A	$885,964.83	N/A	5,124.0	N/A	N/A

Items 1-2 of 2

Figure 6-9. Product categories and sales metrics

Browser-overlay tools [Hack #62] can also be used to evaluate link and conversion success for the different segments (Figure 6-10).

Assuming that you are setting your own cookie as discussed earlier, ensure that the cookie on the order confirmation page is set to count the total number of purchases. Then, using your analytics solution to understand the most popular, most profitable product preferences of each group, use that information to display different promotions on your home page for each of the different segments. By serving more relevant content to different segments, you can expect to increase conversions, average order size, and total revenue.

—Jeff Seacrist and Eric T. Peterson

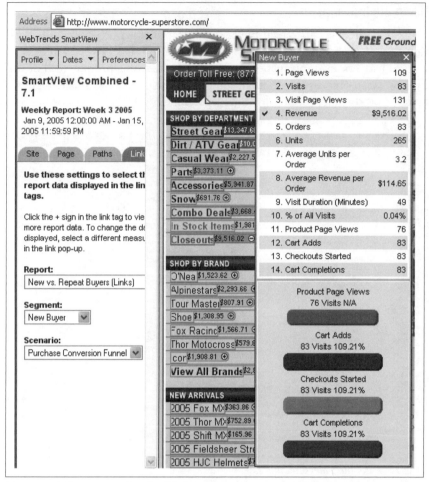

Figure 6-10. Browser overlay for the "New Buyer" segment

 ### Build Your Own Web Measurement Application:
#90 Commerce Data

Fundamental to online retailers successful with web measurement data is the
ability to get non-traffic data into the analysis. In this hack, wel show you how to
add the value of a transaction to the mix and tie it back to your referring sources.

In this hack, we'll return to our sample program and demonstrate how to
extend it to collect additional data. We'll use the example of measuring revenue, but the same method could be used to collect other types of data. Any
data you can access using JavaScript can be passed in the page tag, written
to the logfile, and then analyzed by the logfile reader. For example, you
could report visitors' screen sizes or visitor segments by the same method.

When a visitor to the web site makes a purchase, we want to record that information. We do this by putting additional JavaScript on the page after the transaction is completed—normally the "thank you" page on the web site.

In this hack, we'll assume that you have some way of accessing the revenue amount using JavaScript. How to do that is very dependent on the shopping cart software you use, and we won't cover it in any detail here. Some shopping carts pass the amount back to you when the transaction is finished, whereas others seem to try and make it as hard as possible. As a last resort, you can approximate by using a fixed amount, such as the amount of the average transaction.

The Code: Page Tag and Tag Processor

Assuming that you somehow have a revenue amount available to the JavaScript, you must modify your JavaScript page tag to pass the data to the logging script. Previously the page tag looked like this:

```
document.write('<img src="/cgi-bin/readtag.pl?url='+escape(document.
location)+'&amp;ref='+escape(document.referrer)+'">');
```

To pass the new data, simply modify the code on your "Thank You" page where you confirm the transaction to add the additional field:

```
rev=0.00;  <!-- Change 0.00 to the actual value of the transaction -->
document.write('<img src="/cgi-bin/readtag.pl?url='+escape(document.
location)+'&amp;ref='+escape(document.referrer)+'&amp;rev='+rev+'">');
```

 This should be done only on the thank you page; we'll leave the page tags on the other pages alone.

The next step is to update the script that processes and slogs these requests. We next need to modify the CGI program that reads the page tag and writes the logfile (*readtag.pl*). This is straightforward. We previously wrote five fields using the command:

```
print LF "$time\t$client\t$url\t$ref\t$cookie_val\n";
```

Now we simply modify the script to write either five or six depending whether revenue is present or not. To implement the new functionality, replace the original code line in *readtag.pl* file with this new set of statements:

```
my $rev = $cgi->param('rev');
if (defined($rev)) {
  print LF "$time\t$client\t$url\t$ref\t$cookie_val\t$rev\n";
}
else { print LF "$time\t$client\t$url\t$ref\t$cookie_val\n"; }
```

Once these changes are complete, some of the logfile lines will include an additional field on the end, like the second line here:

```
1104772080 192.168.17.32  /checkout.php   http://www.example.com/addtocart.
php?prodid=17454    192.168.17.32.85261104772101338
1104772091 192.168.17.32  /thankyou.php   http://www.example.com/checkout.
php    192.168.17.32.85261104772101338    39.99
```

The Code: readlog.pl

The next step is to modify the logfile reader to read these types of lines. The following lines should be added to the appropriate classes in this script. The fist step is to modify the parser in the Request constructor to understand the optional additional field. Modify the Request (*Request.pm*) class to look like this:

```
package Request;
use strict;
my $case_insensitive = 0;
sub new {
  my ($invocant, $str) = @_;
  return undef
      unless (my ($time, $host, $file, $referrer, $cookie, $revenue) =
          $str =~
          /^              # start of line
          (1\d{9})\t      # time: ten digits starting with 1
          ([^\t]+)\t      # host: non-empty string
          ([^\t]+)\t      # file: non-empty string
          ([^\t]*)\t      # referrer: possibly empty string
          ([^\t]*)        # cookie: possibly empty string
          (?:\t([\d\.]+))? # optional revenue (tab followed by number)
          $/x);           # end of line
  $file = lc $file if $case_insensitive;
  return bless {
    time => $time,
    host => $host,
    file => $file,
    referrer => $referrer,
    cookie => $cookie,
    revenue => $revenue }
}
```

The Session class needs to know how to calculate the revenue of a session. If there are several revenues in the session, we'll use the last one, rather than adding them, to avoid duplicates if the visitor reloads the thank you page. The risk is that a visitor who does make two purchases will be counted only once, but this is usually a small problem. Modify the Session (*Session.pm*) class to look like this:

```
package Session;
...
sub Revenue {
```

```
  my $self = shift;
  for my $i (reverse 0..$#$self) {  # count backwards through array
    my $req = $self->[$i];
    if (defined ($req->{revenue})) { return $req->{revenue}; }
  }
  return undef;  # revenue never defined
}
```

Finally, the Data (*Data.pm*) class needs to report some statistics from the revenue. There are many useful things that we could report, but as examples, we'll show the total revenue, the conversion rate (i.e., the proportion of sessions with positive revenue), and the amount of revenue generated by each search term. Modify the Data class to look like this:

```
package Data;
...
sub new {
  return bless {
    ...
    total_revenue => 0,
    sessions_with_revenue => 0,
    search_terms_revenue => {},
  };
}
sub AddSession {
  ...
  my $revenue = $sess->Revenue();
  if (defined($revenue) && $revenue > 0)
  {
    $self->{total_revenue} += $revenue;
    ++$self->{sessions_with_revenue};
    if ($search_term) {
      $self->{search_terms_revenue}->{$search_term} += $revenue;
    }
  }
}
sub WriteReport {
  ...
  $self->WriteHash('Search Terms with Revenue', 'search_terms_revenue');
}
sub WriteSummary {
  ...
  printf "Total revenue: \$%.2f\n", $self->{total_revenue};
  printf "Sessions with revenue: %d (%.1f%%)\n",
    $self->{sessions_with_revenue},
    $self->{total_sessions} == 0 ? 0:
    $self->{sessions_with_revenue} / $self->{total_sessions} * 100;
}
```

And that's it. We've successfully retrieved an additional piece of data using JavaScript, passed it to the server in the page tag, written it to the logfile, and reported it in our analysis. Other additional data could be added to the program just as easily.

Running the Code

As always, from the command line, assuming that *page.log* is in the same directory as *readlog.pl*, all you need to do is type:

```
perl readlog.pl page.log
```

Assuming you're collecting data using the rev variable, you will see a report similar to that in Figure 6-11 when you run the code.

Figure 6-11. Search terms with revenue analysis

Hopefully, this hack will suggest other ways you can easily use web measurement applications based on page tags to grab nontraditional web data for processing and analysis.

—Dr. Stephen Turner and Eric T. Peterson

## CHAPTER SEVEN

Reporting Strategies and Key Performance Indicators
Hacks 91–100

Now that you've read a seemingly endless number of hacks describing the data and what you should do with it, all that is left is to communicate the value of that data to your organization. Should be a piece of cake, right?

Then why do so few organizations actually share their web data throughout the company?

Data collected by JupiterResearch indicates that most companies don't share the data they collect about their successes online broadly or frequently enough. By broadly, I mean with enough people in the company; it's not enough to have a small group of webmasters look at the data; you have to get everyone thinking about how the web site is being used to drive business success. In terms of frequency, only 32 percent of companies look at their web data on a daily or weekly basis, while half that number look at the data on an *ad hoc* basis.

You will be successful with your investment in web site measurement only if you're able to get people throughout your company to care about the data. To do this, you have to massage the data into a format they'll understand, present it in a way that speaks directly to their interest in the Internet, and support it with training and higher-order analysis.

Sometimes It's How You Say It

In terms of translating the data into a format that people will understand, perhaps the best analogy is the stock market. Anyone who is interested in playing the market has access to vast volumes of information about every publicly held company that detail how they spend and make money, where the risks are, who the key players are, who they compete with and so on.

So why do people pay for market research services and visit sites like Motley Fool?

Because SEC filings are ridiculously difficult to read and because people like to have complicated information translated into more palatable terms. Unless you're in the securities industry, when is the last time you read a prospectus cover to cover? Compare that to the last time you asked a friend for a stock tip? Your friend's information may not be as complete or correct as a prospectus, but he will provide information in easily understood language, not financial mumbo-jumbo.

You must do the same thing with your web data. You have to become adept at translating the ugly details into something that anyone in your organization will be able to understand. You need to make use of relevant graphs and tables—not necessarily the figures that your vendor provides via their application. Plan on using the language that your company uses, not trying to get everyone to learn how to "talk the talk."

The more you do to make the data palatable, the more likely the data will be consumed. The goal is to create an organization so focused on web data that people look forward to your reports, because they know you'll be providing information they can use to be more successful. While you may never experience that particular level of nirvana, if you're able to simply get people to understand and act on the data, you're winning both the battle *and* the war.

Patience, Patience, Patience

In reality, of course, none of this will happen overnight. People, for the most part, are afraid of complex data. Most people's comfort level with large spreadsheets of numbers is usually very low, unless you're a CPA or, god forbid, a professional data analyst. Keep this in mind as you build and begin to distribute your key performance indicator reports and expect that people will adopt your reports more slowly than you'd like, even if you're producing absolutely brilliant reports.

Every few months, reread the hack on [Hack #91] and use that to set and reset your expectations. Plan on supporting internal data consumers (and don't call them that to their faces, it makes them mad) as much as necessary in the first 90 days, making sure that the KPIs and reports both make sense and are being used. Go as far as cornering people in the hall and asking them about some great insight you provided in the daily KPI report—if you're really into this stuff, people already have you pegged as a geek, so what can it hurt?

The work you do early on will pay you back a thousand-fold down the road when you've managed to transform your organization into one full of data consumers, just waiting to see how the latest round of improvements have positively contributed to the bottom line.

Microsoft Excel: the World's Most Popular Analytics Application

An important thing to consider when you're thinking about how to distribute the data is the need to provide reports in a format that folks are comfortable with. While the application vendors have all done a pretty good job on prettifying their applications, the chances that you'll ever get everyone who needs to use this data to log into the system and successfully navigate to the right reports is, well, zero. This is why I always recommend Microsoft Excel.

Excel is hand's down, by far, the world's most popular and dominant analytics application; sort of the Shaquille O'Neal of number crunching apps. Anyone who has ever used a computer has come in contact with it, and for the most part, business people are used to using Excel for any number of things. Number crunching, project management, data sharing; you name it and I bet Excel has been used. It's even being used to analyze the behavior of Halo 2 players in the videogame world.

Given the choice between forcing people to learn a complex proprietary application or giving them the option of using something they already know and are comfortable with, most people opt for the latter. You should support them in their choice. Plan on building your key performance indicator reports in Excel and look into whether your vendor offers direct-to-Excel export or automated Excel-based reporting (a number, including WebSideStory, WebTrends, Fireclick, and Omniture, currently do).

Excel offers an additional feature that turns out to be nearly critical to most data analysis teams: the ability to easily annotate the data, providing necessary insight. Think about this as the "chicken un-beheader"—if you send everyone a spreadsheet containing *really bad news*, the first thing that happens is everyone runs around like chickens with their heads cut off. Bad news often creates blind panic and blind panic is bad. Now assume that when you present the really bad news that you annotate the report letting everyone know that everything is under control and you expect the problem to be corrected quickly. Voilà! The chickens don't lose their heads, and its business as usual; hence, the chicken "un-beheader."

Again, because this data is nominally complex and almost always new to folks, you need to plan on doing everything possible to increase people's comfort level. Don't reinvent the wheel; use the one you already have.

Distribute Reports Wisely

#91   Don't waste people's time by sending out pages and pages of data

Given all you've learned at this point in the book, I'm sure you're thinking "That's a lot of information to communicate." You're right, it is. Fortunately there are some simple, effective strategies for distributing reports that take advantage of what we know about people's relationships with information. While I'm forced to use some generalities, experience tells me that often these assumptions hold up under scrutiny and can help you make better decisions about who gets what report when.

Give the People What They Want, or Better Yet, What They Need

People have a tendency, when volumes of data are available, to present volumes of data and let the reader sort it out; this is often the case with web measurement data. The problem with this strategy is that it assumes the reader will take the time to figure out which information is relevant to her; this is rarely the case in web measurement, usually because the data is foreign to most people. The best strategy to get people to invest their time is to give them the data they need to do their job and little else. If you take the time to figure out which data is most relevant to a person or group within your company and present that data in language they use and understand, you'll see your efforts pay off, and inevitably your recipients will ask different and, hopefully, better questions.

Use the Same Language Your Audience Uses Whenever Possible

Rather than using the technical jargon used throughout this book, seriously consider translating your reports into the same language your business uses. Other than the fundamental definitions of page view, visit, unique visitors, and referrers [Hack #1], which are important to define clearly for your audience, make sure they understand each term—presenting web site activities in the *lingua franca* of your company is highly recommended. This is essentially an "if it ain't broke, don't fix it" recommendation. Also, keep in mind that some people are more visual than others and that images can augment language in ways you don't expect.

A Picture Says a Thousand Words

While much of the data you're collecting and analyzing is presented back to you in rows and columns, try and keep in mind the value of using images when presenting complex information. You don't have to go out of your way to read Edward Tufte's *The Visual Display of Quantitative Information*

(Graphics Press, 1992), but make use of visual elements whenever appropriate. For example, Figure 7-1 shows how raw data can be transformed into a much more dramatic presentation.

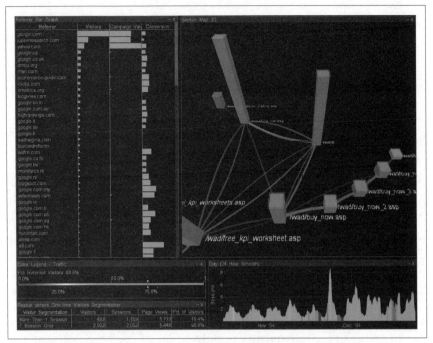

Figure 7-1. Rich presentation in Visual Science's Visual Workstation

Of course, you don't always have to go to such extremes. If you're absolutely unable to visually represent the data, do simple things such as using up and down arrows to represent trends; color "good" numbers in green and "bad" numbers in red [Hack #92]; use bold, italics, and underline strategically to highlight information; and leverage ratios to convey as much information as possible.

Ratios Are Better than Counts

While the difference between a ratio and a key performance indicator [Hack #94] is subtle at best, the difference between a count and a ratio is not. Would you rather know that 1,000 people bought something at your web site yesterday or that 16 percent of all visitors made a purchase? OK, sure, you probably want to know both, but the 1,000 people are presented out of context. "A thousand customers" is great news if you had only 10,000 visitors (a 10 percent conversion rate!) but slightly less good news if you had 1,000,000 visitors. Plus, there is tremendous value in comparing timeframes (this day versus this day last week, for example), which is very difficult to do when presenting only a raw measurement. When in doubt, present both a meaningful ratio and the counts that support it, as shown in Figure 7-2.

Performance Indicator	This Week	Last Week	Percent Change	Warn?
Percent New Visitors	100.0%	100.0%	0.00%	▼
Percent Returning Visitors	100.0%	100.0%	0.00%	▼
Ratio of New to Returning Visitors	1.00	1.00	0.00%	▼
Key Conversion Rates:				
Visit to Purchase	100.0%	100.0%	0.00%	▼
Cart Add to Purchase	100.0%	100.0%	0.00%	▼
Checkout to Purchase	100.0%	100.0%	0.00%	▼
Search to Purchase	100.0%	100.0%	0.00%	▼
New Vistor Conversion Rate	100.0%	100.0%	0.00%	▼
Return Visitor Conversion Rate	100.0%	100.0%	0.00%	▼
Average Order Value (AOV)	$ 1.00	$ 1.00	0.00%	▼
Sales per Visitor	$ 1.00	$ 1.00	0.00%	▼
Customer Retention Rate	100.0%	100.0%	0.00%	▼
Percent of Visits Under 90 Seconds	100.0%	100.0%	0.00%	▼
Key Supporting Metrics:				
Total Orders	2,143	1,832	-16.98%	▼
Total Buyers	2,000	1,699	-17.72%	▼
Total Visitors	13,132	18,322	28.33%	▲
Total Sales Revenue	$12,434	$10,133	-22.71%	▼

Figure 7-2. Key performance indicators and supporting metrics

Distribute Reports Regularly

One of the worst mistakes businesses make regarding web measurement data is to look at it infrequently or only on an *ad hoc* basis. Because this data is not the kind many have experience with, it's important to keep people's attention focused; the best way to do this is by getting reports in front of them frequently enough to generate familiarity and help them do their jobs better. If your marketing staffs tweak their advertising purchases on a weekly basis, make sure their marketing report is in their inbox at the beginning of every week. If your merchandising staffs rotate products every few days, make sure their merchandising reports are delivered every day.

You have to be especially careful regarding the timing of report delivery and consider the previous four recommendations. If you provide too much data, use confusing language, or make them scan ugly tables to mine for actionable information, it won't matter how often you send the report, because it will always end up in the garbage. Conversely, if you do a good job of presenting the information people need to do their jobs in an easily understood format, you'll be generating a report that people expect and rely upon for their ongoing success.

Know If the News Is Good

#92 One of the most common issues in web site meaurement is having the data but not being sure what it means. Knowing whether the news is "good" is central to your company's success with web measurement.

When reviewing metrics, how do you know if "more" is better or worse? It depends on the metric you are looking at and the intent of your site. There are really two aspects of knowing if the news is good. One is understanding the performance of specific metrics: are more page views better or worse? The second is understanding how those metrics compare to those of competitors or other sites driving similar behaviors.

A few metrics are obvious: more sales or leads and a higher average sales price are generally positive (assuming product returns don't increase at the same rate as sales). Other metrics are more challenging. Examples are:

- Page views per visit
- Average visit length
- Visits per visitors during a given timeframe

It's natural to assume that it is a good sign if all three of these metrics increase. But this isn't always the case. It all depends on the goals of the site. If you are running a content site supported by advertising, then yes, you would want to increase all three of those metrics. But if you are managing a lead-generation or online retail site, running these numbers up may not be a positive. For example, optimizing a lead-generation site may increase the number and quality of leads by 50 percent, yet reduce other important KPIs:

The page views per visit dropped.
People were able to find the information they needed in fewer clicks, and the optimized site was able to convert visitors to leads at a faster rate—again, in fewer clicks. In this case, it was a positive that the page views dropped since leads increased significantly. And, from a visitor satisfaction standpoint, it was an improvement.

The average visit length dropped.
In addition to a drop in page views, reflected in less clicks, visitors were spending less time on the site. Again, without focusing on lead conversion, it could be easy to say that the site wasn't as "sticky" as it used to be. In reality, that didn't matter since the conversions were up significantly.

Visits per visitor changed little.
In this example, it didn't change much post-optimization. People normally think that we want site visitors to come back more than once per month, but as you can see, there are cases when that isn't important.

The most important thing is to focus on the key conversions based on your business goals [Hack #38] and ensure that those are moving in the right direction.

Comparing Your Site to Industry Standards and Competitors

"How do we compare to your other clients or the industry in general?" A week does not go by when I don't hear that question. Unfortunately, it can be very tough to answer. There are a few things that can make comparison difficult:

- Different business plans
- Different industries
- Different role of the Web for similar companies in the same industry
- Different site configurations
- Different positions of competitors in the marketplace
- Different mix of clients
- Campaigns and other traffic drivers

You can see how complex it is to get two sites that you can really compare to one another. And then how do you find out about the performance of other sites? There are two primary ways: through research reports and studies or through competitive analysis tools like ComScore (*www.comscore.com*) or Hitwise (*www.hitwise.com*).

Most people have seen the research reports from large research firms or smaller niche analysts that can provide incredible insight into specific industries. ComScore and Hitwise have live panels of millions of web users; they track these visitors as they access sites on the Internet and are then able to combine all of the information. This can help tell the story of your site as well as that of your competitors. Since they are basing this on sampling, we would not want to compare what ComScore says about ZAAZ.com traffic to what our analytics tool says about ZAAZ.com. However, it could make sense to compare the data from ComScore for ZAAZ.com against their data on our competitors. By doing so, we could compare our key metrics against the same key metrics on our competitors' sites.

This competitive information can be used for a lot more than just seeing where you stand against competitors. You can learn more about visitor paths, demographics, the percentage of the overall industry visitors who view your site, and more. In addition, you can evaluate the effectiveness of different portions of your competitors' sites and learn from them to improve your site performance.

When trying to determine whether the news is good, remember that you can always improve your site and business. Focus more on making the small, incremental changes [Hack #2] to the key metrics that drive your business. A plan of ongoing optimization focusing on the right things will always benefit you, no matter what others are doing.

—Jason Burby and Eric T. Peterson

HACK #93   (Don't) Benchmark Your Site

Except in very controlled situations, attempting to compare your conversion rate information to published data almost always creates more problems than it solves and should be avoided.

Many business people seem to have an intense desire to benchmark themselves against market leaders, even if they aren't selling to the same market. Especially for a relatively complex key performance indicator like conversion rate, one dependent on so many variables (for example, marketing strategy and spend, product assortment and pricing, usability of site, or audience), making any comparison except in the most controlled situations is an exercise in futility. I'll explain two situations where you can compare your data to that gathered from another site in a minute, but first here are a few reasons to avoid benchmarking yourself.

First, unless you know exactly where the data is coming from, you might be comparing apples to bowling balls. Given the differences in accuracy observed when comparing different data sources, are you sure you want to make business decisions if you're not sure about the accuracy of someone else's data? If my key comparison is "page views per visit," but I have no idea whether a competitor is rigorous in excluding robot and spider activity [Hack #23] from their data set or whether they use accepted standards to define a visit [Hack #1], how can I be sure their number is any good? The easy answer is that you can't, so comparisons may be misleading.

Second, even if you know the data sources are the same, you still might be comparing apples and oranges. Conversion rate is the most commonly compared measurement—at least it's the one most people ask about most often—but there are a handful of definitions for "conversion rate" [Hack #82]. Depending on whether you're using "order conversion rate" or "buyer conversion rate" and which timeframe you're looking at, a number that sounds like an apple can easily be an orange or worse.

Finally, even if the numbers are the same, you can rarely make anything more than a "gee whiz" comparison. Unless you're able to get data about companies in your vertical market (for example, online sales) and unless you're able to get data about companies in your specific sub-vertical (for example, online booksellers), and unless you're able to get data for sites that have roughly the same average order value (for example, between $25 and $50), and unless you know pretty well how these companies are attempting to attract new visitors, and unless...you get the picture. While you may be able to make a "valid" comparison without a tremendous amount of information, it is extremely unlikely that the comparison will be useful in any meaningful sense.

The Foolproof Benchmarking Hack for Anyone

The easiest way to benchmark your site in a meaningful way, one guaranteed to generate actionable information that can be used in future comparisons, is to benchmark against *your own* site and track *your own* success.

If you establish key performance indicators that are both significant and useful to your business, then you can easily compare those numbers month over month and determine whether the time and effort you've allocated is money well spent. Well-defined key performance indicators [Hack #94], by definition, force you to make comparisons over time, allowing you to view your metrics in the right context.

If in June your order conversion rate is 2 percent, but in July you spend a million dollars in time and effort to improve your site's usability and the quality of your advertising reach, you had better hope that your July conversion rate is better than 2 percent! If your AOV is $35 and you dedicate hundreds of hours to improve your ability to cross-sell and up-sell visitors in the purchase process, you hope that your AOV will go up.

It's all about effort versus improvement and the continuous improvement process [Hack #2]; compare yourself *to* yourself, and you'll always be making a valid and useful comparison.

The Only Way to Benchmark Against External Data

If you *absolutely must* have benchmark data for competitive purposes, there are a few sources for data. Unfortunately, these strategies are vendor dependent, but if your need to benchmark is so overpowering and you're not satisfied with benchmarking against yourself, you may want to give these vendors a look.

Fireclick Index (http://www.fireclick.com). While the page describing the application is chock-full of hyperbole ("The most valuable report ever produced for online businesses"), the Fireclick Index (Figure 7-3) was the web measurement industry's first truly useful benchmarking tool.

Figure 7-3. Benchmarking report from the Fireclick Index

By allowing customers to compare meaningful metrics like order size, first time and returning visitor conversion rate, and shopping cart abandon-ment rate within a handful a handful of verticals and industry segments (such as fashion and apparel, electronics, home and furnishings, and cata-log), Fireclick mitigates the problems described above and delivers at least nominally useful data. More information about the Fireclick Index is avail-able at *http://www.fireclick.com/solutions/fireclick_index.html.*

Coremetrics LIVEmark (http://www.coremetrics.com). Released in early 2005, Coremetrics introduced LIVEmark to their customers as a focused strategy for comparing data to vertical and sub-vertical segments. By enforcing implementation standards within participating customers, Coremetrics is able to provide a great deal of meaningful benchmark information over traf-fic, transactions, on-site search, and marketing campaigns (Figure 7-4).

The applications from Fireclick and Coremetrics both provide carefully con-trolled environments for making comparisons. Both vendors go so far as to double-check implementations for participating web sites to ensure data accuracy and apples-to-apples comparisons.

COREMETRICS :::   Feedback | Help | Logout

Home Page | Topline | Marketing | Merchandising | Site Analysis | Segmentation | Technical Properties | Custom Reports LIVEmark Admin

LIVEmark Summary   Monday 1/10/2005   Download Report   Print Preview   Email Report
Time Period: Monday 1/10/2005

Confidential Client Use Only - Distribution Prohibited

Session Traffic Summary	Your Site	LIVEmark Apparel	vs. LIVEmark Apparel	LIVEmark Retail	vs. LIVEmark Retail
One Page Session %	18.54%	14.30%	29.65%	25.53%	-27.38%
Multi-Page Session %	81.46%	85.70%	-4.95%	74.47%	9.39%
Browser Session %	49.53%	59.96%	-17.39%	53.93%	-8.16%
Shopping Cart Session %	9.64%	10.02%	-3.79%	10.59%	-8.97%
Order Session %	2.68%	4.21%	-36.34%	5.04%	-46.83%
Transactions Summary	**Your Site**	**LIVEmark Apparel**	**vs. LIVEmark Apparel**	**LIVEmark Retail**	**vs. LIVEmark Retail**
Page Views / Session	16.09	20.65	-22.09%	15.07	6.71%
Product Views / Session	2.43	4.62	-47.47%	3.41	-28.85%
Average Items per Order	2.13	2.71	-21.53%	3.88	-45.21%
Average Order Value	$133.60	$94.98	40.66%	$122.06	9.46%
Shopping Cart Conversion %	29.31%	38.18%	-23.23%	45.78%	-35.98%
Shopping Cart Abandonment %	70.69%	61.82%	14.35%	54.22%	30.38%
New Visitor Conversion %	2.01%	3.64%	-44.78%	4.32%	-53.47%
On-Site Search Summary	**Your Site**	**LIVEmark Apparel**	**vs. LIVEmark Apparel**	**LIVEmark Retail**	**vs. LIVEmark Retail**
On-Site Search Session %	0.00%	11.90%	-100.00%	21.58%	-100.00%
On-Site Search Conversion %	2.56%	8.11%	-68.43%	9.29%	-72.44%
Marketing Summary	**Your Site**	**LIVEmark Apparel**	**vs. LIVEmark Apparel**	**LIVEmark Retail**	**vs. LIVEmark Retail**
Direct Load					
% of Site Traffic	61.64%	62.25%	-0.98%	53.34%	15.56%
% of Sales	71.38%	71.08%	0.42%	69.47%	2.75%
Conversion Rate	2.89%	5.07%	-43.00%	6.61%	-56.28%
Natural Search					
% of Site Traffic	9.83%	5.33%	84.43%	9.95%	-1.21%
% of Sales	7.39%	5.04%	46.63%	7.05%	4.82%
Conversion Rate	2.17%	4.35%	-50.11%	4.48%	-51.56%
Referrals					
% of Site Traffic	31.92%	12.13%	163.15%	8.81%	262.32%
% of Sales	24.72%	9.68%	155.37%	5.95%	315.46%
Conversion Rate	1.77%	1.50%	18.00%	2.09%	-15.31%
Other					
% of Site Traffic	0.00%	21.19%	-100.00%	27.27%	-100.00%
% of Sales	0.00%	14.79%	-100.00%	16.86%	-100.00%
Conversion Rate	-	3.06%	-	3.38%	-

Figure 7-4. Benchmarking data from Coremetrics LIVEmark

Use Key Performance Indicators
#94

Key performance indicators are a powerful way to present complex information that works to maximize the use of web measurement data within your organization.

A key performance indicator (KPI) is any ratio that summarizes two or more important measurements and is tied *directly* to your business objectives [Hack #38]. Examples include ratios like your order conversion rate (orders divided by visits) or the average number of page views per visit: numbers that, when they change significantly, prompt someone to pick up the phone, send an email, instant message, or walk down the hall and say, "Something is going on; we need to look into this more deeply right away!" The use of key performance indicators is a powerful and advanced strategy that can dramatically increase your ability to get executive buy-in for your metrics reporting strategy [Hack #91].

A handful of really, truly useful key performance indicators is listed in Table 7-1. These are the kinds of useful ratios that are presented on a daily basis to captains of industry like Michael Dell, Jeffery Bezos, and Meg Whitman: CEOs who clearly get the power of the Internet and understand that every minute counts in an increasingly competitive world.

Table 7-1. Really, truly useful key performance indicators

Order conversion rate	Buyer conversion rate	Cart conversion rate
Checkout start rate	Revenue per visit	Revenue per visitor
Average order value	Visits per visitor	Page views per visit
Percent committed visitors	Lead conversion rate	Home page bailout rate
Average number of items per purchase	Average time spent on site	Percent file take

While Table 7-1 provides a handful of examples, there are hundreds of other potentially valuable measures. Your central challenge is to figure out which ones are best for your business. Here are some recommendations to consider:

Refer back to your business objectives
> Any ratio that speaks directly to your company's business objectives [Hack #38] and will drive action is a good KPI, as are any ratios that are direct measurements of key activities associated with your business goals.

Figure out which indicators are really "key"
> George Orwell once wrote that "all numbers are created equal, but some are more equal than others" (or something like that); clearly Mr. Orwell was a web measurement guru in his spare time. While the KPIs most valuable to specific business models are covered later in this chapter, determining which numbers are "more equal than others" is a great place to start. In general, any number or ratio that senior managers ask about on a regular basis should be considered important.

Make sure your indicators promote action
> The best KPIs are those that, when people look at them and realize they've gone down from week to week, make people freak out and call meetings. The numbers that make people the most nervous are the best candidates, always. Conversely, if you're thinking about a number but cannot think of any action you would take if that number absolutely tanks, set that number aside.

When in doubt, simply consult the hacks describing specific key performance indicators for online retail [Hack #96], advertising and content [Hack #97], customer support [Hack #98], and lead generation [Hack #99].

Best Practices for Defining Key Performance Indicators

Assuming you're still nodding your head and you're thinking to yourself, "yeah, I need to make up some KPIs right away," here are a handful of best practices that you should follow.

Use KPIs to drive action. The most important thing any key performance indicator does is get someone to take a closer look at your visitor's behavior. Since you'll be using KPIs to compare data day to day or week to week, any time you see a strong decrease or a surprising increase, you need to be asking yourself, "why did that happen?" and, "what impact will that change have on my business?" Make sure that you do everything in your power to highlight significant changes, using colors, fonts, and in-your-face warning messages when necessary (Figure 7-5).

[Your Company Logo Goes Here]

WEB ANALYTICS DEMYSTIFIED

Key Performance Indictator Worksheet
Commerce Business Model

Last Updated: [Last Updated Date]

Performance Indicator	This Week	Last Week	Percent Change	Warn?
Percent New Visitors	178.6%	100.0%	78.57% ▲	
Percent Returning Visitors	138.7%	100.0%	38.71% ▲	
Ratio of New to Returning Visitors	4.50	1.00	350.00% ▲	
Key Conversion Rates:				
Visit to Purchase	280.4%	100.0%	180.39% ▲	
Cart Add to Purchase	159.0%	100.0%	59.02% ▲	
Checkout to Purchase	835.0%	100.0%	735.04% ▲	
Search to Purchase	22.7%	100.0%	-77.31% ▼	ALERT
New Vistor Conversion Rate	65.3%	100.0%	-34.69% ▼	ALERT
Return Visitor Conversion Rate	85.7%	100.0%	-14.29% ▼	
Average Order Value (AOV)	$ 37.97	$ 1.00	3697.15% ▲	
Sales per Visitor	$ 0.32	$ 1.00	-68.47% ▼	ALERT
Customer Retention Rate	8977.1%	100.0%	8877.14% ▲	
Percent of Visits Under 90 Seconds	16.2%	100.0%	83.76% ▲	

Figure 7-5. Key performance indicator worksheet

Present KPIs visually whenever possible. You should give serious consideration to how you present the information, and make an attempt to, well, make it interesting. Strange as it sounds, overburdened senior executives often respond to visual representations that present complex information in a simple, effective format. Some analytics vendors allow you to present KPIs using tachometers, thermometers, trended graphs, and the like, as illustrated in Figure 7-6.

Use the language of the business to increase familiarity. Another nice benefit of using key performance indicators is that you're able to use your own words to

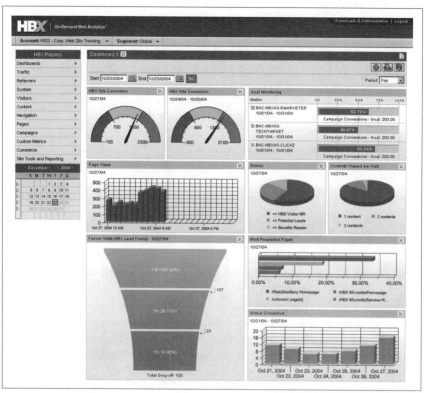

Figure 7-6. KPI dashboard

describe the numbers, not the words used in your measurement application. It sounds simple, but this can be very important; you don't want to force people inside your organization to learn new names for ideas they're already familiar with. For example, if people are familiar with "average sale value" (ASV) not "average sale price" (ASP) use average sale value in your report. Familiarity with the data lowers the barrier to understanding and use.

Explain the how and why of KPIs. Since the use of KPIs is pretty advanced, many of the folks you provide them to will be unfamiliar and will require further explanation. Two simple things you can do to help are to provide personalized training and a glossary with every KPI report. The training will allow folks to ask questions (and help you determine whether they get it), and the glossary will save you time because these folks will have something to refer to (other than you) if they forget what you told them.

While it will take a little extra work to build KPIs and get them implemented into your reporting program, experience shows it's well worth it. Everything you do to make web measurement data more palatable helps. By maximizing the information content and presentation of the numbers you provide, you can dramatically increase people's interest and use of the data.

HACK #95 Know the Difference Between a KPI and a Measurement

All key performance indicators are numbers, but not all numbers are key performance indicators.

There is a longstanding argument in the web measurement community about whether raw measurements like "number of leads" or "total orders taken" can be key performance indicators. The easy answer is no, measurements are not key performance indicators, at least not well-defined key performance indicators [Hack #94].

The rationale for this statement is that raw measurements alone do not contain enough information to drive action, an essential element of a well-defined KPI. If you tell me that I gathered "1,000 leads" or took "10,000 orders," I have no idea if that is good or not, because you haven't presented the numbers in the context of how much work it took to get those leads or orders. This is why we look at leads per visitor, orders per visit, or even better, leads per marketing dollar spent and orders per referring source. As you can see, each of these KPIs drives an action (for example, "get more visitors," "drive more visits," "spend fewer marketing dollars," or "find more referring sources like *this*!").

Key performance indicators are all about creating context and conveying more information than is possible via a single number. Feel free to provide the raw numbers that make up the KPI beside or below the ratio if it makes you feel better (Figure 7-7). Over time, you'll realize that the number is nice, but it doesn't help you make any decisions you wouldn't make otherwise, provided you're using your KPIs correctly.

The exception to always using ratios is reporting revenue and sales numbers. Because we're all so focused on increasing revenue or decreasing operational costs, reporting those numbers in your KPI report will save you from having to answer the question, "How much money did we generate or save during this timeframe?" Still, consider using great indicators like revenue per visitor, revenue per visit, sales per search, and savings per call deflected to provide additional context whenever possible.

Performance Indicator	This Week	Last Week	Percent Change	Warn?
Percent New Visitors	100.0%	100.0%	0.00%	▼
Percent Returning Visitors	100.0%	100.0%	0.00%	▼
Ratio of New to Returning Visitors	1.00	1.00	0.00%	▼
Key Conversion Rates:				
Visit to Purchase	100.0%	100.0%	0.00%	▼
Cart Add to Purchase	100.0%	100.0%	0.00%	▼
Checkout to Purchase	100.0%	100.0%	0.00%	▼
Search to Purchase	100.0%	100.0%	0.00%	▼
New Vistor Conversion Rate	100.0%	100.0%	0.00%	▼
Return Visitor Conversion Rate	100.0%	100.0%	0.00%	▼
Average Order Value (AOV)	$ 1.00	$ 1.00	0.00%	▼
Sales per Visitor	$ 1.00	$ 1.00	0.00%	▼
Customer Retention Rate	100.0%	100.0%	0.00%	▼
Percent of Visits Under 90 Seconds	100.0%	100.0%	0.00%	▼
Key Supporting Metrics:				
Total Orders	2,143	1,832	-16.98%	▼
Total Buyers	2,000	1,699	-17.72%	▼
Total Visitors	13,132	18,322	28.33%	▲
Total Sales Revenue	$12,434	$10,133	-22.71%	▼

Figure 7-7. Present both raw numbers and well-formed KPIs

HACK #96 Key Performance Indicators for Online Retailers

Online retailers, perhaps more than any other business model, should review key performance indicators on a regular basis to mine for changes in visitor interests and identify emerging sales opportunities.

The key performance indicators that I recommend for online retailers are a relatively straightforward bunch; it's all about conversion and value. While you may be tempted to build out a complex report that provides every type of information possible, fight that temptation. Remember, most people aren't going to read a long, complex report full of numbers [Hack #91]. By focusing your efforts on the truly *key* indicators and providing a report similar to Figure 7-8, you will dramatically increase the readership and use of this report (and you cannot act upon something you don't even read, right?).

One important thing to keep in mind when you're thinking about KPIs for online retail is seasonality. Sometimes a big decrease in key indicators means nothing more than the holidays are over and everyone is enjoying their toys. As with any web measurement report, always consider the following in as much context as is available, including time of year and other external factors.

Basic Key Performance Indicators for Online Retailers

The following key performance indicators should be considered core to the regular reporting for any online retailer. Each assumes a constant period of time, e.g., the previous day or the previous week, unless otherwise noted.

Key Performance Indictator Worksheet			Last Updated: [Last Updated Date]	
Commerce Business Model				
Performance Indicator	**This Week**	**Last Week**	**Percent Change**	**Warn?**
Percent New Visitors	100.0%	100.0%	0.00%	▼
Percent Returning Visitors	100.0%	100.0%	0.00%	▼
Ratio of New to Returning Visitors	1.00	1.00	0.00%	▼
Key Conversion Rates:				
Order Conversion Rate	100.0%	100.0%	0.00%	▼
Buyer Conversion Rate	100.0%	100.0%	0.00%	▼
Cart Add to Purchase	100.0%	100.0%	0.00%	▼
Checkout to Purchase	100.0%	100.0%	0.00%	▼
Search to Purchase	100.0%	100.0%	0.00%	▼
New Vistor Conversion Rate	100.0%	100.0%	0.00%	▼
Return Visitor Conversion Rate	100.0%	100.0%	0.00%	▼
Average Order Value (AOV)	$ 1.00	$ 1.00	0.00%	▼
Sales per Visitor	$ 1.00	$ 1.00	0.00%	▼
Customer Retention Rate	100.0%	100.0%	0.00%	▼
Percent of Visits Under 90 Seconds	100.0%	100.0%	0.00%	▼
Key Supporting Metrics:				
Total Orders	2,143	1,832	-16.98%	▼
Total Buyers	2,000	1,699	-17.72%	▼
Total Visitors	13,132	18,322	28.33%	▲
Total Sales Revenue	$12,434	$10,133	-22.71%	▼

Figure 7-8. KPI worksheet for online retailers

Sales per visitor. The ratio of sales per visitor is a simple proxy for your order conversion rate [Hack #37] that frames your ability to sell online in easy to understand terms. The greater the percentage of sales relative to the total number of visitors you attract, the better job you're doing.

Average order value (AOV). The average order value (AOV) is simply defined as the total revenue you took in divided by the total number of orders it took to get that revenue. Depending on the type of products you sell, your AOV may be either very stable month over month or fluctuate wildly from day to day or week to week. The former case is characteristic of higher priced, higher consideration items, the latter characteristic of sites that sell low-cost items or the overstock model of "buy what we have today since it will be gone tomorrow."

As with any good KPI, your AOV is made interesting when it changes dramatically. Any time this happens, make sure you figure out why the change occurred and what effect that change will have on your online business.

Percent new and returning visitors. The percent of new and returning visitors are numbers calculated by your web measurement solution and describe how much of your audience you've originally acquired and how many people you've managed to get to return at least one time after their first visit. If, for some reason, your application doesn't provide the percentages, see [Hack #97] to learn how to make the necessary calculation.

While it's hard to be too specific about what percentage of new and returning visitors is best for online retailers, there are a few general rules to keep in mind:

- If you're spending significantly on acquisition marketing, you want the lion's share of your visitors to be new. Even if you've got a ton of returning visitors, significant marketing expenditure should bring large numbers of new visitors. If it doesn't, take a look at your marketing strategy.

- All other things being equal, the ideal ratio of new to returning visitors for online retailers is roughly 70:30. You always want to be adding new visitors to your visitor mix, and if you're able to get 30 percent of your visitors to return, then you're doing a great job, depending on what you sell and the frequency with which your customers purchase.

Ratio of new to returning visitors. This ratio, simply defined as the total number of new visitors divided by the total number of returning visitors, provides another view of your audience mix. The calculation yields a number between zero and n (with n being some positive integer that can, in theory, be very high if nobody ever returns to your site). This indicator quickly tells you whether you're acquiring, retaining, or basically neutral regarding your visitors.

Smaller numbers indicate that you're retaining more visitors than you attract, something referred to as *visitor retention mode*. The smaller the number, the better the job you're doing at retaining visitors. Because online retailers depend so heavily on attracting new visitors, you rarely see this number below 1.0 on healthy retail sites.

Larger numbers indicate that you're attracting more visitors than you retain, something referred to as *visitor acquisition mode*. Say, for example, the calculation yields a ratio of new to returning visitors of 5.0; this tells you that for every visitor you retain, you acquire five new visitors. In theory the number can be very large, but high numbers paint a picture of poor customer retention.

Much like the 70:30 ideal split of new to returning visitors, the optimal ratio is between about 1.2 and 2.5, both indicating a constant influx of new visitors but not at the expense of returning visitors.

Customer retention rate. Your customer retention rate—sometimes called percent returning customers—is like your percent returning visitors, but it is specific to people who have made a previous purchase. It is, unfortunately, difficult to calculate without your web measurement application's assistance and likely the use of cookies [Hack #15], but it is worth including in your KPI report because it is so important to your online business.

While the need to constantly attract new visitors to your retail web site is obvious, it is just as important to get people to return and purchase again.

Your customer retention rate is usually a direct measure of how good a job you do *after* the purchase is made: do you ship on time, do the products arrive on time, are they the right products, and is your customer support helpful and friendly when needed? These questions speak to your ability to "delight your customers." Any time your customer retention rate spikes up, figure out why. Any time your customer retention rate dips, figure out why and fix the problem.

Advanced Key Performance Indicators for Online Retailers

The following metrics are more advanced but should be seriously considered, in addition to the basic indicators. The most important advanced KPIs are your bevy of conversion rates.

Order conversion rate. Your order conversion rate is the number of orders taken divided by the number of visits to the web site. While this is a fairly raw, top-line success metric, order conversion rate is important to watch for substantial changes that may indicate poor marketing acquisition efforts (for example, you just paid for a bunch of traffic that isn't converting at all).

Buyer conversion rate. Your buyer conversion rate is the number of purchasers divided by the total number of unique visitors to the site. Depending on what you sell, your order and buyer conversion rates may be very similar or relatively divergent. When these numbers are different, i.e., order conversion is higher, you know that you're getting short-term repeat visits that are purchasing; when buyer conversion is higher, or people are returning but not buying.

Cart add to purchase conversion rate. Cart add to purchase conversion rates are calculated by dividing the number of purchases by the number of cart starts (on a per-visit basis). You may need to hack your measurement application to get the number of cart starts by visit, but you don't want to calculate this number using page views, as it can be dramatically overstated if you do (assuming that every time a visitor looks at his shopping cart another page view is logged).

The greater your ability to get visitors to start carts, the greater the likelihood they'll successfully complete those carts; however, sometimes you'll see an increase in cart starts but no change in total purchases. Often, this indicates that people are carting items to check the price or shipping charges, both indicators of poor usability.

Checkout-to-purchase conversion rate. The ratio of purchases to checkouts started (again, on a per-visit basis) is a gross indicator of ease of use in your checkout process. It is a reasonable assumption that once a visitor clicks the

"Checkout" button, she actually intends to make the purchase. Since no business converts 100 percent of its carts, changes in this rate can help you understand which changes you're making in marketing acquisition or process design have a positive (or negative) impact on visitor success.

Search to purchase conversion rate. If you have some type of onsite or internal search [Hack #64], you should be monitoring your search to purchase conversion rate—the number of purchases driven by search divided by the total number of searches executed (measured on a page view basis). To make this calculation, you'll likely need to use either visitor segmentation tools [Hack #48] or an internal campaign [Hack #61] to track a visitor who searches through to a purchase. Still, because when search is done well it has such a positive impact on purchase behavior, you want to make this measurement.

New and returning visitor conversion rates. While you may want to measure conversion over a variety of visitor segments [Hack #48], the minimum segmentation you should monitor is new versus returning visitors. Differentiating these conversion rates will help you better understand how quickly you're likely to convert visitors as they engage with your site. If your new visitor conversion rate is very high, you might be selling low cost, low consideration items that visitors easily purchase. If your return visitor conversion rate is high, perhaps your visitors are browsing around the Internet comparison shopping, eventually settling on you when they're ready to make their purchase.

Percent of visits less than 90 seconds. The percent of visits under 90 seconds is a valuable indicator of the interest your visitors have in your products or services; in general, the higher the percentage, the worse the job you're doing. I use 90 seconds as a rough proxy for the minimum amount of time a visitor needs to do or learn anything meaningful on the average site; you may want to lower the threshold to 60 seconds, or increase it to 120 seconds, depending on how quickly people are able to navigate to actual products.

To make the calculation, you'll need to find the "time spent per visit" or "time spent on site" report—the report that tells you the number of visits broken down by time spent (Figure 7-9). Add up the number of visits less than 90 seconds and then divide by the total number of visits to the site.

Using Figure 7-9 as an example, and assuming we had 5,000 total visits, the calculation would be:

(465 + 401 + 246 Visits 90 Seconds or Less) / 5,000 Total Visits = 0.2224 = 22.2% of visits were less than 90 seconds

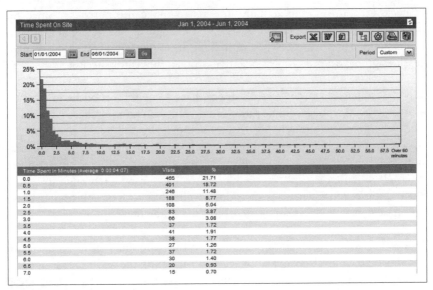

Figure 7-9. Time spent on site report

If your particular measurement application doesn't support the level of granularity afforded by WebSideStory's HBX, do your best. The essence of the KPI is an attempt to identify how many visits are too short to be meaningful.

Other Important Measurements

Finally, in the online retail model, it is important to provide raw numbers as well as performance indicators in all reports. Reporting on your total orders, buyers, visitors, and sales revenue will likely placate those within your organization who *absolutely need* to see the raw numbers. By providing these numbers with otherwise well-formed KPIs, you'll increase the likelihood that your reports will be used.

For a sample key performance indicator worksheet, built in Microsoft Excel from the measurements recommended in this hack, visit the author's web site at *http://www.webanalyticsdemystified.com/kpi_worksheet.*

<p>

HACK
#97
Key Performance Indicators for Advertising and Content Sites

> Companies that make money from online advertising should be primarily focused on depth of visit, visitor retention, and loyalty.

Content sites generally make money by selling other companies access to their visitor base, usually in the form of some type of advertising unit impression. Regardless of the specific strategy for presenting the ad—banners, rich-media, text, email—advertising buyers always look to get their message in front of the right audience the right number of times to generate that all-important "click."

Because the audience is so important, the key performance indicators for content and advertising sites are primarily focused on visits and visitor loyalty. Build a report similar to Figure 7-10 that you automate and send out to anyone responsible for the relationship you have with your audience or your advertisers.

[Your Company Logo Goes Here]

**WEB ANALYTICS
DEMYSTIFIED**

Key Performance Indictator Worksheet
Advertising Business Model

Last Updated: [Last Updated Date]

Performance Indicator	This Week	Last Week	Percent Change	Warn?
Number of Page Views	1	1	0.00%	▼
Number of Visits	1	1	0.00%	▼
Percent New Visitors	100.0%	100.0%	0.00%	▼
Percent Returning Visitors	100.0%	100.0%	0.00%	▼
Ratio of New to Returning Visitors	1.00	1.00	0.00%	▼
Percent of Visits Less Than 90 Seconds	100.0%	100.0%	0.00%	▼
Average Time Spent on Site	0:00:01:00	0:00:01:00	0.00%	▼
Average Pages Viewed per Visit	100.0%	100.0%	0.00%	▼
Average Visits per Visitor	100.0%	100.0%	0.00%	▼
Percent Committed Visits	100.0%	100.0%	0.00%	▼
Key Conversion Rates:				
Newsletter Sign-up	100.0%	100.0%	0.00%	▼
Alert Feature Sign-up	100.0%	100.0%	0.00%	▼
Page "Stickiness" for Key Pages				
Home Page	50.0%	50.0%	0.00%	▼

Figure 7-10. Advertising KPIs and raw data

Basic Key Performance Indicators for Content Sites

The following key performance indicators should be considered core to the regular reporting for any content or advertising site. Each assumes a constant period of time—for example, the previous day or the previous week, unless otherwise noted.

Average pages viewed per visit. Defined simply as the total number of pages viewed divided by the total number of visits to the site, average pages viewed per visit is a key indicator of your visitor's attraction to your content and, by extension, a proxy for the profitability of your site on a per-visit basis. To monetize this KPI, simply multiply the result by your average advertising CPM:

(Total Pages Viewed / Total Visits) * (Average CPM / 1,000) = Average Value per Visit

You divide your average CPM by 1,000 to convert your cost per thousand to the average cost of a single page view to an advertiser. Needless to say, this number is going to be very, very small. It becomes more interesting when you multiply by the total number of visits to your site, especially in the context of "what if we increased the average number of pages viewed per visit?" As an example, consider the following valuation for a visit for a fictitious site:

(100,000 Pages Viewed / 10,000 Visits) * ($35 Average CPM / 1,000) = 10 Pages Viewed per Visit * $0.035 per Page View = $0.35 per Visit

What if you could increase the average number of pages viewed per visit by three?

13 Pages Viewed per Visit * $0.035 per Page View = $0.46 per Visit

A 28 percent increase in revenue per visit, which doesn't sound like much until you consider 10,000 daily visits, which yields an average increase of $4,600 per day. Your job is to figure out how to increase the average number of pages viewed per visit using this KPI as a guide to how you're doing.

Average visits per visitor. Because loyalty, frequency, and recency [Hack #85] are important to any web site trying to make money online, the ratio of average visits per visitor is another important performance indicator. The calculation will always yield a number greater than one, and in general, the larger the number, the more loyal your audience.

Average visits per visitor are difficult to directly monetize, but good salespeople will use this ratio when encouraging advertisers to purchase available impressions. The general pitch is something like "We get 1,000,000 visitors per month and our average visitor returns five times a month and views 12 pages per visit."

Percent new and returning visitors. The percent of new and returning visitors are numbers calculated by your web measurement solution and describe how much of your audience you've managed to get to return at least one time after their first visit. If, for some reason, your application doesn't provide the percentages I recommend using, simply divide the number of new or returning visitors by the total number of visitors to get each percentage, respectively.

While it's hard to be too specific about what the best ratio of new to returning visitors is for content sites, there are a few general rules to keep in mind:

- If you're spending significantly on acquisition marketing, you want the lion's share of your visitors to be new. Even if you've got a ton of returning visitors, significant marketing expenditure should bring large numbers of new visitors. If it doesn't, take a look at your marketing strategy.

- All other things being equal, the ideal ratio of new to returning visitors for content sites is roughly 60/40. You always want to add new visitors to your visitor mix, and if you're able to get 40 percent of your visitors to return, then you're doing a great job.

- If you have the best, most exclusive content and everyone knows about you, don't worry if your ratio of new to returning visitors is more like 40/60. Some sites, such as eBay and ESPN, are so well-known and so relatively unique, even though they do a great job of adding new visitors, they'll always have more loyal returning visitors.

Ratio of new to returning visitors. This ratio, simply defined as the total number of new visitors divided by the total number of returning visitors, provides another view of your audience mix. The calculation yields a number between zero and n (with n being some positive integer that can, in theory, be very, very high if nobody ever returns to your site). This indicator quickly tells you whether you're acquiring, retaining, or basically neutral regarding your visitors.

Smaller numbers indicate that you're retaining more visitors than you attract, something referred to as *visitor retention mode*. The smaller the number, the better the job you're doing at retaining visitors. Very small numbers should create concern since you're not bringing in fresh blood.

Larger numbers indicate that you're attracting more visitors than you retain, something referred to as *visitor acquisition mode*. Say, for example, the calculation yields a ratio of new to returning visitors of 2.0: this tells you that for every visitor you retain, you acquire two new visitors. In theory, the number can be very large, but high numbers paint a picture of poor customer retention.

Much like the 60/40 ideal split of new to returning visitors, the optimal ratio is between about 0.80 and 1.5, the former slightly describing healthy visitor retention and the latter healthy visitor acquisition. The ratio is attractive because it's easily trended and, once you get used to using it, the number tells you a great deal about your audience very quickly.

Average time spent on site. Similar to the percentages of new and returning visitors, the average time visitors spend on your site is calculated by your measurement application. A relatively simple number, average time spent is fundamental to content sites, since often more time equals more impressions and a greater connection with the content.

Watch for dramatic changes in the average time your visitors are spending on your site, because they can indicate a significant change your audience. Often, a large decrease can indicate poor acquisition marketing that brought a large number of visitors who were uninterested in your content and left quickly. Also keep in mind that, especially if you're a news site, significant stories can impact or skew the measurement.

Advanced Key Performance Indicators for Content Sites

The following metrics are more advanced but should be seriously considered in addition to the basic indicators.

Percent of visits less than 90 seconds. The percent of visits under 90 seconds is a valuable indicator of the interest your visitors have in your content; in general, the higher the percentage, the greater the number of uninterested visitors to the site. Although there are no hard and fast rules, 90 seconds is a rough proxy for the minimum amount of time a visitor needs to do or learn anything meaningful on the average site; you may want to lower the threshold to 60 or even 30 seconds, depending on your site. While the visitors may not truly be *uninterested*, when they spend very little time, it's unlikely they're going to spend enough time to truly connect with your content (or advertising content). For details on how to calculate this valuable metric see [Hack #96].

Percent committed visits. Committed visits, especially in the content and advertising model, are those visits made up of a relatively large number of page views. Depending on your site, the number of pages that defines "committed" will vary, but in general, it's between 5 and 10 pages (providing nominal revenue, per the average page views per visit KPI). Obviously, if your site monetizes page views, you want as many committed visits as possible.

Most measurement applications provide the data you need to calculate this KPI in a "path length" or "depth of visits" report (Figure 7-11). To make the calculation, simply add the number of visits over your particular threshold and divide by the total number of visits.

Using Figure 7-11 as an example and assuming we had 1,000 total visits to the site and a threshold of six or more pages, the calculation would be:

> (110 Visits to 6 Pages + 74 Visits to 7 Pages + 35 Visits to 8 Pages + 21 Visits to 9 Pages + 9 Visits to 10 Pages + 4 Visits to 11 Pages) / 1,000 Total Visits = 0.253 = 25.3% Committed Visits

While you can adjust the threshold that defines "committed," you want to be careful to set it high enough to be meaningful and not change it once it's set.

"Stickiness" for key pages. The stickiness of the first page in a visit should keep visitors interested and encourage them to click more deeply into the site. Built from two page reports—the entry page report, describing the

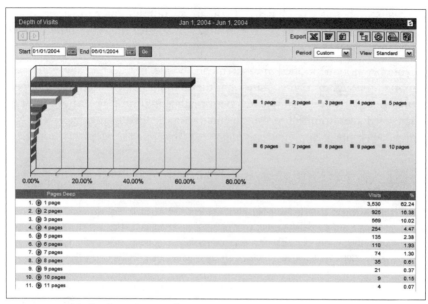

Figure 7-11. Depth of visits report

number of visits that begin at a given page, and the single-access pages reports, describing the number of visits in which the page is the only one a visitor sees—stickiness is one minus the ratio of single access to entry pages:

1.00 – (Single Access Page Visits / Entry Page Visits)

The result of the calculation will be a percentage, and higher percentages are better than lower, indicating greater stick on the page in question. It is recommended that you make this measurement only for important landing pages like your home page, your campaign landing pages, and the top five percent of entry pages from search engines [Hack #43].

Like many of the other KPIs described in this hack, page stickiness provides an indicator of changes in audience make-up. If the "stick" of a key entry page drops suddenly, many of your other KPIs will likely be affected. Also, make sure to not just set-and-forget this list—keep an eye on your entry page report and make sure to adjust which pages you track if you change your marketing campaigns.

Other Important Measurements

In addition to the KPIs discussed here, don't forget to keep careful track of any important conversion rates such as subscription sign-up or registration events. You should also track the number of visits you get from your top 10 referring sites, your top 10 entry pages, and the top 10 search keywords visitors are using to find your site. If you have internal search, track the top 10 internal searches as well. Finally, if you are spending money in specific local markets to drive traffic to your web site, you should track the top 10 cities by visitors.

All of the aforementioned measurements, while not technically KPIs, are important enough to content sites that they should be delivered with the performance report. For a sample key performance indicator worksheet, built in Microsoft Excel from the measurements recommended in this hack, visit the author's web site at *http://www.webanalyticsdemystified.com/kpi_worksheet*.

HACK #98 Key Performance Indicators for Customer Support Sites

The surest path to lowering customer support costs is making sure that people are successful using your online support content. The surest way to do this is to regularly monitor a handful of support key performance indicators, watching for problems and monitoring the effect of changes.

The customer support business model is often overlooked by both vendors and businesses themselves when it comes to web measurement. Often, companies that have a significant support presence and very significant customer support costs fail to actively work to optimize their support web sites. Perhaps it's because so often, support sites are deployed using packaged applications that are difficult to modify or because support sites are so dependent on search. Regardless of the cause, there is a fantastic opportunity for companies to lower operating expenses by ensuring that customers are able to self-service their support needs, rather than making an expensive phone call.

Basic Key Performance Indicators for Customer Support Sites

The following key performance indicators should be considered core to the regular reporting for any customer support site. Each assumes a constant period of time, for example, the previous day or the previous week, unless otherwise noted, and most KPIs assume that you're able to segment or otherwise isolate traffic to your support site if that site is part of a larger site (which is common).

Average pages viewed per visit. Defined simply as the total number of pages viewed divided by the total number of visits to the site, average pages viewed per visit is a strong indicator of the level of confusion and frustration of your customers. In contrast with the same performance indicator for content sites [Hack #97], a higher ratio of page views to visits is not necessarily good news.

The ideal customer support experience is one where visitors arrive, quickly find the solution to their problem, and leave satisfied. The longer a visitor is forced to hunt around for his answer, the more frustrated he is likely to become, often leading directly to a frustrated customer talking to your customer support staff. If yours is a well-designed site, one that has good search and easy-to-read answers, you're likely to see lower average numbers of page views per visit. If your customer support site is confusing or lacking somehow, you'll see a higher average (and your goal should be reducing that average).

Percent new and returning visitors. Usually directly calculated by your measurement application, I recommend watching these percentages as a guide to how your business is growing and whether your customers are satisfied with your support site. Depending on the type of support you offer, the ideal situation is one where customers repeatedly use your site. If your percentage of return visitors is consistently low, you may want to consider checking your call-center volumes and, if they're consistently high, start asking your support customers if they've tried your web site.

Remember that the cost savings associated with having a support site revolves primarily around ongoing call deflection. If a new customer has a question and is able to find a satisfactory answer on your web site she's likely to use the site again; the opposite is also true. Also, as a caution, when you're examining these percentages, be sure to look at a long enough period of time to allow customers to need support more than once.

Average time spent on site. Similar to the percentages of new and returning visitors, the average time visitors spend on your site is calculated by your measurement application. Average time spent should be used the same way as average page views per visitor—the ideal customer support visit is a short one. The longer the "average" visitor spends, the greater the likelihood that he's struggling to find an answer to his question. Especially when coupled with a high average page views per visit ratio, a long time spent on site can indicate frustration.

Really advanced systems are able to combine traffic data with customer support data by assigning a common unique user identifier [Hack #5] to join the two data sets. In this situation, companies are able to validate page view per visit and time spent measurements and begin to identify which types of customer problems are unlikely to be resolved online (and do something about it!)

Advanced Key Performance Indicators for Customer Support Sites

The following metrics are more advanced but should be seriously considered in addition to the basic indicators, especially those covering internal search.

Percent "zero results" searches. While the subtleties of measuring internal search are many [Hack #64], one of the fundamental performance indicators for support sites is the percentage of searches that result in, well, no results (Figure 7-12). Calculated as the total number of "zero" or no results searches divided by the total number of searches executed, because searches that don't have results frustrate customers like nothing else, this metric is very important.

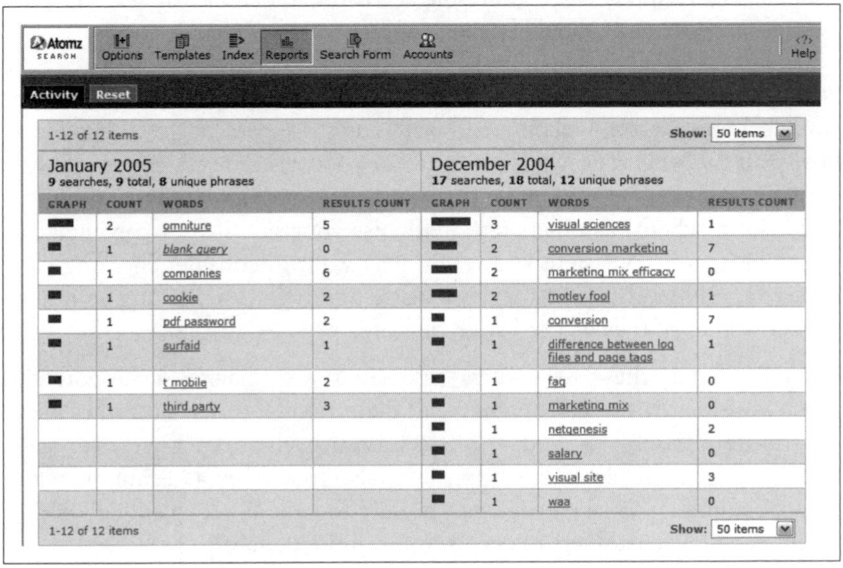

GRAPH	COUNT	WORDS	RESULTS COUNT	GRAPH	COUNT	WORDS	RESULTS COUNT
	2	omniture	5		3	visual sciences	1
	1	blank query	0		2	conversion marketing	7
	1	companies	6		2	marketing mix efficacy	0
	1	cookie	2		2	motley fool	1
	1	pdf password	2		1	conversion	7
	1	surfaid	1		1	difference between log files and page tags	1
	1	t mobile	2		1	faq	0
	1	third party	3		1	marketing mix	0
					1	netgenesis	2
					1	salary	0
					1	visual site	3
					1	waa	0

Figure 7-12. Sample search phrases

To make the calculation, you'll need the ability to differentiate "failed" searches from those that generate at least one result for your web measurement application. Often, search engines will return this in the query string or to the results page in a "results count" variable. Make the calculation using a page view count, allowing for the possibility that a visitor may search repeatedly and still get no results.

Considering that when customers search at your support site, they already have a product name and a pretty good idea of what the item is supposed to do, it is inexcusable for a site to return no results. Any increase in this percentage should prompt you to review your internal search logs looking for zero result searches, making adjustments to your search engine to return results whenever possible.

Support satisfaction rate. If you are actively measuring customer satisfaction, either using your own technology or by working with a vendor like Usability Sciences, Foresee Results, or OpinionLab, I highly recommend that you include some measurement of visitor satisfaction (Figure 7-13) as a key performance indicator.

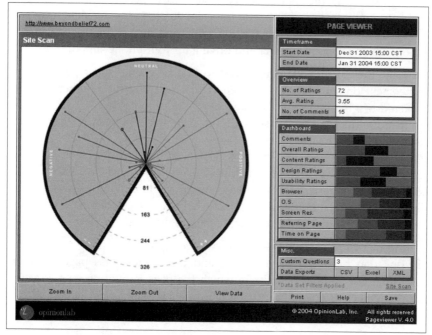

Figure 7-13. Customer satisfaction measurement

Percent "zero yield" search results. When a customer is searching for an answer, presenting her with no results is bad but presenting her with confusing results that she doesn't believe will answer her question is worse. When faced with too many or hard to differentiate results, searchers often back up and search again without exploring any of the results, hence the result set "yields" no clicks.

Measuring zero results searches is complicated but valuable; measuring "zero yield" searches is very complicated but significantly more valuable. Defined as the number of search result sets that didn't generate clicks divided by the total number of search results returned (measured in page views), this KPI strongly depends on your web measurement solution having fairly robust click-tracking abilities.

Again, any increase in the percentage of zero yield searches should prompt you to examine those searches and critically explore the results set, attempting to identify the reason that a customer would fail to click even one link. A good strategy is to search your offline support database for the same type of information to identify the answers that your support agents are providing and comparing that to the online results set.

Percent of visits less than 90 seconds. The percent of visits under 90 seconds is another valuable indicator of the likelihood that customers are successfully self-servicing their support needs. It is extremely rare that a support problem can be answered online in less than 90 seconds. The higher the percentage of short visits, the greater the likelihood that customers are simply looking up your phone number and driving up your phone support costs.

To make the calculation, you'll need to find the "time spent per visit" or "time spent on site" report—the report that tells you the number of visits broken down by time spent (see [Hack #96] for additional details). Add up the number of visits less than 90 seconds and then divide by the total number of visits to the site.

"Stickiness" for key pages. The stickiness of the first page in a visit should keep visitors interested and encourage them to click more deeply into the site. For support sites, these pages can help retain customers looking for information, preventing them from picking up the telephone.

Built from two page reports—the entry page report, describing the number of visits that begin at a given page, and the single-access pages reports, describing the number of visits in which the page is the only one a visitor sees—stickiness is one minus the ratio of single access to entry pages:

$$1.00 - (\text{Single Access Page Visits} / \text{Entry Page Visits})$$

The result of the calculation will be a percentage, and higher percentages are better than lower, indicating greater stick on the page in question.

"Information find" conversion rate. Your "information find" conversion rate is the ratio of unique visitors viewing content you consider an "answer" divided by all unique visitors. While you may end up with a very high conversion rate and still not be sure whether your customers are satisfied, you can be fairly sure that if this rate is low, something is wrong.

Provided you're successful in segmenting customer support visitors, reasonably you should have a nearly 100 percent conversion rate. Anything less than 50 percent should prompt you to look closely at the usability of your site and the likelihood that support-seeking visitors will be successful. The offline analogy would be someone calling a support hot line and then talking about the weather instead of asking for help.

Other Important Measurements

In addition to the KPIs listed above, you should pay careful attention to the top words and phrases that visitors are entering into your internal search engine. Because most customer support sites are often difficult to effectively navigate, research indicates that visitors have an even higher tendency to search. By carefully watching your top searches you will be able to make sure that these searches are yielding the "right" results and, if you're especially smart, modify top-level support pages to point directly to documents that answer the most pressing customer questions.

You should also watch your top entry pages, especially those driven from search engines, as a proxy for your internal search engine. Remember that the majority of searches on the Internet originate at Google. You want to make sure that you watch for an increase in Google searches for support content the same way as you'll watch for an increase in internal searches.

All of the aforementioned measurements, while not technically KPIs, are important enough to be delivered with the key performance indicator report. For a sample key performance indicator worksheet, built in Microsoft Excel from the measurements recommended in this hack, visit the author's web site at *http://www.webanalyticsdemystified.com/kpi_worksheet*.

HACK #99 Key Performance Indicators for Business Sites (Lead Generation)

It is extremely common that the activity that a web site wants the visitor to take is as simple as taking the next step. Especially for products or services with long and complex sales cycles, getting a qualified lead is as good as gold. Business sites like these have just as good key performance indicators as direct-to-consumer online models.

The majority of business sites on the Internet don't sell anything directly via the Internet; they exist to provide information about their products or services. Automobile manufacturers like Nissan and Porsche, well-known brands like Purina and Procter & Gamble, and even software as service companies like Omniture and Coremetrics, each have a vested interest in providing you information in trade for some personal information (the lead).

The general strategy for lead-generating sites is to provide just enough information to help determine that they're the right solution and then provide multiple contact channels so the visitor can get more engaged (for example, talk to someone in sales). There are, of course, a handful of key performance indicators for lead-generation sites to look for opportunity and monitor for problems.

Basic Key Performance Indicators for Business Sites

The following key performance indicators should be considered core to the regular reporting for any lead-generating site. Each assumes a constant period of time unless otherwise noted.

Lead generation conversion rate. The fundamental measurement of how good a job you're doing. Defined as the number of leads generated divided by the number of unique visitors, your lead generation conversion rate is a strong indicator of the quality of your audience, message, and site design. This KPI does depend on being able to measure when a lead comes in and so is much easier to measure for site-generated leads than leads generated over the phone or via email. Still, keeping track of your "online" lead generation conversion rate is an excellent place to start and is highly recommended.

Average visits per visitor. Simply defined, the ratio of visits per visitor can give you a sense of how interested people are in your products or services. In general, the larger the result, the greater the interest, but keep in mind that you may want to look at a longer timeframe than a day or a week.

For extra credit, segment visitors based on whether they generated an online lead or not, looking at average visits per visitor. Depending on what you're selling and the complexity of the product or sale process, you'll likely see a higher average for visitors submitting leads than those who have not. In this case, you can reasonably determine that people need to spend some time getting to know you before they're willing to ask for more information.

Percent new and returning visitors. The percent of new and returning visitors are numbers calculated by your web measurement solution and describe how much of your audience you've managed to get to return at least one time after their first visit. If, for some reason, your application doesn't provide the percentages I recommend using, simply divide the number of new or returning visitors by the total number of visitors to get each percentage, respectively.

These ratios function much in the same way they do for advertising and content sites [Hack #97]. The more you're spending on marketing, the greater the percentage of new visitors you expect. The more complex the sale, the greater the percentage of returning visitors you expect.

Always keep in mind how KPIs are designed to be used [Hack #94]—the specific numbers you're getting are less important than how those numbers change over time. Remember to tie KPI movement to the marketing and site design changes that you're making to better understand the effects of these changes.

Ratio of new to returning visitors. This ratio, simply defined as the total number of new visitors divided by the total number of returning visitors, provides another view of your audience mix. The calculation yields a number between zero and *n* (with *n* being some positive integer that can, in theory, be very, very high if nobody ever returns to your site). This indicator quickly tells you whether you're acquiring, retaining, or basically neutral regarding your visitors.

Smaller numbers indicate that you're retaining more visitors than you attract, something commonly referred to as *visitor retention mode*. The smaller the number, the better the job you're doing at retaining visitors. Larger numbers indicate that you're attracting more visitors than you retain, something referred to as *visitor acquisition mode*. Say, as an example, the calculation yields a ratio of new to returning visitors of 2.0—this tells you that for every visitor you retain, you acquire two new visitors.

For lead-generating sites the ideal ratio is nearly always greater than one, usually 2.00 or 3.00, since you're major goal is attracting new prospects who will hopefully submit a lead. If yours is a very simple process—say you're offering a newsletter subscription to pet owners—this number can be very high since people don't really need to return and think about your offer. The more complex the process, the lower the result of the calculation.

Average time spent on site. Similar to the percentages of new and returning visitors, the average time visitors spend on your site is calculated by your measurement application. The average time visitors spend is a simple indicator of how interested they are in your products or services and whether they're actively reading information.

If you're concerned that visitors may be struggling with your presentation, consider building an average page views per visit KPI [Hack #98] similar to that used for the customer support model. If you have a high average time spent on site and a high ratio of page views to visits, you can be reasonably assured that visitors are clicking around on your site. If you have a high average time spent but a low ratio of page views to visits, likely visitors are getting confused somewhere (and you should the look at your time spent on pages report for pages on which visitors spend an inordinate amount of time).

Advanced Key Performance Indicators for Business Sites

The following metrics are more advanced but should be seriously considered in addition to the basic indicators.

Average hours to response (online inquiry). One of the single most frustrating things for anyone in the sales process is having to wait for information.

Especially if you've done a good job of providing information on your web site and managed to get the visitor engaged, then interested, and finally committed, making him wait a day or more after submitting his lead is a mistake that often leads to a loss in purchase momentum.

While you'll have to get the data for this key performance indicator from another system, likely your customer relationship database, including it with your online KPIs will help you stay focused on the ultimate goal: getting visitors interested and engaged in the sales process as quickly as possible.

Percent of visits less than 90 seconds. The percent of visits under 90 seconds is a valuable indicator of the interest your visitors have in your content; in general, the higher the percentage the greater the number of uninterested visitors to the site. I use 90 seconds as a rough proxy for the minimum amount of time a visitor needs to do or learn anything meaningful on the average site, you may want to lower the threshold to 60 or even 30 seconds. While the visitors may not truly be *uninterested*, when they spend very little time, it's unlikely they're going to spend enough time to truly connect with your brand.

To make the calculation, you'll need to find the "time spent per visit" or "time spent on site" report—the report that tells you the number of visits broken down by time spent (see Figure 7-9 and "Key Performance Indicators for Online Retailers" [Hack #96] for the details).

Percent interested visits. Depending on your particular sales process, a visitor can be said to be "interested" when she looks at more than a small handful of pages during her visit. As a starting point, consider a visit "committed" (see below) when a visitor looks at more than 10 pages, and "interested" when she looks at five to nine pages: enough pages that she's moved on past just browsing, but not so many that she's totally engaged, working to make sure that your solution is right for her.

Most measurement applications provide the data you need to calculate this KPI in a "path length" or "depth of visits" report (Figure 7-14). To make the calculation, simply add up the number of visits over your particular threshold and divide by the total number of visits.

Using Figure 7-14 as an example and assuming we had 1,000 total visits to the site and a threshold of five to nine page views during the visit, the calculation would be:

(135 Visits to 5 Pages + 110 Visits to 6 Pages + 74 Visits to 7 Pages + 35 Visits to 8 Pages + 21 Visits to 9 Pages) / 1.000 Total Visits = 0.375 = 37.5% Interested Visits

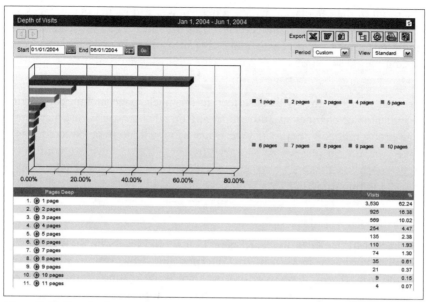

Figure 7-14. Depth of visits report

While you can adjust the thresholds that define "interested" depending on your site and sales process, I would encourage you not to change the calculation once you've made it. The relationship between "uninterested," "interested," and "committed" visits is usually an exponentially declining curve—you have a great number of uninterested visits, a smaller number of interested visits, and a much smaller number of committed visits at any given time.

Percent committed visits. Committed visits are those visits where a visitor is looking at a relatively high number of pages, usually more than 10 for business sites. Most measurement applications provide the data you need to calculate this KPI in a "path length" or "depth of visits" report (see "Percent Interested Visitors" above for the details about making the calculation). For most lead-generating sites, the greater this percentage, the better the news.

"Stickiness" for key pages. The stickiness of the first page in a visit should keep the visitor interested and encourage him to click more deeply into the site. Built from two page reports—the entry page report, describing the number of visits that begin at a given page, and the single-access pages report, describing the number of visits in which the page is the only one a visitor sees—stickiness is one minus the ratio of single access to entry pages:

1.00 – (Single Access Page Visits / Entry Page Visits)

The result of the calculation will be a percentage, and higher percentages are better than lower, indicating greater stick on the page in question. It is highly recommended that you make this measurement only for important landing pages like your home page, your campaign landing pages, and the top five percent of entry pages from search engines [Hack #43].

Like many of the other KPIs described in this hack, page stickiness provides an indicator of changes in audience make-up. If the "stick" of a key entry page drops suddenly, many of your other KPIs will likely be affected. Also, make sure not to just set-and-forget this list—keep an eye on your entry page report and make sure to adjust which pages you track if you change your marketing campaigns.

Other Important Measurements

In addition to the KPIs discussed here, you should track the number of visits you're getting from your top 10 referring sites, your top 10 entry pages, and the top 10 search keywords visitors are using to find your site. If you have internal search, track the top 10 internal searches as well.

All of the aforementioned measurements, while not technically KPIs, are important enough to content sites that they should be delivered with the performance report. For a sample key performance indicator worksheet, built in Microsoft Excel from the measurements recommended in this hack, visit the author's web site at *http://www.webanalyticsdemystified.com/kpi_worksheet*.

HACK #100   Build Your Own Web Measurement Application: Reporting

Now that the application is built and you're collecting and analyzing data, the time has come to think about next steps. We make a handful of suggestions about other things this application could do to improve data collection, performance, or reliability.

As we've gone through the book, we've built a program to collect data from visitors to your web site, and a program to analyze the data and produce some basic statistics. In this final hack, we're going to remind you how to run the application and discuss ways in which it could be extended.

You can get both programs from:

http://www.webanalyticsdemystified.com/byo

You will also find a sample logfile there to allow you to run the second program without waiting to collect any data of your own first.

Running the Application

Remember that this application depends on a small piece of JavaScript [Hack #12] code that is embedded in each page you want tracked. All you need to do is add the following code near the top of the <BODY> element of each of your web pages:

```
<script>
document.write('<img src="/cgi-bin/readtag.pl?url=
  '+escape(document.location)+'&amp;ref='+escape(document.referrer)+'">');
</script>
```

To process the code, you'll use the *readlog.pl* Perl script that we developed throughout most of the book. To execute this program from the command line, assuming that *page.log* is in the same directory as *readlog.pl*, all you need to do (assuming you've already installed the GeoIP modules [Hack #80] is type:

```
perl readlog.pl page.log
```

And again, the sample output will look something like Figure 7-15.

Figure 7-15. Output from the readlog.pl application

Extending This Application

The program really only gives a taste of how web analytics programs work; you're probably already thinking of several great ways you can extend this application, building something that will suit your specific needs, that takes into consideration the other ideas in this book. Here are possible extensions.

Add simple visitor segmentation. The program has no way to segment visitors to compare two groups against each other, or one group against the whole population [Hack #48]. As you've learned while reading the rest of this chapter, the most interesting use of web measurement is usually making comparisons.

It's not very useful to know the raw conversion rate; it's much more useful to know the conversion rate this month compared to last month, or to compare response rates between one campaign and another. You may want to allow segmenting by referrer or entry page, or even add a variable to the JavaScript that allows you to differentiate groups of visitors for your analysis.

Clean up duplicate page names. There is no attempt to combine URLs that correspond to the same file. For example, */products/index.html* is actually the same file as */products/*, and */%7Esret1/* is actually the same as */~sret1/*. These transformations should happen automatically, in the same way as we converted filenames to lowercase on a case-insensitive filesystem. In addition, the user should be able to specify other transformations to apply, such as ignoring certain URL parameters. You may want to build in a transformation filter or table that will resolve these kinds of very common problems.

Improve the reporting. The reporting for the basic system could easily be converted from plain text into a more dynamic HTML format. If you choose to rewrite it in HTML, be careful to encode non-alphanumeric characters in the output to prevent a type of attack known as a cross-site scripting attack. This occurs when a visitor to your web site pretends that his referrer is some nonsense URL that contains malicious JavaScript code. If you were to view the data in a browser without encoding it, you would execute the malicious code. Still, you may want to apply more thoughtful formatting than we did with our bare-bones application.

Add user configuration. At the moment, the program has no way to specify which reports you want to see, or how much data to show in each report, except by editing the source code. You could add the ability to specify these things through command-line arguments using Perl's Getopt::Simple module. Or you could have a text configuration file, or even a graphical user interface.

Improve program efficiency. We have valued code clarity above both speed and memory requirement. This is usually the right choice for the majority of the code. But real web analysis typically deals with very large quantities of data, and in a production environment, certain parts of the code would have to be written to be both faster and less memory intensive. You may even want to take what you've learned in these hacks and rewrite the application in a faster language such as C++.

Add error checking. There is insufficient error checking. While this helps the clarity of the code as a tool for demonstrating major concepts, it would not be appropriate in a production environment. For example, the program assumes that the logfile lines occur in chronological order. If you were to analyze two logfiles and specify them in the wrong order, or even if some corrupt data crept into the logfile, the results would be wrong. Logfiles are typically very large, and errors do creep into them. In addition, malicious visitors can insert arbitrary text into them. So we should be more careful about trusting the data.

Track exits from the site. As we mentioned in [Hack #67], you could extend the data collection to track exits from the site. This would allow you to measure the time spent on the last page of a session. It would also allow you to see where people went when they followed links out of your site.

Add multi-session tracking functionality. Even if the web site uses persistent cookies rather than just session cookies, there is no attempt to remember a visitor who visited yesterday. This is important for understanding the relationship between new and returning visitors and customers [Hack #89], and for attributing purchases to the lead that generated them [Hack #50]. Doing this usually requires saving the visitors in a database on disk because it is not possible to store them all in memory.

You could get the logfile from a remote location via FTP. It would not be difficult to remove the requirement that the *readlog.pl* application lives in the same filesystem as the *page.log* file by using FTP to download the logfile from a remote location. The advantage of doing this would be not having to run a Perl script on your web servers.

—*Dr. Stephen Turner and Eric T. Peterson*

Index

We'd like to hear your suggestions for improving our indexes. Send email to *index@oreilly.com*.

attrition rate, 237
authenticated username, 80
  identifying repeat visitors using, 64
  identifying unique visitors using, 63
authentication server, 79
average order value (AOV), 366
AWStats, 34

RSS tracking application
  data collection for, 45–50
  parsing logfile and generating
    reports, 138–149

Colophon

Our look is the result of reader comments, our own experimentation, and feedback from distribution channels. Distinctive covers complement our distinctive approach to technical topics, breathing personality and life into potentially dry subjects.

The tool on the cover of *Web Site Measurement Hacks* is a combination square, a carpentry tool used primarily to mark and measure 45- and 90-degree angles. Many variations of combination squares are available, but each has the square, used to to measure the accuracy of right angles, as one of its components. While the square may be found in combination with various other tools, the combination square on the cover of *Web Site Measurement Hacks* has a scribe (for transferring the contours of one item onto another) and a level.

Jamie Peppard was the production editor for *Web Site Measurement Hacks*. Linley Dolby was the copy editor and Ann Schirmer was the proofreader. Sarah Sherman, Genevieve d'Entremont, and Darren Kelly provided quality control. Angela Howard wrote the index.

Ellie Volckhausen designed the cover of this book, based on a series design by Edie Freedman. The cover image is a photograph taken from the Comstock CD. Karen Montgomery produced the cover layout with Adobe InDesign CS using Adobe's Helvetica Neue and ITC Garamond fonts.

David Futato designed the interior layout. This book was converted by Keith Fahlgren to FrameMaker 5.5.6 with a format conversion tool created by Erik Ray, Jason McIntosh, Neil Walls, and Mike Sierra that uses Perl and XML technologies. The text font is Linotype Birka; the heading font is Adobe Helvetica Neue Condensed; and the code font is LucasFont's TheSans Mono Condensed. The illustrations that appear in the book were produced by Robert Romano, Jessamyn Read, and Lesley Borash using Macromedia FreeHand MX and Adobe Photoshop CS. This colophon was written by Jamie Peppard.

Keep in touch with O'Reilly

Download examples from our books

To find example files from a book, go to: *www.oreilly.com/catalog* select the book, and follow the "Examples" link.

Register your O'Reilly books

Register your book at *register.oreilly.com*
Why register your books? Once you've registered your O'Reilly books you can:

- Win O'Reilly books, T-shirts or discount coupons in our monthly drawing.
- Get special offers available only to registered O'Reilly customers.
- Get catalogs announcing new books (US and UK only).
- Get email notification of new editions of the O'Reilly books you own.

Join our email lists

Sign up to get topic-specific email announcements of new books and conferences, special offers, and O'Reilly Network technology newsletters at:

elists.oreilly.com

It's easy to customize your free elists subscription so you'll get exactly the O'Reilly news you want.

Get the latest news, tips, and tools

www.oreilly.com

- "Top 100 Sites on the Web"—PC Magazine
- CIO Magazine's Web Business 50 Awards

Our web site contains a library of comprehensive product information (including book excerpts and tables of contents), downloadable software, background articles, interviews with technology leaders, links to relevant sites, book cover art, and more.

Work for O'Reilly

Check out our web site for current employment opportunities:

jobs.oreilly.com

Contact us

O'Reilly Media, Inc.
1005 Gravenstein Hwy North
Sebastopol, CA 95472 USA
Tel: 707-827-7000 or 800-998-9938
   (6am to 5pm PST)
Fax: 707-829-0104

Contact us by email

For answers to problems regarding your order or our products:
order@oreilly.com

To request a copy of our latest catalog:
catalog@oreilly.com

For book content technical questions or corrections: **booktech@oreilly.com**

For educational, library, government, and corporate sales: **corporate@oreilly.com**

To submit new book proposals to our editors and product managers:
proposals@oreilly.com

For information about our international distributors or translation queries:
international@oreilly.com

For information about academic use of O'Reilly books:
adoption@oreilly.com
or visit:
academic.oreilly.com

For a list of our distributors outside of North America check out:
international.oreilly.com/distributors.html

Order a book online

www.oreilly.com/order_new

O'REILLY®

Our books are available at most retail and online bookstores.
To order direct: 1-800-998-9938 • *order@oreilly.com* • *www.oreilly.com*
Online editions of most O'Reilly titles are available by subscription at *safari.oreilly.com*